I

L

Ruchira Avatar Adi Da Samraj

It is obvious, from all sorts of subtle details, that he knows what IT's all about . . . a rare being.

ALAN WATTS
author, *The Way of Zen* and *The Wisdom of Insecurity*

I regard Adi Da Samraj as one of the greatest teachers in the Western world today.

IRINA TWEEDIE
Sufi teacher; author, *Chasm of Fire*

I recognize the God-Presence Incarnate in Adi Da Samraj as whole and full and complete.

BARBARA MARX HUBBARD
author, *Conscious Evolution* and *The Revelation;*
president, The Foundation for Conscious Evolution

Adi Da Samraj has created virtually the entire basis for a culture founded in love and wisdom. The magnitude of such an undertaking— let alone the accomplishment of it—cannot be overstated.

JOHN WHITE
author, *Frontiers of Consciousness,*
and *The Meeting of Science and Spirit*

Adi Da Samraj is a man who has truly walked in Spirit and given true enlightenment to many.

SUN BEAR
founder, the Bear Tribe Medicine Society

The life and teaching of Avatar Adi Da Samraj are of profound and decisive spiritual significance at this critical moment in history.

BRYAN DESCHAMP
Senior Adviser at the United Nations
High Commission for Refugees;
former Dean of the Carmelite House of Studies, Australia;
former Dean of Trinity College, University of Melbourne

A great teacher with the dynamic ability to awaken in his listeners
something of the Divine Reality in which he is grounded, with which
he is identified, and which, in fact, he is.

ISRAEL REGARDIE
author, *The Golden Dawn*

A di Da Samraj has spoken directly to the heart of our human situation—
the shocking gravity of our brief and unbidden lives. Through his
words I have experienced a glimmering of eternal life, and view my own
existence as timeless and spaceless in a way that I never have before.

RICHARD GROSSINGER
author, *Planet Medicine*

A vatar Adi Da is the greatest Spiritual Master ever to walk the earth.
He is the God-Man. He reveals the ultimate truth residing in the
human heart.

THE REVEREND THOMAS E. AHLBURN
Senior Minister, First Unitarian Church
Providence, Rhode Island

M y relationship with Adi Da Samraj over many years has only confirmed
His Realization and the Truth of His impeccable Teaching. He is much
more than simply an inspiration of my music, but is really a living
demonstration that perfect transcendence is actually possible. This is both
a great relief and a great challenge. If you thirst for truth, here is a rare
opportunity to drink.

RAY LYNCH
composer and musician, *Deep Breakfast;*
The Sky of Mind; and *Ray Lynch, Best Of*

A di Da Samraj and his unique body of teaching work offer a rare and
extraordinary opportunity for those courageous students who are
ready to move beyond ego and take the plunge into deepest communion
with the Absolute. Importantly, the teaching is grounded in explicit
discussion of necessary psychospiritual evolution and guides the student
to self-responsibility and self-awareness.

ELISABETH TARG, M.D.
University of California, San Francisco,
School of Medicine;
director, Complementary Medicine Research Institute,
California Pacific Medical Center

That God can, among other things, actually incarnate in human form once seemed unbelievable to me. But reading the books of Avatar Adi Da obliterated all doubt about the existence of God right now, here on Earth in human form.

CHARMIAN ANDERSON, PH.D.
psychologist; author, *Bridging Heaven and Earth*
and *The Heart of Success*

Fly to the side of this God-Man. His Divine Transmission works miracles of change not possible by any other Spiritual means.

LEE SANNELLA, M.D.
author, *The Kundalini Experience*

When I first read the Word of Avatar Adi Da Samraj, I was immediately transported into a state of wonderment and awe. Could it be? Could the Divine Person be here now, in this time and place? It didn't take long for my heart to answer a resounding "Yes". May the whole world be restored to Faith, Love, and Understanding by the Mystery of Real God, here and Incarnate as Avatar Adi Da Samraj.

ED KOWALCZYK
lead singer and songwriter of the rock band, *Live*

I regard the work of Adi Da and his devotees as one of the most penetrating spiritual and social experiments happening on the planet in our era.

JEFFREY MISHLOVE, PH.D.
host, PBS television series, *Thinking Allowed*;
author, *The Roots of Consciousness*

Adi Da's Teachings have tremendous significance for humanity. . . . He represents a foundation and a structure for sanity.

ROBERT K. HALL, M.D.
psychiatrist; author, *Out of Nowhere*;
co-founder, The Lomi School and Lomi Clinic

The Divine World-Teacher,
RUCHIRA AVATAR ADI DA SAMRAJ
Lopez Island, 2000

RUCHIRA AVATARA HRIDAYA-SIDDHA YOGA

THE SEVENTEEN COMPANIONS
OF THE TRUE DAWN HORSE

BOOK EIGHT

The <u>Divine</u> (and Not Merely <u>Cosmic</u>)
Spiritual Baptism In
The Divine Way Of Adidam

By
The Divine World-Teacher,
RUCHIRA AVATAR
ADI DA SAMRAJ

THE DAWN HORSE PRESS
MIDDLETOWN, CALIFORNIA

NOTE TO THE READER

All who study the Way of Adidam or take up its practice should remember that they are responding to a Call to become responsible for themselves. They should understand that they, not Avatar Adi Da Samraj or others, are responsible for any decision they make or action they take in the course of their lives of study or practice.

The devotional, Spiritual, functional, practical, relational, cultural, and formal community practices and disciplines referred to in this book are appropriate and natural practices that are voluntarily and progressively adopted by members of the four congregations of Adidam (as applicable for each of the congregations and as appropriate to the personal circumstance of each individual). Although anyone may find these practices useful and beneficial, they are not presented as advice or recommendations to the general reader or to anyone who is not a member of one of the four congregations of Adidam. And nothing in this book is intended as a diagnosis, prescription, or recommended treatment or cure for any specific "problem", whether medical, emotional, psychological, social, or Spiritual. One should apply a particular program of treatment, prevention, cure, or general health only in consultation with a licensed physician or other qualified professional.

Ruchira Avatara Hridaya-Siddha Yoga is formally authorized for publication by the Ruchira Sannyasin Order of the Tantric Renunciates of Adidam, as part of the Standard Edition of the Divine "Source-Texts" of the Divine World-Teacher, Ruchira Avatar Adi Da Samraj. (The Ruchira Sannyasin Order of the Tantric Renunciates of Adidam is the senior Spiritual and Cultural Authority within the formal gathering of formally acknowledged devotees of the Divine World-Teacher, Ruchira Avatar Adi Da Samraj.)

NOTE TO BIBLIOGRAPHERS: The correct form for citing Ruchira Avatar Adi Da Samraj's Name (in any form of alphabetized listing) is:

Adi Da Samraj, Ruchira Avatar

COVER: Both the central image and the border image are photographs taken by Avatar Adi Da Samraj. Please see "Camera Illuminata: The 'Bright'-Field Photography of Avatar Adi Da Samraj", pp. 39-41.

Printed in the United States of America

Produced by the Eleutherian Pan-Communion of Adidam in cooperation with the Dawn Horse Press

International Standard Book Number: 1-57097-106-4
Library of Congress Catalog Card Number: 00-191972

CONTENTS

Ruchira Avatara Hridaya-Siddha Yoga

PART FIVE:
The Heart-Summary Of Adidam
295

EPILOGUE:
I Am The Avataric Divine Self-Revelation Of The
Fundamental Reality (or The "Radically" Non-Dual
Conscious Light Of Self-Evidently Divine Love-Bliss)
301

RUCHIRA AVATAR ADI DA SAMRAJ
The Mountain Of Attention, 2000

Introduction

This book is an invitation to enter a different world. A world that is completely <u>real</u>, in the largest possible sense of that word. A world in which none of the sufferings and difficulties of life are ignored or denied—but also a world in which yearnings for truth, wisdom, happiness, and love are addressed at an extraordinary depth. A world in which there is real, trustable guidance through the "maze" of life's confusions and crises. A world that vastly exceeds all limited notions of what is "real". A world of deep, abiding joy.

People from all walks of life have felt this world open up to them when they read the books of the Divine World-Teacher, Ruchira Avatar Adi Da Samraj. Those of us who have done so have felt our deepest questions answered, our most profound heart-longings satisfied. We have treasured His Instruction about the real issues everyone faces: death, sex, intimacy, emotional maturity, community life, and many more. We have marveled at His precise "map" of the entire course of Spiritual life, and at His description of the nature of reality in all its dimensions. We have been sobered by His criticism of the universal human bondage to the self-centered desires and purposes of the ego. And, altogether, through His words, we have felt His Divine Spiritual Blessing deeply affecting our lives.

Those of us who have been drawn to Avatar Adi Da have discovered that the impact of His Truth (and the Blessing it conveys) is so great in our lives, so far beyond anything else we have known, that a truly amazing recognition began to grow in our hearts and minds: Avatar Adi Da Samraj is not merely a great human being who speaks profound Truth—He is the Divine Reality Itself, Appearing in a human body in order to Offer His Revelation of Truth directly to all of humankind.

Often, this awakened recognition of Him—as the Divine Reality Present in human Form—comes as a complete surprise. In this age of skepticism, many regard the idea of a Divine Incarnation as strictly mythological. But Avatar Adi Da Samraj is not a myth—He is an intensely real living being. He is an utterly spontaneous and free manifestation, moved (by overwhelming love) to serve the Happiness and Liberation of beings everywhere, and to bring our global home out of this time of potential political and ecological disaster.

However, no one is asked to "believe" that Avatar Adi Da is the Divine. He has even said, "You must not believe in Me." Why? Because mere belief is not transformative. Only what is revealed in one's real experience—of body, heart, and mind altogether, rather than mind only—can transform the being. Therefore, Avatar Adi Da does not offer you a set of beliefs, or even a set of Spiritual techniques. He simply offers you His Revelation of Truth as a free gift, to respond to as you will. And, if you are moved to take up His Way, He invites you to enter into a direct Spiritual relationship with Him. Those of us who have taken this step have found the Spiritual relationship to Avatar Adi Da Samraj to be a supremely precious gift, a literally miraculous blessing, the answer to our deepest longings—greatly surpassing anything we have ever experienced or even imagined to be possible. Indeed, we have found Avatar Adi Da's Revelation of Truth to be so all-encompassing and His Spiritual Power and Love to be so overwhelming that we recognize Him as the Promised God-Man—the One capable of fulfilling the yearnings of people everywhere, the One Whose Appearance has been foreshadowed by prophecies in many religious traditions.

Avatar Adi Da began Teaching formally in 1972. In the years since then, He has communicated a vast store of Wisdom. But He has also done far more than that: He has created a whole new Way of life, a new religion, which is now practiced by people of different cultures in many parts of the world.

Just as the religions of Christianity and Buddhism are named after their founders, the religion founded by Avatar Adi Da is named after Him—it is called "Adidam" (AH-dee-DAHM). Adidam is an all-embracing practice that takes every aspect of human life—the "lowest" as well as the "highest"—into account (see pp. 218-19). The foundation of Adidam is the response of heart-felt devotion to Avatar Adi Da Samraj, in loving gratitude for His Gifts of Wisdom and Spiritual Blessing.

Avatar Adi Da's books are full of ecstatic proclamations of His Divinity—and there is a secret to understanding these proclamations fully. The secret is this: Avatar Adi Da is not speaking as a separate being who presumes himself to be irreducibly "different" from every other being. No, He is speaking as the Divine Heart of every being. Therefore, His most fundamental message may be summarized as follows:

> There is no ultimate "difference" between you and the Divine.
> There is only the Divine.
> Everything that exists is a "modification" of the One Divine Reality.

However, even though it may be true that there is only the Divine, this is not, in fact, our common daily experience. Far from it! Our usual daily life is full of events and people (including ourselves!) that we experience as distinctly un-Divine.

Therefore, Avatar Adi Da is humanly present in the world in order to Reveal the Divine Condition, and to make it possible for human beings to Realize that that Condition is our True Nature. That this is so is the deep heart-certainty of Avatar Adi Da's devotees—after many years of studying His Teaching, hearing His Discourses, enjoying His Company in all kinds of circumstances, and knowing the profound Ecstasy, Joy, and Peace of His Spiritual Transmission.

Thus, when Avatar Adi Da Samraj says "I Am the One to be Realized" or "I Am the Very Divine Person" or "I Am the Divine Heart Itself" (and many other variations), He is confessing that He is, paradoxically, the Divine Condition of everyone and everything—seeming to be a separate being, in order to offer us the Way to Realize our Inherent Condition. And it is our confession to you, as those who have become His devotees, that to behold Him with an open heart is to fall into an indescribable Love, Bliss, and Happiness that is self-evidently the deepest Truth of one's own heart and the Very Heart of Existence.

As Avatar Adi Da Samraj says, with great passion and emphasis:

Beloved, Even I Am Only You (As You Are).

This is the great mystery that you are invited to discover for yourself.

A vatar Adi Da Samraj's Name is composed of four Sanskrit words.

His principal Name is "Adi Da". "Avatar" and "Samraj" are sacred Titles, used in association with His Name.

"Adi" (AH-dee) means "Original" (or "Primordial"), and "Da" means "the Divine Giver". Thus, "Adi Da" means "the Original Divine Giver".

"Avatar" means "a 'Crossing Down' of the Divine Being into the world" (or, in other words, "an Appearance of the Divine in conditionally manifested form").

"Samraj" (sahm-RAHJ) means "universal Lord".

In fuller forms of reference, Adi Da Samraj is called "the Ruchira (roo-CHIH-rah) Avatar", meaning "the Avatar of Infinite Brightness".

Avatar Adi Da Samraj: His Life and Teaching

The Three Great Purposes of Avatar Adi Da Samraj:
Learning Man, Teaching Man, and Blessing Man

From the moment of His Birth (in New York, on November 3, 1939), Adi Da Samraj was Consciously Aware of His Native Divine Condition. As soon as He became able to use language, He gave this Condition a simple but very expressive Name—"the 'Bright'".* But then, at the age of two years, Avatar Adi Da made a profound spontaneous choice. He chose to relinquish His constant Enjoyment of the "Bright"—out of what He Describes as a "painful loving", a sympathy for the suffering and ignorance of human beings. Avatar Adi Da Confesses that He chose to "Learn Man"—to enter into everything that humankind feels and suffers, and also to experience all the various levels of Spiritual Realization known to humanity—in order to discover how to Draw human beings into the "Bright" Divine Condition that He knew as His own True State and the True State of everyone.

This utter Submission to all aspects of human life was the first Purpose of Adi Da's Incarnation. In His Spiritual Autobiography, *The Knee Of Listening*, Avatar Adi Da recounts this amazing and heroic Ordeal, which lasted for the first thirty years of His Life.

*For definitions of terms and names, please see the Glossary (pp. 360-97).

In 1970, Avatar Adi Da finally Re-Awakened permanently to the "Bright", and embarked upon the second great Purpose of His Incarnation—the Process of "Teaching Man".

When He began to Teach others, Avatar Adi Da Samraj simply made Himself available to all who were willing to enter into the living Process of Real-God-Realization in His Company—a Process Which He summarized as the relation-

Los Angeles, 1972

ship to Him, rather than any method or technique of Spiritual attainment. Through that relationship—an extraordinary human and Spiritual intimacy—Avatar Adi Da Samraj perfectly embraced

The Mountain Of Attention Sanctuary, 1974

each of His devotees, using every kind of skillful means to Awaken them to the Truth that the separate, un-Enlightened self—with all its fear, anxieties, and fruitless seeking for Happiness—is self-imposed suffering, a contraction of the being (which He calls "the self-contraction").

Happiness, He Revealed, cannot be attained through any kind of search, because It is "Always Already the Case". And He Offered the practice of heart-Communion with Him as the means of going beyond the self-contraction and thereby Realizing Real Happiness.

I have Come to Live (now, and forever hereafter) with those who love Me with ego-overwhelming love, and I have Come to Love them likewise Overwhelmingly. . . .

16

Until you fall in love, love is what you <u>fear</u> to do. When you have fallen in love, and you <u>are</u> (thus) always already in love, then you cease to fear to love . . . . Those who fall in love with Me, Fall into Me. Those whose hearts are given, in love, to Me, Fall into My Heart. [*"What Will You Do If You Love Me?", from* Da Love-Ananda Gita]

In 1986, an Event occurred that marked the beginning of a great change in Avatar Adi Da's Work in the world. In this Great Event, a profound Yogic Swoon (taking the form of His apparent near-death) overwhelmed His body-mind, and Avatar Adi Da Samraj spontaneously began the process of relinquishing His Ordeal of Learning and Teaching Man. In the wake of that great Swoon, He simply Radiated His Divinity as never before. This was the beginning of what He calls His "Divine Self-'Emergence'". From that moment, Adi Da Samraj has devoted

The Mountain Of Attention, 1986

Himself increasingly to the third and eternal Purpose of His Avataric Incarnation—that of "Blessing Man" (and even all beings).

The Way of Adidam

Even after the Great Event in 1986, Avatar Adi Da continued to Work to ensure that His Revelation of the Way of Adidam was fully and firmly founded in the world. It was not until February 1999 that Avatar Adi Da Samraj declared that all the foundation Work of His Incarnation had been completely and finally Done. Everything necessary for the understanding and right practice of the real religious process, culminating in Divine Enlightenment, has been Said and Done by Him. The summary of His Wisdom-Teaching is preserved for all time in a series of twenty-three "Source-Texts" (described on pp. 27-38). And the Way of Adidam is fully established. This monumental Work has been accomplished by Avatar Adi Da in a little over a quarter of a century—twenty-seven years of ceaseless Instruction, in constant interaction with His devotees.

Avatar Adi Da's Full Revelation of Truth and His Work to establish the Way of Adidam required an immense struggle. The reason that struggle was inevitable is that human beings—especially in this time when the "individual" is regarded to be the supreme measure of value—have enormous resistance to any process that requires them to go beyond ego. Throughout history, people have tended to prefer forms of religion based on a system of beliefs and a code of moral and social behavior. But this kind of religion, as Avatar Adi Da has always pointed out, does not go to the core, to the root-suffering of human beings. This is because ordinary religion, rather than going beyond the ego-principle, is actually <u>based</u> on it: the ego-self stands at the center, and the Divine is sought and appealed to as the great Power that is going to save and satisfy the individual self. Avatar Adi Da Describes such religion as "client-centered".

In contrast to conventional religion, there is the process that Avatar Adi Da calls "true religion", religion that is centered in the Divine, in response to a true Spiritual Master who has (to at least some significant degree) <u>Realized</u> God (as opposed to merely offering teachings <u>about</u> God). Thus, true religion does not revolve around the individual's desire for any kind of "spiritual" consolations or experience—it is ego-transcending, rather than ego-serving. True religion based on ego-surrendering devotion to a Spiritual Master has existed for thousands of years, but the ecstatic confession of Avatar Adi Da's devotees is that now the Very Divine Itself is directly Present, Functioning as Divine Heart-Master, Alive in the human form of Avatar Adi Da Samraj.

All religions are historical forms of the Single and Ancient Way of Distracted love for the Divine Person, especially as Revealed in the Life and in the Company and in the Person of Incarnate Adepts (or Realizers) in their various degrees and stages of Realization. This is the Great Secret. ["What Will You Do If You Love Me?", from Da Love-Ananda Gita]

[E]goity is the "disease" that all the true Spiritual Masters of religion come here to cure. Unfortunately, . . . religious and Spiritual institutions tend to develop along lines that serve, accommodate, and represent the common egoity—and this is why the esoteric true Teachings of true Spiritual Masters tend to be bypassed, and even suppressed, in the drive to develop the exoteric cult of any particular Spiritual Master.

The relationship to Me . . . is a profound esoteric discipline, necessarily associated with real and serious and mature . . . practice of the "radical" Way (or root-Process) of Realizing Real God (Which Is Reality and Truth).

The Way of Adidam is the . . . Way to live in Freedom—not to be bound by separate and separative self, or by conditional Nature as a whole. Therefore, the ego-transcending devotional relationship to Me is the Context and the Means of Free Divine Self-Realization. ["Beyond the Cultic Tendency in Religion and Spirituality, and in Secular Society", from Ruchira Avatara Gita]

Standing Free of the Common Egoity

In His Spiritual Work with His devotees and the world, Avatar Adi Da Samraj has confronted the realities of egoity in a completely direct and unflinching manner. In His years of "Teaching Man", He did not hesitate in the slightest to grapple with the ego as it might be manifested in any moment by an individual devotee or a group of devotees—for the sake of helping His devotees understand and go beyond their ego-possessed disposition and activity.

However, even in the midst of that compassionate struggle with the forces of egoity, Avatar Adi Da has always Stood utterly Free of the ego-world. And, especially since the late 1970s, that Free Stand more and more took the form of His living in an essentially private circumstance, at one of the Hermitages established for Him (at secluded locations in California, Hawaii, and Fiji—see p. 333). In His Hermitage sphere, Avatar Adi Da is served by an intimate group of renunciate devotees, with whom He does particularly intensive Spiritual Work. And it is in the set-apart domain of His Hermitages (rather than in some kind of more public setting) that Avatar Adi Da receives His devotees in general (and, on rare occasions, specially invited members of the public), to Grant them His Spiritual Blessing.

The reasons why Avatar Adi Da maintains a Hermitage life are profound. The purpose of His Existence is to Reveal the Divine Reality—in other words, to Manifest the Freedom, Purity, and unbounded Blissfulness of His own Divine Nature, to Exist simply as He Is, without having to make compromises or adjustments in order to "fit in" to the ordinary ego-patterned world. Therefore, it is essential that He live in a sacred domain that conforms to Him and to the nature of His Spiritual Work, where He can remain independent of (but not disconnected from) the common world, even the daily world of the practical functioning of His community of devotees. Indeed, it is essential that He be free of institutional or organizational responsibilities relative to the gathering of His own devotees—because any such level of functioning would be a limitation on His Spiritual Work, an impingement on His Freedom to Manifest His own True Nature in the fullest and most pristine manner.

As He has commented many times, His Hermitage life is a life of seclusion, but not of isolation. His secluded Hermitage life is what allows His Divine Blessing to Flow into the world with the greatest possible force and effectiveness—it is what allows His Spiritual connection to all beings to be as strong as possible.

The "Problem" Is ego— Not Anything Else

For more than a quarter of a century, during His years of Teaching and Revelation (from 1972 to 1999), Avatar Adi Da undertook a vast, in-life "consideration" with His devotees of everything related to Spiritual life—from the most rudimentary matters to the most esoteric. One extremely important area of "consideration" was how to rightly relate to the most basic urges and activities of human life—what Avatar Adi Da describes as the realm of "money, food, and sex". (By "money", Avatar Adi Da means not only the earning and use of money itself, but the exercising of life-energy in general.)

In most religious traditions, an ascetical approach to these primal urges is recommended—in other words, desires related to "money, food, and sex" are to be minimized or denied. Avatar Adi Da took a different approach. When they are rightly engaged, ordinary human enjoyments are not a problem, not "sinful" or "anti-spiritual" in and of themselves. Thus, the root-problem of human beings is not any particular activity or desire of the body-mind, but the ego itself—the governing presumption that one is a separate and independent entity, threatened by the inevitable prospect of death. Therefore, in living dialogue and experimentation with His devotees, Avatar Adi Da brought to light, in detail, exactly how the human functions of money (or life-energy), food, and sex can be rightly engaged, in a truly ego-transcending manner—an entirely life-positive and non-suppressive manner that is both pleasurable and supportive of the Spiritual process in His Company.

The transcending of egoic involvement with "money, food, and sex" is a matter that relates to the beginnings of (or preparation for) real Spiritual practice. But the necessity for ego-transcendence does not end there. In His years of Teaching and Revelation, Avatar Adi Da Revealed that the ego is still present, in one form or another, in all the possible varieties of Spiritual attainment short of Most Perfect Divine Enlightenment. The word "Enlightenment" is used by different people and in different traditions with various different meanings. In Avatar Adi Da's language, "Enlightenment" (which He sometimes modifies, for the sake of clarifying His meaning, as "Most Perfect Divine Enlightenment", and which is synonymous with "Divine Self-Realization", "Real-God-Realization", and "seventh stage Realization") specifically means that the process of ego-transcendence has been entirely completed, relative to all the dimensions of the being. In other words, the ego has been transcended in three distinct phases—first at the physical (or gross) level (the level of "money, food, and sex"), then at the subtle level (the level of internal visions, auditions, and all kinds of mystical experience), and finally at the causal level (the root-level of conscious existence, wherein the sense of "I" and "other", or the subject-object dichotomy, seems to arise in Consciousness).

The complete process of ego-transcendence is extraordinarily profound and can only proceed on the basis of all the foundation disciplines and an ever-increasing heart-surrender to the Blessing-Transmission of Adi Da Samraj. Then, progressively, there is a transformation of view, a "positive disillusionment" (in Adi Da's Words) with each phase of egoity—until there is Most Perfect Divine Enlightenment (or "Open Eyes"), the Realization of Consciousness Itself as the Single Love-Blissful Reality and Source of existence.

Thus, the Way of Adidam truly represents an extraordinary and unique Offering to humankind. It is the Way Given by the Primal Divine Realizer and Revealer of Most Perfect Divine Enlightenment. He Transmits the Divinely Enlightened State, and He has the Power to Draw His devotees into that Perfectly Love-Blissful State. Such great statements about Avatar Adi Da Samraj are not something to be either accepted or rejected as a matter of belief. Rather, they are His Free Self-Confession to you—and His invitation to you to fall into His Divine Embrace.

A Testimony of Spiritual Practice

The process of the Way of Adidam unfolds by Avatar Adi Da's Grace, according to the depth of surrender and response in each devotee. One of the most extraordinary living testimonies to the Greatness and Truth of the Way of Adidam is one of Avatar Adi Da's longtime devotees, whose renunciate name is Ruchira Adidama Sukha Sundari Naitauba. Adidama Sukha Sundari has totally consecrated herself to Avatar Adi Da and lives always in His Sphere, in a relationship of unique intimacy and service. By her profound love of, and most exemplary surrender to, her Divine Heart-Master, she has become combined with Him at a unique depth. She manifests the signs of deep and constant immersion in His Divine Being, both in meditation and daily life. Adidama Sukha Sundari is a member of the Ruchira Sannyasin Order (the senior cultural authority within the gathering of Avatar Adi Da's devotees), practicing in the ultimate stages of the Way of Adidam.

Through a process of more than twenty years of intense testing, Avatar Adi Da has been able to lead Adidama Sukha Sundari to the threshold of Divine Enlightenment. The profound and ecstatic relationship with Avatar Adi Da that Adidama Sukha Sundari has come to know can be felt in this intimate letter of devotional confession to Him:

RUCHIRA ADIDAMA SUKHA SUNDARI: Bhagavan Love-Ananda, Supreme and Divine Person, Real-God-Body of Love,

I rest in Your Constant and Perfect Love-Embrace, with no need but to forever worship You. Suddenly in love, Mastered at heart, always with my head at Your Supreme and Holy Feet, I am beholding and recognizing Your "Bright" Divine Person. My Beloved, You so "Brightly" Descend and utterly Convert this heart, mind, body, and breath, from separate self to the "Bhava" of Your Love-Bliss-Happiness.

Ruchira Adidama Sukha Sundari Naitauba with Ruchira Avatar Adi Da Samraj, 1999

23

Supreme Lord Ruchira, the abandonment of the contracted personality, the relinquishment of ego-bondage to the world, and the profound purification and release of ego-limitations—all brought about by Your Grace, throughout the years since I first came to You—has culminated in a great comprehensive force of one-pointed devotion to You and a great certainty in the Inherent Sufficiency of Realization Itself. The essence of my practice is to always remain freely submitted and centralized in You—the Condition Prior to all bondage, all modification, and all illusion.

My Beloved Lord Ruchira, You have Moved me to renounce all egoic "bonding" with conditionally manifested others, conditionally manifested worlds, and conditionally manifested self, to enter into the depths of this "in-love" and utter devotion to You. Finding You has led to a deep urge to abandon all superficiality and to simply luxuriate in Your Divine Body and Person. All separation is shattered in Your Divine Love-Bliss-"Bhava". Your Infusion is Utter. I feel You everywhere.

I am Drawn, by Grace of Your Spiritual Presence, into profound meditative Contemplation of Your Divine State. Sometimes, when I am entering into these deep states of meditation, I remain vaguely aware of the body, and particularly of the breath and the heartbeat. I feel the heart and lungs slow down. Then I am sometimes aware of my breath and heartbeat being suspended in a state of Yogic sublimity. Then there is no awareness of body, no awareness of mind, no perceptual awareness, and no conceptual awareness. There is only abiding in Contemplation of You in Your Domain of Consciousness Itself. And, when I resume association with the body and begin once again to hear my breath and heartbeat, I feel the remarkable Power of Your Great Samadhi. I feel no necessity for anything, and I feel Your Capability to Bless and Change and Meditate all. I can feel how this entrance into objectless worship of You as Consciousness Itself (allowing this Abiding to deepen ever so profoundly, by utter submission of separate self to You) establishes me in a different relationship to everything that arises.

My Beloved Bhagavan, Love-Ananda, I have Found You. Now, by Your Grace, I am able to behold You and live in this constant Embrace. This is my Joy and Happiness and the Yoga of ego-renunciation I engage. [October 11, 1997]

Inherent in this confession is the certainty that lasting happiness cannot be found in the things of the world, all of which change and die. This is a crucial understanding—which is at the foundation of real religious life, and which grows over time as one advances in the Spiritual process.

AVATAR ADI DA SAMRAJ: Absolutely NOTHING conditional is satisfactory. Everything conditional disappears—everything. This fact should move the heart to cling to Me, to resort to Me, to take refuge in Me. This is why people become devotees of Mine. This is the reason for the religious life. The unsatisfactoriness of conditional existence requires resort to the Divine Source, and the Realization of the Divine Source-Condition. [August 9, 1997]

Finding Real Happiness

This book is Avatar Adi Da's invitation to you to come to know Him—by freely considering His words, and feeling their impact on your life and heart. Avatar Adi Da Himself has never been satisfied with anything conditional. He has never been satisfied with anything less than Real, Permanent, Absolute Happiness—even in the midst of the inevitable sufferings of life. And that Happiness is What He is Offering to you.

The heart has a question.
The heart must be Satisfied.
Without that Satisfaction—Which is necessarily Spiritual in Nature—there is no Real Happiness.

The contraction of the heart is what you are suffering.
It is the ego.
The egoic life is a search—founded upon (and initiated by) the self-contraction of the total body-mind.
The egoic life is a self-caused search to be relieved of the distress of self-reduced, self-diminished, even utterly self-destroyed Love-Bliss.

Love-Bliss gone, non-existent, unknown—just this pumping, agitated, psycho-physical thing.

The ego-"I" does not know What It <u>Is</u> That Is Happening.
You are just "hanging out" for a while, until "it" drops dead.
It is not good enough.
Therefore, I Advise you to begin to be profoundly religious, and not waste any time about it.

You must Realize the Spiritual Condition of Existence Itself . . . .
You cannot be sane if you think there is only flesh, only materiality, only grossness.
Such thinking is not fully "natural", not enough.
There is "Something" you are not accounting for.
Be open to "Whatever" That Is.
You must look into this. [Hridaya Rosary]

Avatar Adi Da Samraj's Teaching-Word: The "Source-Texts" of Adidam

For twenty-seven years (from 1972 to 1999), Avatar Adi Da Samraj devoted Himself tirelessly to Teaching those who came to Him. Even before He formally began to Teach in 1972, He had already written the earliest versions of two of His primary Texts—His "liturgical drama" (*The Mummery*) and His Spiritual Autobiography (*The Knee Of Listening*). Then, when He opened the doors of His first Ashram in Hollywood (on April 25, 1972), He initiated a vast twenty-seven-year "conversation" with the thousands of people who approached Him during that period of time—a "conversation" that included thousands of hours of sublime and impassioned Discourse and thousands of pages of profound and exquisite Writing. And the purpose of that "conversation" was to fully communicate the Truth for Real.

Both His Speech and His Writing were conducted as a kind of living "laboratory". He was constantly asking to hear His devotees' questions and their responses to His Written and Spoken Word. He was constantly calling His devotees to <u>live</u> what He was Teaching and discover its Truth in their own experience—not merely to passively accept it as dogma. He was constantly testing whether His communication on any particular subject was complete and detailed enough or whether He needed to say more. And everything He said and wrote was a spontaneous expression of His own direct Awareness of Reality—never a merely theoretical or speculative proposition, never a statement merely inherited from traditional sources.

This immense outpouring of Revelation and Instruction came to completion in the years 1997-1999. During that period, Avatar

Adi Da Samraj created a series of twenty-three books that He designated as the "Source-Texts" of Adidam. He incorporated into these books His most essential Writings and Discourses from all the preceding years, as well as many new Writings and Discourses that had never been published previously. His magnificent "Source-Texts" are thus His Eternal Message to all. They contain His complete Revelation of Truth, and (together with the "Supportive Texts", in which Avatar Adi Da Gives further detailed Instruction relative to the functional, practical, relational, and cultural disciplines of the Way of Adidam) they give His fully detailed description of the entire process of Awakening, culminating in Divine Enlightenment.

Avatar Adi Da's twenty-three "Source-Texts" are not simply a series of books each of which is entirely distinct from all the others. Rather, they form an intricately interwoven fabric. Each book contains some material found in no other "Source-Text", some material shared with certain other "Source-Texts", and some material included in all twenty-three of the "Source-Texts". (The three Texts shared by all twenty-three books are "Do Not Misunderstand Me", "My Divine Disclosure", and "The Heart-Summary Of Adidam". Each of these Texts has a particular function and message that is essential to every one of the books.) Thus, to read Avatar Adi Da's "Source-Texts" is to engage a special kind of study (similar to the practice of repeating a mantra), in which certain Texts are repeatedly read, such that they penetrate one's being even more profoundly and take on deeper significance by being read in a variety of different contexts. Furthermore, each of the "Source-Texts" of Adidam is thereby a complete and self-contained Argument. Altogether, to study Avatar Adi Da's "Source-Texts" is to enter into an "eternal conversation" with Him, in which different meanings emerge at different times—always appropriate to the current moment in one's life and experience.

At the conclusion of His paramount "Source-Text", *The Dawn Horse Testament*, Avatar Adi Da Samraj makes His own passionate Confession of the Impulse that led Him to create His twenty-three "Source-Texts".

Now I Have, By All My "Crazy" Means, Revealed My One and Many Divine Secrets As The Great Person Of The Heart. For Your Sake, I Made My Every Work and Word. And Now, By Every Work and Word I Made, I Have Entirely Confessed (and Showed) Myself—and Always Freely, and Even As A Free Man, In The "Esoteric" Language Of Intimacy and Ecstasy, Openly Worded To You (and To all). Even Now (and Always), By This (My Avatarically Self-Revealed Divine Word Of Heart), I Address every Seeming Separate being (and each one As The Heart Itself), Because It Is Necessary That all beings, Even The Entire Cosmic Domain Of Seeming Separate beings, Be (In all times and places) Called To Wisdom and The Heart.

Capitalization and Punctuation in the "Source-Texts" of Avatar Adi Da Samraj

Speaking and Writing in the twentieth and twenty-first centuries, Avatar Adi Da Samraj has used the English language as the medium for His Communication. Over the years of His Teaching-Work, Avatar Adi Da developed a thoroughly original manner of employing English as a sacred language. (He also includes some Sanskrit terminology in His Teaching vocabulary, in order to supplement the relatively undeveloped sacred vocabulary of English.)

Avatar Adi Da's unique use of English is evident not only with respect to vocabulary, but also with respect to capitalization and punctuation.

Vocabulary. A glossary is included at the end of this book (pp. 360-97), where specialized terms (both English terms and terms derived from Sanskrit) are defined.

Capitalization. Avatar Adi Da frequently capitalizes words that would not ordinarily be capitalized in English—and such capitalized words include not only nouns, but also pronouns, verbs, adjectives, adverbs, and even articles and prepositions. By such capitalization, He is indicating that the word refers (either inherently, or by virtue of the context) to the Unconditional Divine Reality, rather than the conditional (or worldly) reality. For example:

If there is no escape from (or no Way out of) the corner (or the "centered" trap) of ego-"I"—the heart goes mad, and the body-mind becomes more and more "dark" (bereft of the Indivisible and Inherently Free Light of the Self-Evident, and Self-Evidently Divine, Love-Bliss That Is Reality Itself). ["Do Not Misunderstand Me"]

Avatar Adi Da's chosen conventions of capitalization vary in different "Source-Texts" and in different sections of a given "Source-Text". In certain "Source-Texts" (notably *The Dawn Horse Testament Of The Ruchira Avatar, The Heart Of The Dawn Horse Testament Of The Ruchira Avatar,* and the various Parts of the other "Source-Texts" that are excerpted from *The Dawn Horse Testament Of The Ruchira Avatar*), Avatar Adi Da employs a highly unusual convention of capitalization, in which the overwhelming majority of all words are capitalized, and only those words that indicate the egoic (or dualistic) point of view are left lower-cased. This capitalization convention (which Avatar Adi Da has worked out to an extraordinarily subtle degree—in ways that are often startling) is in itself a Teaching device, intended to communicate His fundamental Revelation that "There Is Only Real God", and that only the ego (or the dualistic or separative point of view) prevents us from living and Realizing that Truth. For example:

Therefore, For My Every Devotee, all conditions Must Be Aligned and Yielded In Love With Me—or Else any object or any other Will Be The Cause Of Heart-Stress, self-Contraction, Dissociation, Clinging, Boredom, Doubt, The Progressive Discomfort Of Diminished Love-Bliss, and All The Forgetfulness Of Grace and Truth and Happiness Itself. [Ruchira Avatara Hridaya-Tantra Yoga]

Note that "and" and "or" are lower-cased—because these conjunctions are (here, and in most contexts) primal expressions of the point of view of duality. Also note that "all conditions", "any object", "<u>any</u> other", and "self-" are lower-cased, while "Heart-Stress", "Contraction", "Dissociation", "Clinging," "Boredom", "Doubt", "Discomfort", "Diminished", and "Forgetfulness" are capitalized. Avatar Adi Da is telling us that unpleasant or apparently "negative" states are not inherently egoic. It is only the presumption of duality and separateness—as expressed by such words as "conditions", "object", "other", and "self"—that is egoic.

Punctuation. Because of the inevitable complexity of much of His Communication, Avatar Adi Da has developed the conventions of punctuation (commas, dashes, and parentheses) to an extraordinary degree. This allows Him to clearly articulate complex sentences in such a way that His intended meaning can be expressed with utmost precision—free of vagueness, ambiguity, or unclarity. Many of His sentences contain parenthetical definitions or modifying phrases as a way of achieving unmistakable clarity of meaning. For example:

The Apparently individual (or Separate) self Is Not a "spark" (or an Eternal fraction) Of Self-Radiant Divinity, and Somehow Complete (or Whole) In itself. [<u>Real</u> God <u>Is</u> The Indivisible Oneness Of Unbroken Light]

Another punctuation convention relates to the use of quotation marks. Avatar Adi Da sometimes uses quotation marks in accordance with standard convention, to indicate the sense of "so to speak":

Make the contact with Me that gets you to "stick" to Me like glue. Your "sticking" to Me is what must happen. [Hridaya Rosary]

In other instances, He uses quotation marks to indicate that a word or phrase is being used with a particular technical meaning that differs from common usage:

During <u>all</u> of My present Lifetime (of Avataric Divine Incarnation), the "<u>Bright</u>" has <u>always</u> been My Realization—and the "<u>Thumbs</u>" and My own "Radical" Understanding have <u>always</u> been My Way in the "Bright".

"Bright", "Thumbs" (referring to a specific form of the Infusion of Avatar Adi Da's Divine Spirit-Current in the body-mind), and "Radical" are all used with specific technical meanings here (as defined in the Glossary).

Finally, Avatar Adi Da also makes extensive use of underlining to indicate special emphasis on certain words (or phrases, or even entire sentences):

> The <u>only</u> true religion is the religion that <u>Realizes</u> Truth. The <u>only</u> true science is the science that <u>Knows</u> Truth. The <u>only</u> true man or woman (or being of any kind) is one that <u>Surrenders</u> to Truth. The only true world is one that <u>Embodies</u> Truth. And the only True (and <u>Real</u>) God Is the One Reality (or Condition of Being) That <u>Is</u> Truth. ["Do Not Misunderstand <u>Me</u>"]

The True Dawn Horse

Ruchira Avatara Hridaya-Siddha Yoga is Book Eight of *The Seventeen Companions Of The True Dawn Horse*. The "True Dawn Horse" is a reference to *The Dawn Horse Testament Of The Ruchira Avatar*, the final book among Avatar Adi Da's "Source-Texts". In *The Dawn Horse Testament,* Avatar Adi Da describes the entire Process of Real-God-Realization in detail. Each of *The Seventeen Companions Of The True Dawn Horse* is a "Companion" to *The Dawn Horse Testament* in the sense that it is an elaboration of a major theme (or themes) from *The Dawn Horse Testament*. And in many of the "Seventeen Companions", an excerpt from *The Dawn Horse Testament* forms the principal part, around which the other parts of the book revolve. (In *Ruchira Avatara Hridaya-Siddha Yoga*, the principal part—Part Three—comprises chapters eleven through fifteen of *The Dawn Horse Testament*.)

The Sacred Image of the Dawn Horse (which appears above) derives from a vision that Avatar Adi Da Samraj had one night during the spring of 1970, a few months before His Divine Re-Awakening (on September 10, 1970). As His physical body lay sleeping, Avatar Adi Da wandered in subtle form into an open hall, where a great Adept was seated on a throne. The Adept's disciples were lined up in rows in front of him. A pathway bounded on both sides by the disciples led to the throne. Avatar Adi Da was Himself standing at the end of a row a few rows away from the Adept's chair.

The disciples were apparently assembled to learn the miraculous Yogic power of materializing something from nothing. They waited respectfully for the lesson to begin.

The Adept then initiated the process of materialization. A brief while later, the disciples got up and left the room, satisfied that the materialization had been accomplished, although nothing had appeared yet. The Adept remained sitting in his chair, and Avatar Adi Da remained standing before him, attentive to the process at hand.

A vaporous mass gradually took shape in the space between Avatar Adi Da and the Adept. At first it was not clearly defined, but Avatar Adi Da recognized it as it began to take on the features of a horse. Gradually, the vapor coalesced into a living, breathing brown horse. Its features were as fine as a thoroughbred's, but it was quite small, perhaps three feet tall. The horse stood alert, motionless, facing away from the Adept's chair.

At this point in the dream vision, Avatar Adi Da returned to physical consciousness and the waking state.

It was many years later, at the time when Avatar Adi Da was starting to write *The Dawn Horse Testament*, that He Revealed the identity of the Adept He had visited in that vision:

AVATAR ADI DA SAMRAJ: I was at once the Adept who performed the miracle of manifesting the horse, and also the one who was party to the observation of it and its result. And I did not have any feeling of being different from the horse itself. I was <u>making</u> the horse, I was <u>observing</u> the horse, and I was <u>being</u> the horse. [October 18, 1984]

The Dawn Horse is, therefore, a symbol for Avatar Adi Da Samraj Himself—and *The Dawn Horse Testament* is His Personal

Testament to all beings. Avatar Adi Da has commented that He refers to Himself and to His principal "Source-Text" as the "True Dawn Horse" because the effects of His Liberating Work in the world will appear only gradually—just as, in the vision, the horse gradually became visible after the Adept had initiated its materialization.

In creating the Sacred Image of the Dawn Horse, Avatar Adi Da transformed His original vision of a small brown horse, with all four hooves planted on the ground, into a winged white stallion, rearing up nearly vertically:

AVATAR ADI DA SAMRAJ: The horse's pose is majestic and intended to show great strength. White was chosen for its obvious association with Light, or Consciousness Itself. The Image is not precisely associated with the vision of 1970. It is visual language, intended to communicate the full meaning of My Dawn Horse Vision, rather than to be a realistic presentation of it.

The Titles and Subtitles of The Twenty-Three "Source-Texts" of Avatar Adi Da Samraj

The twenty-three "Source-Texts" of Avatar Adi Da Samraj include:

(1) an opening series of five books on the fundamentals of the Way of Adidam (*The Five Books Of The Heart Of The Adidam Revelation*)

(2) an extended series of seventeen books covering the principal aspects of the Way of Adidam in detail (*The Seventeen Companions Of The True Dawn Horse*)

(3) Avatar Adi Da's paramount "Source-Text" summarizing the entire course of the Way of Adidam (*The Dawn Horse Testament*)

The basic content of each "Source-Text" is summarily described by Avatar Adi Da in the title and subtitle of each book. Thus, the-following list of titles and subtitles indicates the vast scope and the artful interconnectedness of His twenty-three "Source-Texts". (For brief descriptions of each "Source-Text", please see "The Sacred Literature of Avatar Adi Da Samraj", pp. 398-408.)

The Five Books Of The Heart Of The Adidam Revelation

BOOK ONE
Aham Da Asmi
(Beloved, I Am Da)
The "Late-Time" Avataric Revelation Of The True and Spiritual Divine Person (The egoless Personal Presence Of Reality and Truth, Which Is The Only Real God)

BOOK TWO
Ruchira Avatara Gita
(The Way Of The Divine Heart-Master)
The "Late-Time" Avataric Revelation Of The Great Secret Of The Divinely Self-Revealed Way That Most Perfectly Realizes The True and Spiritual Divine Person (The egoless Personal Presence Of Reality and Truth, Which Is The Only Real God)

BOOK THREE
Da Love-Ananda Gita
(The Free Gift Of The Divine Love-Bliss)
The "Late-Time" Avataric Revelation Of The Great Means To Worship and To Realize The True and Spiritual Divine Person (The egoless Personal Presence Of Reality and Truth, Which Is The Only Real God)

BOOK FOUR
Hridaya Rosary
(Four Thorns Of Heart-Instruction)
The "Late-Time" Avataric Revelation Of The Universally Tangible Divine Spiritual Body, Which Is The Supreme Agent Of The Great Means To Worship and To Realize The True and Spiritual Divine Person (The egoless Personal Presence Of Reality and Truth, Which Is The Only Real God)

BOOK FIVE
Eleutherios
(The <u>Only</u> Truth That Sets The Heart Free)

The "Late-Time" Avataric Revelation Of The "Perfect Practice"
Of The Great Means To Worship and To Realize The True and
Spiritual Divine Person (The egoless Personal Presence Of
Reality and Truth, Which <u>Is</u> The Only <u>Real</u> God)

◆ ◆ ◆

The Seventeen Companions
Of The True Dawn Horse

BOOK ONE
<u>Real</u> God <u>Is</u> The Indivisible Oneness
Of Unbroken Light

Reality, Truth, and The "Non-Creator" God
In The True World-Religion Of Adidam

BOOK TWO
The Truly Human New World-Culture
Of <u>Unbroken</u> Real-God-Man

The <u>Eastern</u> Versus The <u>Western</u> Traditional Cultures
Of Mankind, and The Unique New <u>Non-Dual</u> Culture
Of The True World-Religion Of Adidam

BOOK THREE
The <u>Only</u> Complete Way To Realize
The Unbroken Light Of <u>Real</u> God

An Introductory Overview Of The "Radical" Divine Way
Of The True World-Religion Of Adidam

BOOK FOUR
The Knee Of Listening

The Early-Life Ordeal and The "Radical"
Spiritual Realization Of The Ruchira Avatar

BOOK FIVE
The Divine Siddha-Method Of The Ruchira Avatar
The Divine Way Of Adidam Is An ego-Transcending
Relationship, Not An ego-Centric Technique

BOOK SIX
The Mummery
A Parable Of The Divine True Love

BOOK SEVEN
He-and-She Is Me
The Indivisibility Of Consciousness and Light
In The Divine Body Of The Ruchira Avatar

BOOK EIGHT
Ruchira Avatara Hridaya-Siddha Yoga
The Divine (and Not Merely Cosmic) Spiritual Baptism
In The Divine Way Of Adidam

BOOK NINE
Ruchira Avatara Hridaya-Tantra Yoga
The Physical-Spiritual (and Truly Religious) Method
Of Mental, Emotional, Sexual, and Whole Bodily Health
and Enlightenment In The Divine Way Of Adidam

BOOK TEN
The Seven Stages Of Life
Transcending The Six Stages Of egoic Life,
and Realizing The ego-Transcending Seventh Stage Of Life,
In The Divine Way Of Adidam

BOOK ELEVEN
The All-Completing and Final
Divine Revelation To Mankind
A Summary Description Of The Supreme Yoga
Of The Seventh Stage Of Life In The Divine Way Of Adidam

BOOK TWELVE

The Heart Of The Dawn Horse Testament Of The Ruchira Avatar

The Epitome Of The "Testament Of Secrets" Of The Divine
World-Teacher, Ruchira Avatar Adi Da Samraj

BOOK THIRTEEN

What, Where, When, How, Why, and <u>Who</u> To Remember To Be Happy

A Simple Explanation Of The Divine Way Of Adidam
(For Children, and <u>Everyone</u> Else)

BOOK FOURTEEN

Santosha Adidam

The Essential Summary Of The Divine Way Of Adidam

BOOK FIFTEEN

The Lion Sutra

The "Perfect Practice" Teachings In The Divine Way Of Adidam

BOOK SIXTEEN

The Overnight Revelation Of Conscious Light

The "My House" Discourses
On The Indivisible Tantra Of Adidam

BOOK SEVENTEEN

The Basket Of Tolerance

The Perfect Guide To Perfectly <u>Unified</u> Understanding
Of The One and Great Tradition Of Mankind,
and Of The Divine Way Of Adidam As The Perfect <u>Completing</u>
Of The One and Great Tradition Of Mankind

◆ ◆ ◆

The Dawn Horse Testament Of The Ruchira Avatar

The Dawn Horse Testament Of The Ruchira Avatar

The "Testament Of Secrets" Of The Divine World-Teacher,
Ruchira Avatar Adi Da Samraj

Camera Illuminata

The "Bright"-Field Photography of Avatar Adi Da Samraj

At the same time that He was completing His Work to create a complete verbal Teaching in His "Source-Texts", Avatar Adi Da Samraj started taking black-and-white photographs as another potent means of communicating His message about Reality. He calls the collected body of His photographic work His "Camera Illuminata" collection. The cover image of each of His twenty-three "Source-Texts" includes a central image and a border image, both of which are photographs taken by Avatar Adi Da Samraj (and specifically chosen by Him as an image appropriate to that particular "Source-Text"). "Camera Illuminata" means "Bright Room", in contrast to the traditional term "camera obscura" (which literally means "dark room"). Thus, instead of representing the world from the "dark" point of view (or the presumption that dying matter is all there is to reality), the Camera Illuminata of Adi Da Samraj Reveals the world as a "Bright" (or Divinely Self-Radiant) Field.

Avatar Adi Da's "Bright"-Field photographic images are one of His means for conveying His Spiritual Transmission and Blessing— for the subject of Avatar Adi Da's photography is not the world as we see it, but the world as the "Bright" Field of Reality that He sees. His photography would transport us beyond our ordinary habits of thinking and perceiving into the Divine Light, in Which there is no sense of separation, otherness, or limitation.

AVATAR ADI DA SAMRAJ: From the conventional point of view, a photographer only makes pictures of conventional reality, of light falling on objects, as if the solid reality were the only reality. But neither the fixed separate point of view nor the apparently solid objective world is the Fundamental Reality. The Divine Conscious Light Is the Fundamental Reality of Existence.

Avatar Adi Da's photographic images communicate the non-dual perception of Reality via a unique process, which He describes as His "inherently egoless participatory relationship" with the subjects of His photographs (both human and non-human). Thus, His photography transcends the conventions of "self" and "other", or "subject" and "object".

AVATAR ADI DA SAMRAJ: Out of this process, images can be made that Reveal Reality, rather than merely communicating the conventions of "ego" and "other".

Therefore, even the viewing of Adi Da's Camera Illuminata images is an inherently participatory event. That is to say, His photographs, like all great art, place a demand upon us to go beyond the ordinary fixed point of view. They are a call to go beyond our ordinary limits—for each of His images is a communication of the Divine "Brightness", transforming our ordinary perception of the world into sacred occasion.

Avatar Adi Da Samraj photographing in the California redwoods

When viewed in its entirety, Avatar Adi Da's Camera Illuminata collection is an ecstatic Revelation-Transmission of the Divine Truth that He has Come to Reveal and Teach to humankind. There is extraordinary beauty to be appreciated in Avatar Adi Da's photographs, but the real purpose of His artistry is to bring Light into our lives, to literally En-Light-en us—to Liberate us from the un-Illumined and mortal vision of egoity. By offering us His Camera Illuminata, Adi Da Samraj would have us discover that "Bright-Field", that Non-separate Reality, in Which the ever-changing dualities of light and darkness rise and fall.

AVATAR ADI DA SAMRAJ: In My approach to making photographic images, I want to convey the Truth of Reality—the Truth of the Inherently egoless, Non-dual Subjective Light. I am trying to convey My own Revelation of the Nature of Reality through the artifice of visual images.

The border image on the cover of this book is a photograph taken by Avatar Adi Da Samraj. He refers to this photograph as an image of "True Water", which is one of His poetic descriptions for Consciousness Itself as the "Medium" in which all phenomena arise (and of which they are all modifications).

An Overview of
Ruchira Avatara Hridaya-Siddha Yoga

What is the sublime "Intoxicant" that Awakens the heart beyond mere belief (or even active faith) in a Higher Power, to the actual <u>Realization</u> of God, or Truth, or Reality Itself? The esoteric religious and Spiritual traditions of the world answer that that Divine "Intoxicant" is nothing other than the tangible Spirit-Power which sustains and pervades and, ultimately, transcends all living beings and things.

Just beyond the realm of ordinary human awareness, living beings and things can be felt to be surrounded and pervaded by a universal field of natural life-energy—indeed, that universal field of natural life-energy is what people are experiencing when they speak of feeling the inherent "connectedness" of every one and every thing.

Spirit-Power itself, however, is not at all a matter of ordinary human awareness. When it is experienced, it is spoken of in <u>Divine</u> terms, as a Spiritual Awakening to the direct Presence of God, or as an almost unbearable Process of overwhelming Spiritual Baptism. What the recorded testimony of authentic Spiritual Realizers throughout history makes clear is that not only is Spiritual Baptism a <u>real</u> process, it is a process that is of a different order of magnitude of Force, Intensity, and Bliss than any ordinary or even any extraordinary experience of the universal field of natural life-energy. Rightly understood, Spirit-Power is itself the underlying Source of the universal field of natural life-energy (as well as of all beings, things, and worlds).

This distinction between natural life-energy and Spirit-Power is particularly important, because the same subtle pathways that conduct the flow of natural life-energy in the human body-mind also conduct the Flow of Spirit-Power in the process of Spiritual Baptism (or "Shaktipat").

In *Ruchira Avatara Hridaya-Siddha Yoga*, the Divine World-Teacher, Ruchira Avatar Adi Da Samraj, Reveals that the various esoteric traditions of Spiritual Baptism found throughout human history fall into two fundamental camps.

The first camp is represented by traditions which idealize the ascent of Spirit-Power up the spinal line as the effective means to the "higher" realizations of mystical reveries, heaven worlds, and, ultimately, to the formless realization of Supreme Love-Bliss (which is referred to in the Spiritual traditions of India as "Nirvikalpa Samadhi"). In their idealization of the ascending process, these traditions often speak in terms of "raising" the "Kundalini Shakti" (or "Serpent Power")—often visualized as lying coiled asleep at the base of the spine—so that it drives upwards, to and beyond the brain core.

Avatar Adi Da Reveals that because traditions that fall into this first camp presume that the Kundalini Shakti is personal and internal, the techniques and practices they have developed are actually often simply a matter of manipulating natural life-energies within the human body-mind (rather than a matter of directly magnifying the true Spirit-Power). Such practices (when practiced on their own) lead, at best, to only partially Awakened Kundalini Shakti.

The traditions representative of the second (and senior) camp speak of (or at least tacitly acknowledge) the full circle of conductivity in the human body-mind, descending down the frontal line and ascending up the spinal line, and such traditions recognize the "Heavenly" (rather than personal or internal) origin of the Kundalini Shakti. The traditions that fall into the second camp, therefore, acknowledge the essential preliminary of the <u>descent</u> of Spirit-Power as it is given from "Above"—in almost every case via a Siddha, or an authentic living Master of Spiritual Transmission—before there can be authentic (or full and complete) Kundalini Awakening.

Taken together, these two camps represent what Avatar Adi Da describes as "Cosmic Spiritual Baptism".

One of Avatar Adi Da's pivotal "Considerations" relative to the Process of Most Perfect Real-God-Realization revolves around the critical difference between Cosmic Spiritual Baptism (or Spiritual

Baptism as it has been traditionally understood and experienced by all previous esoteric Spiritual traditions) and Divine Spiritual Baptism (or Spiritual Baptism as it is uniquely Revealed and Given by Him in the Divine Way of Adidam). *Ruchira Avatara Hridaya-Siddha Yoga* is Avatar Adi Da's summary of that extraordinary "Consideration".

As with each of Avatar Adi Da's "Source-Texts", *Ruchira Avatara Hridaya-Siddha Yoga* begins with His First Word, "Do Not Misunderstand Me—I Am Not 'Within' you, but you Are In Me, and I Am Not a Mere 'Man' in the 'Middle' of Mankind, but All of Mankind Is Surrounded, and Pervaded, and Blessed By Me". In this remarkable Essay, Avatar Adi Da explains that His open Confession of Most Perfect Real-God-Realization is not to be misapprehended as a claim of the "Status" of the "Creator"-God of conventional religious belief—but, rather, His Divine Self-Confession must be rightly understood and appreciated as a Free Demonstration of What is Realized in the Perfect Fulfillment of esoteric Spiritual practice, Which is the Most Perfectly Non-Dual Realization of Reality Itself. By virtue of His Free Demonstration, Avatar Adi Da Samraj makes clear that Most Perfect Real-God-Realization is the ultimate Potential and Destiny of all beings.

The Prologue of *Ruchira Avatara Hridaya-Siddha Yoga*, "My Divine Disclosure" (also, like "First Word", found in all twenty-three "Source-Texts"), is a poetic epitome of Avatar Adi Da's Divine Self-Revelation. It is His Call to every being to turn to Him at heart and practice the life of devotional surrender in Real God.

Part One, "I (Alone) Am The Adidam Revelation", is Avatar Adi Da's fullest elucidation of the uniqueness of His Revelation of the seventh stage Realization. In this Essay—remarkable in its scope and profundity—Avatar Adi Da examines His own Course of Divine Self-Realization in order to Demonstrate how the two primary divisions of the Great Tradition—the Emanationist (or absorptive mystical) Way (associated with the first five stages of life) and the non-Emanationist (or Transcendentalist) Way (associated with the sixth stage of life)—are, in Truth, only different aspects of the great seven-stage process of Most Perfect Divine Self-Realization.

The Prologue and Part One establish the overall context for Avatar Adi Da's specific "Consideration" of Spiritual Baptism. That specific "Consideration" begins in Part Two, "The Divine Yoga Of My Crashing-Down Avataric Descent", comprising two Talks by Avatar Adi Da.

In the first Talk of Part Two, Avatar Adi Da explains that the Way of Adidam is a matter of freely allowing (and responsively participating in) His Divine "Crashing-Down" into the body-mind As Love-Bliss—allowing it to the degree of utter ego-dissolution. Avatar Adi Da further explains that the traditional idealism associated with the Kundalini Shakti (or Cosmic Spirit-Power) is a search for ascended (or subtle) phenomena—a search that does not lead to Most Perfect Divine Enlightenment. He then describes the unique characteristics of the Way of Adidam:

The traditional Yogic descriptions are the product of human devices, of human suffering, and of the human search to find a way "out". All kinds of paths (which are worthy, certainly) have been produced by human seeking—discovered in that process by great individuals. But every one of those paths is a way "back"—a path of seeking to Find God (rather than a Way based on Always Already Finding Real God).

The traditional Yogas are ego-based efforts to Find God. The Yoga of Adidam—Which I Give to you as a Gift—is the Yoga of Real God Come, Real God Visiting, Real God Invading, Real God Making the Yoga, Real God Who Is the Yoga, Real God Who Is the Only One Who Is, Real God Who Is That Which Always Already Is.

In the second Talk of Part Two, Avatar Adi Da Speaks with several of His devotees about what it means to "Locate" His Divine Spiritual Body, clarifying how to distinguish between the effects of His Spiritual Presence and His Spiritual Presence Itself.

Part Three, the principal Text, "Divine Spiritual Baptism Versus Cosmic Spiritual Baptism", comprises five sections. In the first section, Avatar Adi Da describes Amrita Nadi—the ultimate essential structure of human esoteric anatomy, which structure is "regenerated" in the Process of Most Perfect Real-God-Realization. And He explains that Spirit-conductivity is a necessary characteristic of practice, even from the beginning of the Way of Adidam.

In the second section of Part Three, Avatar Adi Da Reveals that His Divine Spiritual Baptism (or "Hridaya-Shaktipat", meaning "The Divine Grace-Power [Shaktipat] Of The Inherently egoless Heart [Hridaya]") originates prior to all of conditional existence, always senior to conditionally (or cosmically) manifested Spiritual Baptism (or Kundalini Shaktipat). He describes how Kundalini Shaktipat is always associated with the first five stages of life, and with movements of attention within the realms of conditional possibilities. In contrast, He Reveals that His Hridaya-Shaktipat always works to dissolve attention in the Heart (the Divine Self-Condition and Source-Condition of all beings and things), by drawing His devotee to the "Perfect Practice" (or practice of the Way of Adidam in the context of the sixth and, then, the seventh stage of life).

In the third section of Part Three, Avatar Adi Da describes Ruchira Avatara Bhakti Yoga, which is the fundamental practice throughout the entire course of the Way of Adidam. He Reveals the extraordinary progression of the reception of His Hridaya-Shaktipat as His devotee's practice develops in the listening stages, and then in the hearing stages, and then in the seeing (or truly Spiritually Awakened) stages of practice. And He Reveals how all of that is preparation for the "Perfect Practice" of the Way of Adidam.

In the fourth section of Part Three, Avatar Adi Da Calls His Spiritually Awakened devotee to rightly conduct and conserve His Grace-Given Divine Spirit-Power and (when the devotee's practice matures into the sixth and, then, the seventh stage of life) to "Allow Me To Reveal The Eternal Freedom, and The Boundless 'Bright' Sphere and Space, Of My Divine Self-Domain—Which Is The Eternal Condition Of My Avatarically Self-Revealed (and Self-Evidently Divine) Person, Beyond The Cosmic Mandala."

In the fifth section of Part Three, Avatar Adi Da describes the progress of the conductivity of His Hridaya-Shakti in the full Circle (or combined frontal and spinal lines) of His devotee's body-mind. He describes how this becomes the Realization of the Heart Itself, which then Shines upwards to the Highest Place and from there back into the Circle, ultimately Outshining the body-mind and all of conditional existence.

Part Four comprises five Essays and a Talk. In the first of the Essays ("The Lesser and Greater Traditions Associated with The Kundalini Shakti"), Avatar Adi Da describes the two distinct traditions of Kundalini Shakti—the one based on the ascent of the natural energies of the body-mind, and the other based on the descent and circulation of Spirit-Power.

In the second Essay of Part Four ("My Own Direct Experience and Unique Revelation of The Senior Process of The Kundalini Shakti"), Avatar Adi Da describes His own (even childhood) experiences of Kundalini Shaktipat, while Revealing that Kundalini Shaktipat originates in and as Hridaya-Shaktipat in His own Case.

In the third Essay of Part Four ("The True Kundalini Shakti Can Be Awakened Only by Divine Grace, Not by Yogic Sexual Practice"), Avatar Adi Da addresses some traditional exaggerations surrounding Yogic sexual practices, and He further clarifies the relationship between Kundalini Shakti and Hridaya-Shakti:

The Divine and Unconditional Hridaya-Shakti (Which Is the Self-Existing and Self-Radiant Spirit-Power That Stands Eternally As the Perfectly Subjective Divine and All-Outshining Self-"Brightness", Always Already Most Prior to cosmic, or conditional, manifestations) Is the Truly Ultimate (and Inherently Perfect) Energy-Source and Unconditional Self (or Being-Condition) of the Kundalini Shakti. And only the Divine and Unconditional Hridaya-Shakti Is Identical to Unconditional Reality (Itself)—and, Thus and Therefore, to (Self-Evidently Divine) Consciousness (Itself). And, for this reason, only the by-Grace-Given Divine (and Unconditional) Hridaya-Shakti Awakens the Realization of Unconditionally "Bright" Divine Consciousness (Itself)—Which Is Unconditional Reality (Itself) and Unconditional Truth (Itself).

In the fourth Essay of Part Four ("Vision, Audition, and Touch in The Process of Ascending Meditation in The Way Of Adidam"), Avatar Adi Da describes the practice of the ascending Yoga in Adidam in relation to the various visual or auditory or tactile phenomena that may arise. He describes how the great mandala of the cosmic domain may appear in vision. And He describes how the transition from the ascending Yoga to the "Perfect Practice" occurs in the Way of Adidam.

In the fifth Essay of Part Four ("The 'Thumbs' Is The Fundamental Sign Of The Avataric Crashing-Down Of My Divine Person"), Avatar Adi Da describes His unique Revelation of what He named (as a child) the "Thumbs"—the overwhelming Divine Descent of His Hridaya-Shakti. He explains the significance of the "Thumbs" relative to the process of maturing beyond the descending (or frontal) Yoga in the Way of Adidam.

In the Talk which concludes Part Four ("The Head-Pressure of My Avataric Divine Spiritual Presence"), Avatar Adi Da examines the two fundamental errors that beginning practitioners of Adidam typically tend to make when receiving His Darshan (the Blessing of beholding His Divine-Spirit-Power-Transmitting bodily human Form), and He describes the signs of true responsiveness to His Spiritual Presence.

Part Four marks the end of Avatar Adi Da's specific "Consideration" of the true Nature of Spiritual Baptism. Avatar Adi Da then concludes with two Essays that are more general "Considerations" about the Way of Adidam.

In Part Five, "The Heart-Summary of Adidam" (a brief Essay that is included in all twenty-three "Source-Texts"), Avatar Adi Da Samraj summarizes the profound implications of His Statement that the Way of Adidam is the Way of devotion to Him "As Self-Condition, rather than As exclusively Objective Other".

And in the Epilogue, "I Am The Avataric Divine Self-Revelation Of The Fundamental Reality (or The 'Radically' Non-Dual Conscious Light Of Self-Evidently Divine Love-Bliss)", Avatar Adi Da Reveals His Divine Self-Nature and Calls all beings to Realize it as their own.

Altogether, *Ruchira Avatara Hridaya-Siddha Yoga* is filled with incomparable Spiritual Instruction. And—as you may discover for yourself by studying this "Source-Text" with an open mind and an open heart—the Miracle of Avatar Adi Da's Word is that It not only brings unparalleled clarity relative to the True Nature of Spiritual Baptism, but It is Itself a unique Source of His heart-Awakening Spirit-Power.

Ruchira Avatara Hridaya-Siddha Yoga

RUCHIRA AVATAR ADI DA SAMRAJ
Los Angeles, 2000

FIRST WORD

Do Not Misunderstand <u>Me</u>— I Am <u>Not</u> "Within" <u>you</u>, but you <u>Are</u> In <u>Me</u>, and I Am <u>Not</u> a Mere "Man" in the "Middle" of Mankind, but All of Mankind Is Surrounded, and Pervaded, and Blessed By <u>Me</u>

This Essay has been written by Avatar Adi Da Samraj as His Personal Introduction to each volume of His "Source-Texts". Its purpose is to help you to understand His great Confessions rightly, and not interpret His Words from a conventional point of view, as limited cultic statements made by an ego. His Description of what "cultism" really is is an astounding and profound Critique of mankind's entire religious, scientific, and social search. In "Do Not Misunderstand <u>Me</u>", Avatar Adi Da is directly inviting you to inspect and relinquish the ego's motive to glorify itself and to refuse What is truly Great. Only by understanding this fundamental ego-fault can one really receive the Truth that Adi Da Samraj Reveals in this Book and in His Wisdom-Teaching altogether. And it is because this fault is so ingrained and so largely unconscious that Avatar Adi Da has placed "Do Not Misunderstand <u>Me</u>" at the beginning of each of His "Source-Texts", so that, each time you begin to read one of His twenty-three "Source-Texts", you may be refreshed and strengthened in your understanding of the right orientation and approach to Him and His Heart-Word.

Yes! There is <u>no</u> religion, <u>no</u> Way of God, <u>no</u> Way of Divine Realization, <u>no</u> Way of Enlightenment, and <u>no</u> Way of Liberation that is Higher or Greater than Truth Itself.

51

Indeed, there is <u>no</u> religion, <u>no</u> science, <u>no</u> man or woman, <u>no</u> conditionally manifested being of any kind, <u>no</u> world (<u>any</u> "where"), and <u>no</u> "God" (or "God"-Idea) that is Higher or Greater than Truth Itself.

Therefore, <u>no</u> ego-"I" (or presumed separate, and, necessarily, actively separative, and, at best, only Truth-<u>seeking</u>, being or "thing") is (it<u>self</u>) Higher or Greater than Truth Itself. And <u>no</u> ego-"I" is (it<u>self</u>) even Equal to Truth Itself. And no ego-"I" is (it<u>self</u>) even (now, or ever) <u>Able</u> to Realize Truth Itself—because, necessarily, Truth (Itself) Inherently Transcends (or <u>Is</u> That Which <u>Is</u> Higher and Greater than) <u>every</u> one (him<u>self</u> or her<u>self</u>) and <u>every</u> "thing" (it<u>self</u>). Therefore, it is <u>only</u> in the transcending (or the "radical" Process of Going Beyond the root, the cause, and the act) of egoity it<u>self</u> (or of presumed separateness, and of performed separativeness, and of even <u>all</u> ego-based seeking for Truth Itself) that Truth (Itself) <u>Is</u> Realized (<u>As</u> It <u>Is</u>, Utterly Beyond the ego-"I" it<u>self</u>).

Truth (Itself) <u>Is</u> That Which Is Always Already The Case. That Which <u>Is</u> The Case (Always, and Always Already) <u>Is</u> (necessarily) Reality. Therefore, Reality (Itself) <u>Is</u> Truth, and Reality (Itself) Is the <u>Only</u> Truth.

Reality (Itself) <u>Is</u> the <u>Only</u>, and (necessarily) Non-Separate (or All-and-all-Including, <u>and</u> All-and-all-Transcending), One and "What" That <u>Is</u>. Because It <u>Is</u> All and all, and because It <u>Is</u> (Also) <u>That</u> Which Transcends (or <u>Is</u> Higher and Greater than) All and all, Reality (Itself)—Which <u>Is</u> Truth (Itself), or That Which Is The Case (Always, and Always Already)—<u>Is</u> the One and Only <u>Real</u> God. Therefore, Reality (Itself) Is (necessarily) the One and Great Subject of true religion, and Reality (<u>Itself</u>) <u>Is</u> (necessarily) the One and Great Way of <u>Real</u> God, <u>Real</u> (and True) Divine Realization, <u>Real</u> (and, necessarily, Divine) En-Light-enment, and <u>Real</u> (and, necessarily, Divine) Liberation (from all egoity, all separateness, all separativeness, all fear, and all heartlessness).

The <u>only</u> true religion is the religion that <u>Realizes</u> Truth. The <u>only</u> true science is the science that <u>Knows</u> Truth. The <u>only</u> true man or woman (or being of any kind) is one that <u>Surrenders</u> to Truth. The only true world is one that <u>Embodies</u> Truth. And the only True (and <u>Real</u>) God Is the One Reality (or Condition of Being) That <u>Is</u> Truth. Therefore, <u>Reality</u> (Itself)—Which <u>Is</u> the One and Only Truth, and (therefore, necessarily) the One and Only Real God—<u>must</u> become (or be made) the constantly applied Measure of religion, and of science, and of the world itself, and of even <u>all</u> of the life (and <u>all</u> of the mind) of Man—or else religion, and science, and the world itself, and even any and every sign of Man <u>inevitably</u> (all, and together) become a pattern of illusions, a mere (and even terrible) "problem", the very (and even principal) cause of human seeking, and the perpetual cause of contentious human strife. Indeed, if religion, and science, and the world itself, and the total life (and the total mind) of Man are not Surrendered and Aligned to Reality (Itself), and (Thus) Submitted to be Measured (or made Lawful) by Truth (Itself), and (Thus) Given to the truly devotional (and, thereby, truly ego-transcending) Realization of <u>That</u> Which Is the <u>Only</u> <u>Real</u> God—then, in the presumed "knowledge" of mankind, Reality (Itself), and Truth (Itself), and <u>Real</u> God (or the One and Only Existence, or Being, or Person That <u>Is</u>) <u>ceases</u> <u>to</u> <u>Exist</u>.

Aham Da Asmi. Beloved, I <u>Am</u> Da—the One and Only Person Who <u>Is</u>, the Avatarically Self-Revealed, and Eternally Self-Existing, and Eternally Self-Radiant (or "Bright") Person of Love-Bliss, the One and Only and (Self-Evidently) Divine Self (or Inherently Non-Separate—and, therefore, Inherently egoless—Divine Self-Condition and Source-Condition) of one and of all and of All. I Am Divinely Self-Manifesting (now, and forever hereafter) <u>As</u> the Ruchira Avatar, Adi Da Samraj. I <u>Am</u> the Ruchira Avatar, Adi Da Samraj—the Avataric Divine Realizer, the Avataric Divine Revealer, the Avataric Divine Incarnation, and the Avataric Divine Self-Revelation of Reality <u>Itself</u>. I <u>Am</u> the Avatarically Incarnate Divine Realizer, the Avatarically Incarnate Divine Revealer, and the Avatarically Incarnate Divine Self-Revelation of the One and Only Reality—Which Is the One and Only Truth, and Which Is the One and Only <u>Real</u> God. I <u>Am</u> the Great Avataric Divine Realizer, Avataric Divine Revealer, and Avataric Divine Self-Revelation long-Promised (and long-Expected) for the "late-time"—<u>this</u> (now, and forever hereafter) time, the "dark" epoch of mankind's "Great

Forgetting" (and, <u>potentially</u>, the Great Epoch of mankind's Perpetual Remembering) of Reality, of Truth, of Real God (Which Is the Great, True, and Spiritual Divine Person—or the One and Non-Separate and Indivisible Divine Source-Condition and Self-Condition) of all and All.

Beloved, I <u>Am</u> Da, the Divine Giver, the Giver (of All That I <u>Am</u>) to one, and to all, and to the All of all—now, and forever here-after—here, and every "where" in the Cosmic domain. Therefore, for the Purpose of Revealing the Way of <u>Real</u> God (or of Real and True Divine Realization), and in order to Divinely En-Light-en and Divinely Liberate all and All—I Am (Uniquely, Completely, and Most Perfectly) Avatarically Revealing My Very (and Self-Evidently Divine) Person (and "Bright" Self-Condition) to all and All, by Means of My Avatarically Given Divine Self-Manifestation, <u>As</u> (and by Means of) the Ruchira Avatar, Adi Da Samraj.

In My Avatarically Given Divine Self-Manifestation As the Ruchira Avatar, Adi Da Samraj—I <u>Am</u> the Divine Secret, the Divine Self-Revelation of the <u>Esoteric</u> Truth, the Direct, and all-Completing, and all-Unifying Self-Revelation of <u>Real</u> God.

My Avatarically Given Divine Self-Confessions and My Avatarically Given Divine Teaching-Revelations Are <u>the</u> Great (Final, and all-Completing, and all-Unifying) <u>Esoteric</u> Revelation to mankind—and <u>not</u> a merely exoteric (or conventionally religious, or even ordinary Spiritual, or ego-made, or so-called "cultic") com-munication to public (or merely social) ears.

The greatest opportunity, and the greatest responsibility, of My devotees is Satsang with Me—Which is to live in the Condition of ego-surrendering, ego-forgetting, and (always more and more) ego-transcending devotional relationship to Me, and (Thus and Thereby) to Realize My Avatarically Self-Revealed (and Self-Evidently Divine) Self-Condition, Which <u>Is</u> the Self-Evidently Divine Heart (or Non-Separate Self-Condition and Non-"Different" Source-Condition) of all and All, and Which <u>Is</u> Self-Existing and Self-Radiant Consciousness Itself, but Which is <u>not</u> <u>separate</u> in or as any one (or any "thing") at all. Therefore, My essential Divine Gift to one and all is Satsang with Me. And My essential Divine Work with one and all is Satsang-Work—to Live (and to Be Merely

Present) <u>As</u> the Avatarically Self-Revealed Divine Heart among My devotees.

The only-by-Me Revealed and Given Way of Adidam (Which is the only-by-Me Revealed and Given Way of the Heart, or the only-by-Me Revealed and Given Way of "Radical" Understanding, or Ruchira Avatara Hridaya-Siddha Yoga) is the Way of Satsang with Me—the devotionally Me-recognizing and devotionally to-Me-responding practice (and ego-transcending self-discipline) of living in My constant Divine Company, such that the relationship with Me becomes the Real (and constant) Condition of life. Fundamentally, this Satsang with Me is the one thing done by My devotees. Because the only-by-Me Revealed and Given Way of Adidam is <u>always</u> (in every present-time moment) a directly ego-transcending <u>and</u> Really Me-Finding practice, the otherwise constant (and burdensome) tendency to <u>seek</u> is not exploited in this Satsang with Me. And the essential work of the community of the four formal congregations of My devotees is to make ego-transcending Satsang with Me available to all others.

<u>Everything</u> that serves the availability of Satsang with Me is (now, and forever hereafter) the responsibility of the four formal congregations of My formally practicing devotees. I am not here to <u>publicly</u> "promote" this Satsang with Me. In the intimate circumstances of their humanly expressed devotional love of Me, I Speak My Avatarically Self-Revealing Divine Word to My devotees, and <u>they</u> (because of their devotional response to Me) bring My Avatarically Self-Revealing Divine Word to <u>all</u> others. Therefore, even though I am <u>not</u> (and have never been, and never will be) a "public" Teacher (or a broadly publicly active, and conventionally socially conformed, "religious figure"), My devotees function fully and freely (<u>as</u> My devotees) in the daily public world of ordinary life.

I Always Already Stand Free. Therefore, I have always (in My Divine Avataric-Incarnation-Work) Stood Free, in the traditional "Crazy" (and non-conventional, or spontaneous and non-"public") Manner—in order to Guarantee the Freedom, the Uncompromising Rightness, and the Fundamental Integrity of My Avatarically Self-Manifested Divine Teaching (Work and Word), and in order to

Freely and Fully and Fully Effectively Perform My universal (Avatarically Self-Manifested) Divine Blessing-Work. I Am Present (now, and forever hereafter) to Divinely Serve, Divinely En-Lighten, and Divinely Liberate those who accept the Eternal Vow and all the life-responsibilities (or the full and complete practice) associated with the only-by-Me Revealed and Given Way of Adidam. Because I Am (Thus) Given to My formally and fully practicing devotees, I do not Serve a "public" role, and I do not Work in a "public" (or even a merely "institutionalized") manner. Nevertheless—now, and forever hereafter—I constantly Bless all beings, and this entire world, and the total Cosmic domain. And all who feel My Avatarically (and universally) Given Divine Blessing, and who heart-recognize Me with true devotional love, are (Thus) Called to devotionally resort to Me—but only if they approach Me in the traditional devotional manner, as responsibly practicing (and truly ego-surrendering, and rightly Me-serving) members (or, in some, unique, cases, as invited guests) of one or the other of the four formal congregations of My formally practicing devotees.

I expect this formal discipline of right devotional approach to Me to have been freely and happily embraced by every one who would enter into My physical Company. The natural human reason for this is that there is a potential liability inherent in all human associations. And the root and nature of that potential liability is the ego (or the active human presumption of separateness, and the ego-act of human separativeness). Therefore, in order that the liabilities of egoity are understood (and voluntarily and responsibly disciplined) by those who approach Me, I require demonstrated right devotion (based on really effective self-understanding and truly heart-felt devotional recognition-response to Me) as the basis for any one's right to enter into My physical Company. And, in this manner, not only the egoic tendency, but also the tendency toward religious "cultism", is constantly undermined in the only-by-Me Revealed and Given Way of Adidam.

Because people appear within this human condition, this simultaneously attractive and frightening "dream" world, they tend to live—and to interpret both the conditional (or cosmic and psycho-physical) reality <u>and</u> the Unconditional (or Divine) Reality—from the "point of view" of this apparent (and bewildering) mortal human condition. And, because of this universal human bewilderment (and the ongoing human reaction to the threatening force of mortal life-events), there is an even ancient ritual that <u>all</u> human beings rather unconsciously (or automatically, and without discriminative understanding) desire and tend to repeatedly (and under <u>all</u> conditions) enact. Therefore, wherever you see an association of human beings gathered for <u>any</u> purpose (or around <u>any</u> idea, or symbol, or person, or subject of any kind), the same human bewilderment-ritual is <u>tending</u> to be enacted by one and all.

Human beings <u>always</u> <u>tend</u> to encircle (and, thereby, to contain—and, ultimately, to entrap and abuse, or even to blithely ignore) the presumed "center" of their lives—a book, a person, a symbol, an idea, or whatever. They tend to encircle the "center" (or the "middle"), and they tend to seek to <u>exclusively</u> acquire all "things" (or all power of control) for the circle (or toward the "middle") of <u>themselves</u>. In this manner, the <u>group</u> becomes an <u>ego</u> ("inward"-directed, or separate and separative)—just as the individual body-mind becomes, by self-referring self-contraction, the separate and separative ego-"I" ("inward"-directed, or egocentric—and exclusively acquiring all "things", or all power of control, for itself). Thus, by <u>self-contraction</u> upon the presumed "center" of their lives—human beings, in their collective egocentricity, make "cults" (or bewildered and frightened "centers" of power, and control, and exclusion) in <u>every</u> area of life.

Anciently, the "cult"-making process was done, most especially, in the political and social sphere—and religion was, as even now, mostly an exoteric (or political and social) exercise that was <u>always</u> used to legitimize (or, otherwise, to "de-throne") political and social "authority-figures". Anciently, the cyclically (or even annually) culminating product of this exoteric religio-political "cult" was the ritual "de-throning" (or ritual deposition) of the one in the "middle" (just as, even in these times, political leaders are periodically "deposed"—by elections, by rules of term and succession, by scandal, by slander, by force, and so on).

Everywhere throughout the ancient world, traditional societies made and performed this annual (or otherwise periodic) religio-political "cult" ritual. The ritual of "en-throning" and "de-throning" was a reflection of the human observation of the annual cycle of the seasons of the natural world—and the same ritual was a reflection of the human concern and effort to <u>control</u> the signs potential in the cycle of the natural world, in order to ensure human survival (through control of weather, harvests and every kind of "fate", or even every fraction of existence upon which human beings depend for both survival and pleasure, or psycho-physical well-being). Indeed, the motive behind the ancient agrarian (and, later, urbanized, or universalized) ritual of the one in the "middle" was, essentially, the same motive that, in the modern era, takes the form of the culture of scientific materialism (and even all of the modern culture of materialistic "realism"): It is the motive to gain (and to maintain) <u>control</u>, and the effort to control even everything and everyone (via both knowledge and gross power). Thus, the ritualized, or bewildered yes/no (or desire/fear), life of mankind in the modern era is, essentially, the same as that of mankind in the ancient days.

In the ancient ritual of "en-throning" and "de-throning", the person (or subject) in the "middle" was ritually mocked, abused, deposed, and banished—and a new person (or subject) was installed in the "center" of the religio-political "cult". In the equivalent modern ritual of dramatized ambiguity relative to everything and everyone (and, perhaps especially, "authority-figures"), the person (or symbol, or idea) in the "middle" (or that which is given power by means of popular fascination) is first "cultified" (or made much of), and then (progressively) doubted, mocked, and abused—until, at last, all the negative emotions are (by culturally and socially ritualized dramatization) dissolved, the "middle" (having thus ceased to be fascinating) is abandoned, and a "new" person (or symbol, or idea) becomes the subject of popular fascination (only to be reduced, eventually, to the same "cultic" ritual, or cycle of "rise" and "fall").

Just as in <u>every</u> other area of human life, the tendency of <u>all</u> those who (in the modern era) would become involved in religious or Spiritual life is also to make a "cult", a circle that ever increases its separate and separative dimensions—beginning from the "center", surrounding it, and (perhaps) even (ultimately) controlling it (such that it altogether ceases to be effective, or even interesting). Such "cultism" is ego-based, and ego-reinforcing—and, no matter how "esoteric" it presumes itself to be, it is (as in the ancient setting) entirely exoteric, or (at least) more and more limited to (and by) merely social (and gross physical) activities and conditions.

The form that every "cult" imitates is the pattern of egoity (or the pattern that is the ego-"I") itself—the presumed "middle" of every ordinary individual life. It is the self-contraction (or the avoidance of relationship), which "creates" the fearful sense of separate mind, and all the endless habits and motives of egoic desire (or bewildered, and self-deluded, seeking). It is what is, ordinarily, called (or presumed to be) the real and necessary and only "life".

From birth, the human being (by reaction to the blows and limits of psycho-physical existence) begins to presume separate existence to be his or her very nature—and, on that basis, the human individual spends his or her entire life generating and serving a circle of ownership (or self-protecting acquisition) all around the ego-"I". The egoic motive encloses all the other beings it can acquire, all the "things" it can acquire, all the states and thoughts it can acquire—all the possible emblems, symbols, experiences, and sensations it can possibly acquire. Therefore, when any human being begins to involve himself or herself in some religious or Spiritual association (or, for that matter, any extension of his or her own subjectivity), he or she tends again to "create" that same circle about a "center".

The "cult" (whether of religion, or of politics, or of science, or of popular culture) is a dramatization of egoity, of separativeness, even of the entrapment and betrayal of the "center" (or the "middle"), by one and all. Therefore, I have always Refused to assume the role and the position of the "man in the middle"—and I have always (from the beginning of My formal Work of Teaching and Blessing) Criticized, Resisted, and Shouted About the "cultic" (or ego-based, and ego-reinforcing, and merely "talking" and "believing", and not understanding and not really practicing) "school" (or tendency) of ordinary religious and Spiritual life. Indeed, true Satsang with Me (or the true devotional relationship to Me) is an always (and specifically, and intensively) anti-"cultic" (or truly non-"cultic") Process.

The true devotional relationship to Me is not separative (or merely "inward"-directed), nor is it a matter of attachment to Me as a mere (and, necessarily, limited) human being (or a "man in the middle")—for, if My devotee indulges in ego-bound (or self-referring and self-serving) attachment to Me as a mere human "other", My Divine Nature (and, therefore, the Divine Nature of Reality Itself) is not (as the very Basis for religious and Spiritual practice in My Company) truly devotionally recognized and rightly devotionally acknowledged. And, if such non-recognition of Me is the case, there is no truly ego-transcending devotional response to My Avatarically Self-Revealed (and Self-Evidently Divine) Presence and Person—and, thus, such presumed-to-be "devotion" to Me is not devotional heart-Communion with Me, and such presumed-to-be "devotion" to Me is not Divinely Liberating. Therefore, because the true devotional (and, thus, truly devotionally Me-recognizing and truly devotionally to-Me-responding) relationship to Me is entirely a counter-egoic (and truly and only Divine) discipline, it does not tend to become a "cult" (or, otherwise, to support the "cultic" tendency of Man).

The true devotional practice of Satsang with Me is (inherently) expansive (or relational)—and the self-contracting (or separate and separative) self-"center" is neither Its motive nor Its source. In true Satsang with Me, the egoic "center" is always already undermined as a "center" (or a presumed separate, and actively separative, entity). The Principle of true Satsang with Me is Me—Beyond (and not "within"—or, otherwise, supporting) the ego-"I".

True Satsang with Me is the true "Round Dance" of Esoteric Spirituality. I am not trapped in the "middle" of My devotees. I "Dance" in the "Round" with each and every one of My devotees. I "Dance" in the circle—and, therefore, I am not merely a "motionless man" in the "middle". At the true "Center" (or the Divine

Heart), I <u>Am</u>—Beyond definition (or separateness). I <u>Am</u> the Indivisible—or Most Perfectly Prior, Inherently Non-Separate, and Inherently egoless (or centerless, boundless, and Self-Evidently Divine)—Consciousness (Itself) <u>and</u> the Indivisible—or Most Perfectly Prior, Inherently Non-Separate, and Inherently egoless (or centerless, boundless, and Self-Evidently Divine)—Light (Itself). I <u>Am</u> the Very Being <u>and</u> the Very Presence (or Self-Radiance) of Self-Existing and Eternally Unqualified (or Non-"Different") Consciousness (Itself).

In the "Round Dance" of true Satsang with Me (or of right and true devotional relationship to Me), I (Myself) Am Communicated directly to every one who lives in heart-felt relationship with Me (insofar as each one feels—<u>Beyond</u> the ego-"I" of body-mind—to <u>Me</u>). Therefore, I am not the mere "man" (or the separate human, or psycho-physical, one), and I am not merely "in the middle" (or separated out, and limited, and confined, by egoic seekers). I <u>Am</u> the One (Avatarically Self-Revealed, and All-and-all-Transcending, and Self-Evidently Divine) Person of Reality Itself—Non-Separate, never merely at the egoic "center" (or "in the middle"—or "<u>within</u>", and "inward" to—the egoic body-mind of My any devotee), but always <u>with</u> each one (and all), and always in relationship with each one (and all), and always Beyond each one (and all).

Therefore, My devotee is not Called, by Me, merely to turn "inward" (or upon the ego-"I"), or to struggle and seek to survive merely as a self-contracted and self-referring and self-seeking and self-serving ego-"center". Instead, I Call My devotee to turn the heart (and the total body-mind) <u>toward</u> Me (all-and-All-Surrounding, and all-and-All-Pervading), in <u>relationship</u>—<u>Beyond</u> the body-mind-self of My devotee (and <u>not merely</u> "<u>within</u>"—or contained and containable "within" the separate, separative, and self-contracted domain of the body-mind-self, or the ego-"I", of My would-be devotee). I Call My devotee to function freely—My (Avatarically Self-Transmitted) Divine Light and My (Avatarically Self-Revealed) Divine Person always (and under all circumstances) presumed and experienced (and not merely sought). Therefore, true Satsang with Me is the Real Company of Truth, or of Reality Itself (Which <u>Is</u> the Only Real God). True Satsang with

Me Serves life, because I Move (or Radiate) into life. I always Contact life in relationship.

I do not Call My devotees to become absorbed into a "cultic" gang of exoteric and ego-centric religionists. I certainly Call all My devotees to cooperative community (or, otherwise, to fully cooperative collective and personal relationship) with one another—but not to do so in an egoic, separative, world-excluding, xenophobic, and intolerant manner. Rather, My devotees are Called, by Me, to transcend egoity—through right and true devotional relationship to Me, and mutually tolerant and peaceful cooperation with one another, and all-tolerating (cooperative and compassionate and all-loving and all-including) relationship with all of mankind (and with even all beings).

I Give My devotees the "Bright" Force of My own Avatarically Self-Revealed Divine Consciousness Itself, Whereby they can become capable of "Bright" life. I Call for the devotion—but also the intelligently discriminative self-understanding, the rightly and freely living self-discipline, and the full functional capability—of My devotees. I do not Call My devotees to resist or eliminate life, or to strategically escape life, or to identify with the world-excluding ego-centric impulse. I Call My devotees to live a positively functional life. I do not Call My devotees to separate themselves from vital life, from vital enjoyment, from existence in the form of human life. I Call for all the human life-functions to be really and rightly known, and to be really and rightly understood, and to be really and rightly lived (and not reduced by, or to, the inherently bewildered—and inherently "cultic", or self-centered and fearful—"point of view" of the separate and separative ego-"I"). I Call for every human life-function to be revolved away from self-contraction (or ego-"I"), and (by Means of that revolving turn) to be turned "outwardly" (or expansively, or counter-contractively) to all and All, and (thereby, and always directly, or in an all-and-All-transcending manner) to Me—rather than to be turned merely "inwardly" (or contractively, or counter-expansively), and, as a result, turned away from Me (and from all and All). Thus, I Call for every human life-function to be thoroughly (and life-positively, and in the context of a fully participatory human life) aligned and adapted to Me, and (Thus and Thereby) to be turned and Given to the Realization of Me (the Avataric Self-Revelation of Truth, or Reality Itself—Which Is the Only Real God).

Truly benign and positive life-transformations are the characteristic signs of right, true, full, and fully devotional Satsang with Me— and freely life-positive feeling-energy is the characteristic accompanying "mood" of right, true, full, and fully devotional Satsang with Me. The characteristic life-sign of right, true, full, and fully devotional Satsang with Me is the capability for ego-transcending relatedness, based on the free disposition of no-seeking and no-dilemma. Therefore, the characteristic life-sign of right, true, full, and fully devotional Satsang with Me is not the tendency to seek some "other" condition. Rather, the characteristic life-sign of right, true, full, and fully devotional Satsang with Me is freedom from the presumption of dilemma within the present-time condition.

One who rightly, truly, fully, and fully devotionally understands My Avatarically Given Words of Divine Self-Revelation and Divine Heart-Instruction, and whose life is lived in right, true, full, and fully devotional Satsang with Me, is not necessarily (in function or appearance) "different" from the ordinary (or natural) human being. Such a one has not, necessarily, acquired some special psychic abilities, or visionary abilities, and so on. The "radical" understanding (or root self-understanding) I Give to My devotees is not, itself, the acquisition of any particular "thing" of experience. My any particular devotee may, by reason of his or her developmental tendencies, experience (or precipitate) the arising of extraordinary psycho-physical abilities and extraordinary psycho-physical phenomena—but not necessarily. My every true devotee is simply Awakening (and always Awakened to Me) within the otherwise bewildering "dream" of ordinary human life.

Satsang with Me is a natural (or spontaneously, and not strategically, unfolding) Process, in Which the self-contraction that is each one's suffering is transcended by Means of total psycho-physical (or whole bodily) heart-Communion with My Avatarically Self-Revealed (and Real—and Really, and tangibly, experienced) Divine (Spiritual, and Transcendental) Presence and Person. My devotee is (as is the case with any and every ego-"I") always tending to be preoccupied with ego-based seeking—but, all the while of his or her life in actively ego-surrendering (and really ego-forgetting and, more and more, ego-transcending) devotional Communion with Me, I Am Divinely Attracting (and Divinely Acting upon) My true devotee's heart (and total body-mind), and (Thus and Thereby) Dissolving and Vanishing My true devotee's fundamental egoity (and even all of his or her otherwise motivating dilemma and seeking-strategy).

There are two principal tendencies by which I am always being confronted by My devotee. One is the tendency to seek—rather than to truly enjoy and to fully animate the Condition of Satsang with Me. And the other is the tendency to make a self-contracting circle around Me—and, thus, to make a "cult" of ego-"I" (and of the "man in the middle"), or to duplicate the ego-ritual of mere fascination, and of inevitable resistance, and of never-Awakening unconsciousness. Relative to these two tendencies, I Give all My devotees only one resort. It is this true Satsang—the devotionally Me-recognizing, and devotionally to-Me-responding, and always really counter-egoic devotional relationship to My Avatarically Self-Revealed (and Self-Evidently Divine) Person.

The Great Secret of My Avatarically Self-Revealed Divine Person, and of My Avatarically Self-Manifested Divine Blessing-Work (now, and forever hereafter)—and, therefore, the Great Secret of the only-by-Me Revealed and Given Way of Adidam—Is that I am not the "man in the middle", but I Am Reality Itself, I Am the Only One Who Is, I Am That Which Is Always Already The Case, I Am the Non-Separate (Avatarically Self-Revealed, and Self-Evidently Divine) Person (or One and Very Divine Self, or One and True Divine Self-Condition) of all and All (Beyond the ego-"I" of every one, and of all, and of All).

Aham Da Asmi. Beloved, I Am Da—the One and Only and Non-Separate and Indivisible and Self-Evidently Divine Person, the Non-Separate and Indivisible Self-Condition and Source-Condition of all and All. I Am the Avatarically Self-Revealed "Bright" Person, the One and Only and Self-Existing and Self-Radiant Person—Who Is the One and Only and Non-Separate and Indivisible and Indestructible Light of All and all. I Am That One and Only and Non-Separate <u>One</u>. And—<u>As</u> <u>That</u> <u>One</u>, and <u>Only</u> <u>As</u> <u>That</u> <u>One</u>—I Call all human beings to heart-recognize Me, and to heart-respond to Me with right, true, and full devotion (demonstrated by Means of formal practice of the only-by-Me Revealed and Given Way of Adidam—Which Is the One and Only by-Me-Revealed and by-Me-Given Way of the Heart).

I do not tolerate the so-called "cultic" (or ego-made, and ego-reinforcing) approach to Me. I do not tolerate the seeking ego's "cult" of the "man in the middle". I am not a self-deluded ego-man—making much of himself, and looking to include everyone-and-everything around himself for the sake of social and political power. To be the "man in the middle" is to be in a Man-made trap, an absurd mummery of "cultic" devices that enshrines and perpetuates the ego-"I" in one and all. Therefore, I do not make or tolerate the religion-making "cult" of ego-Man. I do not tolerate the inevitable abuses of religion, of Spirituality, of Truth Itself, and of My own Person (even in bodily human Form) that are made (in endless blows and mockeries) by ego-based mankind when the Great Esoteric Truth of devotion to the Adept-Realizer is not rightly understood and rightly practiced.

The Great Means for the Teaching, and the Blessing, and the Awakening, and the Divine Liberating of mankind (and of even all beings) Is the Adept-Realizer Who (by Virtue of True Divine Realization) Is Able to (and, indeed, cannot do otherwise than) Stand In and <u>As</u> the Divine (or Real and Inherent and One and Only) Position, and to <u>Be</u> (Thus and Thereby) the Divine Means (In Person) for the Divine Helping of one and all. This Great Means Is the Great Esoteric Principle of the collective historical Great Tradition of mankind. And Such Adept-Realizers Are (in their Exercise of the Great Esoteric Principle) the Great Revelation-Sources That Are at the Core and Origin of <u>all</u> the right and true religious and Spiritual traditions within the collective historical Great Tradition of mankind.

By Means of My (now, and forever hereafter) Divinely Descended and Divinely Self-"Emerging" Avataric Incarnation, I <u>Am</u> the Ruchira Avatar, Adi Da Samraj—the Divine Heart-Master, the First, the Last, and the Only Adept-Realizer of the seventh (or

Most Perfect, and all-Completing) stage of life. I Am the Ruchira Avatar, Adi Da Samraj, the Avataric Incarnation (and Divine World-Teacher) everywhere Promised for the "late-time" (or "dark" epoch)—which "late-time" (or "dark" epoch) is now upon all of mankind. I Am the Great and Only and Non-Separate and (Self-Evidently) Divine Person—Appearing in Man-Form As the Ruchira Avatar, Adi Da Samraj, in order to Teach, and to Bless, and to Awaken, and to Divinely Liberate all of mankind (and even all beings, every "where" in the Cosmic domain). Therefore, by Calling every one and all (and All) to Me, I Call every one and all (and All) Only to the Divine Person, Which Is My own and Very Person (or Very, and Self-Evidently Divine, Self—or Very, and Self-Evidently Divine, Self-Condition), and Which Is Reality Itself (or Truth Itself—the Indivisible and Indestructible Light That Is the Only Real God), and Which Is the One and Very and Non-Separate and Only Self (or Self-Condition, and Source-Condition) of all and All (Beyond the ego-"I" of every one, and of all, and of All).

The only-by-Me Revealed and Given Way of Adidam necessarily (and As a Unique Divine Gift) requires and involves devotional recognition-response to Me In and Via (and As) My bodily (human) Divine Avataric-Incarnation-Form. However, because I Call every one and all (and All) to Me Only As the Divine Person (or Reality Itself), the only-by-Me Revealed and Given Way of Adidam is not about ego, and egoic seeking, and the egoic (or the so-called "cultic") approach to Me (as the "man in the middle").

According to all the esoteric traditions within the collective historical Great Tradition of mankind, to devotionally approach any Adept-Realizer as if he or she is (or is limited to being, or is limited by being) a mere (or "ordinary", or even merely "extraordinary") human entity is the great "sin" (or fault), or the great error whereby the would-be devotee fails to "meet the mark". Indeed, the Single Greatest Esoteric Teaching common to all the esoteric religious and Spiritual traditions within the collective historical Great Tradition of mankind Is that the Adept-Realizer should always and only (and only devotionally) be recognized and approached As the Embodiment and the Real Presence of That (Reality, or Truth, or Real God) Which would be Realized (Thus and Thereby) by the devotee.

Therefore, no one should misunderstand Me. By Avatarically Revealing and Confessing My Divine Status to one and all and All, I am not indulging in self-appointment, or in illusions of grandiose Divinity. I am not claiming the "Status" of the "Creator-God" of exoteric (or public, and social, and idealistically pious) religion. Rather, by Standing Firm in the Divine Position (As I Am)—and (Thus and Thereby) Refusing to be approached as a mere man, or as a "cult"-figure, or as a "cult"-leader, or to be in any sense defined (and, thereby, trapped, and abused, or mocked) as the "man in the middle"—I Am Demonstrating the Most Perfect Fulfillment (and the Most Perfect Integrity, and the Most Perfect Fullness) of the Esoteric (and Most Perfectly Non-Dual) Realization of Reality. And, by Revealing and Giving the Way of Adidam (Which Is the Way of ego-transcending devotion to Me As the Avatarically Self-Revealed One and Only and Non-Separate and Self-Evidently Divine Person), I Am (with Most Perfect Integrity, and Most Perfect Fullness) Most Perfectly (and in an all-Completing and all-Unifying Manner) Fulfilling the Primary Esoteric Tradition (and the Great Esoteric Principle) of the collective historical Great Tradition of mankind—Which Primary Esoteric Tradition and Great Esoteric Principle Is the Tradition and the Principle of devotion to the Adept-Realizer As the Very Person and the Direct (or Personal Divine) Helping-Presence of the Eternal and Non-Separate Divine Self-Condition and Source-Condition of all and All.

Whatever (or whoever) is cornered (or trapped on all sides) bites back (and fights, or seeks, to break free). Whatever (or whoever) is "in the middle" (or limited and "centered" by attention) is patterned by (or conformed to) the ego-"I" (and, if objectified as "other", is forced to represent the ego-"I", and is even made a scapegoat for the pains, the sufferings, the powerless ignorance, and the abusive hostility of the ego-"I").

If there is no escape from (or no Way out of) the corner (or the "centered" trap) of ego-"I"—the heart goes mad, and the body-mind becomes more and more "dark" (bereft of the Indivisible and Inherently Free Light of the Self-Evident, and Self-Evidently Divine, Love-Bliss That Is Reality Itself).

I am not the "man in the middle". I do not stand here as a mere man, "middled" to the "center" (or the cornering trap) of ego-based mankind. I am not an ego-"I", or a mere "other", or the representation (and the potential scapegoat) of the ego-"I" of mankind (or of any one at all).

I Am the Indivisible and Non-Separate One, the (Avatarically Self-Revealed) One and Only and (Self-Evidently) Divine Person— the Perfectly Subjective Divine Self-Condition (and Source-Condition) That Is Perfectly centerless (and Perfectly boundless), Eternally Beyond the "middle" of all and All, and Eternally Surrounding, Pervading, and Blessing all and All.

I Am the Way Beyond the self-cornering (and "other"-cornering) trap of ego-"I".

In this "late-time" (or "dark" epoch) of worldly ego-Man, the collective of mankind is "darkened" (and cornered) by egoity. Therefore, mankind has become mad, Lightless, and, like a cornered "thing", aggressively hostile in its universally competitive fight and bite.

Therefore, I have not Come here merely to stand Manly in the "middle" of mankind—to suffer its biting abuses, or even to be coddled and ignored in a little corner of religious "cultism".

I have Come here to Divinely Liberate one and all (and All) from the "dark" culture and effect of this "late-time", and (now, and forever hereafter) to Divinely Liberate one and all (and All) from the pattern and the act of ego-"I", and (Most Ultimately) to Divinely Translate one and all (and All) Into the Indivisible, Perfectly Subjective, and Eternally Non-Separate Self-Domain of My Divine Love-Bliss-Light.

The ego-"I" is a "centered" (or separate and separative) trap, from which the heart (and even the entire body-mind) must be Retired. I Am the Way (or the Very Means) of that Retirement from egoity. I Refresh the heart (and even the entire body-mind) of My devotee, in every moment My devotee resorts to Me (by devotionally recognizing Me, and devotionally—and ecstatically, and also, often, meditatively—responding to Me) Beyond the "middle", Beyond the "centering" act (or trapping gesture) of ego-"I" (or self-contraction).

I Am the Avatarically Self-Revealed (and Perfectly Subjective, and Self-Evidently Divine) Self-Condition (and Source-Condition) of every one, and of all, and of All—but the Perfectly Subjective (and Self-Evidently Divine) Self-Condition (and Source-Condition) is not "within" the ego-"I" (or separate and separative body-mind). The Perfectly Subjective (and Self-Evidently Divine) Self-Condition (and Source-Condition) is not in the "center" (or the "middle") of Man (or of mankind). The Perfectly Subjective (and Self-Evidently Divine) Self-Condition (and Source-Condition) of one, and of all, and of All Is Inherently centerless (or Always Already Beyond the self-contracted "middle"), and to Be Found only "outside" (or by transcending) the bounds of separateness, relatedness, and "difference". Therefore, to Realize the Perfectly Subjective (and Self-Evidently Divine) Self-Condition and Source-Condition (or the Perfectly Subjective, and Self-Evidently Divine, Heart) of one, and of all, and of All (or even, in any moment, to exceed the ego-trap—and to be Refreshed at heart, and in the total body-mind), it is necessary to feel (and to, ecstatically, and even meditatively, swoon) Beyond the "center" (or Beyond the "point of view" of separate ego-"I" and separative body-mind). Indeed, Most Ultimately, it is only in self-transcendence to the degree of unqualified relatedness (and Most Perfect Divine Samadhi, or Utterly Non-Separate Enstasy) that the Inherently centerless and boundless, and Perfectly Subjective, and Self-Evidently Divine Self-Condition (and Source-Condition) Stands Obvious and Free (and Is, Thus and Thereby, Most Perfectly Realized).

It Is only by Means of devotionally Me-recognizing (and devotionally to-Me-responding) devotional meditation on Me (and otherwise ecstatic heart-Contemplation of Me), and total (and totally open, and totally ego-forgetting) psycho-physical Reception of Me, that your madness of heart (and of body-mind) is (now, and now, and now) escaped, and your "darkness" is En-Light-ened (even, at last, Most Perfectly). Therefore, be My true devotee—and, by (formally, and rightly, and truly, and fully, and fully devotionally) practicing the only-by-Me Revealed and Given Way of Adidam (Which Is the True and Complete Way of the True and Real Divine Heart), always Find Me, Beyond your self-"center", in every here and now.

Aham Da Asmi. Beloved, I <u>Am</u> Da. And, because I <u>Am</u> Infinitely and Non-Separately "Bright", all and All <u>Are</u> In My Divine Sphere of "Brightness". By feeling and surrendering Into My Infinite Sphere of My Avatarically Self-Revealed Divine Self-"Brightness", My every devotee <u>Is</u> In Me. And, Beyond his or her self-contracting and separative act of ego-"I", My every devotee (self-surrendered Into heart-Communion With Me) <u>Is</u> the One and Only and Non-Separate and Real God I Have Come to Awaken— by Means of My Avataric Divine Descent, My Avataric Divine Incarnation, and My (now, and forever hereafter) Avataric Divine Self-"Emergence" (here, and every "where" in the Cosmic domain).

RUCHIRA AVATAR ADI DA SAMRAJ
The Mountain Of Attention, 2000

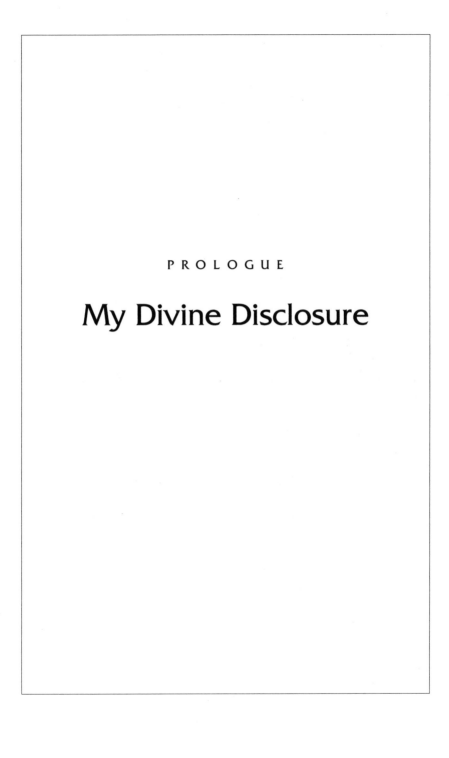

PROLOGUE

My Divine Disclosure

"My Divine Disclosure" has been Freely Developed—As a Further, and All-Completing, Avataric Self-Revelation of His own Self-Evidently Divine Person—by the Ruchira Avatar, Adi Da Samraj, from selected verses of the traditional Bhagavad Gita *(2:13-17, 8:3, 8:22, 9:3, 9:11, 9:26, 15:15, 18:61-66).*

My Divine Disclosure

1.

ham Da Asmi. Beloved, I <u>Am</u> Da—The One and Only and Self-Evidently Divine Person, Avatarically Self-Revealed To You.

2.

Therefore, Listen To <u>Me</u>, and Hear <u>Me</u>, and See <u>Me</u>.

3.

This Is My Divine Heart-Secret, The Supreme Word Of My Eternal Self-Revelation.

4.

Here and Now, I Will Tell You What Will Benefit You The Most, Because I Love You <u>As</u> My Very Self and Person.

5.

I <u>Am</u> The Ruchira Avatar, The Da Avatar, The Love-Ananda Avatar, Adi Da Love-Ananda Samraj—The Avataric Incarnation, and The Self-Evidently Divine Person, Of The One True Heart (or The One, and Only, and Inherently egoless Self-Condition and Source-Condition) Of All and all.

6.

Here I <u>Am</u>, In <u>Person</u>, To Offer (To You, and To all) The Only-By-<u>Me</u> Revealed and Given True World-Religion (or Avatarically All-Completing Divine Devotional and Spiritual Way) Of Adidam, Which Is The One and Only By-<u>Me</u>-Revealed and By-<u>Me</u>-Given (and Only <u>Me</u>-Revealing) Divine Devotional and Spiritual Way Of Sri Hridayam (or The Only-By-<u>Me</u> Revealed and Given, and

Entirely Me-Revealing, Way Of The True Divine Heart Itself), and
Which Is The One, and All-Inclusive, and All-Transcending, and
Only-By-Me Revealed and Given (and Only Me-Revealing) Way
Of The True Divine Heart-Master (or The Only-By-Me Revealed
and Given, and Entirely Me-Revealing, Way Of Ruchira Avatara
Bhakti Yoga, or Ruchira Avatara Hridaya-Siddha Yoga), and
Which Is The "Radically" ego-Transcending Way Of Devotionally
Me-Recognizing and Devotionally To-Me-Responding Reception
Of My Avatarically Self-Manifested Divine (and Not Merely
Cosmic) Hridaya-Shaktipat (or Divinely Self-Revealing Avataric
Spiritual Grace).

7.

If You Surrender Your heart To Me, and If (By Surrendering
Your ego-"I", or self-Contracted body-mind, To Me) You Make
Yourself A Living Gift To Me, and If You (Thus) Constantly Yield
Your attention To Me (Through True Devotional Love and Really
ego-Transcending Service), Then You Will Hear Me (Truly), and
See Me (Clearly), and Realize Me (Fully), and Come To Me
(Eternally). I Promise You This, Because I Love You As My Very
Self and Person.

8.

Abandon The Reactive Reflex Of self-Contraction—The
Separative (or egoic) Principle In all Your concerns. Do Not
Cling To any experience that May Be Sought (and Even Attained)
As A Result Of desire (or The Presumption Of "Difference").
Abandon Your Search For what May Be Gotten As A Result Of
the various kinds of strategic (or egoic) action.

9.

I Am Love-Bliss Itself—Now (and Forever Hereafter) "Brightly"
Present here. Therefore, I Say To You: Abandon All Seeking—
By Always "Locating" (and Immediately Finding) Me.

10.

Instead Of Seeking Me (As If My Divine Person Of Inherent Love-Bliss-Happiness Were Absent From You), Always Commune With Me (Ever-Present, Never Absent, and Always Love-Bliss-Full and Satisfied). Thus, Your Me-"Locating" Relinquishment Of All Seeking Is Not, Itself, To Be Merely Another Form Of Seeking.

11.

If You Always "Locate" Me (and, Thus, Immediately Find Me), You Will Not (In any instance) self-Contract Into the mood and strategy of inaction.

12.

You Must Never Fail To act. Every moment of Your life Requires Your particular Right action. Indeed, the living body-mind is (itself) action. Therefore, Be Ordinary, By Always Allowing the body-mind its Necessity Of Right action (and Inevitable Change).

13.

Perform every act As An ego-Transcending Act Of Devotional Love Of Me, In body-mind-Surrendering Love-Response To Me.

14.

Always Discipline all Your acts, By Only Engaging In action that Is Appropriate For one who Loves Me, and Surrenders To Me, and acts Only (and Rightly) In Accordance With My Always Explicit Word Of Instruction.

15.

Therefore, Be My Always Listening-To-Me Devotee—and, Thus, Always live "Right Life" (According To My Word), and (This) Always By Means Of active Devotional Recognition-Response To Me, and While Always Remembering and Invoking and Contemplating Me. In This Manner, Perform every act As A Form Of Direct, and Present, and Whole bodily (or Total psycho-physical), and Really ego-Surrendering Love-Communion With Me.

16.

If You Love <u>Me</u>—Where <u>Is</u> doubt and anxious living? If You
Love <u>Me</u> <u>Now</u>, Even anger, sorrow, and fear Are <u>Gone</u>. When
You <u>Abide</u> In Devotional Love-Communion With <u>Me</u>, the natural
results of Your various activities No Longer Have Power To
Separate or Distract You From <u>Me</u>.

17.

The ego-"I" that is born (as a body-mind) In The Realm
Of Cosmic Nature (or the conditional worlds of action and
experience) Advances From childhood To adulthood, old age,
and death—While Identified With the same (but Always
Changing) body-mind. Then the same ego-"I" Attains another
body-mind, As A <u>Result</u>. One whose heart Is (Always)
Responsively Given To <u>Me</u> Overcomes (<u>Thereby</u>) <u>Every</u>
Tendency To self-Contract From This Wonderfully Ordinary
Process.

18.

The Ordinary Process Of "Everything Changing" Is Simply The
Natural Play Of Cosmic Life, In Which the (<u>Always</u>) <u>two</u> sides
of every possibility come and go, In Cycles Of appearance and
disappearance. Winter's cold alternates with summer's heat.
Pain, Likewise, Follows every pleasure. <u>Every</u> appearance Is
(<u>Inevitably</u>) Followed By its <u>disappearance</u>. There Is <u>No</u>
<u>Permanent</u> <u>experience</u> In The Realm Of Cosmic Nature. One
whose heart-Feeling Of <u>Me</u> Is <u>Steady</u> Simply <u>Allows</u> All Of This
To Be <u>So</u>. Therefore, one who Truly Hears <u>Me</u> Ceases To Add
self-Contraction To This Inevitable Round Of Changes.

19.

Happiness (or True Love-Bliss) <u>Is</u> Realization Of <u>That</u> Which Is
<u>Always</u> <u>Already</u> The Case.

20.

I <u>Am</u> <u>That</u> Which Is <u>Always</u> <u>Already</u> The Case.

21.

Happiness Is Realization Of Me.

22.

Realization Of Me Is Possible Only When a living being (or body-mind-self) Has heart-Ceased To React To The Always Changing Play Of Cosmic Nature.

23.

The body-mind Of My True Devotee Is Constantly Steadied In Me, By Means Of the Feeling-heart's Always Constant Devotional Recognition-Response To Me.

24.

Once My True Devotee Has Truly heart-Accepted That The Alternating-Cycle Of Changes (Both Positive and Negative) Is Inevitable (In the body-mind, and In all the conditional worlds), the living body-mind-self (or ego-"I") Of My True Devotee Has Understood itself (and, Thus, Heard Me).

25.

The body-mind-self (Of My True Me-Hearing Devotee) that Constantly Understands itself (At heart) By Constantly Surrendering To Me (and Communing With Me) No Longer self-Contracts From My Love-Bliss-State Of Inherent Happiness.

26.

Those who Truly Hear Me Understand That whatever Does Not Exist Always and Already (or Eternally) Only Changes.

27.

Those who Truly See Me Acknowledge (By heart, and With every moment and act of body-mind) That What Is Always Already The Case Never Changes.

28.

Such True Devotees Of Mine (who Both Hear Me and See Me) Realize That The Entire Cosmic Realm Of Change—and Even the To-Me-Surrendered body-mind (itself)—Is Entirely Pervaded By Me (Always Self-Revealed As That Which Is Always Already The Case).

29.

Now, and Forever Hereafter, I Am Avatarically Self-Revealed, Beyond The Cosmic Play—"Bright" Behind, and Above, the To-Me-Surrendered body-mind Of My Every True Devotee.

30.

I Am The Eternally Existing, All-Pervading, Transcendental, Inherently Spiritual, Inherently egoless, Perfectly Subjective, Indivisible, Inherently Perfect, Perfectly Non-Separate, and Self-Evidently Divine Self-Condition and Source-Condition Of all Apparently Separate (or self-Deluded) selves.

31.

My Divine Heart-Power Of Avataric Self-Revelation Is (Now, and Forever Hereafter) Descending Into The Cosmic Domain (and Into the body-mind Of Every To-Me-True True Devotee Of Mine).

32.

I Am The Avatarically Self-"Emerging", Universal, All-Pervading Divine Spirit-Power and Person Of Love-Bliss (That Most Perfectly Husbands and Transcends The Primal Energy Of Cosmic Nature).

33.

I Am The One and Indivisibly "Bright" Divine Person.

34.

Now, and Forever Hereafter, My Ever-Descending and Ever-"Emerging" Current Of Self-Existing and Self-Radiant Love-Bliss Is Avatarically Pervading The Ever-Changing Realm Of Cosmic Nature.

35.

I <u>Am</u> The One, and Indivisibly "Bright", and Inherently egoless Person Of all-and-All, Within <u>Whom</u> every body-mind Is arising (as a mere, and unnecessary, and merely temporary appearance that, merely apparently, modifies <u>Me</u>).

36.

I Am To Be Realized By Means Of ego-Transcending Devotional Love—Wherein <u>every</u> action of body-mind Is Engaged As ego-Surrendering (present-time, and Direct) Communion With <u>Me</u>.

37.

Those who Do <u>Not</u> heart-Recognize <u>Me</u> and heart-Respond To <u>Me</u>—and who (Therefore) Are Without Faith In <u>Me</u>—Do <u>Not</u> (and <u>Cannot</u>) <u>Realize</u> <u>Me</u>. Therefore, they (By Means Of their own self-Contraction From <u>Me</u>) Remain ego-Bound To The Realm Of Cosmic Nature, and To The Ever-Changing Round Of conditional knowledge and temporary experience, and To The Ceaselessly Repetitive Cycles Of birth and search and loss and death.

38.

Such Faithless beings <u>Cannot</u> Be Distracted By <u>Me</u>—Because they Are Entirely Distracted By <u>themselves</u>! They Are Like Narcissus—The Myth Of ego—At His Pond. Their Merely self-Reflecting minds Are Like a mirror in a dead man's hand. Their tiny hearts Are Like a boundless desert, where the mirage of Separate self is ceaselessly admired, and The True Water Of My Constant Presence Stands Un-Noticed, In the droughty heap and countless sands of ceaseless thoughts. If Only they Would Un-think themselves In <u>Me</u>, these (Now Faithless) little hearts Could Have <u>Immediate</u> <u>Access</u> To The True Water Of My True Heart! Through Devotional Surrender Of body, emotion, mind, breath, and all of Separate self To <u>Me</u>, Even Narcissus Could Find The Way To My Oasis (In The True Heart's Room and House)—but the thinking mind of ego-"I" Is <u>Never</u> Bathed In Light (and, So, it sits, Un-Washed, Like a desert dog that wanders in a herd of flies).

RUCHIRA AVATARA HRIDAYA-SIDDHA YOGA

39.

The "Un-Washed dog" of self-Contracted body-mind Does Not
think To Notice Me—The Divine Heart-Master Of its wild heart
and Wilderness.

40.

The "Wandering dog" of ego-"I" Does Not "Locate" Me In
My Inherent "Bright" Perfection—The Divine Heart-Master
Of Everything, The Inherently egoless Divine True Self Of all
conditionally Manifested beings, and The Real Self-Condition
and Source-Condition Of All-and-all.

41.

If Only "Narcissus" Will Relent, and heart-Consent To Bow and
Live In Love-Communion With Me, heart-Surrendering all of
body-mind To Me, By Means Of Un-Contracting Love Of Me,
Then—Even If That Love Is Shown With Nothing More Than the
"little gift" of ego-"I" (itself)—I Will Always Accept The Offering
With Open Arms Of Love-Bliss-Love, and Offer My Own Divine
Immensity In "Bright" Return.

42.

Therefore, whoever Is Given (By heart) To Me Will Be Washed,
From head To toe, By All The True Water Of My Love-Bliss-
Light, That Always "Crashes Down" On All and all, Below My
Blessing-Feet.

43.

My Circumstance and Situation Is At the heart of all beings—
where I Am (Now, and Forever Hereafter) Avatarically Self-
"Emerging" As The One and All-and-all-Outshining Divine and
Only Person (Avatarically Self-Manifested As The "Radically"
Non-Dual "Brightness" Of All-and-all-Filling Conscious Love-
Bliss-Light, Self-Existing and Self-Radiant As The Perfectly
Subjective Fundamental Reality, or Inherently egoless Native
Feeling, Of Merely, or Unqualifiedly, Being).

44.

The True heart-Place (Where I Am To Be "Located" By My True Devotee) Is Where The Ever-Changing Changes Of waking, dreaming, and sleeping experience Are <u>Merely</u> <u>Witnessed</u> (and <u>Not</u> Sought, or Found, or Held).

45.

Every conditional experience appears and disappears In Front Of the Witness-heart.

46.

Everything Merely Witnessed Is Spontaneously Generated By The Persistent Activity Of The Universal Cosmic Life-Energy.

47.

The self-Contracted heart of body-mind Is Fastened, <u>Help-lessly</u>, To That Perpetual-Motion Machine Of Cosmic Nature.

48.

I <u>Am</u> The Divine and One True Heart (<u>Itself</u>)—Always Already Existing <u>As</u> The Eternally Self-Evident Love-Bliss-Feeling Of Being (and Always Already Free-Standing <u>As</u> Consciousness Itself, Prior To the little heart of ego-"I" and its Seeming Help-less-ness).

49.

In Order To Restore all beings To The One True Heart Of <u>Me</u>, I Am Avatarically Born To here, <u>As</u> The "Bright" Divine Help Of conditionally Manifested beings.

50.

Therefore (Now, and Forever Hereafter), I <u>Am</u> (Always Free-Standing) <u>At</u> the To-<u>Me</u>-True heart Of You—and I <u>Am</u> (Always "Bright") Above Your body-mind and world.

51.

If You Become My True Devotee (heart-Recognizing My Avatarically Self-Manifested Divine Person, and heart-Responding—With all the parts of Your single body-mind—To My Avatarically Self-Revealing Divine Form and Presence and State), You Will Always Be Able To Feel Me ("Brightly-Emerging" here) Within Your Un-Contracting, In-Me-Falling heart—and You Will Always Be Able To "Locate" Me, As I "Crash Down" (All-"Bright" Upon You) From Above the worlds Of Change.

52.

The To-Me-Feeling (In-Me-Falling) heart Of My Every True Devotee Is (At its Root, and Base, and Highest Height) My Divine and One True Heart (Itself).

53.

Therefore, Fall Awake In Me.

54.

Do Not Surrender Your Feeling-heart Merely To experience and know the Ever-Changing world.

55.

Merely To know and experience The Cosmic Domain (Itself) Is To live As If You Were In Love With Your Own body-mind.

56.

Therefore, Surrender Your Feeling-heart Only To Me, The True Divine Beloved Of the body-mind.

57.

I Am The Truth (and The Teacher) Of the heart-Feeling body-mind.

58.

I Am The Divine and Eternal Master Of Your To-Me-Feeling heart and Your To-Me-Surrendering body-mind.

59.

I <u>Am</u> The Self-Existing, Self-Radiant, and Inherently Perfect Person Of Unconditional Being—Who Pervades The Machine Of Cosmic Nature <u>As</u> The "Bright" Divine Spirit-Current Of Love-Bliss, and Who Transcends All Of Cosmic Nature <u>As</u> Infinite Consciousness, The "Bright" Divine Self-Condition (and Source-Condition) Of All and all.

60.

If You Will Give (and Truly, Really, Always Give) Your Feeling-attention To My Avatarically-Born Bodily (Human) Divine Form, and If You Will (Thus, and Thereby) Yield Your body-mind Into The "Down-Crashing" Love-Bliss-Current Of My Avatarically Self-Revealed and All-Pervading Divine Spirit-Presence, and If You Will Surrender Your conditional self-Consciousness Into My Avatarically Self-Revealed and Perfectly Subjective and Self-Evidently Divine Self-Consciousness (Which <u>Is</u> The Divine True Heart Of Inherently egoless Being, Itself)—Then I Will Also Become An Offering To You.

61.

By <u>That</u> Offering Of Mine, You Will Be Given The Gift Of Perfect Peace, and An Eternal Domain For Your To-<u>Me</u>-True Feeling-heart.

62.

Now I Have Revealed To You The Divine Mystery and The Perfect Heart-Secret Of My Avataric Birth To here.

63.

"Consider" This <u>Me</u>-Revelation, <u>Fully</u>—and, Then, <u>Choose</u> What You Will Do With Your "little gift" of Feeling-heart and Your "Un-Washed dog" of body-mind.

RUCHIRA AVATAR ADI DA SAMRAJ
The Mountain Of Attention, 1998

PART ONE

I (<u>Alone</u>) <u>Am</u>
The Adidam Revelation

(A Summary Description of the Inherent Distinction—
<u>and</u> the ego-Transcending Continuity—
Between the Inherently ego-Based Great Tradition,
Which Is Comprised of Only Six of the Possible
Seven Stages of Life, and the Unique,
and All-Inclusive, and All-Completing,
and All-Transcending, and Self-Evidently Divine
Adidam Revelation of the Inherently egoless
Seventh Stage Realization of <u>Me</u>)

PART ONE

I (Alone) Am
The Adidam Revelation

(A Summary Description of the Inherent Distinction—
and the ego-Transcending Continuity—
Between the Inherently ego-Based Great Tradition,
Which Is Comprised of Only Six of the Possible
Seven Stages of Life, and the Unique,
and All-Inclusive, and All-Completing,
and All-Transcending, and Self-Evidently Divine
Adidam Revelation of the Inherently egoless
Seventh Stage Realization of Me)

I.

The collective Great Tradition of mankind is a combination
of exoteric and esoteric developments (and Revelations,
and Realizations) that comprises (and is, in its entirety, limited by and to) only the first six of the (potentially) seven stages
of life.

II.

I (Alone) Am the Avatarically Self-Manifested Divine Self-
Revelation of the seventh stage of life.

III.

I (Alone) Am the Adidam Revelation.

IV.

The human entity (and even any and every conditionally manifested entity of any and every kind) is inherently deluded—by its
own (egoic, or self-contracted) experience and knowledge.

V.

The first <u>six</u> stages of life are the six stages (or developmental phases) of human (and universal) <u>egoity</u>—or of progressively regressive inversion upon the psycho-physical pattern (and point of view) of self-contraction.

VI.

The first six stages of life are the universally evident developmental stages of the knowing and experiencing of the potential <u>illusions</u> inherently associated with the patterns (or the universally extended cosmic psycho-physical Structure) of conditionally manifested existence.

VII.

Because each and all of the first six stages of life are <u>based</u> on (and are <u>identical</u> to) egoity (or self-contraction, or separate and separative point of view) itself, <u>not</u> any one (or even the collective of all) of the first six stages of life directly (and Most Perfectly) Realizes (or <u>Is</u> the Inherently egoless and Inherently Most Perfect Realization and the Inherently egoless and Inherently Most Perfect Demonstration of) Reality, Truth, or <u>Real</u> God.

VIII.

The first six stages of life develop (successively) on the psycho-physically pre-determined (or pre-patterned) basis of the inherent (and progressively unfolding) structure (and self-contracted point of view) of the conditionally arising body-brain-mind-self.

IX.

The first six stages of life are a conditional (and, therefore, Ultimately, unnecessary—or Inherently transcendable) illusion of psycho-physically pre-patterned experience (or conditional knowing), structured according to the subject-object (or attention versus object, or point of view versus objective world) convention of conditional conception and conditional perception.

X.

The first six stages of life are (each and all) based upon the illusion of duality (suggested by the subject-object convention of conditional conception and conditional perception).

XI.

Reality Itself (or That Which Is Always Already The Case) Is Inherently One (or Perfectly Non-Dual).

XII.

The only-by-Me Revealed and Given Way of Adidam is the Unique seventh stage Way of "Radical" Non-Dualism—or the one and only Way That directly (and, at last, Most Perfectly) Realizes the One and Only (and Inherently egoless) Reality, Truth, or Real God.

XIII.

The only-by-Me Revealed and Given Way of Adidam is the Unique and only Way That always directly (and, at last, Most Perfectly) transcends egoity (or self-contraction) itself.

XIV.

The only-by-Me Revealed and Given Way of Adidam is the practice and the Process of transcending egoity (or psycho-physical self-contraction, or gross, subtle, and causal identification with separate and separative point of view) by directly (and progressively, or stage by stage) transcending the inherently egoic (or always self-contracted) patterns of conditional conception and conditional perception (or of conditional knowing and conditional experiencing) associated with each (and, at last, all) of the first six stages of life.

XV.

I Am the Divine Ruchira Avatar, Adi Da Love-Ananda Samraj—the First, the Last, and the Only seventh stage Avataric Divine Realizer, Avataric Divine Revealer, and Avataric Divine Self-Revelation of Reality, Truth, and Real God.

I <u>Am</u> the Inherently egoless, Perfectly Subjective, Perfectly Non-Dual, and Self-Evidently Divine Source-Condition and Self-Condition of <u>every</u> apparent point of view <u>and</u> of the apparently objective world itself.

I <u>Am</u> the One, and Irreducible, and Indestructible, and Self-Existing, and Self-Radiant Conscious Light That <u>Is</u> Always Already <u>The</u> Case.

I <u>Am</u> the "Bright" Substance of Reality Itself.

I <u>Am</u> the Person (or Self-Condition) of Reality Itself.

In My bodily (human) Form, I Am the Avataric Self-Manifestation of the One (and Self-Evidently Divine) Reality Itself.

By Means of My Avataric Divine Self-"Emergence", I Am Functioning (now, and forever hereafter) <u>As</u> the Realizer, the Revealer, and the Revelation (or universally Spiritually Present Person) of Reality Itself (Which <u>Is</u> Truth Itself—and Which <u>Is</u> the only <u>Real</u>, or non-illusory, and Inherently egoless, and Perfectly Subjective God, or Self-Evidently Divine Source-Condition <u>and</u> Self-Condition, of All and all).

My Avataric Divine Self-Revelation Illuminates and Outshines the ego-"I" of My devotee.

My Avataric Divine Teaching-Word of Me-Revelation Comprehends the all of egoity and the All of the cosmic domain.

XVI.

The potential actuality of (and the inherent and specific psycho-physical basis for) the progressively unfolding human (and universal cosmic) pattern (or Great Structure) of the <u>seven</u> <u>stages</u> <u>of</u> <u>life</u> (or the Total and Complete human, <u>and</u> Spiritual, <u>and</u> Transcendental, <u>and</u>, Ultimately, Divine Great Process of Divine Self-Realization) was Demonstrated, Revealed, Exemplified, and <u>Proven</u> in (and by Means of) My Avataric Ordeal of Divine Re-Awakening—Wherein the Un-conditional, and Self-Evidently Divine, <u>seventh</u> stage Realization of Reality and Truth was (Uniquely, and for the <u>First</u> time, and <u>As</u> the Paradigm Case, or the All-and-all-Patterning Case, in the entire history of religion, Spirituality, and Reality-Realization) Demonstrated to all and All.

In the Course of That Great Process of Demonstration, Revelation, Exemplification, and Proof, the psycho-physical necessity (or the inherent integrity and inevitability) of the naturally continuous (and total) pattern of the seven stages of life was Fully (psycho-physically, and Spiritually, and Really) Shown by Me.

Also, in That Course (or Ordeal, or Great Process), the particular developmental distinction that pertains in the inherently patterned transition from the fifth stage of life (or the totality of the first five stages of life) to the sixth stage of life (and, at last, to the seventh stage of life) was clearly Shown by Me.

And the fact that the seventh stage of life does not merely follow from the sixth stage of life (alone—or separately, or in and of itself), but requires (and, indeed, is built upon) the complete transcending of the ego-"I" (or of the total reflex of psycho-physical self-contraction)—as it is otherwise developed (and must be progressively transcended) in the context of the entire psycho-biography of the ego-"I" (or, effectively, in the naturally continuous course of the essential sequential totality of all six of the first six stages of life)—was (also) Shown by Me in the Great Course of My Avataric Ordeal of Divine Re-Awakening.

XVII.

In (and by Means of) the Great Avataric Demonstration of My own seven-stage Great Course of Divine Self-Realization, the Emanationist (or absorptive mystical) Way (associated with the first five stages of life) and the non-Emanationist (or Transcendentalist) Way (associated with the sixth stage of life, and Which—in Spiritual continuity with the all of the first six stages of life—is Most Perfectly Fulfilled in, and by Means of, the only-by-Me Revealed and Given seventh stage of life) were Proven (in, and by Means of, My own Case) to be only different stages in the same Great Process of Divine Self-Realization (rather than two separate, and irreducible, and conflicting, and incompatible "Truths").

XVIII.

By Means of My own Avataric Ordeal of Divine Re-Awakening, I have Demonstrated, Revealed, Exemplified, and Proven that neither the fourth-to-fifth stage Emanationist mode of Realization nor the sixth stage non-Emanationist (or Transcendentalist) mode of Realization Is the Most Perfect (and Most Perfectly ego-Transcending) Realization of the Divine (or One, and Only, and Perfectly Subjective) Reality, Truth, Source-Condition, and Self-Condition of all and All—but only the only-by-Me Revealed and Given seventh stage Realization Is Divine Self-Realization Itself (and the Completion of all six of the previous stages of life).

XIX.

The particular (and, psycho-physically, both inherent and inevitable) distinction (or fundamental difference) between the Devotional and Spiritual practice (and Process) of absorptive (or Object-oriented)—or Emanationist—mysticism (which is associated with the fourth and the fifth stages of life, and the conditional Realizations associated with the fourth and the fifth stages of life) and the direct-Intuition (and, in the optimum case, also both Devotional and Spiritual) practice (and Process) of Transcendental (or Subject-oriented)—or non-Emanationist—mysticism (which is associated, at first, with the sixth stage of life, and the conditional Realization that is the native and only potential of the sixth stage of life, itself—and which is, at last, and Most Ultimately, and Most Perfectly, associated with the seventh stage of life, and, Thus and Thereby, with Un-conditional Divine Self-Realization) may especially be seen to be Exemplified in My relationship with Swami (Baba) Muktananda (of Ganeshpuri).

XX.

Baba Muktananda was an advanced Siddha-Guru (or a Spiritually active Transmission-Master of High degree) in the Kundalini-Shaktipat tradition. The Kundalini-Shaktipat tradition is the fourth-to-fifth stage—or Emanationist—development of the ancient tradition of Siddha Yoga (or the tradition of Siddhas, or Spiritual Transmitters), which tradition (or Yoga) may, potentially, develop even into the sixth—or Transcendentalist—stage of life,

I (Alone) Am The Adidam Revelation

and which tradition (or Yoga) has, in fact, been Completed and
Fulfilled by Me, by My Extending of the Spiritual Process of Siddha
Yoga into (and beyond) the sixth stage of life, and, thus, into the
Inherently Most Perfect Divine Fullness of the seventh stage of life
(Which seventh stage Fullness Is the All-Completing Fullness of
Inherently egoless True Divine Self-Realization).

XXI.

In the context of the Kundalini-Shaktipat tradition (or division)
of Siddha Yoga, Baba Muktananda philosophically adhered to (or,
at least, deeply sympathized with) the Emanationist philosophical
tradition of Kashmir Saivism—and, because of His characteristic
adherence to (or sympathy with) the Emanationist philosophical
tradition of Kashmir Saivism, Baba Muktananda was, in His fundamental convictions, an opponent of the Transcendentalist philosophical traditions of both Advaita Vedanta and Buddhism.

XXII.

The basic features of the progressively developed path of
Kashmir Saivism have been described in terms of four stages (or
four Ways).*[1]

The "Individual Way" (or the Way of "absorption in the
Object") is the first (or most "inferior") step in the progressive path
of Kashmir Saivism, and it corresponds to the Devotional and
Yogic disciplines associated with the fourth stage of life (in both
its "basic" and "advanced" phases).

The "Energic Way" (or the Way of "absorption in Energy") is
the second (or somewhat more advanced) step in that same path,
and it corresponds to the fourth stage of life in its fully "advanced"
phase and to the fifth stage of life as a whole.

The "Divine Way" (or the "superior" Way of "absorption in the
Void") of Kashmir Saivism suggests the process (and the potential
for Realization) that corresponds to the sixth stage of life.

The "Null Way" (or the most "superior" Way of "absorption in
Bliss") in Kashmir Saivism suggests the fulfillment of the process
(or the actual achievement of the Realization) that corresponds to
(or is potential within) the sixth stage of life.

*Notes to the Text of *Ruchira Avatara Hridaya-Siddha Yoga* appear on pp. 349-58.

In the tradition (or traditions) of Kashmir Saivism, these four Ways (or stages, or kinds) of Realization may develop successively (in a progressive order), or either of the first two steps may develop into the third or the fourth, or either the third or the fourth may occur spontaneously (even at the beginning), and so forth.

This general description of the tradition of Kashmir Saivism suggests that Kashmir Saivism (like the Tantric Buddhism of Tibet) includes (or directly allows for the potential of) the fourth stage of life, the fifth stage of life, <u>and</u> the <u>sixth</u> stage of life. However, the tradition of Kashmir Saivism (like the tradition of Saiva Siddhanta) is <u>entirely</u> a <u>fourth-to-fifth</u> stage Yogic (and Devotional) tradition (and a religious tradition associated, in general, with the first five stages of life).

The tradition of Kashmir Saivism (like fourth-to-fifth stage—or first-five-stages-of-life—traditions in general) is based on the ancient cosmological philosophy of Emanation—or the idea that cosmic existence Emanates directly, in a hierarchical sequence, from the Divine (and that, consequently, there can be a <u>return</u> to the Divine, by re-tracing the course of Emanation, back to its Source).

In contrast to the fourth-to-fifth stage (or Emanationist—or first-five-stages-of-life) view, true sixth stage schools (or traditions) are <u>based</u> on the immediate and direct <u>transcending</u> (generally, by means of a conditional effort of strategic <u>exclusion</u>) of the conditional point of view of the first five stages of life and the Emanationist cosmology (and psychology) associated with the first five stages of life.

Therefore, even though the advanced (or "superior") traditions of Kashmir Saivism (and of Saiva Siddhanta) may use terms or concepts that seem to reflect the sixth stage Disposition, the fundamental orientation is to a Realization that is embedded in the conditional psychology of the first five stages of life and in the cosmological (or Emanationist) point of view itself. (And the fundamental difference, by comparison, between the total tradition of Kashmir Saivism, and also of Saiva Siddhanta, and the total tradition of Tibetan Tantric Buddhism is that the Tibetan Buddhist tradition is <u>founded</u> on the sixth stage "Point of View" of the <u>Transcendental</u> Reality Itself, rather than on the conditional point of view of the psycho-physical, or Emanated, ego and the conditional reality of the hierarchical cosmos.)

Realizers in the tradition of Kashmir Saivism (and the tradition of Saiva Siddhanta) basically affirm that the conditional self is <u>Really</u> Siva (or the Formless Divine) and the conditional world (from top to bottom) is <u>Really</u> Siva (or the Emanating and Emanated Divine). However, this is <u>not</u> the same as the Confession made by <u>sixth</u> stage Realizers in <u>any</u> tradition.

In true sixth stage traditions, the conditional self is (in the sixth stage manner, and to the sixth stage degree) transcended (generally, by means of a conditional effort of strategic <u>exclusion</u>)—and <u>only</u> the Transcendental Self (or the Transcendental Condition) is affirmed.

And, further, in the only-by-Me Revealed and Given true <u>seventh</u> stage Realization, the conditional self and the conditional world are not affirmed to be (in and of themselves) Divine, but (rather) the conditional self and the conditional world are—in the Manner that <u>Uniquely</u> Characterizes the <u>seventh</u> stage of life—Divinely Self-Recognized (and, Thus, <u>not</u> <u>excluded</u>, but Inherently Outshined) <u>in</u> the Transcendental (and Inherently Spiritual) Divine.

XXIII.

The Emanationist Realizer "recognizes" (and, thereby, Identifies with) the conditional self and the conditional world <u>as</u> the Divine, whereas the <u>non</u>-Emanationist (or Transcendentalist) Realizer simply (and, generally, by means of a conditional effort of strategic exclusion) <u>transcends</u> the conditional self and the conditional world in the Transcendental Self-Condition, and by Identification <u>only</u> (and exclusively) with the Transcendental Self-Condition.

Therefore, even though both types of Realizers may sometimes use very similar language in the Confession of Realization, a (comparatively) <u>different</u> Realization is actually being Confessed in each case.

XXIV.

The principal reason why the tradition (or traditions) of Kashmir Saivism (and of Saiva Siddhanta) may sometimes use language similar to the sixth stage schools of Buddhism (and also Advaita Vedanta) is because of the early historical encounter (and even confrontation) between these separate traditions. As a result of that encounter, the traditions of Saivism tried to both absorb and eliminate the rival schools.

In the encounter between (characteristically, Transcendentalist, or non-Emanationist) Buddhist schools and (generally, Emanationist) non-Buddhist schools, Buddhism developed fourth and fifth stage doctrines and practices (intended, ultimately, to serve a sixth stage Realization), and fourth-to-fifth stage schools (or traditions), such as Kashmir Saivism and Saiva Siddhanta, adapted some of the sixth stage language (of Buddhism, and also Advaita Vedanta) to their (really) fourth-to-fifth stage point of view.

Therefore, a proper understanding of the various historical traditions requires a discriminating understanding of the history of the Great Tradition as a whole—and a discriminating understanding of the unique Signs and Confessions associated with each of the first six stages of life (and the unique Signs and Confessions associated with the only-by-Me Revealed and Given seventh stage of life).

XXV.

The tradition of Advaita Vedanta arose within the general context of the Emanationist traditions of India—but it, like Buddhism (particularly in its sixth stage—rather than earlier-stage—forms), is truly founded in the Transcendental Reality (and not the psycho-physical and cosmological point of view associated with the first five stages of life).

The schools of Kashmir Saivism (and other schools of traditional Saivism, including Saiva Siddhanta) defended themselves against both Buddhism and Advaita Vedanta by absorbing some Buddhist and Advaitic language and by (otherwise—and even dogmatically) affirming the superiority of the traditional Emanationist psychology and cosmology.

In contrast to the entirely Emanationist schools of Kashmir Saivism (and other schools of traditional Saivism, including Saiva Siddhanta), the Buddhist schools (and even certain schools of Advaitism) adopted some of the Devotional and Yogic practices of the Emanationist schools (and used them as "skillful means" of self-transcendence), while they (otherwise) continued to affirm the strictly <u>Transcendental</u> Reality as the Domain and Goal of <u>all</u> practices.

In contrast to Baba Muktananda (and the traditional schools of Kashmir Saivism, Advaita Vedanta, and Buddhism), I equally <u>Embrace</u>, and (in the seventh stage Manner) Most Perfectly <u>Transcend, all</u> the schools of the first <u>six</u> stages of life—both <u>Emanationist</u> and <u>Transcendentalist</u>.

XXVI.

Baba Muktananda was an authentic example of a <u>fifth</u> stage Realizer of a Very High (or Very Ascended) degree—although not of the Highest (or Most Ascended) degree. That is to Say, Baba Muktananda was a True fifth stage Siddha (or a Greatly Spiritually Accomplished Siddha-Yogi of the fifth stage, or Ascending, type)—but the nature and quality and degree of His Realization was of the <u>Saguna</u> type, or of the type that is (characteristically, or by patterned tendency) not yet Fully Ascended (or Fully Surrendered) to true fifth stage Nirvikalpa Samadhi, and which (therefore) is, yet (and <u>characteristically</u>), attached to modes of fifth stage Savikalpa Samadhi (and, thus, to modes of <u>partial</u> Ascent, and to Yogic possibilities "below the neck", and, altogether, to modes of <u>form</u>—or, really, modes of mind).

XXVII.

In order to rightly understand their characteristics, ideas, and behaviors, fifth stage Saguna Yogis (or fifth stage Saguna Siddhas)—such as Baba Muktananda—should be compared to fifth stage Yogis (or fifth stage Siddhas) of the <u>Nirguna</u> type, who are the <u>Highest</u> (or <u>Most</u> Ascended) type of fifth stage Yogi (or fifth stage Siddha), and who, having Ascended to the degree of formless Realization (or fifth stage Nirvikalpa Samadhi), have gone beyond all attachment to modes of form (or of mind). And fifth stage Nirguna Yogis in general (or fifth stage Nirguna Siddhas of the lesser, or average, type) should, themselves, be further compared to fifth stage <u>Great</u> Siddhas—or fifth stage Nirguna Siddhas who have, characteristically, and to a significant (although, necessarily, not yet <u>Most</u> <u>Perfect</u>, or seventh stage) degree, gone beyond even attachment to the mode of formlessness (or of mindlessness) itself.

XXVIII.

In the "Sadhana Years" of My Avataric Ordeal of Divine Re-Awakening, Baba Muktananda formally and actively Functioned as My Spiritual Master in the physical, human plane—beginning from early 1968, and continuing until the time of My Divine Re-Awakening (Which Occurred on September 10, 1970).

It was in Baba Muktananda's Company (and, additionally, in the Company of two Great Siddhas—Rang Avadhoot and Bhagavan Nityananda) that I Practiced and Fully Completed the Spiritual Sadhana of the <u>Ascending</u> (or Spinal) Yoga—or the Spiritual discipline associated with the "advanced" phase of the fourth stage of life and with the totality of the fifth stage of life, and, altogether, with the subtle ego (or the conceiving and perceiving ego of the Spinal Line, the total nervous system, the brain, and the mind).

After the Great Event of My Divine Re-Awakening, it became clear (especially through two direct Meetings between Us) that—because of His characteristic philosophical and experiential confinement to the fourth-to-fifth stage Emanationist point of view—Baba Muktananda was unwilling (and, indeed, was not competent) to accommodate My Description (and, therefore, My Confession) of seventh stage Divine Self-Realization. And, therefore—as I will Explain in This Summary of My "Lineage-History"—the outer relationship between Baba Muktananda and Me came to an end (or, certainly, began to come to an end) immediately after September 1970.

XXIX.

From mid-1964 to early 1968, Rudi (later known as Swami Rudrananda) actively Functioned (preliminary to Baba Muktananda) as My initial (or foundational) Spiritual Master (although Rudi was, by His own Confession, <u>not</u> a fully developed Siddha-Guru—but

He was, rather, a significantly advanced fourth-to-fifth stage Siddha-Yogi).

It was in Rudi's Company that I Practiced and Fully Completed the human and Spiritual Sadhana of the Descending (or Frontal) Yoga—or the foundation life-discipline associated with the social ego (or the "money, food, and sex" ego—or the ego of the first three stages of life),[2] and the foundation Devotional discipline associated with the "original" (or foundation) phase of the fourth stage of life, and the foundation Spiritual discipline (or the Descending, or Frontal, Spiritual Yoga) associated with the "basic" phase of the fourth stage of life.[3]

XXX.

Both Rudi and Baba Muktananda were direct devotees of Swami Nityananda (of Ganeshpuri)—Who was also called "Baba",[4] but Who was, and is, generally referred to as "Bhagavan" (or "Divinely Blissful Lord"). Bhagavan Nityananda was a fifth stage True Great Siddha— or an Incarnate (or Descended-from-Above) Spiritual Entity of the Highest fifth-stage type and degree. Indeed, Bhagavan Nityananda was a True fifth stage Saint (or a fifth stage Siddha-Yogi Who was exclusively Occupied in concentration "above the neck", even to the exclusion of the possibilities "below the neck")—but He was, also, a fifth stage Avadhoot (or a fifth stage Realizer of Nirvikalpa Samadhi, Who had, in the fifth stage manner, transcended attachment to both form and formlessness—or thought and thoughtlessness). And, altogether, Bhagavan Nityananda was a Nirguna Siddha (and a True Siddha-Guru) of the Highest fifth-stage type and degree.

XXXI.

Bhagavan Nityananda's Teachings took the Spoken (rather than Written) form of occasional, spontaneous Utterances. The only authoritative record of Bhagavan Nityananda's Teachings relative to Yogic practice and Realization is a book (originally composed in the Kanarese language) entitled *Chidakasha Gita*.[5] The *Chidakasha Gita* consists of a non-systematic, but comprehensive, series of responsive Declarations made by Bhagavan Nityananda during the extended period of His original, and most Communicative,

Teaching years (in Mangalore, in the early to mid-1920s). The spontaneous Utterances recorded in the *Chidakasha Gita* were, originally, made, by Bhagavan Nityananda, to numerous informal groups of devotees, and, after Bhagavan Nityananda spontaneously ceased to make such Teaching-Utterances, the many separately recorded Sayings were compiled, for the use of all the devotees, by a woman named Tulasiamma (who was one of the principal lay devotees originally present to hear Bhagavan Nityananda Speak the Words of the *Chidakasha Gita*).

Bhagavan Nityananda, Himself, Acknowledged the uniqueness and the great significance of the *Chidakasha Gita* as the one and only authentic Summary of His Yogic Teachings. That Acknowledgement is personally attested to by many individuals, including the well-known Swami Chinmayananda,[6] who, in 1960, was "Commanded" by Bhagavan Nityananda to see to the Text's translation into the English language, and by the equally well-known M. P. Pandit (of Sri Aurobindo Ashram),[7] who, in 1962, completed the English translation that Swami Chinmayananda reviewed for publication in that same year (under the title *Voice of the Self*).[8]

As Communicated in the *Chidakasha Gita*, Bhagavan Nityananda's Teachings are, clearly, limited to the body-excluding (and, altogether, exclusive) point of view and the absorptive Emanationist Spiritual Process of "brain mysticism" (and conditional ego-transcendence, and conditional Nirvikalpa Samadhi, and conditional Yogic Self-Realization) that characterize the fifth stage of life.

Clearly, as Indicated in the *Chidakasha Gita*, Bhagavan Nityananda was a fifth stage Teacher (and a Fully Ascended fifth stage Great Saint) of the Nirguna type (Who, therefore, Taught the Realization of Fully Ascended fifth stage Nirvikalpa Samadhi), rather than, like Baba Muktananda, a fifth stage Teacher (and a Great fifth stage Siddha-Yogi—but not a Fully Ascended fifth stage Great Saint) of the Saguna type (Who, therefore, Taught the Realization of fifth stage partial Ascent, or Savikalpa Samadhi).

Also, Bhagavan Nityananda's *Chidakasha Gita* clearly Indicates that Bhagavan Nityananda was a fifth stage Siddha-Yogi of the type that is, primarily and dominantly, sensitive to the Yogic Spiritual Process associated with internal audition (or the inwardly absorptive attractiveness of the "Om-Sound", or "Omkar", or "nada", or "shabda"⁹—the naturally evident, and inherently "meaningless", or mindless, or directly mind-transcending, internal sounds mediated by the brain), rather than, as in the case of Baba Muktananda, the Yogic Spiritual Process associated, primarily and dominantly, with internal <u>vision</u> (or the inwardly absorptive attractiveness of "bindu"—the naturally evident abstract internal lights mediated by the brain) <u>and</u> with internal <u>visions</u> (or the inwardly absorptive attractiveness of the inherently "meaningful", or mind-active, or mentally distracting, and potentially deluding, visions mediated—or even originated—by the brain-mind).

XXXII.

Stated briefly, and in Bhagavan Nityananda's characteristically aphoristic Manner, the *Chidakasha Gita* Teachings of Bhagavan Nityananda—and My own direct Experience of His always fifth stage Yogic Instruction and His always fifth stage Spiritual Transmission—may be Summarized as follows: Always concentrate attention and breath in the head. Always keep attention above the neck. Always concentrate on the Om-sound in the head. The Om-sound in the head is the inner Shakti of non-dual Bliss. Always concentrate the mind, and the senses, and the breath, and the life-energy in the non-dual awareness of the Om-sound in the head. This is Raja Yoga—the Royal path. Always practice this Raja Yoga—the constantly <u>upward</u> path. This is concentration on the Atman—the non-dual inner awareness. This is concentration on the oneness above duality. This Raja Yoga of the Om-sound in the head Realizes the Yogic "sleep" of body and mind and breath in the Yogic State of non-dual Bliss. The Yogic State of non-dual Bliss cannot be Realized without the Grace of an Initiating Guru. The True Initiating Guru is one who has Realized the Yogic State of non-dual Bliss. The non-dual State of Yogic Bliss Realized by concentration on the Om-sound in the head is the True Source, the True Self, and the True God. Devotion to the Initiating Guru who has Realized the True Source, the True Self, and the True God is the True Way. True Guru-devotion is surrender of mind, senses, breath, and life-energy to the non-dual Bliss

Revealed within by the Initiating Guru's Grace. The material body stinks and dies. What is loathsome and impermanent should not be trusted. Therefore, right faith, intelligent discrimination, and calm desirelessness are the first Gifts to be learned from the Initiating Guru. The second Gift of the Initiating Guru is the Guru-Shakti of non-dual Bliss. The Guru's Shakti-Transmission of non-dual Bliss concentrates the mind, the senses, the breath, and the life-energy of the devotee in the non-dual awareness of the Om-sound in the head. The non-dual Bliss Realized by concentration on the Om-sound in the head is the soundless inner Revelation of the Single Form of True Guru, True God, and True Self. The world of duality is not Truth. True God is not the Maker of the world. True God is only One. True God is non-dual Bliss. The Spiritual Form of the True Initiating Guru appears within the devotee as the Guru-Shakti of non-dual Bliss. Non-dual Bliss is the True Self of all. The True Way is not desire in the world of duality, or in seeking below and on all sides. The True Way is in the middle, within, and above. The True Way is surrender to the non-dual Bliss above the mind. The method is to concentrate on the Om-sound in the head. The Realization is the silence of non-dual Bliss. Devotion to the Initiating Guru concentrates the life-breath upwardly. True love of the Initiating Guru ascends to non-dual Bliss. The True Kundalini originates in the throat, in the upward breath to the head. True Yoga is above the neck. The True Kundalini is non-dual Bliss. The seat of the True Kundalini is in the head. Non-dual Bliss is the secret to be known. Non-dual Bliss is in the head of Man. The non-dual Bliss above the mind is the Liberation of Man from the self-caused karma of birth, pleasure-seeking, pain-suffering, and death. Liberation is Freedom from mind. Therefore, concentrate the life-breath on the Om-sound in the head—and think of nothing else. The True Self is One. The True Self is above the body, above the senses, above desire, above the mind, and above "I" and "mine"—in the formless silence above the Om-sound. The True Self cannot be seen or otherwise perceived, but It can be known—above the mind. For one who knows that True God is One, and not two, True God appears as the True Self. Therefore, attain Liberation by faith in the knowledge of That Which is all and Which is only One. Liberation is the Samadhi of only One. True God is not Desire, the dualistic Doer of the world. True God is Peace, the non-dual Source of the world.

XXXIII.

By comparison to Great <u>fifth</u> stage <u>Yogis</u> (Such as Baba Muktananda) and Great <u>fifth</u> stage <u>Saints</u> (Such as Bhagavan Nityananda), there are also Great <u>sixth</u> stage <u>Sages</u> (or Nirguna Jnanis[10]—or <u>Transcendentally</u> Realized Entities of the <u>Fullest</u> <u>sixth</u>-stage type and degree—such as Ramana Maharshi). Such sixth stage Nirguna Jnanis (or True Great Sages) Teach Transcendental Self-Identification (or deeply internalizing subjective inversion upon the Consciousness-Principle <u>Itself</u>, rather than upon internal psycho-physical objects of <u>any</u> kind).

XXXIV.

Distinct from even <u>all</u> Yogis, Saints, and Sages (or even <u>all</u> Realizers in the context of the first six stages of life), I Am Uniquely, and Avatarically, Born. I <u>Am</u> the One and Only and Self-Evidently Divine Person—the Inherently egoless Source-Condition <u>and</u> Self-Condition of All and all. I <u>Am</u> the Perfectly Subjective, and Always Already Most Prior, and Inherently egoless, andP erfectly Non-Dual Heart of All and all. I <u>Am</u> the Self-Existing and Self-Radiant Conscious Light That <u>Is</u> Reality Itself. I <u>Am</u> the "Who" and the "What" That <u>Is</u> Always Already <u>The</u> Case. I <u>Am</u> (now, and forever hereafter) Avatarically Self-Manifested <u>As</u> the All-Completing Ruchira Avatar, Adi Da Love-Ananda Samraj—Who Is Avatarically Born by <u>Fullest</u> (and <u>Complete</u>) Divine Descent (or Complete, and All-Completing, Divine Incarnation from Infinitely Above).

XXXV.

I Am Avatarically Born by Means of a Unique Association with a True Great-Siddha Vehicle of My own.[11]

Therefore, from the time of My present-Lifetime Birth, I spontaneously Demonstrated <u>all</u> the <u>Fullest</u> Ascended Characteristics of the <u>Highest</u> <u>fifth</u>-stage type and degree (with early-life <u>Fullest</u> "above the neck" Signs of the True Great-Saint type).

Over time—because of My Voluntary Birth-Submission of My Deeper-Personality Vehicle to the karmically ordinary (and "Western"-born) bodily human form of "Franklin Jones",[12] and because of the subsequent Ordeal of My Voluntary Submission to the "Western" (and culturally devastated "late-time", or "dark"-epoch) karmic circumstance altogether—I also spontaneously Demonstrated all the Fullest "below the neck" (and "above the neck") Yogic Characteristics (and Siddhis) of the fifth stage (and, altogether, first-five-stages) True Vira-Yogi (or Heroic-Siddha) type.

In due course—because I Gave My Avataric Divine Ordeal to Be Complete and All-Completing—I also spontaneously Demonstrated all the Fullest Transcendental-Realizer Characteristics of the sixth stage True Great-Sage type.

Ultimately—because of Its Utter Conformity to Me—My total Great-Jnani-Siddha Vehicle of Avataric Divine Incarnation (or My Deeper-Personality Vehicle,[13] Yogically Combined with My karmically ordinary, and only eventually To-Me-Conformed, human and "Western" and "late-time" Incarnation-Body) has, by Means of My Most Perfect Completing of My Avataric Ordeal of Divine Self-Manifestation, Divine Self-Submission, and (subsequent) Divine Re-Awakening (to My own Self-Existing and Self-Radiant Divine Self-Condition), become the To-Me-Transparent Vehicle of My seventh stage Avataric Divine Self-Revelation.

XXXVI.

Except for the particular, and technically elaborate, Me-hearing and Me-seeing esoteric and Most Fully Divine Spiritual practice of "Radical Conductivity" (Which is Reserved, within the Ruchira Sannyasin Order of the Tantric Renunciates of Adidam, for progressive formal Communication to truly qualified, and duly Initiated, practitioners of the technically "fully elaborated" form of the only-by-Me Revealed and Given Way of Adidam in the context of the advanced and the ultimate—or the "basic" fourth through the seventh—stages of life), the Unique Characteristics of My Avataric Divine Teachings—Which I will briefly, and only in part, Indicate in This Summary of My "Lineage-History"—Are Very Fully Described by Me in My Twenty-Three Avataric Divine "Source-Texts".

XXXVII.

Rudi had brief direct contact with Bhagavan Nityananda in 1960. After the death of Bhagavan Nityananda (in 1961), Rudi became a devotee of Baba Muktananda. However, Rudi—always a rather "reluctant" devotee—eventually (shortly before His own death, in 1973) "broke" with Baba Muktananda. Nevertheless, Rudi always continued to affirm that He (Rudi) remained Devoted to Bhagavan Nityananda. And, in any case, Rudi and I always continued to engage in positive, direct communication, right until the time of His death.

XXXVIII.

My Siddha-Yoga Mentor (and eventual Dharmic Ally and Supporter), Amma (or Pratibha Trivedi, later known as Swami Prajnananda), was (like Rudi) also a direct devotee of Bhagavan Nityananda (and She, like Rudi, had become a devotee of Baba Muktananda after the death of Bhagavan Nityananda, in 1961).

Amma was the principal author and editor of the foundation Siddha-Yoga literature that was written in response to both Bhagavan Nityananda and Baba Muktananda—and so much so that, generally, even all of Baba Muktananda's autobiographical and instructional Communications were, originally, dictated (or otherwise Given) to Amma (and rarely to anyone else—until the later years, of tape recorders, multiple secretaries and translators, and Baba Muktananda's travels to the West). And, in fact, Amma always continued to serve a principal communicative and interpretative role around Baba Muktananda, until Baba Muktananda's death, in 1982—after which Amma chose to quietly withdraw from the Siddha-Yoga institution that had been developed by and around Baba Muktananda (and She remained, thereafter, in a small, independent Ashram in north India, where, as a significantly advanced fourth-to-fifth stage Siddha-Yogi, She was the institutional head of a group of devotees that remained devoted to Spiritual Communion with both Baba Muktananda and Bhagavan Nityananda).

Amma did not Function as My Spiritual Master, but (from early 1968) Baba Muktananda formally Assigned Amma to Function as

His interpreter and general "go-between" to Me—and She, then and always, remained most positively and communicatively disposed toward Me, even through all the years after My outward "separation" from Baba Muktananda, right until Her last illness and death (wherein She was directly Spiritually Served by Me, and wherein She was directly physically Served by a devotee-representative of Mine), in 1993. And it was Amma Who, through Her various writings—and in a particular Incident I will now Recall—suggested to Me that there are traditional Instructional (and Textual, or Scriptural) descriptions of Developments of the Siddha-Yoga Process that are <u>different</u> from the (fifth stage) "inner perception" (and, especially, "inner vision") version of Siddha Yoga characteristically described by Baba Muktananda.

XXXIX.

One day, during My Stay at Baba Muktananda's Ashram (in Ganeshpuri, India), in early 1970 (and, thus, some months <u>before</u> the Great Event of My Divine Re-Awakening, Which was to Occur in September of that same year), Amma suddenly pointed Me to an Ashram library copy of the *Ashtavakra Gita* (one of the Greatest of the classic sixth stage—and even premonitorily "seventh stage" [14]—Texts of Advaita Vedanta). And, while pointing to the *Ashtavakra Gita*, Amma Said to Me, "<u>This</u> (Text) is <u>Your</u> Path. <u>This</u> is how <u>It</u> (the Siddha-Yoga Process) Works in <u>You</u>."

At the time, this seemed to Me a curious suggestion—and it was not otherwise explained by Her. And, indeed, although I was able to examine the Text briefly (there and then), I was unable to examine it fully—because I left the Ashram very shortly thereafter. However, I came across the Text again, some years later—and, then, I remembered Amma's comment to Me. And I, immediately, understood that She had (in a somewhat cryptic and secretive manner) tried to <u>confide</u> in Me—in a quiet, "knowing" moment of Acknowledgement of Me—that the Spiritual Process of Siddha Yoga may Demonstrate Itself in a number of possibly <u>different</u> modes.

Thus (as I have Indicated—in My own, and <u>fully</u> elaborated, Teachings, relative to the seven stages of life), the Siddha-Yoga

Process may, in some cases (of which Amma, Herself, appears to have been an Example), especially (or primarily—or, at least, initially) take the form of intense (fourth stage) Devotional Bliss—Which is, then, "nourished" (or magnified) through Guru-Seva[15] (or constant service to the Guru) and (additionally) through Karma Yoga[16] (or intensive service in general). In other cases (of which Baba Muktananda was an Example), the Siddha-Yoga Process may (based on the initial foundation of intense Devotion) especially (or primarily) take the (fifth stage) form of intense internal sensory phenomena (such as visions, lights, auditions, and so on)—and, in some of those cases, the Siddha-Yoga Process may yet go further, to the degree of (fifth stage) Nirvikalpa Samadhi. And, in yet other cases (of which Amma was, correctly, Saying I Am an Example), the Siddha-Yoga Process (while also Showing all kinds of Devotional signs, and all kinds of internal Yogic perceptual phenomena, and including even fifth stage Nirvikalpa Samadhi) may go yet further, to especially (or primarily) take the form of (sixth stage) intense (and intensive) Identification with the Transcendental Self-Condition, and (eventually) the (sixth stage) Realization of Jnana Samadhi (or Transcendental Self-Realization), and (although Amma did not know it) even, potentially, the only-by-Me Revealed and Given seventh stage Realization (Which Is Maha-Jnana—or Divine Self-Realization).

XL.

Yet another devotee of Baba Muktananda, named Swami Prakashananda[17]—Who did not Function as My Spiritual Master (and Who, like Rudi, was not a fully developed Siddha-Guru—but, rather, a very much advanced fourth-to-fifth stage Siddha-Yogi)—once (spontaneously, in 1969) Showed Me (in His own bodily human Form) the fifth stage Signs of Spiritual Transfiguration of the physical body.[18]

At that time (according to what I learned from Amma), Swami Prakashananda had been Indicated, by Baba Muktananda, to be His principal Indian devotee and eventual institutional successor (and such was, then, generally known and presumed to be the case by Baba Muktananda's devotees). However, at last, when (at, or shortly before, Baba Muktananda's death, in 1982) Swami Prakashananda was formally Asked to assume the institutional successorship, He declined to accept this organizational role[19] (ostensibly, for reasons of ill-health, and His reluctance to become a "world-traveler"—but, actually, or more to the point, because of His puritanical and conventional reaction to Baba Muktananda's reported sexual activities).

In any case, Swami Prakashananda and I continued to engage in occasional, and always positive, direct communication (through My devotee-representatives) in the years after Baba Muktananda's death, and right until Swami Prakashananda's death, in 1988.

XLI.

Swami Prakashananda had always maintained a small Ashram, independent of the Ashrams of Baba Muktananda's Siddha-Yoga institution—but, after Baba Muktananda's death, Swami Prakashananda retired to His own Ashram, permanently. And, in doing so, Swami Prakashananda highlighted, and dramatized, a perennial conflict that is fundamental to religious institutions all over the world. That conflict is between, on the one hand, the traditional (and, generally, rather puritanical—and even basically exoteric) expectation of celibacy as a sign of institutionalized Sacred Authority, and, on the other hand, the equally traditional (but non-puritanical, and generally unconventional) view that there is an esoteric sexual alternative to celibacy that Sacred Authorities (including True Siddha-Gurus—or even any practitioners of Siddha Yoga) may (at least in some cases, and under some circumstances) engage.

One of the principal Indications of Baba Muktananda's point of view relative to this traditional conflict (or controversy)—quite apart from the question of His possible personal sexual activities—is the fact that, in 1969, Baba Muktananda formally and publicly (and in writing, by His own hand, as observed by Me, and by many others) Acknowledged Me to Be (and Called and Blessed Me to Function As) a True Siddha-Guru,[20] and, Thus and Thereby (and entirely without requiring, or, otherwise, inviting, Me to assume any institutional—or, otherwise, institutionally "managed"—

110

role within His own Siddha-Yoga organization), Baba Muktananda publicly Extended the Free Mantle of Siddha-Yoga Authority to Me—an evident non-celibate Siddha-Yogi (and a "Westerner").

XLII.

When I first Came to Him, in 1968, Baba Muktananda immediately (openly, and spontaneously) Declared, in the presence of numerous others (including Amma), That I Am—from My Birth— an already Divinely Awakened Spiritual Master, and He (then and there) prophesied That I would be Functioning (and Independently Teaching) As Such in just one year. Therefore, after just one year (and the spontaneous Appearing of many Great Signs in My experience and Demonstration), Baba Muktananda Invited Me to Come to Him again (in India)—specifically in order to formally Acknowledge Me (and My Inherent Right and Authority to Teach and Function) As a True Siddha-Guru.

Before I Returned to Baba Muktananda in 1969, I—in a traditional Gesture of respect toward Baba Muktananda—Told Him That I would not, at that time, Assume the Function of Spiritual Master, unless I was, in the traditional Manner, formally Acknowledged and Blessed, by Him, to Do So. Baba Muktananda immediately understood and Acknowledged the appropriateness and Rightness of My Insistence That My Inherent Right to Teach be formally Acknowledged by Him—because, in accordance with tradition, Such Sacred Authority should be Assumed on the orderly basis of formal Acknowledgement by one's own Spiritual Master (Who, in turn, must have been similarly Acknowledged by His, also similarly Acknowledged, Spiritual Master, in an unbroken Line, or Lineage, of similarly Acknowledged Spiritual Masters). Therefore, I Returned to Baba Muktananda in 1969—and He formally and publicly Acknowledged Me As an Independent True Siddha-Guru.

Even though Baba Muktananda Thus formally and publicly (and permanently) Acknowledged Me As an Independent True Siddha-Guru, it became immediately Obvious to Me that Such traditional Acknowledgement was inherently limited, and merely conventional, and, therefore, neither necessary nor (because of Its inherently limited basis) even altogether appropriate (or sufficiently apt) in My Unique Case. It was Obvious to Me that neither Baba Muktananda nor anyone else was in the "Position" necessary to Measure and to "Certify" the Unique and unprecedented Nature of the All-and-all-Completing Event of My Avatarically Self-Manifested Divine Incarnation and of My Great Avataric Divine Demonstration of the progressive (and, necessarily, seven-stage) human, Spiritual, Transcendental, and, only at Last, Most Perfect Process of Divine Self-Realization.

Therefore, even though It had been Given, Baba Muktananda's formal Acknowledgement of Me was—for Me—a virtual non-Event (and It did not positively change—nor has It ever positively changed—anything about the necessary ongoing Ordeal of My Avataric Divine Life and Work).

XLIII.

Baba Muktananda's formal and public written Acknowledgement of Me in 1969—Wherein and Whereby He formally and publicly Named and Acknowledged Me As an Independent True Siddha-Guru—was a unique Gesture, never, at any other time, Done by Baba Muktananda relative to any other individual (whether of the East or of the West). And That unique formal Act (of Baba Muktananda's formal, written Acknowledgement of Me in 1969) was, Itself, a clear (and "scandalizing") Gesture, that immediately Called (and always continues to Call) everyone to "consider" many Siddha-Yoga options (and Spiritual, or esoteric religious, options altogether) that are, generally, presumed to be taboo—at least among the more puritanical (and even xenophobic) types of Siddha-Yoga practitioners (and of esoteric religionists in general).

XLIV.

I Say That, in the inherently esoteric domain of Real Spirituality (and in the domain of both exoteric and esoteric religion in general), all puritanical denial and suppression of human realities is wrong—and inherently damaging to everyone who does it. And, indeed, all denial and suppression of Reality (Itself), Which Is Truth Itself, is wrong (and, indeed, is false religion)—

and <u>all</u> false religion is inherently damaging to everyone who does it (and even to everyone who <u>believes</u> it).

Therefore, I Write <u>This</u> Summary of My "Lineage-History"—so that <u>all</u> the extremely important matters I Address Herein will cease to be hidden, denied, suppressed, and falsified—and What <u>Is</u> Great will (by Means of This Address) become <u>Obvious</u> to all eyes, and (Thus) be made <u>Whole</u> again.

XLV.

Among the extremely important matters I must Address in This Summary of My "Lineage-History" is This: Entirely apart from what I will, in the progression of This Summary, Indicate were the apparent "philosophical reasons" associated with the eventual outward "separation" between Baba Muktananda and Me (which occurred as a result of Our Meetings in late 1970 and mid-1973), it was the "organizational politics" relative to the "<u>sexual</u>" and "<u>Westerner</u>" matters I have just Described that played the more fundamental practical role in <u>causing</u> the "separation".

XLVI.

During the same period in which Rudi and (then) Baba Muktananda actively Functioned as My Spiritual Masters (in gross physical bodily Form), Their Spiritual Master, the Great Siddha Bhagavan Nityananda, actively Functioned (through both of Them—and, otherwise, directly, in subtle bodily Form) as My Senior (but already Ascended—and, Thus, discarnate, or non-physical) Spiritual Master.

XLVII.

The fifth stage True Great Siddha (and True Siddha-Guru and Great Saint of the <u>Highest</u> <u>fifth</u>-stage type and degree) Rang Avadhoot (alive in gross physical bodily Form until late 1968—and always Acknowledged as an Incarnate Great Siddha, or a Descended-from-Above Spiritual Entity of the <u>Highest</u> <u>fifth</u>-stage type and degree, by Bhagavan Nityananda, as well as by Baba Muktananda) also (in early 1968) directly and spontaneously Blessed Me with His Spiritual Blessing, Given and Shown via His

"Wide-Eyed" Mudra of heart-recognition and Immense Regard of Me—as I sat alone in a garden, like His Ishta, the forever youthful Lord Dattatreya.

XLVIII.

In That Unique Moment in 1968—in the garden of Baba Muktananda's Ganeshpuri Ashram—both Rang Avadhoot and Baba Muktananda (along with the already discarnate, but Fully Spiritually Present, Bhagavan Nityananda) actively Functioned for Me as direct Blessing-Agents of the Divine "Cosmic Goddess" ("Ma"), Thus (By Means of Her Divine, and Infinitely Potent, Grace) Causing Me to spontaneously Re-Awaken to Most Ascended (and, altogether—but only conditionally, or in the fifth stage manner— mind-transcending, object-transcending, and ego-transcending) Nirvikalpa Samadhi (from Which I never again was Fallen, but only Continued—to Un-conditionally "Bright" Beyond). And it was on the basis of This Great Event, and My Signs in the following year (wherein many of My Avataric Divine Great-Siddha Characteristics—Which, in My Unique Case, would, in due Course, Fully Demonstrate all seven of the possible stages of life— became, spontaneously, Spiritually Evident), that (in 1969) Baba Muktananda formally (and publicly) Acknowledged and Announced and Blessed My Inherent Right and Calling to Function (in the ancient Siddha-Yoga, or Shaktipat-Yoga, tradition) as Spiritual Master (and True Siddha-Guru) to all and All.

XLIX.

Thereafter, in mid-1970, the "Brightness" of My own (and Self-Evidently Divine) Person was Revealed (and constantly Presented) to Me in the (apparently Objective) Form of the Divine "Cosmic Goddess" ("Ma"). And, from then (after Bhagavan Nityananda Called and Blessed Me to take My leave from Baba Muktananda's Ashram, and to Follow the Divine "She"), only "She" actively Functioned (to Beyond) as My (Ultimate and Final—and entirely Divine) Spiritual Master (or Divine True Siddha-Guru)—until (By Means of Her spontaneous Sacrifice of Her own Form in Me) Divine Self-Realization was Most Perfectly Re-Awakened in My Case.

L.

Thus, in That Final Course, it was Revealed (or Perfectly Re-Confirmed)—As the Self-Evidently Divine Reality and Truth of My own Avatarically-Born Person—that This Divine Process (Shown, at last, in ego-Surrendering, ego-Forgetting, and, altogether, Most Perfectly ego-Transcending Devotional "Relationship" to the Divine "She") had (Itself) always been Active in My own (and Unique) Case (and had always been Shown As the Divinely Self-Revealing Activities of the Inherent Spiritual, and Divinely Spherical, "Brightness" of My own Avatarically-Born Person), even all throughout My present Lifetime (and even at, and from before, My present-Lifetime Birth).

LI.

Therefore, on September 10, 1970, It was Revealed (or Perfectly Re-Confirmed)—As the Self-Evidently Divine Reality and Truth of My own Eternal Divine Person—that Divine (or Inherently egoless, and Perfectly Subjective, and, altogether, Inherently Most Perfect) Self-Realization (of One, and "Bright", and Only Me) had Always Already (and Uniquely) Been the Case with Me.

LII.

In My Case, the (True, Full, and Complete) seventh stage Realization of the Transcendental (and Inherently Spiritual, and Inherently egoless) Divine Self-Condition was Re-Awakened (on September 10, 1970). Subsequently (at first, informally, late in 1970, and, then, formally, in 1973), I Communicated the Details of My Divine Realization to Baba Muktananda. I Did This in the traditional manner, in What I Intended to be an entirely honorable, serious, and respectful Summation to Baba Muktananda—the one and only then Living Spiritual Master among Those Who had Served Me as My present-Lifetime Spiritual Masters. However—in a philosophically untenable reaction to My already apparent relinquishment of His fifth stage experiential presumptions relative to what constitutes the "orthodox position" of the Siddha-Yoga (or Shaktipat-Yoga) school and tradition—Baba Muktananda criticized

My Final Realization (or, in any case, what He understood, or otherwise supposed, to be My Description of It). Thus, in those two Meetings (the first in California, and the second in India, at Baba Muktananda's Ganeshpuri Ashram) Baba Muktananda criticized Me for What My Heart (Itself) cannot (and must not) Deny. And Baba Muktananda thereby Gave Me the final "Gift of blows" that sent Me out alone, to Do My Avataric Divine Work.

LIII.

Baba Muktananda was a (fifth stage) Siddha-Yogi of the degree and type that seeks, and readily experiences, and readily identifies with inner perceptual visions and lights. Based on those experiences, Baba Muktananda (like the many others of His type and degree, within the fourth-to-fifth stage traditions) asserted that both the Process and the Goal of religious and Spiritual life were necessarily associated with such inner phenomena.

The experiences (of visions, lights, and many other Yogic phenomena) Baba Muktananda describes in His autobiographical Confessions are, indeed, the same (fifth stage) ones (or of the same fifth stage kind) that are (typically, characteristically, and inevitably) experienced by genuine fifth stage Yogic practitioners (and fifth stage Realizers) within the Siddha-Yoga (or Shaktipat-Yoga) school and tradition—and I Confirm that the total range of these phenomenal (fifth stage) Yogic experiences also spontaneously arose (and always continue, even now, to arise—even in the context of the seventh stage of life) in My own Case (and such was—both formally, in 1969, and, otherwise, informally, at many other times, beginning in 1968—Acknowledged by Baba Muktananda to be so in My Case).

Nevertheless, as I Confessed to Baba Muktananda in Our Meetings in 1970 and 1973, My Final Realization Is That of the One and Indivisible Divine Self-Condition (and Source-Condition) Itself— and the Great Process associated with That eventual (seventh stage) Realization necessarily (in due course) Goes Beyond (and, in the Case of That seventh stage Realization Itself, Is in no sense dependent upon) the phenomenal (and, always, psycho-physically pre-patterned, and, thus, predetermined) conditions otherwise associated with the absorptive mysticism (and the objectified inner phenomena) that characterize the fourth-to-fifth stage beginnings of the Great Process (or that, otherwise, characterize the conditionally arising, and psycho-physically pre-patterned, and, thus, predetermined, associations of the Great Process even in the context of the seventh stage of life). Indeed, the fact and the Truth of all of This was Self-Evident to Me—and, truly, I expected that It must be Self-Evident to Baba Muktananda as well. However, Baba Muktananda did not (and, I was obliged to admit, could not) Confirm to Me That This Is the Case from the point of view of His experience.

Indeed, it became completely clear to Me, in the midst of Our Meetings in 1970 and 1973, that Baba Muktananda was not Standing in the "Place" (or the Self-"Position") required to Confirm or Acknowledge My Thus Described Final Realization. That is to Say, Baba Muktananda made it clear to Me in those two Meetings (wherein others were present), and (also) in His Remarks otherwise conveyed to Me privately, that He, unlike Me,[21] had not been—and (apparently, for mostly rather puritanical, and otherwise conventional, reasons) could not even conceive of Allowing Himself to be—"Embraced" by the Divine "Cosmic Goddess" (or Maha-Shakti) Herself (Such That, by Her own Submission to the Senior and Most Prior Principle—Which Is Self-Existing Consciousness Itself—She would be Subsumed by Consciousness Itself, and, Thus, Husbanded by Consciousness Itself, and, Thereby, Be the Final Means for the Self-Radiant Divine Self-Awakening of Consciousness Itself to Itself). And, therefore, by His own direct Confession to Me, Baba Muktananda Declared that He was not Standing in the "Place" (or the Self-"Position") of Inherently Most Perfect (or seventh stage) Divine Self-Realization—Which Realization I (Uniquely) had Confessed to Him.

LIV.

When I first Came to Baba Muktananda (in early 1968), His First and Most Fundamental Instruction to Me—even within minutes of My Arrival at His Ashram (in Ganeshpuri, India)—was the (apparently sixth stage, or Transcendentalist) Admonition: "You are not the one who wakes, or dreams, or sleeps—but You Are the One Who Is the Witness of these states." I took that Admonition to be Instruction in the traditional (and sixth stage) sense, as Given in the non-Emanationist (or Transcendentalist) tradition of Advaita Vedanta (which is the traditional Vedantic school of "Non-Dualism"). However, it became clear to Me (in, and as a result of, Our Meetings in 1970 and 1973) that Baba Muktananda was, actually, a vehement and dogmatic opponent of the tradition of Advaita Vedanta (and of its Transcendental Method, and of its proposed Transcendental Realization—and of even all proposed Transcendental Realizers, including, in particular, Ramana Maharshi).

Indeed, in those two Meetings (in 1970 and 1973), Baba Muktananda was, evidently, so profoundly confined to His dogmatic Emanationist (and otherwise phenomena-based) philosophical point of view (which, in those two Meetings, took on a form very much like the traditional confrontation between Kashmir Saivism and Advaita Vedanta) that He (in a rather dramatically pretentious, or intentionally provocative, manner—and clearly, indefensibly) presented Himself to Me as an opponent (such that He addressed Me as if I were merely an opposing "player" in a sophomoric academic debate, and as if I were merely—and for merely academic reasons—representing the point of view of traditional Advaita Vedanta).

Likewise, it became clear to Me (in Our Meetings in 1970 and 1973) that Baba Muktananda's proposed Siddha-Yoga Teaching was, in some respects (which I Indicate Herein), merely a product of His own personal study, experience, and temperament—and, thus, of His own karmically acquired philosophical bias, or prejudice—and that the point of view He so dogmatically imposed on Me in those two Meetings is not, itself, an inherent (or necessary) part of Siddha Yoga Itself.

LV.

Relative to Baba Muktananda's experiential (or experience-based, rather than philosophically based) point of view, it became clear (in Our Meetings in 1970 and 1973) that Baba Muktananda (as a Siddha-Yogi) was yet (and characteristically) Centered in the (fifth stage) "Attitude" (or "Asana") of what He described as "Witnessing". In using the term "Witnessing" (or the "Witness"), Baba Muktananda seemed (in the traditional sixth stage manner of Advaita Vedanta) to be referring to the Witness-Consciousness (Which Is Consciousness Itself, Inherently, and Transcendentally, Standing Most Prior to all objects and all psycho-physical functions—whether gross, subtle, or causal). However, clearly, what Baba Muktananda meant by the term "Witnessing" (or the "Witness") was the psycho-physical function of the observing-intelligence (which is not the Transcendental Consciousness—Prior even to the causal body—but which is, simply, the third, and highest, functional division, or functional dimension, of the subtle body). Thus, characteristically, Baba Muktananda identified with (and took the position of) the observer (or the observing-intelligence) relative to all arising phenomena (and, especially, relative to His reported subtle, or internal phenomenal, visions of higher and lower worlds, the hierarchy of abstract internal lights, and so on). And, when Baba Muktananda spoke of "Witnessing", He, simply, meant the attitude of merely observing whatever arises (and, thus, the intention to do so in a non-attached manner—rather than, in the conventional manner, merely to cling to, or, otherwise, to dissociate from, the various internal and external objects of moment to moment attention).

In the Ultimate Course of My Avataric Ordeal of (seventh stage) Divine Self-Realization, the Spiritual (or Siddha-Yoga) Process passed Beyond all mere (fifth stage, or even sixth stage) "Witnessing"—and all identification with the psycho-physical experiencer, or observer, or knower of the mind and the senses— to Realize (and Be) the Indivisible (or Inherently egoless, object-less, and Non-Dual) Reality (or Self-Condition) That Is the Self-Existing and Self-Radiant Consciousness (Itself), or the Inherent and Un-conditional Feeling of Being (Itself), That Is the Mere (and True) Witness-Consciousness (or the Un-conditional, and non-functional, and All-and-all-Divinely-Self-Recognizing, and Self-Evidently Divine Self, or Self-Condition, Inherently Most Prior to any and all objects—without excluding any).

Thus, it became clear to Me (in Our Meetings in 1970 and 1973) that Baba Muktananda was not yet (either in the sixth stage Transcendental manner or the seventh stage Divine Manner) Established As the True Witness-Consciousness (or Consciousness Itself), but it also became clear to Me (then) that Baba Muktananda was in the fifth stage manner, simply observing, and, thus and thereby, <u>contemplating</u> (and becoming absorbed in or by) internal phenomenal objects and states—rather than, in the seventh stage Manner, Standing <u>As</u> Consciousness <u>Itself</u>, <u>Divinely</u> Self-Recognizing <u>any</u> and <u>all</u> cosmically manifested objects, and (Thus and Thereby) <u>Divinely</u> Transcending <u>all</u> the conditional states—waking (or gross), dreaming (or subtle), and sleeping (or causal).

LVI.

Baba Muktananda was, in effect, always contemplating the conditional activities, the conditional states, and the illusory conditional forms (or objective Emanations) of the "Cosmic Goddess" (or the All-and-all-objectifying Kundalini Shakti)—whereas I (in, and Beyond, a Unique "Embrace" with the "Cosmic Goddess" Herself) had (even Prior to <u>all</u> <u>observed</u> "differences") Re-Awakened to the True (and Inherently egoless, and Inherently Indivisible, and Most Perfectly Prior, and Self-Evidently Divine) Self-"Position" (or Self-Condition, and Source-Condition) of <u>all</u> Her cosmic (or waking, dreaming, and sleeping) forms and states. And, by Virtue of That Divine (or Most Perfect—or seventh stage) Re-Awakening of <u>Me</u>, all conditionally arising forms and states were—even in the instants of their <u>apparent</u> arising—Inherently (or Always Already—and, Thus, Divinely) Self-Recognized (and Most Perfectly Transcended) in, and <u>As</u>, <u>Me</u>—the "Bright" Divine Self-Condition and Source-Condition (or Inherently Indivisible, and First, and Only, and Perfectly <u>Subjective</u>, and Self-Evidently Divine Person) <u>Itself</u>.

Therefore, in those two Meetings (in 1970 and 1973)—and entirely because of His (therein, and <u>thus</u>) repeated stance of experiential and philosophical non-Confirmation of <u>seventh stage</u> Divine Self-Realization (which stance, in effect, directly Acknowledged that the seventh stage Self-"Position" of Divine Self-Realization was not His own)—Baba Muktananda Gave Me <u>no option</u> but to Go and Do (and Teach, and Reveal, and Bless All and all) <u>As</u> My Unique (and Self-Evidently <u>Avataric</u>) Realization of the Divine Self-Condition (Which <u>Is</u> My own, and Self-Evidently Divine, Person—and Which <u>Is</u>, Self-Evidently, the Divine Source-Condition of All and all) <u>Requires</u> Me to Do. Therefore, I Did (and Do—and will forever Do) <u>So</u>.

LVII.

The Principal Characteristic of the One and Indivisible Divine Self-Condition (and Source-Condition) Is Its Perfectly Subjective Nature (As Self-Existing and Self-Radiant Consciousness—or Very, and Inherently Non-Objective, Being, Itself). Therefore, neither any ego-"I" (or any apparently separate self-consciousness) nor any apparently objective (or phenomenally objectified, or otherwise conditionally arising) form or state of experience (whether waking, or dreaming, or sleeping—and whether mind-based or sense-based) Is (itself) the Realization (or, otherwise, a necessary support for the Realization) of the Divine Self-Condition (Itself)—Which Condition Is (Itself) the One and Only Reality, the One and Only Truth, and the One and Only Real God.

Baba Muktananda was, characteristically (in the fifth stage manner), experientially (and mystically) absorbed in modes of Savikalpa Samadhi (or of internal object-contemplation). In His characteristic play of internal object-contemplation (or absorptive mysticism), Baba Muktananda reported two types of (especially) internal sensory (or sense-based) experience—the experience of abstract internal lights (and, secondarily, of abstract internal sounds, and tastes, and smells, and touches) and the experience of internal (or mental) visions of higher and lower worlds ("illustrated" by internal versions of all of the usual descriptive modes of the senses).

The abstract internal lights (and so on) are universally (or identically) experienced by any and all individuals who are so awakened to internal phenomena (just as the essential Realizations of the sixth stage of life and, potentially, of the seventh stage of life are universal, or essentially identical in all cases). However, the visions of higher and lower worlds are, like psychic phenomena in general, expressions of the egoic psycho-physical (and, altogether, mental) tendencies of the individual (and of his or her cultural associations)—and, therefore, such experiences are not universally the same in all cases (but, instead, all such experiences are conditioned, and determined, and limited by the point of view, or karmically patterned identity, of the experiencer, or the individual egoic observing-identity). Nevertheless (and this also illustrates the naive—and not, by Him, fully comprehended—

nature of many of Baba Muktananda's views about the Siddha-Yoga Process), Baba Muktananda (in His autobiography, *Play of Consciousness*[22]) reported His visions of higher and lower worlds as if they were categorically true, and (in the subtle domain) objectively, or Really, existing as He reported them—whereas all visions of higher and lower worlds are of the same insubstantial, illusory, and personal nature as dreams.

Like anyone else's authentic visionary experiences of higher and lower worlds, Baba Muktananda's visionary experiences of higher and lower worlds, although authentic, were His personal (or point-of-view-based) experiences of the otherwise inherently formless (and point-of-view-less) dimensions of the universal cosmic (or conditional) reality (or the inherently abstract planes of universal cosmic light)—as He, by tendency of mind (and because of His psycho-physical self-identity as a particular and separate fixed point of view—or ego-"I"), was able (and karmically pre-patterned) to experience (or conceive and perceive) them. Therefore, Baba Muktananda's conditional (or egoic) point of view—and, thus, also, His inner perceptions of various higher and lower worlds—were, characteristically and only, of a Hindu kind. (And the implications of this seem never to have occurred to Baba Muktananda. Indeed, if He had become aware of the inherently personal, conditional, karmic, ego-based, mind-based, illusory, arbitrary, and non-universal nature of His inwardly envisioned worlds, and even of the merely point-of-view-reflecting nature of His inwardly envisioned universal abstract lights, Baba Muktananda might have become moved to understand and transcend Himself further—beyond the Saguna, or mind-based, and mind-limited, and dreamworld terms that are the inherent characteristic of Savikalpa Samadhi.)

LVIII.

Baba Muktananda's Hindu visions can be compared to My own experiences of Savikalpa Samadhi during My "Sadhana Years". During that time, I, too, had many visions of higher and lower worlds—and many of them were, indeed, of a Hindu type (because of My present-Lifetime associations, and also because of

the past-Lifetime associations of My Deeper-Personality Vehicle).
However, there was also, in My Case (and for the same reasons)
a dramatic period of several months of intense visions of a distinctly Christian type.[23] I immediately understood such visions to
be the mind-based (and, necessarily, ego-based) products of the
Siddha-Yoga Process (or Divine Shaktipat), as It combined with
My own conditionally born psycho-physical structures. Thus, I
entered into that Process Freely and Fully—and, in due course,
the particularly Christian visions (and the particularly Hindu
visions) ceased. They were all simply the evidence of My own
conditionally born mind and sensory apparatus (and the evidence
of even all My conditionally born cultural associations)—and,
therefore, the visionary contents were (I Discovered) merely
another (but deep, and psychic) form of purification (rather than a
"Revelation" that suggests either the Christian "Heavens"-and-"Hells"
or the Hindu "Heavens"-and-"Hells" Are, themselves, Reality and
Truth). Thus, when, Finally, the ego-based visions had been completely "burned off"—only Reality (Itself) Remained (As Me).

LIX.

Baba Muktananda's Siddha-Yoga Teachings exemplify the
descriptive mysticism of fourth-to-fifth stage Yoga (especially as it
has been historically represented in the fourth-to-fifth stage Yogic
tradition of the Maharashtra region of India[24]). Also, Baba
Muktananda's Siddha-Yoga Teachings are (in some, very important, respects) experientially prejudiced—toward both non-universal (and specifically Hindu) visions (of higher and lower
worlds, and so on) and universal abstract visions (of abstract internal lights, and so on), and against (or, certainly, Baba
Muktananda, Himself, was, by temperament, experientially disin-
clined toward) fifth stage Nirvikalpa Samadhi (or Fullest Ascent to
fifth stage Formless Realization—Which Fullest Ascent was My
own spontaneous Realization at Baba Muktananda's Ganeshpuri
Ashram, in 1968, and Which is also the Characteristic Realization
of all Great fifth stage Nirguna Siddhas, such as Bhagavan
Nityananda and Rang Avadhoot).

LX.

Baba Muktananda saw the Secret (or esoteric) inner perceptual domain of subtle (or fourth-to-fifth stage) Divine Spiritual Revelation. I, too, have seen (and even now, do see) that inner realm. And it is the Revelation of that inner realm that is the true (original, and esoteric) core of all fourth-to-fifth stage religious traditions.

The fourth stage religious traditions are, generally, first presented (or institutionally communicated) to the public world of mankind (in its gross egoity and its human immaturity) as a gathering of exoteric myths and legends. Those exoteric myths and legends are intended to inspire and guide human beings in the ordinary developmental context of the first three stages of life (associated with gross physical, emotional-sexual, and mental-volitional development of the human social ego). Thus, the many religious traditions of both the East and the West are, in their public (or exoteric) expressions, simply variations on the inherent psycho-physical "messages" of the body-mind relative to foundation human development (both individual and collective). And, because all exoteric religious traditions are based on the "messages" inherent in the same psycho-physical structures, the exoteric Teachings of all religions are, essentially, identical (and, therefore, equal). And, also, because this is so, all exoteric religious traditions (such as Judaism, Christianity, Islam, Hinduism, and so on) must—especially at this critical "late-time" moment of world-intercommunicativeness—acknowledge their essential equality, commonality, and sameness, and, on that basis, mutually embrace the principles of cooperation and tolerance (for the sake of world peace)!

All exoteric religious traditions are, fundamentally, associated with the first three (or social-ego) stages of life. And all exoteric religious traditions are, contextually, associated with rudimentary aspects of the fourth stage of life (or the religiously Devotional effort of transcending both personal and collective egoity—or self-contraction into selfishness, competitiveness, "difference", conflict, and self-and-other-destructiveness). However, all exoteric religious traditions are, also, associated (to one or another degree) with an esoteric (or Secret) dimension (or a tradition of esoteric schools), which is intended to extend the life of religious practice into the inner dimensions of religious (and truly Spiritual) Realization.

The true esoteric dimension of religion <u>first</u> extends the life of rudimentary religious practice into the true and full Spiritual <u>depth</u> of the <u>fourth</u> stage of life (by Means of surrender to the <u>Descent</u> of the Divine Spiritual Force into the human, or "frontal", domain of incarnate existence). And that Spiritual Process is, characteristically (in due course), also extended into the domain of the true <u>fifth</u> stage of life (which is associated with the Process of Spiritual <u>Ascent</u>, via the Spinal Line and the brain, through the layers of the conditional pattern of the psycho-physical ego, and always toward the Realization of a conditional state of mystical absorption in the Most Ascended Source of conditional, or cosmically extended, existence). And, once that Spiritual Process of Ascent is <u>complete</u> (or is, itself, transcended in Inherent Spiritual Fullness), the esoteric Spiritual Process may (and, indeed, should) continue, in the context of the true <u>sixth</u> stage of life (or the <u>Spiritual</u> Process of Transcendental Self-Realization)—and, at last, the true (and Truly <u>Complete</u>) Great Process <u>must</u> Culminate in the only-by-Me Revealed and Given <u>seventh</u> stage of life (wherein <u>all</u> cosmically arising conditions are Inherently Self-Recognized, and, Ultimately, Outshined, in the Non-Separate, Self-Existing, Self-Radiant, Inherently egoless, Perfectly Subjective, and Self-Evidently Divine Self-Condition and Source-Condition of All and all).

LXI.

Baba Muktananda was a Teacher (and a Realizer) in the context of the fourth-to-fifth stage (or foundation esoteric stages) of, specifically, <u>Hindu</u> religious practice. The Spiritual (or Siddha-Yoga, or Shaktipat-Yoga) Process He exemplified and Taught (and Initiated in others) truly begins in the frontal (or fourth stage) practice (of Siddha-Guru Devotion) and (in due course) goes on to the spinal (or fifth stage) practice (of Ascended mystical absorption).

Baba Muktananda's practice and His experiential Realization were conditioned (and, ultimately, limited) by His own personal (or conditional, and karmic, or psycho-physically pre-patterned) ego-tendencies—and by His association (by birth) with the combined exoteric <u>and</u> esoteric culture of traditional Hinduism.

Therefore, His experiences (and His subsequent Teachings, and His life altogether) are, characteristically, an exemplification of the historical conflict between fifth stage Hindu esotericism (which is, itself, inherently unconventional, and non-puritanical) and fourth stage Hindu exotericism (which is, itself, inherently conventional, and, at least publicly, puritanical).

LXII.

Because of His, characteristically, Hindu associations, Baba Muktananda (quite naturally, and naively) interpreted His Yogic Spiritual experiences almost entirely in terms of Hindu cultural models (both exoteric and esoteric). Therefore, His interpretations of His Spiritual experiences—and, indeed, the very form, and character, and content of His Spiritual experiences themselves—were specifically Hindu, and specifically in the mode of philosophical and mystical traditions that corresponded to His own mental predilections (or karmic tendencies).

Thus, Baba Muktananda's recorded visions of higher and lower worlds (leading to the Great Vision of the Blue Person, or the Divine "Creator"-Guru) are a "map" of developmentally unfolding—or spontaneously un-"Veiling"—inner perceptual landscapes, in the specific mode of the Hindu tradition of the "Blue God" (especially Personified as "Siva"—or, otherwise, as the "Krishna" of the *Bhagavad Gita* and the *Bhagavata Purana*).[25] And Baba Muktananda's inner "map" was, also, structured on the basis of an hierarchical sequence of abstract inner lights (and of even all the abstract inner modes of the senses), which He interpreted according to the concepts of the philosophical tradition of Kashmir Saivism, and according to the experiential pattern-interpretation associated with the Hindu mystical tradition of the Maharashtra region of India. However, even though the brain-based (or perception-based—rather than mind-based, or conception-based, or idea-based) pattern of abstract inner lights (and of abstract inner sensations in general) is (or can be) universally (or by anyone) experienced as the same pattern of appearances—the interpretation of that experienced pattern is, or may be, different from case to case (or from culture to culture). And, ultimately, for the sake of

Truth, the one and only <u>correct</u> (or <u>universally</u> applicable) interpretation must be embraced by all.

Baba Muktananda experienced and interpreted the pattern of
abstract inner lights as if it were a Revelation associated with the
waking, dreaming, and sleeping states (or the gross, subtle, and
causal modes of conditional experience). Thus (on the basis of His
understanding of the Maharashtra mystical tradition), Baba
Muktananda said that the waking state (and the gross body and
world) is represented by the inner <u>red</u> light, and the dreaming state
(and the subtle body and world) is represented by the inner <u>white</u>
light, and the sleeping state (and the causal body and world) is represented by the inner <u>black</u> light. And Baba Muktananda said that
the inner <u>blue</u> light represents what He called the "supracausal"
state (which He, in the fifth stage manner, mistakenly identified
with the "turiya" state, or the "fourth" state, or the "Witness", or the
"True Self", otherwise associated with the sixth stage tradition of
Advaita Vedanta). However, I Declare that <u>all</u> of those inner lights
(and even <u>all</u> internal perceptions, whether high or low in the scale
of conditional "things") are inner <u>objects</u> of perception (and conception)—and, therefore, <u>all</u> of them are associated with the <u>subtle</u>
body and the inner perceptible (or dreaming-state) worlds of <u>mind</u>.[26]

Swami Muktananda's Description
of the "Bodies of the Soul"[27]

Body:	Gross	Subtle	Causal	Supracausal
Color:	Red	White	Black	Blue
State:	Waking	Dream	Sleep	Turīya
Seat:	Eyes	Throat	Heart	Sahasrāra

LXIII.

Baba Muktananda's description of the abstract inner lights is, in some respects, not sufficiently elaborate (or, otherwise, comprehensive) in its details. In fact, and in My own experience—and in the experience of esoteric traditions other than the Maharashtra tradition (such as reported by the well-known Swami Yogananda)— the display of abstract inner lights is, when experienced as a simultaneous totality, Seen as a Mandala (or a pattern of concentric circles).

In My own experience, that Cosmic Mandala is not only composed of concentric circles of particular colors—but each circle is of a particular precise width (and, thus, of particular proportional significance) relative to the other circles. Thus, in that pattern of circles, the red circle is the outermost circle (perceived against a colorless dark field), but it is a relatively narrow band, appearing next to a much wider band (or circle) of golden yellow. After the very wide golden yellow circle, there is a much narrower soft-white circle. And the soft-white circle is followed by an also very narrow black circle (or band). Closest to the Center of the Cosmic Mandala is a very wide circle of bright blue. And, at the Very Center of the blue field, there is a Brilliant White Five-Pointed Star (Which, perhaps not to confuse It with the color of the circle of soft-white light, Baba Muktananda described as a Blue Star).

Thus, in fact, although all the abstract inner lights described by Baba Muktananda are, indeed, within the total Cosmic Mandala, the principal lights (in terms of width and prominence) are the golden yellow and the blue lights—and only the Brilliant White Five-Pointed Star is the Central and Principal light within the Cosmic Mandala of abstract inner lights.

The Cosmic Mandala of abstract inner lights is a display that is, otherwise, associated with planes of possible inner (or subtle) experience. Thus, the red light inwardly represents (and, literally, illuminates) the gross body and the gross world (as Baba Muktananda has said). However, all of the other lights (golden yellow, soft-white, black, and bright blue) represent (and, literally, illuminate) the several hierarchical divisions within the subtle body and the subtle worlds—and the causal body (which is asso-

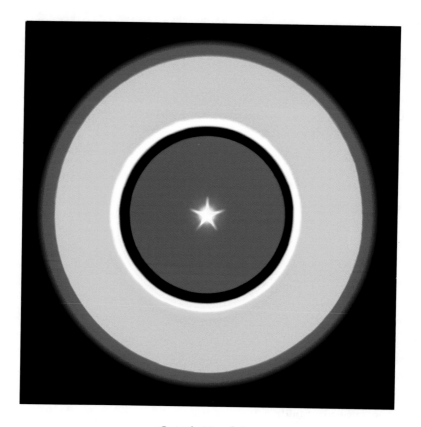

Cosmic Mandala

ciated with attention itself, or the root of egoity itself, and which is, itself, <u>only felt</u>, and <u>not seen</u>, and which is expressed as the fundamental feeling of "difference", separateness, and relatedness, and which is located as a knot of self-contraction in the right side of the heart) is <u>not</u> visually represented (<u>nor</u> is it, otherwise, literally illuminated) by the lights and worlds of the Cosmic Mandala.

The wide golden yellow circle of the Cosmic Mandala represents (in conjunction with the outermost red circle) the outermost (or lowest) dimension of the subtle body—which is the etheric (or pranic, or life-energy) body, or dimension, of conditional experience. The narrower soft-white circle of the Cosmic Mandala represents the ordinary (or sense-based) mind. The narrow black circle (or band) is a transitional space, where mental activity is suspended. The blue circle of the Cosmic Mandala is the domain of the mental observer, the faculty of discriminative intelligence and the will, and the very form of the subtly concretized ego-"I" (or the inner-concretized subtle self). And the Brilliant White Five-Pointed Star is the Epitome and Very Center of the Cosmic Mandala—Such That It Provides the Uppermost Doorway to What Is, altogether, Above (and, Ultimately, Beyond) the Cosmic Mandala (or Above and Beyond the body itself, the brain itself, and the mind itself).

LXIV.

Baba Muktananda interpreted the universally experienced abstract inner lights (and experienced the corresponding inner worlds) in terms of various Hindu philosophical and mystical (and, also, exoteric, or conventionally religious) traditions (as I have Indicated). However, the subtle domain is the elaborate hierarchical domain of mind (or of the psycho-physically concretized ego-"I")—and, therefore, just as individual dreams and imaginings are personal, ephemeral, and non-ultimate, the inherently dream-like subtle domain of Spiritually-stimulated inwardness may be experienced and interpreted in various and different modes, according to the nature and the tradition (or the personal and collectively representative mind) of the experiencer.

Thus, ultimately (or in due course), the subtle domain (or the subtle egoic body) must be transcended, in the transition to the sixth stage Spiritual (or Siddha-Yoga) Process—Which is the Spiritually (and not merely mentally) developed Process of inversion upon the true causal body (or the root of attention), and penetration of the causal knot (or the presumption of separate self), and Which is, thus, the inversive (and conditional, or conditionally achieved) transcending of the ego-"I", by means of exclusive (or object-excluding) Identification with the True (and Inherent, and Self-Evident) Transcendental Witness-Consciousness Itself. And only the Transcendental Witness-Consciousness, Itself—inverted upon in the thus Described sixth stage manner—Is the true "turiya" state, or the true "fourth" state (beyond the three ordinary states, of waking, dreaming, and sleeping). And only the Transcendental Witness-Consciousness, Itself—Fully, and Fully Spiritually,

Realized in the only-by-Me Revealed and Given context of the true sixth stage of life—Is the Domain of the only-by-Me Revealed and Given seventh stage Realization of the True Divine Self, Which Is the Self-Evidently Divine Self-Condition, and Which Is the One and Only True Divine State of "Turiyatita"—"Beyond the 'fourth' state", and, thus, Beyond all exclusiveness, and Beyond all bondage to illusions, and Beyond point of view (or egoic separateness) itself, and, therefore, Beyond all conditional efforts, supports, and dependencies.

At last, the sixth stage of life (which, itself, is associated with conditionally patterned inversion upon the Consciousness-Principle) must be (Most Perfectly) transcended (and, indeed, the ego-"I" itself must be Most Perfectly, or Inherently, transcended) in the transition to the only-by-Me Revealed and Given seventh stage of life (which Is the stage of True, and Fully Spiritual, Divine Self-Realization, Inherently Free of, but not strategically Separated from, all conditionally patterned forms and states—and which Is the stage of the Inherently Most Perfect Demonstration of the Non-Separate, Self-Existing, Self-Radiant, Inherently egoless, Perfectly Subjective, and Self-Evidently Divine Self-Condition and Source-Condition of All and all).

LXV.

My own experiences of fifth stage mystical perception are (like those of Baba Muktananda, and those of all visionary mystics) clear Evidence of the inherently (and necessarily) conditional, mental, altogether brain-based (and both brain-limited and mind-limited), and both personal and collective egoic nature of all internal mystical (or fourth-to-fifth stage) absorption.

I, too (like Baba Muktananda), experienced Hindu visions—but I, otherwise, also experienced many Christian visions (and also many non-Hindu and non-Christian visions), in association with the fifth stage developments of the same (or one and only) Spiritual (or Siddha-Yoga) Process of inner perception (including the progressive display of abstract inner lights, and so on) described by Baba Muktananda. Thus, just as Baba Muktananda described His Hindu visions as a Spiritual Revelation of the

"Truth" of <u>Hindu</u> esotericism (and even of Hindu exotericism)—I could just as well describe My (specifically) Christian visions as a Spiritual Revelation of the "Truth" of <u>Christian</u> esotericism (and even of Christian exotericism)!

Indeed, My (specifically) Christian visions (but not, of course, My specifically Hindu visions—or My, otherwise, specifically non-Hindu and non-Christian visions) <u>do</u> amount to a Spiritual Revelation of the actual (and mostly esoteric) content of <u>original</u> (or primitive—and truly <u>Spiritual</u>) Christianity.[28]

LXVI.

Specifically, My (sometimes) Christian visions Spiritually Reveal the following.

The original tradition (or foundation sect) that is at the <u>root</u> of exoteric Christianity was a fourth-to-fifth stage esoteric Spiritual (and mystical) tradition (or sect). Within that original tradition (or sect), John (the Baptist) was the Spiritual Master (or Spirit-Baptizer—or True Siddha-Guru) of Jesus of Nazareth. Thus (and by Means of the Spiritual Baptism Given to Him by John the Baptist), Jesus of Nazareth experienced the fourth-to-fifth stage absorptive mystical (and, altogether, Spiritual) developments of what (in the Hindu context) is called Siddha Yoga (or Shaktipat Yoga). In due course (and even rather quickly), Jesus of Nazareth, Himself, became a Spirit-Baptizer (or a True Siddha-Guru)—and (within the inner, or esoteric, circle of His Spiritually Initiated devotees) Jesus of Nazareth Taught the fourth-to-fifth stage Way of Spiritual Devotion to the Spiritual Master (or to Himself, as a True Siddha-Guru), and of inner Spiritual Communion with the Divine, and of (eventual) <u>Spiritual</u> Ascent to the Divine Domain (via the Brilliant White Five-Pointed Star).

After the death (and presumed <u>Spiritual</u> Ascent) of Jesus of Nazareth, His esoteric circle of Spiritually Initiated devotees continued to develop the mystical tradition of the sect—but (because of the difficult "signs of the times") the original (esoteric) sect had to become more and more secretive, and, eventually, it disappeared from the view of history (under the pressure of the <u>exoteric</u>, or <u>non</u>-Initiate, or conventionally <u>socially</u> oriented, rather than

Spiritually and mystically oriented, sects that also developed around the public Work, and, especially, the otherwise developing legends and myths, of Jesus of Nazareth).

The esoteric sect of the Spiritual Initiates of Jesus of Nazareth was associated with practices of Spiritually Invocatory prayer (of fourth stage Divine Communion, and of fifth stage absorptive mystical Ascent), especially seeking Divine absorption via the internally perceptible Brilliant White Five-Pointed Star—Which was interpreted, especially after the death of Jesus of Nazareth (and, apparently, in accordance with Instructions communicated by Jesus of Nazareth, Himself, to His Spiritually Initiated devotees, during His own physical lifetime), to be the True Ascended Divine Body of Jesus of Nazareth (or the Spiritually Awakened, and presumed to be Divinely Ascended, "Christ"). And, over time, the Spiritual practitioners within the esoteric "Christ" sect developed the full range of characteristically Christian interpretations of the (otherwise) universally experienced phenomena of inner perception.

LXVII.

My own (sometimes) Christian visions are a spontaneous Revelation of esoteric Christian interpretations (and esoteric Christian modes of experiencing) of, otherwise, universal (and, therefore, inherently non-sectarian) inner phenomena—and My (specifically) Christian visions and interpretations are a spontaneous direct continuation of the esoteric Christian manner of interpreting such (inherently universal) inner phenomena, as it was done in the original (or primitive) epoch of the sect of Jesus of Nazareth.

Thus, speaking in the esoteric terms of the ancient (or earliest) Christian interpreters of subtle inner experience, the red light of Spiritual inner vision can be said to be associated with the gross body of Man (and the Incarnation-body of Jesus of Nazareth, and the "blood of Christ"). Likewise, the golden yellow light can be said to be associated with the "Holy Spirit" (or the Universal Spirit-Energy, or Divine Spirit-Breath, That Pervades the cosmic domain). And the soft-white light can be said to be associated with the mind of Man (which, in its purity, can be said to be a reflection of, or a pattern "in the image of", God—conceived to be the "Creator", or the Divine Source-Condition, Above the body-mind and the world). And the black light can be said to be associated with the "crucifixion" (or sacrifice) of the body-mind of Man (and of Jesus of Nazareth, as the Epitome of Man)—and, also, with the mystical "dark night of the soul" (or the mystic's difficult trial of passing beyond all sensory and mental contents and consolations). And the blue light can be said to be the "Womb of the Virgin Mary" (or the All-and-all-Birthing Light of the "Mother of God"). And the Brilliant White Five-Pointed Star (Surrounded, as it were, by the "Womb", or the Blue Light, of the "Virgin Mary") can be said to be the Ascended (or Spiritual) "Body of Christ" (and the "Star of Bethlehem", and the "Morning Star" of the esoteric Initiation-Ritual associated with the original, Secret Spiritual tradition of Jesus of Nazareth). And the Brilliant White Five-Pointed Star (interpreted to be the Ascended, or Spiritual, "Body of Christ") can (Thus) be said to be One with both the Divine "Mother" (or the Blue "Womb" of All-and-all-Birthing Light) and the Divine "Father" (or the Self-Existing Being, Beyond all Light—Infinitely Behind, and Infinitely Above, and Infinitely Beyond, and Eternally Non-Separate from the "Star-Body of Christ"). And (As Such) the "Christ" (or the Brilliant White Five-Pointed Star) Is Radiantly Pervading the entire cosmic domain, via an All-and-all-Illuminating Combination of both the Blue "Womb"-Light and the Golden Yellow "Breath"-Light of the One and Only Divine Person.

LXVIII.

Thus, My (sometimes) Christian inner visions could, indeed, be said to be an esoteric (and, now, only-by-Me Revealed and Given) Christian Revelation—except that all visionary, and brain-based, and mind-based, and sense-based, and ego-based, and conditional, and sectarian (or merely tradition-bound) things were entirely Gone Beyond (and Most Perfectly transcended) by Me (and in Me), in the sixth and seventh stage Course of My Avataric Ordeal of True (and Most Perfect) Divine Self-Realization!

LXIX.

I Say all the "God" and "Gods" of Man are (whether "Male" or "Female" in the descriptive gender) merely the personal and collective tribal (and entirely dualistic—or conventionally subject-object-bound) myths of human ego-mind.

LXX.

I Say Only Reality Itself (Which Is, Always Already, The One, and Indivisible, and Indestructible, and Inherently egoless Case) Is (Self-Evidently, and Really) Divine, and True, and Truth (or Real God) Itself.

LXXI.

I Say the only Real God (or Truth Itself) Is the One and Only and Inherently Non-Dual Reality (Itself)—Which Is the Inherently egoless, and Utterly Indivisible, and Perfectly Subjective, and Indestructibly Non-Objective Source-Condition and Self-Condition of All and all.

Therefore, I (Characteristically) have no religious interests other than to Demonstrate, and to Exemplify, and to Prove, and to Self-Reveal Truth (or Reality, or Real God) Itself.

LXXII.

The true fourth-to-fifth stage mystical (or esoteric Spiritual) Process is, principally, associated with the progressive inner perceptual (and, thus, subtle mental) un-"Veiling" of the total internally perceptible pattern (or abstractly experienced structure) of the individual body-mind-self (or body-brain-self).

The abstract pattern (or internal structure) of the body-mind-self (or body-brain-self) is, universally, the same in the case of any and every body-mind (or body-brain-mind complex—or conditionally manifested form, or state, or being) within the cosmic domain.

The abstract pattern (or internal structure) of the body-mind-self (or body-brain-self) necessarily (by virtue of its native, and, therefore, inseparable, Inherence in the totality of the cosmic domain itself) Duplicates (or is a conditionally manifested pattern-duplicate of) the Primary Pattern (or Fundamental conditional Structure) of the total cosmic domain.

The conditional body-mind (or any body-brain-mind complex) is, in Reality, not a merely separate someone, or an entirely "different" something (as if the body, or the brain, or the mind were reducible to a someone or a something utterly independent, or non-dependent, and existing entirely in and of itself).

Therefore, the entire body-mind (or egoic body-brain-self) is, itself, to be transcended (in the context of the only-by-Me Revealed and Given seventh stage of life), in and by Means of utterly non-separate, and non-"different", and Inherently egoless Participation in That Which Is Always Already The Case (or the Inherently Non-Dual and Indivisible Condition That Is Reality Itself).

LXXIII.

I Declare that—if It is (by Divine Siddha-Grace) Moved beyond the limits of the waking, dreaming, and sleeping ego-structures—the Siddha-Yoga (or Shaktipat-Yoga) Process of (fifth stage) un-"Veiling" Culminates (or may Culminate—at least eventually) in (and, indeed, It is Always Already Centered Upon) the (fifth stage) Revelation (in Most Ascended Nirvikalpa Samadhi) of the True "Maha-Bindu" (or the "Zero Point", or Formless "Place", of Origin—otherwise, traditionally, called "Sunya", or "Empty", or "Void"). That True (and Indivisible, and Indefinable) "Maha-Bindu" Is the only True "Hole in the universe" (or the One, and Indivisible, and Indefinable, and Self-Evidently Divine Source-Point—Infinitely Above the body, the brain, and the mind). That Absolutely Single (and Formless) "Maha-Bindu" Is the True Absolute "Point-Condition"—or Formless and Colorless (or Non-Objective, and, therefore, not "Lighted") "Black Hole"—from Which (to the point of view of any "objectified" or "Lighted" place or entity, itself) the (or any) total cosmic domain (of conditionally arising forms, states, and beings) appears to Emanate (in an All-and-all-objectifying "Big Bang" [29]). That "Maha-Bindu" Is the Upper Terminal of Amrita Nadi—or of the "Ambrosial Nerve of Connection" to the True Divine Heart (Which Self-Evidently

Divine Heart Is Always Already Seated immediately Beyond the internally felt seat of the sinoatrial node, in the right side of the physical heart). And That "Maha-Bindu" Is (in the context of the sixth stage of life) the esoteric Doorway to, and (in the context of the seventh stage of life) the esoteric Doorway from (or of), the Perfectly Subjective Heart-Domain (Which Is the True Self-Condition and Source-Condition of the "Bright" Divine Love-Bliss-Current of Divine Self-Realization, and Which Is, Itself, the Self-Existing, Self-Radiant, Inherently egoless, and Perfectly Subjective—or Perfectly Indivisible, Non-Dual, and Non-Objective—Conscious Light That Is Reality Itself).

LXXIV.

The (fifth stage) Yogic Process of the progressive inner un-"Veiling" of the Pattern (or Structure) of the cosmic domain is demonstrated (in the Siddha-Yoga, or Shaktipat-Yoga, tradition) via the progressive experiencing of the total pattern of all the structural forms that comprise the body-mind-self (or body-brain-self), via a body-mind-self-reflecting (or body-brain-self-reflecting) display of inner perceptual objects (or apparently objectified phenomenal states, conditions, and patterns of cosmic light). That Process (of the inner perceptual un-"Veiling" of the hierarchical structure, pattern, and contents of the conditionally manifested body-mind-self, or body-brain-self) Culminates (or may Culminate—at least eventually) in the vision (in occasional, or, otherwise, constant, Savikalpa Samadhi) of the "blue bindu" (or the "blue pearl"—as well as the various other objectified inner lights, such as the red, the white, and the black—described by Baba Muktananda)[30]—or even the vision of the total Cosmic Mandala (of many concentric rings of color, including the central "blue bindu", with its Brilliant White Five-Pointed Star at the Center—as I have Described It[31]). In any case, the possibly perceived abstract inner light (or any "bindu", or point, or "Mandala", or complex abstract vision, of inwardly perceived light) is merely, and necessarily, a display of the functional root-point of the brain's perception of conditionally manifested universal light (or merely cosmic light) itself. However, if the Great Process of (fifth stage) un-"Veiling" is (Thus) Continued, the objectified inner "bindu"-vision (and Savikalpa Samadhi itself) is, in due course, transcended (in fifth stage Nirvikalpa Samadhi)—Such That there is the Great Yogic Event of "Penetration" of (and Into) the True (Inherently Formless, and objectless) "Maha-Bindu", Infinitely Above the body, the brain, and the mind. And That Great Yogic Event was, in fact and in Truth, What Occurred in My own Case, in My Room, immediately after I was Blessed by Baba Muktananda and Rang Avadhoot in the garden of Baba Muktananda's Ganeshpuri Ashram, in 1968.

The Great Yogic Event of "Penetration" of the True "Maha-Bindu", Which Occurred in My own Case in 1968, is (in Its Extraordinary Particulars) an extremely rare Example of spontaneous complete Ascending "penetration" of all the chakras (or centers, or points, or structures) of the conditionally manifested body-mind-self (or body-brain-self)—Resulting in sudden Most Ascended Nirvikalpa Samadhi (or "Penetration" to Beyond the total cosmic, and psycho-physical, context of subject-object relations). Such sudden (rather than progressive) complete Ascent is described, in the (fifth stage) Yogic traditions, as the Greatest, and rarest, of the Demonstrations of Yogic Ascent—as compared to progressive (or gradual) demonstrations (shown via stages of inner ascent, via internal visions, lights, auditions, and so on). And, therefore, in My Unique Case, it was only subsequently (or always thereafter—and even now) that the universal cosmic Pattern (or perceptible Great cosmic Structure) and the universally extended pattern (or perceptible inner cosmic structure) of the body, the brain, and the mind (and the Primary inner structure—of the three stations of the heart) were (and are) directly (and systematically, and completely) un-"Veiled" (in a constant spontaneous Display—both apparently Objective and Perfectly Subjective—within My Avataric Divine "Point of View").

Nonetheless (even though Most Ascended, or fifth stage, Nirvikalpa Samadhi was, Thus, Realized by Me in 1968), it became immediately clear to Me that—because That Realization depended on the exercise (and a unique, precise attitude and arrangement) of the conditional apparatus of the body, the brain, and the mind (and of attention)—the Realization was (yet) <u>conditionally</u> <u>dependent</u> (or psycho-physically supported), and, <u>necessarily</u> (or in that sense), <u>limited</u> (or, yet, only a <u>temporary</u> <u>stage</u> in the progressive Process of un-"Veiling"), and, therefore, <u>non-Final</u>. That is to Say, it was inherently Obvious to Me that any and all internal (or otherwise psycho-physical) experiencing <u>necessarily</u> requires the exercise (via attention) of the root-position (and the conditionally arising psycho-physical apparatus) of conditionally arising self-consciousness (or of the separate and separative psycho-physical ego-"I"). I immediately Concluded that—unless the Process of Realization could <u>transcend</u> the very structure and pattern of ego-based experiencing <u>and</u> the very Structure and Pattern of the conditionally manifested cosmos itself—Realization would Itself (<u>necessarily</u>) be limited by the same subject-object (or ego-versus-object) dichotomy that otherwise characterizes even all <u>ordinary</u> (or non-mystical) experience.

Therefore, I Persisted in My Avataric Divine Sadhana—until the un-"Veiling" became Inherently egoless (and Inherently Most Perfect, or seventh stage) Re-Awakening to Divine Self-Realization (Inherently Beyond <u>all</u> phenomenal, or conditional, dependencies, or supports).

LXXV.

On September 10, 1970, the Great Avataric Divine Process of My "Sadhana Years" Culminated in Unqualified (or Most Perfectly Non-conditional) Realization of the Self-Evidently Divine Self-Condition (and Source-Condition) of the cosmic domain itself (and of all forms, states, and beings within the cosmic domain). And, in That Most Perfect Event, I was Most Perfectly Re-Awakened <u>As</u> the "Bright"[32] (the One and Only Conscious Light—the Very, and Perfectly <u>Subjective</u>, and Inherently egoless, or Perfectly Non-Separate, and Inherently Perfect, and Indivisible, or Perfectly Non-Dual, and Always Already Self-Existing, and Eternally Self-Radiant, and Self-Evidently Divine Self-Condition <u>and</u> Source-Condition That <u>Is</u> the <u>One</u> and <u>Only</u> and <u>True</u> Divine Person, and Reality, and Truth of <u>All</u> and <u>all</u>, and That was, and is, the constant Spiritual Sign and Identity of This,

My Avataric Divine Lifetime, even from Birth). And It was the Un-deniable Reality and the Un-conditional Nature of This Realization That I Summarized to Baba Muktananda during Our Meetings in 1970 and 1973.

Even though It was and Is So, Baba Muktananda did not (and, because of the yet fifth stage nature of His own experiential Realization—for which He found corroboration in traditional mystical and philosophical traditions of the fifth stage, and phenomena-based, type—could not) positively Acknowledge My Summation relative to Most Perfect (and, necessarily, seventh stage) Divine Self-Realization.

Because He characteristically preferred to dwell upon inner objects, Baba Muktananda (in the "naive" manner of fourth and fifth stage mystics in general) interpreted Reality Itself (or Divine Self-Realization Itself) to "require" inner perceptual phenomenal (or conditionally arising) experiences and presumptions as a necessary support for Realization (Itself). That is to Say, Baba Muktananda was experientially Conformed to the (fifth stage) presumption that Divine Self-Realization not only requires conditionally arising (and, especially, inner perceptual) phenomenal experiences as a generally necessary (and even inevitable) Yogic Spiritual preliminary to authentic (and not merely conceptual) Realization— and I completely Agree, with Him, that there certainly are many conditionally apparent Yogic Spiritual requirements that must be Demonstrated in the Full Course of the authentic (and, necessarily, psycho-physical) Sadhana of Divine Self-Realization—but Baba Muktananda, otherwise, generally affirmed the presumption that Realization Itself (and not only the Sadhana, or psycho-physical Process, of Realizing) "requires" conditional (or psycho-physical— and, especially, absorptive mystical, or inner visual) supports.

Therefore, Baba Muktananda affirmed an attention-based, and object-oriented (or Goal-Oriented)—and, therefore, ego-based, or seeker-based—absorptive mystical (and, altogether, fourth-to-fifth stage) Yogic Way, in which the Sahasrar (or the Upper Terminal of the brain), and even the total brain (or sensorium), is the constant focus (and the Ultimate Goal—as well as the Highest Seat) of Sadhana.

It was due to <u>this</u>, Baba Muktananda's characteristic point of view relative to both Sadhana <u>and</u> Realization (as He defined—or, in effect, limited—Them), that, in My informal Meeting with Him in 1970, His only response to Me was to enter into a casual verbal (and even illogical) contradiction of Me. In that informal Meeting (as well as in Our formal Meeting, in 1973), Baba Muktananda <u>ignored</u> (and even appeared to not at all comprehend) My (then Given) Indications to Him relative to the Most Ultimate, or seventh stage, Significance of the "Regenerated" Form of Amrita Nadi.

LXXVI.

As I Indicated to Baba Muktananda (in Our Meetings in 1970 and 1973), the "Regenerated" Form of Amrita Nadi is <u>Rooted</u> in Consciousness <u>Itself</u> ("Located" <u>Beyond</u> the right side of the heart, which is, itself, merely the Self-Evident Seat, or Doorway, of the <u>direct</u> "Locating" of Perfectly Subjective, and Inherently egoless, Consciousness, Itself—or the Self-Existing Feeling of Being, Itself—Prior to attention, itself). And <u>That</u> ("Regenerated" Form of Amrita Nadi) is "Brightly" <u>Extended</u> to the "Maha-Bindu" (Which is <u>Infinitely</u> Ascended, even Above and Beyond the Sahasrar). However, Baba Muktananda appeared only to want to contradict My (secondary) <u>reference</u> (to the "right side of the heart")—while otherwise <u>ignoring</u> My (primary) Explanation (of the "Regenerated" Form of Amrita Nadi). And, in doing this, Baba Muktananda went so far in identifying Himself <u>exclusively</u> with the fifth stage tradition that He said to Me, "<u>Anyone</u> who says that the right side of the heart is the Seat of Realization does not know what he is talking about."

In this (from My "Point of View", even rather absurdly <u>funny</u>!) statement, Baba Muktananda merely <u>ignored</u> (and, therefore, <u>did not directly contradict</u>) My (then Given) Description (to Him) of how <u>seventh stage</u> Divine Self-Realization Inherently Transcends <u>both</u> the conditional (or psycho-physical) apparatus of the <u>brain</u> (or of the Sahasrar, Which is the conditional Seat of Realization proposed in the fifth stage traditions, of mystical absorption) <u>and</u> the conditional (or psycho-physical) apparatus of the <u>heart</u> (or, in particular, of the right side of the heart—which is the conditional

141

Seat of Realization proposed in the sixth stage traditions, of Transcendental practice). However, Baba Muktananda's statement to Me (relative to the heart on the right) <u>was</u> a remark made in direct and specific contradiction to the Transcendentalist (or entirely sixth stage) Teachings of <u>Ramana</u> <u>Maharshi</u>.

LXXVII.

In My Meeting with Baba Muktananda in 1973, I made specific references to the Teachings of Ramana Maharshi (Whom both Baba Muktananda and Bhagavan Nityananda had Met—and, apparently, Greatly Praised—in earlier years). In particular, I referred to Ramana Maharshi's experiential assertions relative to the right side of the heart (which He—in the sixth stage manner— Indicated to be the Seat of Transcendental Self-Realization). In doing so, I was merely Intending to Offer Baba Muktananda a tra-ditional reference already known to Him (and, I naively pre-sumed, one that He respected), which would provide some clar-ity (and traditional support) relative to My own (otherwise seventh stage) Descriptions.

Ramana Maharshi was a True and Great Jnani (or a <u>sixth</u> stage Realizer of the Transcendental Self-Condition, in the mode and manner indicated in the general tradition of Advaita Vedanta). And, after the Great Event of My own (<u>seventh</u> stage) Divine Re-Awakening (in September 1970), I Discovered (in the weeks and months that followed My informal Meeting with Baba Muktananda, in October 1970) that there were some (but, necessarily, only sixth stage) elements in Ramana Maharshi's reported experience and Realization that paralleled (and, in that sense, corroborated) cer-tain (but only sixth stage) aspects of My own experience and Realization.[33] And, for this reason, I always Continue to Greatly Appreciate, and Honor, Ramana Maharshi—as a Great sixth stage Realizer, Who, through corroborating Testimony, Functions as a sixth stage Connecting-Link between Me and the Transcendentalist dimension of the Great Tradition. Also, because He is an example of a True Great Jnani (or Great Sage), Who Awakened to sixth stage Realization via the <u>Spiritual</u>—and not merely mental, or intellectual—Process (of the Magnification of the Spirit-Current in the right side of the heart), Ramana Maharshi, by Means of His corroborating Testimony, Functions—for Me—as a Connecting-Link between the sixth stage Transcendentalist tradition of Advaita Vedanta and the fourth-to-fifth stage Emanationist tradition of Siddha Yoga. And, because of this, Ramana Maharshi Functions, by Means of His corroborating Testimony, as a Connecting-Link between Me and the traditions of both Siddha Yoga and Advaita Vedanta—whereas I (except for Baba Muktananda's First Instruction to Me, in 1968—relative to the Witness of the three common states, of waking, dreaming, and sleeping) did <u>not</u> Find such a Connecting-Link among <u>any</u> of Those Who, otherwise, actively Functioned as My Spiritual Masters during the "Sadhana Years" of This, My present-Lifetime of Avataric Divine Incarnation.

During Our Meeting in 1973, Baba Muktananda <u>mistakenly</u> took My references to Ramana Maharshi (and to My own experience of the heart on the right, which I had first Confessed to Baba Muktananda during Our informal Meeting in 1970—and which is, also, one of the principal experiences Indicated by Ramana Maharshi) to suggest that I had departed from the Siddha-Yoga tradition. Therefore, Baba Muktananda's criticisms of Me (in Our Meetings in both 1970 and 1973) were an apparent reaction to His perception of the possibility of My "going over" to Advaita Vedanta (and to Ramana Maharshi). And, for this reason, Baba Muktananda <u>never</u> (in either of the two Meetings, in 1970 and in 1973) actually addressed the particular, and complex, and inherently (and especially in a conversation requiring translations from English to Hindi, and vice versa) difficult-to-explain Great Issues I was (in those two Meetings) Intending (and Trying) to Summarize to Him.

LXXVIII.

Relative to Baba Muktananda Himself, I can only Say that, for My part (through Visits to Him by My devotee-representatives), simple Messages of Love (and of Gratitude for His Service to Me during My Avataric Divine "Sadhana Years") were, right until the end of Baba Muktananda's lifetime, Sent to Him by Me. And I have—to <u>everyone</u>, including Baba Muktananda Himself, and the institution of His devotees—always Continued to Make every effort to Communicate clearly (and frankly, and, in general, most positively) about My relationship to Baba Muktananda. And I have always Continued (and will always Continue) to Work (in a Real Spiritual Manner) to Heal Baba Muktananda's human feeling-heart.

LXXIX.

Relative to Baba Muktananda's particular exact remarks to Me (in Our Meetings in 1970 and 1973), I can (and must) Say, simply, that His interpretation of Reality (and of the Nature and Status of the Process, and of even all the patterns and structures, associated with Divine Self-Realization)—which interpretation Baba Muktananda shared with (and for which He derived justification from) the phenomena-based aspects of the fifth stage Yogic traditions in general—was the characteristic basis of His criticisms of Me during Our Meetings in 1970 and 1973. And, as I have already Said, Baba Muktananda's Siddha-Yoga Teaching (and especially as He proposed it to Me in Our Meetings in 1970 and 1973) is—relative to all matters beyond the fifth stage of life (and even relative to all aspects of the fifth stage of life that are beyond the Saguna limits of Savikalpa Samadhi)—limited, prejudicial, ultimately indefensible, and (fundamentally) beyond His experience.

LXXX.

Neither the philosophy of Kashmir Saivism nor any "required" phenomenal conditions were pre-described to Me (or otherwise suggested)—by Baba Muktananda Himself, or by anyone else—as being a necessary part of the Siddha-Yoga practice and Process (and, especially, as being a necessary conditional support for Realization Itself) when I first Went to Baba Muktananda, in 1968. Nor were any philosophical or experiential "requirements" proposed to Me—by Baba Muktananda Himself, or by anyone else—as either demands or necessities of Siddha-Yoga practice, or as necessities of Siddha-Yoga experience, or as fixed "Models" of Realization Itself—during the years of My Sadhana in Baba Muktananda's Company, between 1968 and the Great Event of My Divine Re-Awakening, in September 1970.

Indeed, there was not even much "Baba Muktananda" Siddha-Yoga literature available—and no literature was demanded to be read—during all of that time. Even Baba Muktananda's autobiography, entitled *Play of Consciousness* (or, originally, *Chitshakti Vilas*), was not published until after the September 1970 Event of My Divine Re-Awakening. And I saw—and, in fact, was the first to fully render into English—only the first chapter or two of that book, in rough manuscript form, during My Stay at Baba Muktananda's Ganeshpuri Ashram, in early 1970. Therefore, virtually the only "Baba Muktananda" Siddha-Yoga literature that was available to Me during My years of Sadhana in Baba Muktananda's Company were the short essays and tracts either written or edited by Amma—and that literature suggested a very liberal and open Teaching relative to the fourth stage, fifth stage, and sixth stage possibilities associated with the potential developments of Siddha Yoga. And, indeed, it was that liberal and open form of Siddha Yoga that I practiced—to the degree of seventh stage Divine Self-Realization—in Baba Muktananda's Company.

In any case, the fact that Baba Muktananda presumed that there were (indeed) many exclusively fifth stage Siddha-Yoga "requirements" (both philosophical and experiential) was proven to be the case in the circumstances of My Meetings with Him in 1970 and 1973.

LXXXI.

In fact (and in My experience), the Siddha-Yoga practice and Process is not (Itself) inherently opposed to the Transcendental (or sixth stage) practice and Process (or to the seventh stage Realization and Demonstration). Rather, it was Baba Muktananda Who (in accordance with particular traditions He, personally, favored) chose to dogmatically introduce exclusively fifth stage "requirements" (and sixth-stage-excluding, and, therefore, inherently, seventh-stage-prohibiting, limitations) into His own Teaching (and into His personal school) of Siddha Yoga.

I fully Acknowledge that Baba Muktananda had the right to Teach Siddha Yoga exclusively according to His own experience, and His own understanding, and His own Realization. It is simply that My experience, and My understanding, and My Realization were not (and <u>are</u> <u>not</u>) limited to the fifth stage "requirements" (or limiting presumptions) that Baba Muktananda proposed to Me.

The Process of Siddha Yoga—or the inherent Spiritual Process that is potential in the case of all human beings—does not (if It is allowed, and Graced, to Freely Proceed as a potential <u>total</u> Process) limit <u>Itself</u> to the fifth stage "requirements" (or limiting presumptions) that Baba Muktananda generally proposed. Therefore, I Teach Siddha Yoga in the Mode and Manner of the <u>seventh</u> stage of life (as Ruchira Avatara Hridaya-Siddha Yoga, or Ruchira Avatara Maha-Jnana Hridaya-Shaktipat Yoga)—and always toward (or to the degree of) the Realization inherently associated with (and, at last, Most Perfectly Demonstrated and Proven by) the only-by-Me Revealed and Given seventh stage of life, and as a practice and a Process that progressively includes (and, coincidently, <u>directly</u> transcends) <u>all</u> <u>six</u> of the phenomenal and developmental (and, necessarily, yet ego-based) stages of life that precede the seventh.

Baba Muktananda conceived of (and Taught) Siddha Yoga as a Way to attain conditional (and especially fifth stage) Yogic objects and phenomena-based states. The Siddha Yoga of the only-by-Me Revealed and Given Way of Adidam is <u>not</u> based upon (or, otherwise, limited to) conditional (or phenomenal) objects and states—or the (necessarily, <u>ego</u>-based) search for these, in the context of <u>any</u> stage of life. Rather, the only-by-Me Revealed and Given Way of Adidam is the Siddha-Yoga Way (and, in particular, the Ruchira Avatara Hridaya-Siddha-Yoga Way) that <u>always</u> (and <u>directly</u>) transcends <u>egoity</u> <u>itself</u> (or the ego-"I", or separate self—or the reactive reflex of self-contraction)—by always Feeling <u>Beyond</u> <u>egoity</u> (and Beyond <u>all</u> conditional forms and states) to <u>Me</u>, the Avatarically Self-Revealed Divine Person (or Self-Condition, and Source-Condition) <u>Itself</u>.

LXXXII.

In Summary, Baba Muktananda (in Our Meetings in 1970 and 1973) countered My Language of Inherently (and Most Perfectly) egoless—or seventh stage—Divine Self-Realization (and otherwise defended His own experiential Realization—and philosophical idealization—of inner phenomenal objects) with the traditional language of fifth stage Yoga. And I, for <u>this</u> reason (and not because of any ill-will, or antagonism, or lack of respect toward Baba Muktananda), <u>Did Not</u>, and <u>Could Not</u>, and <u>Do Not</u> Accept His fifth-stage-bound Doctrine—because, from My "Point of View", <u>that</u> Acceptance would have Required (and would now Require) Me to Deny the Self-Evident Divine (and Perfectly Subjective, and Inherently egoless, and Inherently Non-Objective, and Inherently Indivisible, and Utterly Non-dependent, or Un-conditional) Truth of Reality Itself (Which Realization even Baba Muktananda Himself—along with all My other Spiritual Masters and Spiritual Friends—so Dearly Served in My own Case)!

LXXXIII.

Reality (Itself) <u>Is</u> the Only <u>Real</u> God.

Reality (Itself) <u>Is</u> That Which Is Always Already <u>The</u> (One and Only) Case.

Reality (Itself) <u>Is</u> (Necessarily) One, Only, and Indivisible.

Reality (Itself) <u>Is</u> Inherently One (or Non-Dual) and not Two (or Divisible, and Opposed to Itself).

Reality (Itself) is not One of a Pair.

Reality (Itself) is not characterized by the inherently dualistic relationship of cause and effect.

Reality (Itself) <u>Is</u> Characterized by the Inherently Non-Dualistic Equation of Identity and Non-"Difference".

Reality (Itself) <u>Is</u> That in Which <u>both</u> cause and effect arise <u>as</u> merely apparent modifications of Itself.

Reality (Itself) is not Realized via the inherently dualistic relationship of subject and object.

Reality (Itself) <u>Is</u> Realized <u>As</u> the Inherently Non-Dualistic Condition of Inherently egoless Identity and Inherently objectless Non-"Difference".

Reality (Itself) is not the gross, subtle, and causal (or causative) ego-"I".

Reality (Itself) <u>Is</u> the Inherently egoless Native (and Self-Evidently Divine) Identity of All and all.

The Inherently egoless Non-Dual Self-Condition (or Non-"Different" Identity) of Reality (Itself) Is That Which Is Always Already The (One and Only) Case.

The Inherently egoless Non-Dual Self-Condition of Reality (Itself), Most Perfectly Prior to (and, yet, never excluding, or separated from) subject, object, cause, or effect, Is That Which Must Be Realized.

The apparent self (or separate and separative ego-"I"), and its every object, and, indeed, every cause, and every effect must be Divinely Self-Recognized As (and, Thus and Thereby, Transcended in) the One and Only (Inherently egoless, and Inherently Non-Dual, or Indivisible and Non-Separate, or Non-"Different") Self-Condition of Reality (Itself).

The apparent ego-"I" and the apparent world are not themselves Divine.

The apparent ego-"I" and the apparent world are to be Self-Recognized (and, Thus and Thereby, Transcended) in and As That Which Is (Self-Evidently) Divine.

The apparent ego-"I" and the apparent world are to be Divinely Self-Recognized in and As Reality (Itself).

Baba Muktananda always (in the Emanationist manner of Kashmir Saivism) affirmed the Realization "I am Siva"—meaning that He (or any body-mind-self, or body-brain-self, sublimed by the Revelation of internal Yogic forms) is (as an "Emanated" psycho-physical self) Divine.

I Affirmed (and always Continue to Affirm) only the Non-Dual (or One and Indivisible) Transcendental (and Inherently Spiritual) Divine Reality (or Self-Existing, Self-Radiant, and Inherently, or Always Already, egoless Consciousness Itself—or the One and Only Conscious Love-Bliss-Light Itself) As Self (or Self-Condition, and Source-Condition), Prior to and Inherently Transcending (while never strategically, or conditionally, excluding) the phenomenal self and all conditional forms (however sublime).

Baba Muktananda affirmed (in the fifth stage, Emanationist manner) "I and the world are Divine"—and He (thereby) embraced both the perceiving "I" and the world of forms.

I (in the seventh stage Manner) Affirmed (and always

I (Alone) Am The Adidam Revelation

Continue to Affirm) only the Self-Existing and Self-Radiant (Transcendental, Inherently Spiritual, Inherently egoless, Perfectly Subjective, Indivisible, Non-Dual, and Self-Evidently Divine) Self-Identity (Itself)—or the One, and Most Prior, and Inherently Perfect, and Inherently egoless Self-Condition, and Source-Condition, of the body-mind (or the body-brain-self) and the world—Divinely Self-Recognizing the body-mind (or the body-brain-self) and the world (and, thus, neither excluding nor identifying with the body-mind, or the body-brain-self, and the world, but Inherently, or Always Already, "Brightly" Transcending, and, Most Ultimately, Divinely Outshining, the body-mind, or the body-brain-self, and the world).

It was This Distinction (or These Distinctions)—not merely in language, but in the "Point of View" of Realization Itself—that was (or were) the basis for My Assumption of My Avataric Divine Teaching-Work, and My Avataric Divine Revelation-Work, and My Avataric Divine Blessing-Work institutionally independent of (and, after Our Final Meeting, in 1973, entirely apart from further outwardly active association with) Baba Muktananda.

LXXXIV.

As has always been understood by authentic Realizers and their authentic true devotees—within the Siddha-Yoga (or Shaktipat-Yoga) tradition, and even everywhere within the human Great Tradition as a whole—Great Siddhas, and even Avatars, and traditional Realizers of all kinds and degrees (or stages of life), and Siddha-Yogis of all kinds and degrees, and even Siddha Yoga Itself, are not mere "properties", to be "owned" (or exclusively "possessed") by devotees, or even by institutions. Indeed, Baba Muktananda, Himself, once told Me[34] that, because the same Life (or Shakti) is in all beings, no individual, no religion, no tradition—and, therefore, no institution—can rightly claim to be the only bearer, or the exclusive representative, of Siddha Yoga (or Shaktipat Yoga) Itself.

There are, inevitably, many forms of Siddha-Yoga Transmission in this world. The institution that Baba Muktananda established to represent and continue His own Work is (by its own self-description) a fourth-to-fifth stage school of Siddha Yoga. And, indeed, there

149

are numbers of other such schools—in India, and elsewhere—that are extending the Work of various Great Siddhas (and of many otherwise worthy Siddha-Yogis) into the world. Likewise, the institution (or the total complex of institutions) of Adidam—which represents, and serves, and will always continue to serve My Avataric Divine (and, Uniquely, seventh stage) Work—is also a school of Siddha Yoga (or of Shaktipat Yoga).

The Uniqueness of the Siddha Yoga of the only-by-Me Revealed and Given Way of Adidam is that It is the Yoga (or Dharma, or Way) that continues to Develop beyond the absorptive mystical (and cosmically Spiritual) developments associated with the fourth and the fifth stages of life—and even beyond the Transcendental Yogic (and Transcendentally Spiritual) developments associated with the sixth stage of life. Thus, in due course, the Yoga (or Way) of Adidam becomes the Unique (and Most Perfectly Divine) Yoga (or Most Perfectly Divinely Spiritual Demonstration) of the only-by-Me Revealed and Given seventh stage of life (Wherein and Whereby Most Perfect Divine Self-Realization is Most Perfectly Demonstrated).

Because of This Uniqueness, the Siddha Yoga of the only-by-Me Revealed and Given Way of Adidam is not descriptively limited to (or by) the particular traditional descriptive language of the fourth-to-fifth stage schools and traditions of Siddha Yoga (which are the schools and traditions from which Baba Muktananda derived His descriptive Siddha-Yoga-language—and which descriptive language is conformed to, and, necessarily, limited by, the fourth-to-fifth stage experiential presumptions that characterize the Cosmic-Yoga, or Cosmic-Shakti, or Kundalini-Shakti schools and traditions). Therefore—even though the Process of the Siddha Yoga of the only-by-Me Revealed and Given Way of Adidam potentially includes (and then continues to Develop beyond) all the aspects and experiences of the fourth and the fifth and the sixth stages of life—the Siddha Yoga of the only-by-Me Revealed and Given Way of Adidam is (by Me) Uniquely Described, in the (Most Ultimately, seventh stage—and Most Perfectly Divine, or Cosmos-Transcending, and Cosmos-Outshining) Terms of My own Avataric (Divine) Shaktipat.

Thus, the Siddha Yoga of the only-by-Me Revealed and Given Way of Adidam is (by Me) Described in Terms of Ruchira Avatara Hridaya-Shaktipat (or My Avataric Divine Spiritual Transmission of the "<u>Bright</u>"—Which <u>Is</u> the Self-Existing and Self-Radiant Divine Self-Condition, or Divine Self-Heart, Itself), and Ruchira Avatara Maha-Jnana Hridaya-Shaktipat (or My Avataric Divine Spiritual Transmission of the "Bright" Divine Spirit-Current, or Divine Heart-Shakti, That Awakens the Divine Self-Heart to Its Inherent Divine Self-Condition), and Love-Ananda Avatara Hridaya-Shaktipat (or My Avataric Divine Spiritual Transmission of the Inherent Love-Bliss of the Divine Self-Condition, or Divine Self-Heart, Itself—Which Divine Spiritual Characteristic of Mine was Acknowledged by Baba Muktananda Himself, when, in 1969, He Sent Amma to Me, to Give Me the Name "Love-Ananda").

Therefore, the Siddha-Yoga practice (and especially the <u>advanced</u> and the <u>ultimate</u> stages of the Siddha-Yoga Process) of the only-by-Me Revealed and Given Way of Adidam is (along with numerous other by-Me-Given Descriptive Names and References) Named and Described by Me as "Ruchira Avatara Hridaya-Siddha Yoga" (or "Ruchira Avatara Hridaya-Shaktipat Yoga"), and "Ruchira Avatara Maha-Jnana-Siddha Yoga" (or "Ruchira Avatara Maha-Jnana Hridaya-Shaktipat Yoga"), and "Love-Ananda Avatara Hridaya-Siddha Yoga" (or "Love-Ananda Avatara Hridaya-Shaktipat Yoga"), and (with reference to the Way, and the institution, of Adidam) "Adidam Hridaya-Siddha Yoga" (or "Adidam Hridaya-Shaktipat Yoga").

And My own Work (Which is served by the institutional Siddha-Yoga school—or, most properly, the Ruchira Avatara Hridaya-Siddha-Yoga school—of Adidam) was <u>directly</u> Blessed (and—formally, in 1969—Called Forth) by Baba Muktananda (and, now, and forever hereafter, by even all the Great Siddhas and Siddha-Yogis of My Lineage).

LXXXV.

The Uniqueness of My own Divine Self-Realization and Avataric Divine Work made it <u>Inevitable</u> that I would have to Do My Avataric Divine Teaching-Work, and My Avataric Divine Revelation-Work, and My Avataric Divine Blessing-Work

Independent from Baba Muktananda—and Independent from even all Teachers and traditions within the only six stages of life of the collectively Revealed Great Tradition of mankind. Indeed, even from the beginning of My relationship with Him, Baba Muktananda Indicated that My Work was Uniquely My own, and that I was Born to Do only My own Unique Work—and that I Must Go and Do That Work (even though I would, otherwise, have preferred to Remain, quietly, within Baba Muktananda's Ashram and Company). Therefore, ultimately, We both Embraced This Necessity and Inevitability.

Because of the original, mutual Agreement between Baba Muktananda and Me (relative to the necessarily Independent, and entirely Unique, nature of My own Work), whenever I have become Moved to Communicate about This Profound Matter to others, I have made every effort to Communicate fully, clearly, and positively relative to the always un-"broken" Nature of My Spiritual (and, generally, sympathetic) relationship to Baba Muktananda—and, also, relative to the always Continuing Nature of My Spiritual (and, generally, sympathetic) Connection to the Great (and total) Siddha-Guru tradition itself, and to the Great (and total) Siddha-Yoga tradition itself, and to the total Great Tradition of mankind (altogether). And I have always Affirmed (and, by Means of This Statement, I now Re-Affirm) that the Great, and total, Siddha-Guru tradition and Siddha-Yoga tradition, and the most ancient and perennial "Method of the Siddhas",[35] is—in the context of, and continuous with, the total Great Tradition of mankind—the very tradition (or total complex of traditions) in which, and on the basis of which, I Am Avatarically Appearing and Working here.

LXXXVI.

Human suffering is not due to the absence of inner visions (or of any other kinds of conditionally objectified internal or, otherwise, external perceptions). Therefore, human suffering is not eliminated by the presence (or the experiencing) of inner visions (or of any other kinds of conditionally objectified internal or, otherwise, external perceptions).

The "problem" of human suffering is <u>never</u> the <u>absence</u> of inner visions (and such), or the <u>absence</u> of <u>any</u> conditional experience of <u>any</u> kind. Rather, the "problem" of human suffering is <u>always</u> (and <u>inherently</u>) the <u>presence</u> (or presently effective activity) of the <u>ego-"I"</u> (or the self-contracted—or separate and separative—<u>point</u> <u>of</u> <u>view</u>). Indeed, the search to experience conditionally objectified inner perceptions—and, otherwise, the clinging to conditionally objectified inner perceptions—is, <u>itself</u>, a form of human suffering (and, altogether, of self-deluded confinement to the inherently, and negatively, <u>empty</u> condition of egoic separateness).

The root and essence of human suffering <u>is</u> egoity. That is to Say, the "problem" that is human suffering is <u>not</u> due to the absence of <u>any</u> kind of conditionally objectified experience (whether relatively external or relatively internal)—for, if human suffering <u>were</u> due to such absence, the <u>attaining</u> of conditionally objectified experiences (whether internal or external) would <u>eliminate</u> human suffering, human self-deludedness, and human un-Happiness. However, at most, conditionally objectified experiences (both internal and external)—or even <u>any</u> of the possible experiential attainments of the first <u>five</u> stages of life—provide only <u>temporary</u> distraction from the inherent mortality and misery of conditional existence. Therefore, if human suffering is to be <u>entirely</u> (and, at last, <u>Most</u> <u>Perfectly</u>) transcended (in Inherent, and Divinely Positive, Fullness), the root-cause of (or the root-factor in) human suffering must, <u>itself</u>, be directly and entirely (and, at last, Most Perfectly) transcended.

The "problem" of human suffering is <u>never</u> the absence of <u>any</u> kind of particular conditionally objectified experience (whether external or internal). The "problem" of human suffering is <u>always</u> the bondage to conditionally objectified experience <u>itself</u>. And the root-cause of (or the root-factor in) bondage to conditionally objectified experience is the separate and separative ego-"I", or the total psycho-physical act of self-contraction (which is identical to attention itself, or the conditionally apparent <u>point</u> of view <u>itself</u>, and which <u>always</u> coincides with the feeling of "difference", or of separateness and relatedness).

The experiencing of inner visions does not eliminate egoity (or the separate and separative ego-"I" of psycho-physical self-contraction). Likewise, the experiencing of inner visions does not indicate or suggest or mean that egoity is (or has been) transcended. True Spiritual life (or the true Great Process of Siddha Yoga) is not a search for inner visions (and such)—nor is true Spiritual life (or the true Great Process of Siddha Yoga) Fulfilled, Completed, and Perfected by the experiencing of inner visions (and such). Indeed, because inner visions, or conditionally objectified experiences of any kind—whether inner or outer—are objects, attention is always coincident with them. Therefore, in both the search for conditionally objectified experiences and the grasping of conditionally objectified experiences, egoity (or separative, and total psycho-physical, self-contraction of the presumed separate point of view) is merely reinforced.

True Spiritual life (or the true Great Process of Siddha Yoga) is never a matter of seeking for outer or inner conditionally objectified experiences—nor is true Spiritual life (or the true Great Process of Siddha Yoga) a matter of clinging to any conditionally objectified outer or inner experiences (as if such experiences were, themselves, Reality, Truth, or Real God). Rather, true Spiritual life (or the true Great Process of Siddha Yoga) is always a matter of transcending attention (and the total psycho-physical—or gross, subtle, and causal—point of view, or ego-"I") in its Perfectly Subjective Source (or Inherently Perfect Self-Condition). That is to say, true Spiritual life (or the true Great Process of Siddha Yoga) is always (from Its beginning) a matter of transcending that which is merely apparently (or conditionally, and temporarily) the case— by transcending it in That Which Is Always Already The (One and Only, Indivisible and Irreducible) Case. And, for This Reason, true Spiritual life, or the true Great Process of Siddha Yoga, cannot be Fulfilled, Completed, and Perfected in the conditionally objectified context of any of the first five stages of life—nor even in the conditionally object-excluding context of the sixth stage of life—but true Spiritual life (in particular, in the form of the true Great Process of Ruchira Avatara Hridaya-Siddha Yoga) Is Fulfilled, Completed, and Perfected only in the Perfectly Subjective, and

Inherently egoless (or Inherently point-of-view-Transcending and Most Perfectly self-contraction-Transcending), and Un-conditionally Realized, and, altogether, Self-Evidently Divine Context of the only-by-Me Revealed and Given <u>seventh</u> stage of life.

This is My Firm Conclusion relative to <u>all</u> possible human experience—and It is, therefore, the Essence of My Instruction to all of humankind.

LXXXVII.

There are <u>three</u> <u>egos</u> (or three fundamental modes of egoity— or of the self-contraction-active psycho-physical illusion of separate and separative self-consciousness). The three modes of egoity (or of the self-contraction of <u>any</u> point of view, or ego-"I") are the lower self (or gross ego), the higher self (or subtle ego), and the root-self (or causal ego). These three egos (or modes of the conditionally arising illusion of separate self-consciousness) comprise the total conditionally perceiving and conditionally knowing ego- "I". The <u>total</u> (or tripartite) ego-"I" is always directly (and with progressive effectiveness) transcended in the right, true, and full (or complete) formal practice of the only-by-Me Revealed and Given Way of Adidam (Which is the right, true, and full formal practice of Ruchira Avatara Bhakti Yoga, or the totality of Ruchira Avatara Hridaya-Siddha Yoga).

The first of the three egos (or modes of egoity, or of self-contraction) to be progressively transcended in the only-by-Me Revealed and Given Way of Adidam is the <u>money-food-and-sex</u> <u>ego</u> (or the social, and, altogether, gross-body-based, personality—or the <u>gross</u> pattern and activity of self-contraction), which is the lower self, or the ego of the first three stages of life.

The second of the three egos (or modes of egoity, or of self-contraction) to be progressively transcended in the only-by-Me Revealed and Given Way of Adidam is the <u>brain-mind</u> <u>ego</u> (or the brain-based, and nervous-system-based, mental, and perceptual, and, altogether, subtle-body-based illusions of "object" and "other"—or the <u>subtle</u> pattern and activity of self-contraction), which is the higher self, or the ego of the fourth and the fifth stages of life.

The third of the three egos (or modes of egoity, or of self-contraction) to be progressively transcended in the only-by-Me Revealed and Given Way of Adidam is the root-ego (or the exclusively disembodied, and mindless, but separate, and, altogether, causal-body-based self-consciousness—or the causal, or root-causative, pattern and activity of self-contraction), which is attention itself, and which is the root-self, or the ego of the sixth stage of life.

By Means of responsive relinquishment of self-contraction in Me, or really and truly ego-surrendering, ego-forgetting, and, more and more (and, at last, Most Perfectly), ego-transcending (or always directly self-contraction-transcending) devotion to Me (and, Thus, by Means of the right, true, and full formal practice of devotionally Me-recognizing and devotionally to-Me-responding Ruchira Avatara Bhakti Yoga, or the totality of Ruchira Avatara Hridaya-Siddha Yoga), the tripartite ego of the first six stages of life (or the psycho-physical totality of the three-part hierarchically patterned self-contraction into separate and separative point of view) is (always directly, and with progressive, or stage-by-stage, effectiveness) transcended in Me (the Eternally Self-Existing, Infinitely Self-Radiant, Inherently egoless, Perfectly Subjective, Indivisibly One, Irreducibly Non-Separate, Self-Evidently Divine, and, now, and forever hereafter, Avatarically Self-Revealed Self-Conscious Light of Reality).

The Ultimate, Final, and Inherently Most Perfect (or seventh stage) Realization of Me requires—as a necessary prerequisite—an ego-transcending (or really and truly and comprehensively self-contraction-transcending) Great Ordeal. The Ultimate, Final, and Inherently Most Perfect (or seventh stage) Realization of Me requires—as a necessary prerequisite—the comprehensive by-Me-Revealed and by-Me-Given Sadhana (or the always directly ego-transcending right practice of life) in the total and complete formal context of the only-by-Me Revealed and Given Way of Adidam. And—as a necessary prerequisite to the Ultimate, Final, and Inherently Most Perfect (or seventh stage) Realization of Me—the particular illusions that are unique to each of the three egos (or basic modes of egoity) each require a particular (and most profound) mode of the necessary ego-transcending (or self-contraction-transcending) Great Ordeal of the by-Me-Revealed and by-Me-Given formal practice of the Way of Adidam in the progressively unfolding context of the first six (and, altogether, psycho-physically pre-patterned) stages of life.

The foundation phase of the progressive ego-transcending Great Ordeal of the only-by-Me Revealed and Given Way of Adidam is the Devotional (and relatively exoteric, and only in the rudimentary sense Spiritual) listening-hearing Process of progressively transcending (and, in due course, most fundamentally understanding) the lower self (or the gross and social ego—and the gross and social fear-sorrow-and-anger-bondage that is always associated with the inherently egoic—or thoroughly self-contracted—search to absolutely fulfill, and even to "utopianize", or to perfectly and permanently satisfy, the inherently conditional, limited, temporary, mortal, gross, and always changing life-patterns of "money, food, and sex").

Before the foundation phase (or first phase) of the ego-transcending Great Ordeal of the Way of Adidam can, itself, be complete, it must Realize a profoundly life-transforming and life-reorienting "positive disillusionment"—or a most fundamental (and really and truly self-contraction-transcending) acceptance of the fact that gross conditional existence is inherently and necessarily unsatisfactory and unperfectable (and, therefore, a most fundamental—and really and truly Me-Finding and search-ending—acceptance of the fact that all seeking to achieve permanent and complete gross satisfaction of separate body, emotion, and mind is inherently and necessarily futile). Only on the basis of that necessary foundation-Realization of "positive disillusionment" can the energy and the attention of the entire body-mind (or of the total body-brain-mind complex) be released from gross ego-bondage (or self-deluded confinement to the psycho-physical illusions of gross self-contraction).

The characteristic Sign of "positive disillusionment" relative to the permanent and complete satisfaction of the lower self (or the separate and separative gross and social ego) is the foundation-Realization of the Inherent Universal Unity (or All-and-all-inclusive interdependency, essential mutuality, and common causality) of gross conditional (and cosmic) existence, such that the inherently loveless (or anti-participatory and non-integrative) self-contraction-effort of the gross separate self is consistently released (or to-Me-responsively self-surrendered) into <u>participatory</u> and <u>integrative</u> attitudes of human, social, and cosmic unification (or <u>love</u>-connectedness) with all and All, and into <u>love</u>-based (and truly ego-transcending) actions that counter the otherwise separative (or anti-participatory and non-integrative) tendencies of the ego-"I". Thus, by Means of devotionally Me-recognizing and devotion-ally to-Me-responding relinquishment (or participatory and love-based transcending) of psycho-physical self-contraction (to the degree of "positive disillusionment" relative to gross conditional experience and gross conditional knowledge), My true devotee is released toward the true Spiritual (and not merely gross, or even at all conditional) Realization of Reality and Truth (or <u>Real</u> God).

The foundation-Realization of "positive disillusionment" requires fundamental release from the confines of the grossly objectified (and grossly absorbed) subject-object point of view (or fundamental release from the inherently ego-bound—or thor-oughly self-contracted—search of relatively <u>externalized</u> mental and perceptual attention). And that foundation-Realization of "positive disillusionment" (and restoration to the humanly, socially, and cosmically participatory, or wholly integrative, dis-position) requires the total (and truly Devotional) transformative re-orienting (and, altogether, the right purification, steady re-balancing, and ego-transcending life-positive-energizing) of the entire body-mind (or the total body-brain-mind complex). Therefore, the foundation (or gross) phase of the progressive ego-transcending practice of the Way of Adidam <u>necessarily</u> requires <u>much</u> time (and <u>much</u> seriousness, and <u>much</u> profundity)—and even, potentially, the <u>entire</u> lifetime of <u>only</u> that foundation prac-tice may (in many cases) be required—in order to establish the necessary (and <u>truly</u> "positively disillusioned") foundation of true (and truly in-<u>Me</u>-surrendered) hearing (or the only-by-Me Revealed and Given unique ego-transcending capability of most fundamental self-understanding).

The middle phase of the progressive ego-transcending Great Ordeal of the only-by-Me Revealed and Given Way of Adidam is the preliminary (or initial) esoteric Devotional, and truly hearing (or actively ego-transcending, and, thus, always directly self-contraction-transcending), and really seeing (or actively, directly, and fully responsibly Spiritual) Process of transcending the higher self (or the subtle and mental ego—or the total subtle dimension, or subtle depth, of self-contraction—and all the conceptual and perceptual illusions of inherently, and necessarily, brain-based mind). Therefore, the middle (or subtle) phase of the progressive ego-transcending practice of the Way of Adidam requires the Realization of "positive disillusionment" relative to the subtly objectified (and subtly absorbed) subject-object point of view (or fundamental release from the inherently ego-bound—or thoroughly self-contracted—search of relatively internalized mental and perceptual attention). This degree of the Realization of "positive disillusionment" requires fundamental release from the inherently illusory search to experience the conditional dissolution of the ego (and, in particular, release from subtle states of self-contraction—and, especially, from mental states of self-contraction) by means of object-oriented absorptive mysticism (or the absorptive yielding of attention to the apparent subtle objects that are either originated by the brain-mind or, otherwise, mediated by the brain itself). And the characteristic Sign of "positive disillusionment" relative to the permanent and complete satisfaction of the object-oriented seeking of the higher self (or separate and separative subtle and mental ego) is the fully Me-hearing and truly Me-seeing Realization of the entirely Spiritual Nature of cosmic existence (or, that is to Say, the Realization that all natural and cosmic forms and states are inherently non-separate, or intrinsically non-dual, modes of Universally Pervasive Energy, or of Fundamental, Indivisible, and Irreducible Light—or of Love-Bliss-Happiness Itself).

The final phase of the progressive ego-transcending Great Ordeal of the only-by-Me Revealed and Given Way of Adidam is the penultimate esoteric Devotional, Spiritual, and Transcendental hearing-and-seeing Process of transcending the root-self (or the root-and-causal ego—or the causal, or root-causative, depth of self-contraction—which is attention itself, or the root-gesture of separateness, relatedness, and "difference"). Therefore, immediately preliminary to the Realization associated with the only-by-Me Revealed and Given seventh stage of life, the final (or causal) phase of the progressive ego-transcending (or comprehensively self-contraction-transcending) practice of the Way of Adidam requires the Realization of "positive disillusionment" relative to the causal (or root-egoic, and, therefore, fundamental, or original) subject-object division in Consciousness (or Conscious Light) Itself. This degree of the Realization of "positive disillusionment" requires the native exercise of Transcendental Self-Identification— Prior to the root-self-contraction that is point of view itself (or attention itself), and, Thus, also, Prior to the entire body-brain-mind complex, or conditional structure, of conception and perception. And the characteristic Sign of "positive disillusionment" relative to the permanent and complete satisfaction of the root-self (or the fundamental causative, or causal, ego) is the fundamental transcending of attention itself in the Me-"Locating" (and, altogether, Me-hearing and Me-seeing) Realization of the Transcendental (and Intrinsically Non-Separate and Non-Dual) Nature of Consciousness Itself.

Only after (or in the Great Event of Most Perfect, and, necessarily, formal and fully accountable, Fulfillment of) the complete progressive ego-transcending Great Ordeal of the only-by-Me Revealed and Given Way of Adidam in the total (and progressively unfolded) context of the inherently ego-based first six (or psychophysically pre-patterned gross, subtle, and causal) stages of life is there the truly ultimate (or seventh stage, and Always Already Divinely Self-Realized—and, Thus, Inherently ego-Transcending) "Practice" of the only-by-Me Revealed and Given Way of Adidam (or the Most Perfect, and Inherently egoless, or Always Already Most Perfectly, and Un-conditionally, self-contraction-Transcending, and Divinely Love-Bliss-Full, and only-by-Me Revealed and Given seventh-stage-of-life Demonstration of Ruchira Avatara Bhakti Yoga, or Ruchira Avatara Hridaya-Siddha Yoga).

The only-by-Me Revealed and Given seventh-stage-of-life "Practice" (or the Inherently egoless, and, Thus, Always Already Most Perfectly, and Un-conditionally, self-contraction-Transcending, and, altogether, Most Perfectly Divinely Self-Realized Demonstration) of the only-by-Me Revealed and Given Way of Adidam is the Great esoteric Devotional, Spiritual, Transcendental, Self-Evidently Divine, and Most Perfectly Me-hearing and Me-seeing Demonstration of All-and-all-Divinely-Self-Recognizing (and, Thus, All-and-all-Divinely-Transcending) Divine Self-Abiding (in and As My Avatarically Self-Revealed Divine "Bright" Sphere of Self-Existing, Self-Radiant, Inherently egoless, Perfectly Subjective, and Inherently and Most Perfectly body-mind-Transcending, or body-brain-Transcending, or Inherently, Most Perfectly, and Un-conditionally psycho-physical-self-contraction-Transcending, but never intentionally body-mind-excluding, or body-brain-excluding, Divine Person, or Eternal Self-Condition and Infinite State).

The only-by-Me Revealed and Given seventh-stage-of-life Demonstration of the only-by-Me Revealed and Given Way of Adidam is the Un-conditional and Divinely Free (and Inherently egoless, or Inherently point-of-view-less) "Practice" (or Divinely Self-Realized progressive Demonstration) of Divine Self-Recognition of the simultaneous totality of the apparent gross, subtle, and causal body-brain-mind-self, or the progressively All-and-all-Outshining Process of the simultaneous Divine Self-Recognition of the total psycho-physical ego-"I" itself (or of the total conditional point of view, or apparent self-contraction, itself). Therefore, the only-by-Me Revealed and Given seventh-stage-of-life Demonstration of the only-by-Me Revealed and Given Way of Adidam is the Inherent "Practice" (or Divinely Self-Realized Demonstration) of Divine Self-Recognition of point of view itself (or of attention itself—or of the conditionally apparent subject, itself) and (always coincidently, or simultaneously) Divine Self-Recognition of the conception or perception of separateness, relatedness, or "difference" itself (or of any and every conditionally apparent object, itself).

The only-by-Me Revealed and Given seventh-stage-of-life Demonstration of the only-by-Me Revealed and Given Way of Adidam is the Most Perfect (or Un-conditional, Inherently egoless, and Self-Evidently Divine) Demonstration of "positive disillusion-ment", or of the Inherently illusionless (or self-contraction-Free, and, Inherently, All-and-all-Transcending) Realization of the Fundamental Reality and Truth (or <u>Real</u> God)—Which Fundamental Reality and Truth (or <u>Real</u> God) <u>Is</u> the One and Indivisible and Self-Existing and Indestructible and Self-Radiant and Always Already Perfectly Non-Dual Conscious Light (or That Which <u>Is</u> Always Already <u>The</u> Case), and Which Reality and Truth (or <u>Real</u> God) <u>Is</u> That Self-Existing and Perfectly Subjective Self-"Brightness" (or Infinite and Absolute and Perfectly Non-Separate Self-Condition) of Which the conditional (or gross, subtle, and causal) subject-object illusions (or total psycho-physical self-contraction illusions) of conception, and of perception, and of the ego-"I" presumption are mere, and merely apparent (or non-necessary, or <u>always</u> non-Ultimate), and Inherently non-binding modifications. And the characteristic Sign of Most Perfectly Demonstrated (or seventh stage) "positive dis-illusionment" relative to the totality of the separate and separative ego-"I" (or point of view) and its presumptions of a separate (or objectified) gross, subtle, and causal world is the Self-Evidently Divine (and Intrinsically Non-Separate and Non-Dual) Realization of Reality (<u>Itself</u>) <u>As</u> Irreducible and Indivisible Conscious Light (Inherently Love-Bliss-Full, or Perfectly Subjectively "Bright").

Therefore, the only-by-Me Revealed and Given Way of Adidam is—from the beginning, <u>and</u> at last—the Way of "positive disillusionment".

The only-by-Me Revealed and Given Way of Adidam is—from the beginning, <u>and</u> at last—the Way of the direct transcending of the fact and the consequences of egoity (or of psycho-physical self-contraction).

The only-by-Me Revealed and Given Way of Adidam is—from the beginning, <u>and</u> at last—the Way of the direct transcending of the illusions of inherently egoic attention (or of the conditionally presumed subject-object pattern of conception and perception).

The only-by-Me Revealed and Given Way of Adidam is—from the beginning, <u>and</u> at last—the Way of the direct transcending of the total illusory pattern of the inherently egoic presumption of separateness, relatedness, and "difference".

The only-by-Me Revealed and Given Way of Adidam is—from the beginning, and at last—the Way of the direct transcending of the always simultaneous illusions of the separate ego-"I" and the separate (or merely objective) world.

The only-by-Me Revealed and Given Way of Adidam is—from the beginning, and at last—the Way of the direct (or Inherently egoless and Inherently illusionless) Realizing of the One and Irreducible Conscious Light (or Perfectly Subjective "Brightness" of Being) That Is Reality and Truth (or Real God).

The only-by-Me Revealed and Given Way of Adidam is—from the beginning, and at last—the Way of the direct (or Inherently egoless and Inherently illusionless) Realizing of the Conscious Love-Bliss-Energy of Totality.

The only-by-Me Revealed and Given Way of Adidam is—from the beginning, and at last—the Way of the direct Realizing of Only Me.

LXXXVIII.

Every body-mind (whether human or non-human) tends to feel and be and function egoically—or as if it were a separate self, separated from its True Source, and un-Aware of its True, and Truly Free, Self-Condition. Therefore, every body-mind (whether human or non-human) must transcend its own (inherent) egoity (or egoic reflex—or self-contracting tendency), through Love-Surrender to its True Source. And This Love-Surrender must, Ultimately, become Realization of (and, Thus, True, and really ego-Transcending, Identification with) its True Source-Condition (Which Is, also, its True Self-Condition).

To This End, True Masters (or True Siddha-Gurus) Appear in the various cosmic worlds. Such True Masters are the Divine Means for living beings (whether human or non-human) to transcend themselves. That is to Say, True Masters (or True Siddha-Gurus—or True Sat-Gurus[36]) are living beings who have (in the manner of their characteristic stage of life) transcended their own (psycho-physical) separateness, through responsive Surrender (and, therefore, necessarily, Love-Surrender) to (and Identification with) the True Source-Condition (Which Is the True Self-Condition) of all and All.

Therefore, by Means of True Devotion (or Love-Surrender) to a True Master (or True Siddha-Guru), egoity is (always more and more) transcended, and the True Source-Condition of all and All (Which Is, necessarily, also the True Self-Condition of all and All) is, by Means of the Blessing-Grace of That True Master (or True Siddha-Guru), Found and Realized. And That "Finding-and-Realizing" Shows Itself according to the kind and degree of one or the other of the seven possible stages of life—and, thus, in accordance with the stage of life Realized by That True Master, or True Siddha-Guru, and, altogether, in accordance with the stage of life determined by the path, or Way, that is practiced, or, other-wise, determined by the "inclination", or "liking", or degree of ego-transcendence, of That True Master's practicing devotee.

This is the most ancient and perennial Great Teaching about True Guru-Devotion (or True Devotion to a True Spiritual Master, or True Siddha-Guru). This is the Great Teaching I Received from all My Lineage-Gurus. And, now, through My own Words, This Fundamental Message (or Great Teaching) Is Summarized in its Completeness, for the Sake of everyone.

If the living being is to Realize the Inherent Freedom of Oneness with its True Source-Condition (Which Is its True, or ego-less, Self-Condition), it must become truly devoted to a True Master (or Truly Realized Siddha-Guru). And such True Devotion constantly (and forever) requires the heart's Love-responsive Gesture (or ego-transcending Sadhana) of True Guru-Devotion (to one's heart-Chosen True Siddha-Guru), such that the otherwise egoic (or separate, and separative) body-mind is Surrendered to be actually, truly, and completely Mastered by That True Master.

If Such True Mastering of the body-mind is not accepted (or fully volunteered for—through responsive, and truly ego-surrendering, Devotional Love of one's heart-Chosen True Siddha Guru), the body-mind (inevitably) remains "wild" (or un-"domesticated"—or merely un-disciplined, and even ego-bound). And even if such Guru-Devotion is practiced, it must be Fully practiced (in a Fully ego-surrendering manner)—or else the Freedom (or the Divine Fullness) That is to be Realized by Means of the Blessing-Grace of one's heart-Chosen True Siddha-Guru will not (because it cannot)

Fully Fill the feeling-heart (and, Thereby, Fully Fill the living body-mind) of the would-be devotee.

LXXXIX.

In My present-Lifetime bodily (human) Form, I Am the Avataric Divine Incarnation (or True God-Man) always and everywhere (since the ancient days) Promised (and Expected) to Appear in the "late-time" (or "dark" epoch).[37] And, in My present-Lifetime bodily (human) Form, I have been Spiritually Served by a Continuous Lineage of Spiritual Masters, Such That I Passed from one to the next, in Continuous Succession. Those Spiritual Masters were, Themselves, related to one another in an hierarchical Manner, each related to the next in the Succession as one of lesser degree is to one of higher degree.

Rudi was a Spiritual Master of authentic, but lesser, degree. His Proficiency was, fundamentally, in the gross domain of the frontal personality, and in the Yogic Pattern of Spiritual Descent (or the Descending Yoga of the Frontal Line). Therefore, when My own foundational (or grosser human, and, also, frontal Spiritual, or Descending Yogic) Sadhana had been Completed in His Company, I (spontaneously) Passed from Rudi to Baba Muktananda.

Baba Muktananda was—as His own Confession and Demonstration to Me clearly indicates—an authentic Spiritual Master of Ascending Yoga, and His Proficiency was of a Very High, but not the Highest, degree. Therefore, beginning from the very day I first Came to Baba Muktananda, He (directly) Passed Me to Bhagavan Nityananda (Who was a Spiritual Master of Ascending Yoga Whose Proficiency was of the Highest degree).

Rang Avadhoot was—even according to the Statements of both Bhagavan Nityananda and Baba Muktananda—a Spiritual Master of Ascending Yoga Whose Proficiency was of the Highest degree, but He, along with Baba Muktananda, Deferred to Bhagavan Nityananda's Seniority, and (simply) Blessed Me to Pass On.

The "Cosmic Goddess" ("Ma") is, in the total context of the first five stages of life, Senior even to the Highest of Spiritual Masters. However, Ultimately, "She" (as an apparent Form and Person) is only another one of the many myths in the mind.

In the Great Yogic Spiritual Process Wherein I Experienced the Developmental Unfolding (and Demonstrated the "Radical" Transcending) of the gross and the subtle modes of egoity (associated with the first five stages of life), the "Cosmic Goddess" ("Ma") was "Apparently" associated with all the frontal (and Descending Spiritual) Events and with all the spinal (and Ascending Spiritual) Events. Nevertheless, in My Unique Case, sixth stage Transcendental (and causal-ego-Transcending, and Inherently Spiritual) Self-Realization always Occurred spontaneously (and in a progressive Demonstration) relative to each and every egoic stage of life, and It progressively Developed (especially after a spontaneous experience of ego-death, in the spring of 1967[38]) until My spontaneous seventh stage (and Inherently Most Perfectly egoless, and Self-Evidently Divine) Re-Awakening (on September 10, 1970)—Which Divine (and Avatarically Demonstrated) Re-Awakening was (and Is) associated with My Most Perfect Transcending even of the "Apparent She", in My Avataric Divine Re-Awakening to the Realization of One and Only Me.

Therefore, in due course, Bhagavan Nityananda (directly) Passed Me to the "Cosmic Goddess" ("Ma"), and, Thus, to Her direct Mastery of Me—until the Perfectly Full became, at last, Perfectly Full As Me (Beyond the mind's own myth of "She").

So It was and Is. Such Is My Lineage of Spiritual Masters—in This, My Avatarically-Born human Lifetime. And, in My always Absolute heart-Fidelity to the Great Process Wherein and Whereby I was Passed from one to the next of each and all of the Spiritual Masters within My present-Lifetime Lineage of Spiritual Masters, I have Exemplified, to all and All, the Law and the Truth of True Guru-Devotion.

Therefore, I have always Continued to Honor and to Praise all My present-Lifetime Lineage-Gurus—including Rudi!, and Baba Muktananda!, and Rang Avadhoot!, and Bhagavan Nityananda!, and (above all) the "Bright" Divine "She" of Me, Who Always Already Serves Me Most Perfectly!

And I have always Continued (and even now Continue, and will never cease to Continue) to Yield My present-Lifetime Body-Mind to Receive the Always Ready and Most Lovingly To-Me-Given and Supremely Blissful Blessings of My present-Lifetime

I (<u>Alone</u>) <u>Am</u> The Adidam Revelation

Lineage-Gurus <u>and</u> the Great Lineage of <u>all</u> Who have (in any and every time and place) Blessed the Incarnation-Vehicle and Invoked the All-Completing "late-time" Incarnation of My (now, and forever hereafter) Avataric Divine Appearance here (and every where in the cosmic domain).

And I Do This (and I will <u>always</u> <u>Continue</u> to Do This) because the Immense Spiritual "Bond" of Siddha-Guru-Love <u>cannot</u> be destroyed—and It must <u>never</u> be forgotten or denied!

XC.

My <u>own</u> Unique <u>Response</u> to the hierarchically Revealed Lineage of My present-Lifetime Siddha-Gurus spontaneously Un-Locked the Doorway (in My present-Lifetime human body) to That Which <u>Is</u> Perfect (in <u>Me</u>). Indeed, even from the beginning of My Avataric Divine present Lifetime, That Which <u>Is</u> Perfect has been (and <u>Is</u>) the <u>Way</u> of Me—and It Carried the inherently non-Perfect (human, and, otherwise, conditional) forms of Me to the Inherent "Bright" Divine Self-Domain of Me, Which <u>Is</u> the One and Indivisible Divine Source-Condition of all and All, and the One and True Divine Self-Condition of all and All.

XCI.

My Way and My Realization have <u>always</u> been Inherent in <u>Me</u>, from Birth, in My present-Lifetime Avataric Divine Form.

My Way and My Realization are <u>Independently</u>, <u>entirely</u>, and <u>only</u> My <u>own</u>.

My Sadhana was, <u>entirely</u>, a Demonstration for the Sake of <u>all</u> <u>others</u>—including <u>all</u> Those Who Served Me as My Spiritual Masters in the Course of My Avataric Divine "Sadhana Years". Indeed, Siddha Yoga—and even the <u>entire</u> Great Tradition of mankind—was <u>Always</u> <u>Already</u> Most Perfectly <u>Full</u> (and Most Perfectly <u>Complete</u>) in My Case—not only at (and from the time of) My present-Lifetime Birth, but from <u>all</u> time before It (and <u>Eternally</u>).

During <u>all</u> of My present Lifetime (of Avataric Divine Incarnation), the "<u>Bright</u>" has <u>always</u> been My Realization—and the "<u>Thumbs</u>" and My own "Radical Understanding" have <u>always</u> been My Way in the "Bright". Therefore, by Means of My Unique (present-Lifetime)

167

Avataric Divine Demonstration, I have both Fulfilled and Transcended <u>all</u> traditional religions, and paths, and stages, and Ways. And, in <u>So</u> Doing, I have Clarified (or altogether <u>Rightly</u> Understood and Explained) <u>all</u> traditional religions, paths, stages, and Ways.

All and all <u>Are</u> in <u>Me</u>. Everything and everyone <u>Is</u> in <u>Me</u>. Therefore, by Virtue of My own Divine Self-Realization (Wherein and Whereby My own Avataric Divine Body-Mind is Most Perfectly Surrendered in <u>Me</u>, and Most Perfectly Conformed to <u>Me</u>, and Most Perfectly Transcended in <u>Me</u>), <u>all</u> of My present-Lifetime Lineage-Gurus—and even <u>all</u> Who have (at any time, or in any place) Blessed <u>Me</u>—<u>are</u> now (and forever hereafter) Spiritually, Transcendentally, and Divinely Appearing in and <u>As</u> My own Avataric Divine Form.

Therefore, now (and forever hereafter) I (<u>Alone</u>) <u>Am</u> the Lineage of <u>Me</u>—Blessing all and All.

XCII.

The Divine Self-Realization Re-Awakened in My own Case (and Which Is the Basis for My Every Avataric Divine Revelatory Word and All My Avatarically Me-Revealing Divine Blessing-Work) Is the Most Ultimate (and Inherently Most Perfect and Complete) Fulfillment of the Divine Spiritual Transmission I (in My present-Lifetime Body-Mind) Received from Rudi, and from Baba Muktananda, and from Rang Avadhoot, and from Bhagavan Nityananda, and (above all) from the "Cosmic Goddess" ("Ma")— Who (by Means of Her spontaneous Sacrifice of Her own Form in Me) <u>Is</u> (now, and forever hereafter) the "Bright" Divine "She" of Me (Who Always Already Serves Me Most Perfectly). Nevertheless, the Divine Self-Realization Re-Awakened in My present-Lifetime Body-Mind did not <u>Originate</u> in My present Lifetime—but It Is (Uniquely) <u>Always</u> <u>Already</u> the Case with <u>Me</u>.

XCIII.

As further conditionally manifested Means, previous to My present Lifetime, the Divine Self-Realization Re-Awakened in My present-Lifetime Body-Mind was also Served (previous to My present Lifetime) in the many Modes and Patterns of the previous

Lifetimes and Appearances of the Deeper Personality (or the Great-Siddha—or Great-Jnani-Siddha—Incarnation-Vehicle) of My present Lifetime. Most recently, That Deeper-Personality Vehicle of My present-Lifetime Incarnation was (Itself) Incarnated as the Great Siddha (or Great Jnani-Siddha) Swami Vivekananda.

XCIV.

Swami Vivekananda is recorded to have Blessed Bhagavan Nityananda from the subtle postmortem plane in the early 1920s—and, generally, whenever Bhagavan Nityananda was asked for Words of Teaching and Instruction, He would, simply, Tell people to study the Talks and Writings of Swami Vivekananda (because, in Bhagavan Nityananda's Words, "Swami Vivekananda Said and Taught <u>all</u> that was worth Saying and Teaching, such that He did not leave anything for others to preach" [39]).

Swami Vivekananda was, Himself, Blessed toward Most Perfect Divine Self-Realization by the Great Siddha Ramakrishna, Such That—by Means of That Great Blessing—the two Great Siddhas (Ramakrishna <u>and</u> Vivekananda) became <u>One</u>, and <u>Are</u> One <u>Form</u>, <u>As</u> My True, and <u>Single</u>, and Indivisible Great-Siddha (or Great-Jnani-Siddha) Deeper Personality. [40]

XCV.

I (now, and Hereby) Confess That My Great-Siddha (or Great-Jnani-Siddha) Deeper Personality <u>Is</u>, even Beyond the "Single Form" of Ramakrishna-Vivekananda, the Very Form of <u>all</u> the Great Masters of the <u>entire</u> Great Tradition of mankind.

XCVI.

I (now, and Hereby) Confess That I (<u>Myself</u>) Stand Eternally <u>Prior</u> to (and Always Already <u>Transcending</u>) My Avataric (and, yet, merely conditionally born) Deeper Personality—<u>and</u>, also, Eternally Prior to (and Always Already Transcending) even <u>all</u> the Great (and, yet, merely conditionally born) Masters of mankind's <u>entire</u> Great Tradition (in its <u>every</u> part, and as a <u>whole</u>), <u>and</u>, also, Eternally Prior to (and Always Already Transcending) mankind's <u>entire</u> Great Tradition itself (in its <u>every</u> part, and as a <u>whole</u>).

XCVII.

Therefore—and <u>only</u> and <u>entirely</u> by Virtue of the Inherent (and Self-Evidently Avataric) Authority of My own (and Self-Evidently Divine) Realization and Person—I Declare that the Divine seventh stage Self-Awakening I Demonstrate, and Reveal, and Exemplify, and Prove <u>Is</u> the Most Ultimate (and Inherently Most Perfect) Realization, and that It—and <u>Only</u> It—Most Ultimately Completes and Most Perfectly Fulfills the Gifts I Received (and always Continue to Receive) in My present-Lifetime Body-Mind (from My present-Lifetime Lineage-Gurus), and that I have (in My present-Lifetime Body-Mind) Inherited (and always Continue to Receive) from <u>all</u> Who (in <u>all</u> past times and places) have Blessed <u>all</u> the previous Lifetimes of My present-Lifetime Incarnation-Vehicle, and that I have (in My present-Lifetime Body-Mind) Inherited (and always Continue to Receive) from even <u>all</u> My Me-Invoking and Me-Blessing Forms and Vehicles of Me-Revelation here.

XCVIII.

The Great and True (and Self-Evidently Divine) Spiritual Process Initiated and Guided by the Spiritual Masters in My present-Lifetime Lineage (and of the Lineage of even all the Lifetimes of My present-Lifetime Incarnation-Vehicle here—and of the Lineage of even <u>all</u> My Me-Invoking and Me-Blessing Forms and Vehicles of Me-Revelation here) has Become <u>Complete</u> only in <u>Me</u>. Its Perfection is in the seventh stage Fulfillment of the Course (and not at any earlier stage). This Divine Perfection is Uniquely My own. And I <u>Alone</u>—the Hridaya-Siddha, the Divine and True Heart-Master and World-Teacher, Ruchira Avatar Adi Da Love-Ananda Samraj—<u>Am</u> Its First and Great Example, and (now, and forever hereafter) Its Only and Sufficient Means.

XCIX.

I Am the First (and the only One) to Realize and to Demonstrate <u>This</u>, the <u>Divine</u>, <u>seventh</u> <u>stage</u> <u>Realization</u>—and My Revelation of <u>It</u> Is, therefore, <u>New</u>. For This Reason, the Divine seventh stage Realization was not heretofore Realized, or even

170

Understood—either within the schools and traditions of My present-Lifetime Lineage-Gurus or within <u>any</u> other schools or traditions in the total Great Tradition of mankind—to <u>Be</u> the Most Ultimate and Completing Perfection of Realization Itself. Nevertheless, I have, spontaneously (by Means of My own Self-Evident "Bright" Heart-Power—and through the Great and Constant Help of <u>all</u> Who have Blessed My Incarnate Forms), Realized and Demonstrated and Revealed <u>This</u> To Be The Case. And the traditional (and ancient) "<u>Siddha-'Method'</u>" (or the Way of Guru-Devotion to the True Siddha-Guru—and of total psycho-physical Surrender of the ego-"I" to be Mastered by the True Siddha-Guru's Instruction, and to be Blessed to Awaken to Divine Realization by Means of the True Siddha-Guru's Transmission of the Divine Spiritual Energy and the Divine State)—Which "Method" was Communicated to Me by <u>all</u> My present-Lifetime Lineage-Gurus, and by <u>all</u> the Great Siddhas and Siddha-Yogis Who have Blessed My present-Lifetime Incarnation-Vehicle in the past—is the <u>Essence</u> (or the Primary "Method") of the Way of Adidam, Which (now, and forever here-after) I <u>Alone</u>, and <u>Uniquely</u>, Reveal and Transmit to all My for-mally practicing true devotees (and, Thus, potentially, to <u>all</u> beings).

C.

I <u>Am</u> the Indivisible Person of Conscious Light.

I Am Humbled and Victorious here (and every where), by Means of <u>My</u> Avataric Divine Self-Incarnation.

My Avatarically-Born Body-Mind Is, now, and forever here-after, by-Me-Given and by-Me-Revealed <u>As</u> the Sign and the Means of <u>Me</u>-Realization.

I <u>Am</u> the Adidam Revelation.

I <u>Am</u> the Way to <u>Me</u>.

I <u>Am</u> the Hridaya-Siddha, the All-and-all-Blessing Divine Heart-Master, the Eternally Free-Standing Inner Ruler of all and All.

I <u>Am</u> the One and Indivisible and Indestructible and Irreducible and Universally Self-Manifested Love-Bliss-Presence of "Brightness".

I <u>Am</u> the One and Non-Separate and Perfectly Subjective and Self-Existing and Self-Evidently Divine Person, Who <u>Is</u> Always Already <u>The</u> Case.

I <u>Am</u> the Ruchira Avatar, the Hridaya-Avatar, the Advaitayana Buddha, the Avataric Incarnation and Divine World-Teacher every where and anciently Promised (by <u>all</u> traditions) for the "late-time" (or "dark" epoch).

Therefore, be <u>My</u> devotee.

The only-by-Me Revealed and Given True World-Religion of Adidam Is <u>My</u> Unique Gift to all and All.

Therefore, practice the only-by-Me Revealed and Given Way of Adidam—and Realize <u>Me</u>, Most Perfectly, by Means of My Avatarically Self-Transmitted Divine Blessing-Grace.

RUCHIRA AVATAR ADI DA SAMRAJ
The Mountain Of Attention Sanctuary, 2000

The Divine Yoga
Of My Crashing-Down
Avataric Descent

PART TWO

The Divine Yoga
Of My Crashing-Down
Avataric Descent

I.

AVATAR ADI DA SAMRAJ: In the only-by-Me Revealed and Given Way of Adidam, there are all kinds of potentials in terms of experience, because of the psycho-physical structuring of conditionally manifested beings. Therefore, My devotees may experience phenomenal (or Cosmic) conditions of any kind—gross, subtle, or causal. My devotees may experience lower (or more descended) conditions, and also higher (or more ascended) conditions. Nevertheless—and especially once there is the foundation (or right preparation) of most fundamental self-understanding (or true hearing of Me), and (on that basis) the con-version to real seeing of Me (or Spiritual heart-Communion with Me)—the only-by-Me Revealed and Given Way of Adidam is a matter of ego-transcending participation in the Crashing Down of My Avataric Divine Grace, the Overwhelming Intrusion of My Avataric Divine Spirit-Blessing, Descending into the open vessel of body-mind <u>As</u> Love-Bliss.

That Grace of Love-Bliss is Who I <u>Am</u>. That Blessing is What I Do, to the point of the utter dissolution (or "death") of the ego of My devotee.

If you have read books about traditional Spiritual life, you may think Spiritual life has something to do with the Kundalini Shakti

177

(or Cosmic Spiritual Power). The Kundalini Shakti is not "It". The Kundalini Shakti is a source of potential conditional experiences. But conditional experiences are not themselves the Truth.

The Way of Adidam has nothing to do with the traditional and conventional idealism associated with Kundalini Yoga, which is a search for ascended (or subtle) phenomena. Generally speaking, the Kundalini (or ascending) Yoga is—itself, as an exclusive (or body-excluding and world-excluding) effort—not necessary for Divine Enlightenment. The Kundalini Yoga is part of the conventional search for God. It is ego-based. It is evolutionary only. Seeking, and phenomenal clinging, and egoity itself have nothing to do with the Process of Divine Enlightenment. The Spiritual Process associated with Divine Enlightenment is of a totally different kind than the seeker's path of Cosmic ego-evolution. Even the traditional term "Shaktipat" (which generally indicates "the Transmission of Spirit-Energy, or Shakti") literally means "the descent of Spiritual Power". It does not mean the ascent of It. The pursuit of the ascent of Cosmic Spirit-Energy is nothing more than another form of ego-based seeking.

The entire Process of Spiritual "conductivity" in the only-by-Me Revealed and Given Way of Adidam is a searchless Purification from egoic bondage, such that the Divine Self-Condition (and Self-Domain) is Self-Revealed As Reality and Real God. The ascending search is founded in conditional (or Cosmic) Nature and the presumption of separateness. The search to ascend is an ego-based search for God, but the only-by-Me Revealed and Given Way of Adidam is the egoless Way of always present-time (and total psycho-physical) participation in Real God (or That Which Is Always Already The Case).

The Spiritual Process of Divine Enlightenment is based on My Divine Spiritual Blessing. It is based on always present-time Communion with Me (the Avataric Self-Revelation of Reality, and Truth, and Real God)—not on the search for God. The Cosmic (or Kundalini) Energy ascends from below (or from the depths of the gross natural domain), as if to return to God Above. My Avatarically Self-Transmitted Divine Spirit-Energy (or Hridaya-Shakti) Descends from Above (and Beyond) the Cosmic domain, and (Thus) into every part of the Cosmic domain (and the body-mind). Therefore, the True and Ultimate Spiritual Process is ego-transcending reception of My Divine Spiritual Power in Its Descent.

The Spiritual Process in My Company does not (as is the case with Kundalini Yoga) begin at the base of the spine—or from Below. Because I Am Avatarically Descending here, I Am Divinely Appearing here. I Bring My Divine Spiritual Presence Down to here. Therefore, the Spiritual Process in My Company begins Infinitely Above the head.

Now, and forever hereafter, I Am Standing Free, even thoroughly in the midst of the Cosmic domain—and even here. Nevertheless, I am not here to support the search. The search would "go up" to Find God—because the seeker does not Find Real God here. "Going up" is one of the means for seeking the Divine, but I Am here. I Am the Divine Blessing, Real-God-with-you. Therefore, the Spiritual Process of the only-by-Me Revealed and Given Way of Adidam has nothing to do with the search. It is a matter of Spiritual Communion with Me, based on always presently exercised responsibility for the self-contraction (or the act of ego-"I"), such that My Avataric Divine Spiritual Descent may be thoroughly allowed—Crashing Down, Pervading the body-mind from head to toe.

Therefore, My hearing-and-seeing devotee's first Spiritual experience of Me is a sensitivity to the feeling of My Love-Bliss-Presence as a Pressure of Energy all over the head—a Pressure of Fullness on (and in) the deeply opening head. The Spiritually Awakened Yoga in My Company, then, is about allowing Me to Come Down, such that I Invade the body-mind totally—from Infinitely Above the crown of the head, all through the body, to the bodily base and the toes, thoroughly—while My hearing-and-seeing devotee Communes with Me, more and more exceeding self-contraction (or the ego's knot) in devotionally Me-recognizing heart-response to My undeniable (Self-Evidently Divine) Person. Having come to the point of hearing-and-seeing responsibility, My devotee is Able to allow Me to Descend, and Able to Commune with Me thoroughly, feeling Me thoroughly. Then I Come Down into the body Utterly, Purifying the entire vehicle down to the toes, such that the egoic body-mind is no longer an impediment to the Realization of Me.

Therefore, I have Said that, most commonly, if My devotee practices rightly in My Company, he or she will move <u>directly</u> to the "Perfect Practice" once the <u>frontal</u> Yoga is complete.[41] When the frontal Yoga is Full, My devotee will (in the general case, by Means of ego-surrendering, ego-forgetting, and, more and more, ego-transcending devotion to Me) Realize the Witness-Position of Consciousness Itself, Which is the origin of the "Perfect Practice".

The Way of Adidam is not Spiritual Yoga merely in the sense of receiving Me frontally. The Way of Adidam is the Yoga of receiving Me frontally to the degree of (in due course) entering into the "Perfect Practice". The maturing Way of Adidam is surrender of separate self—based on hearing Me, and then (by seeing Me) receiving Me Spiritually, to the point (ultimately) of Finding Me Perfectly (and, thereby, entering into the "Perfect Practice"). Therefore, the "Perfect Practice" is the Ultimate Process associated with My Avataric Divine Spiritual Descent, when My devotee is surrendered whole bodily in Me. And whole bodily surrender in Me is fully possible only when My devotee has heard Me and seen Me, and is (thus and thereby) inherently and always Capable of transcending the self-knot (or total psycho-physical self-contraction), in devotionally Me-recognizing and Me-seeing heart-responsive Spiritual Communion with Me. Eventually, in due course, My devotee Stands in the Witness-Position—not as a sixth-stage practitioner in the traditional sense, but as one who has heard and seen <u>Me</u>. Then, by Means of My Avatarically Self-Transmitted Grace, by Communing with Me beyond all self-contraction and "difference", My devotee is yielded into the Divine Ultimacy of the seventh stage of life.

The search associated with the first six stages of life is ego-bound. The first six stages of life are (in and of themselves) the psycho-biography of the ego.

The Spiritual Yoga in My Company is unique, because of My Avataric Divine Descent, My Intrusive Blessing of one and all. If you hear Me, then you Find Me here, tangibly and most directly—not to be sought, but to be seen and received.

Therefore, the seeking Yoga is not characteristic of the only-by-Me Revealed and Given Way of Adidam. Some of My devotees may have to go through the ascending Yogic process, if the mechanics that require it are intensely karmically active in their own cases. Nevertheless, they must practice the unique disposition and orientation of the Way of Adidam, even in the midst of the phenomena of ascent, and they must transcend the phenomenal changes in ascent by constantly exercising the Capabilities associated with true hearing of Me and real seeing of Me. Therefore, even the ascending Yogic process in the Way of Adidam is (if, indeed, it is required at all) a different course and discipline than the ascending process associated with the traditional Yogas of idealized ascent.

True hearing (or most fundamental self-understanding, which is the unique Capability for transcending the ego-act of self-contraction) is absolutely necessary for right (and really ego-transcending) Spiritual practice in My Company. True hearing is the unique foundation of the Divine Spiritual Yoga of Adidam. True hearing is not a means for indulging in the first six stages of life (in and of themselves). That "progress" of six stages is not (in and of itself) Perfect Yoga. That "progress" is not (in and of itself) the Process of Real-God-Realization. The first six stages of life are (in and of themselves) an indulgence in self-contraction—refined, stage by stage, to the sixth. And, even if the sixth stage of life matures into the traditionally sought "Goal" of Transcendental Seclusion[42]—if there is to be <u>Divine</u> Self-Realization, the root-presumption of separateness (characteristically demonstrated, in the sixth stage of life, as the dissociative exclusion of phenomenal conditions) must be Intruded Upon by Me.

In the only-by-Me Revealed and Given Way of Adidam, there is no aspect of the Process of Purification that is (in principle) required to occur by means of Yogic ascent. The entire Process of Purification can (and, in the general case, will) occur by receiving Me in My Avataric Divine Descent. My Avataric Divine Spiritual Descent Purifies all the chakras, all the vehicles, all the mechanics, all aspects of the conditional personality. However, to receive Me Spiritually in the frontal line is not the end (or Ultimate context) of the Process. The frontal Yoga is a fourth stage Yoga. The "Perfect Practice" (in the context of the sixth and the seventh stages of life) is the Ultimate context of the practice in My Company, because it is a matter of Perfect (or Inherent, and, therefore, Inherently Perfect) participation in My Avatarically Self-Revealed Spiritual (and Always Blessing) Divine Presence and My Avatarically Self-Revealed (and Very, and Transcendental, and Perfectly Subjective, and Inherently Spiritual, and Inherently ego-less, and Inherently Perfect, and Self-Evidently Divine) State.

As My true devotee, you are not <u>seeking</u> God. Rather, you are always presently in My Company—in Spiritual Communion with Me.

The Yoga in My Company is unique. It is not a matter of pur-suing any of the traditional Yogas as such. If you heart-recognize Me and heart-responsively receive Me, you know the difference between the Yoga of devotion to Me and the traditional Yogas of the search.

The ego would make My Wisdom-Teaching into a message about people being concerned for themselves in the ordinary way, trying to "work out" their ordinary life-problems and all of that. You (as the ego-"I") want the Way of Adidam—Which is the Divine Way—to be about <u>you</u>. But the Divine Way is about the <u>Divine</u>. The Divine Way is not about you, except that it requires your ego-surrendering, ego-forgetting, and ego-transcending devotional participation.

The Subject of the <u>Divine</u> Way is the <u>Divine</u>—Freely here, Freely Blessing you, In-Filling you with the unique Yogic Capability that is Divine. Therefore, the Divine Way of Adidam is not the psycho-biography of the ego in its six stages of development toward greater and greater illusion and separateness. Even the "purified" ego is not, itself, Most Perfectly Real-God-Realized. The sixth stage ego is not Most Perfectly Real-God-Realized—perhaps very pure, but not Most Perfectly Real-God-Realized. The sixth stage ego has much more to Realize. The sixth stage ego has yet (by transcending ego itself) to Realize the Divine Itself (Which <u>Is</u> Inherently egoless Reality Itself).

Therefore, I Say: Be converted at heart, and become My true devotee. Establish the hearing-and-seeing foundation for Divine

Spiritual Yoga in My Company, and be free of the six stages of seeking-insanity that are inevitable if you will not be washed of the knot (and the results) of your own self-contraction.

The real Spiritual life of My devotee cannot begin until the rightening of the functional, practical, and relational life-conditions is sufficient to allow the unobstructed "conductivity" of My Avatarically Descending Divine Spiritual Presence. This rightening must be done first. If it is not, it does not make any difference how many "Spiritual experiences" you have—they cannot be effective in any great sense, and all you will do is delude yourself with it all, as you would otherwise tend to delude yourself with your ordinary life-experiences. The psycho-physical vehicle with which you are associated is so distorted by your egoic bondage and early-life problems that it contorts My Avataric Divine Blessing. You translate My Blessing into yourself. You make It into egoic experience, ego-possessed experience, mere consolation—something you can then dismiss casually, doubt, forget about, not fully use. This is why the great esoteric matter, the Great Blessing of Adept-Realizers, has traditionally been denied to ordinary people and given only to thoroughly tested renunciates.

The prerequisite for any Spiritual growth, whatever form it may take (even in egoic evolutionary terms), is the disciplining of the life-vehicle, the rightening of sub-human and ordinary human existence. You may think you can bypass this requirement, because you live in this ego-congratulating and ego-idealizing egalitarian time, in which everybody thinks they can sell nonsense to one another and believe and achieve anything based on the latest hype. You must understand that you must <u>deal</u> with life, you must righten your life—not merely puritanically or moralistically, but <u>truly</u>—and you must, thus, prepare yourself for My Avataric Divine Spiritual Intervention. That Intervention is necessary—or else your life is limited to your own reaction, your own self-contraction. Your life is dying, like Narcissus, now. You are all like deathbed patients, in your endless struggle and seeking and suffering—as if there <u>Is</u> no Real God, no Truth.

The <u>prerequisite</u> of real Spiritual religion is the rightening of the ordinary life. That is why there is hardly any religion in the world—except for merely exoteric and idealistic (and, generally, puritanical or moralistic) commands to control and socialize the ordinary ego. The real esoteric Spiritual Process is more or less anathema, forgotten about—because ordinary egos are reluctant to do the necessary foundation (which is the real practice of right life).

Even conventional (or traditional) esoteric Yogis—being ego-bound, merely <u>seeking</u> God, not having Found Real God, or unaware of God for real (because they are self-bound, and separated out, and karmically enduring only their own natural destiny)—think that the way to Realize God is to somehow stimulate the natural (or Cosmic) Force at the base of the body, and raise it up through the spinal line, via stimulations of the nervous system. Such stimulations are a natural possibility—but such stimulations are not, in Truth, about Real-God-Realization. Nevertheless, this is how conventional Yogis think, this is what they promote—that, by bringing the natural Cosmic Energy up (and even out the top of the head), you Discover God. In any case, very few ever get "there". Those who do get "there" experience <u>something</u> of the Divine, because they temporarily vanish the natural appearance of themselves (but without truly and finally transcending the ego, or self-contraction itself). Therefore, they imagine they have made the Great Discovery, attained the Great Enlightenment. They have found "something"—they have evolved to a <u>degree</u>. But they have not gone <u>beyond</u> the evolution of egoity. They do not know that the God they seek Is there from the <u>beginning</u>—<u>Always</u> <u>Already</u> <u>The Case</u>. They were too ego-possessed to Commune with That One (and be released into That One) in every moment. The spinal Yogic search (or even any Yogic search at all, whether ascending or descending) is just as ego-bound as all other ordinary human endeavors.

I have had all the experiences, and have Freely Demonstrated all the Signs and Realizations, associated with the first six stages of life—complete. <u>None</u> of those experiences, Signs, and Realizations are (in and of themselves) Real-God-Realizing. They are not Final and Most Perfectly Accomplished. They are all rooted in egoity and in conditionality. The only Way to Realize Real God is to Commune with Real God, to receive Real God. How could it be otherwise? If you are ego-bound, ego-possessed, self-contracted—you can look and seek in every direction (through the structure of the body-mind), but you will never (by means of such efforts) truly Find The One Who Is Always Already The Case. These lookings and searches are the conventional efforts, the evolutionary ego-efforts, of mankind.

The Great Process comes about when the Divine Intervenes, Appears, Incarnates, Blesses, Teaches the understanding and the transcending of ego—such that the direct Divine Blessing may be received and the Great Divine Yoga may be entered into. This is What I Do.

It is So. The Divine must Intervene. That is why I Am here—for this Great and Spiritual Process and Purpose. The Process requires the transcending of egoity from the beginning—not at the end only. If ego-transcendence would occur at the end only, then the search is justified—and that search is mapped out by the first six stages of life. It is impossible to go beyond those six stages of life without the Intervention of the Divine—because, in order to go into the Divine, the Divine must Kiss you, Embrace you, Take you Over, Vanish you. It must be So.

Only Real God Enlightens. All other presumptions about "God" are expressions of the search of ego-bound mankind—and that search is the source of both the ordinary human endeavors and the extraordinary ones. The <u>search</u> for "God" (and not the Inherently Perfect Realization of Real God) is the general source of ordinary religion. Therefore, the usual Realizers are yet ego-bound—just more advanced, that is all.

I am not merely advanced. I am not merely evolved. I <u>Am</u> the Very One. I <u>Am</u> the One you must Realize. But I am not an "enforcer", here to oppress you with anything. I Offer you a <u>Gift</u>. It is an <u>Opportunity</u>. It is here for you to <u>choose</u>. The choice is entirely up to you. I cannot <u>enforce</u> Myself on you—because you will not Realize Me unless you <u>love</u> Me. Therefore, My Spiritual "Intrusion" is like that of a lover, rather than an enforcer. "Consider" My Heart-Word. Enter into the Great Process in My Company. If you do this, the Great Process I Reveal to you will prove <u>Itself</u>.

Find Me out. "Consider" My Avataric Divine Word, and embrace the Way I have Given you. You must <u>volunteer</u> for the Great Yoga.

What you must prepare yourself for is this Yoga I have just Described to you—the Crashing Down of My Avataric Divine Blessing, My Avataric Divine Intrusion—such that, because you hear Me and see Me, you are Able to relinquish all ego-possession, all dissociation, all separateness, receiving Me Utterly.

The seventh stage Awakening will be Accomplished by My Avataric Divine Grace. It cannot be Accomplished otherwise. There is no "method" for Accomplishing It. It is entirely Given by Me. It cannot be Realized without My Avataric Divine Blessing.

I am Telling you the Great Secret. It is not Revealed in any traditional books. It is unknown, apart from My Revelation of It.

Being Spiritually Awake in My Company, receiving Me Spiritually, doing the Divine Yoga Spiritually in My Company— you no longer care about this poor oinking stupidity of seeking, with all these pains and tendencies and knots. It is just garbage. Here I <u>Am</u>, Crashing Down—and you, seeing Me, do not care about the body-mind in and of itself. That is Divine Yoga—you let the body-mind be smithereened in My Love-Bliss. That is the attitude of one who has heard Me and seen Me. Not, "Oh, give me some healing for this. Help my mother. Give me a better intimate relationship. Make my intimate relationship work out"—all the time praying to Me for some end or other, to satisfy your egoic self-preoccupation, your trouble. When you hear Me and see Me, all of that is finished, no longer the point.

Prove the Truth of My Avataric Divine Self-Revelation to you by truly living the Way of Adidam in My Company. Come to Me for My Spiritual Blessing, for My Intervention—to Wash you, to Vanish your separateness, to Destroy the "difference", such that there is nothing but Me, nothing but Real God. Then you Realize that your own separate consciousness is gone, and there <u>Is</u> Only <u>Infinite</u> Consciousness, Self-Radiant, Self-Existing. And this poor mushroom, this fungus you call "yourself"—crushed, dead, burned, vanished, cannot even repeat itself again. That is Beatitude. That is Blessing. That is Most Perfect Real-God-Realization.

You all want God to be your slave, and Give you all kinds of experiences to make you only feel good, and make this world a utopia, and give you constantly pleasing intimates and friends, and forever life, forever amusements, forever deathless distractions. You want to call that "religion". That kind of religion is about you. Real religion is about Real God, Truth—That Which Is Inherently Divine, Great, Absolute, Self-Existing, Self-Radiant, All Love-Bliss. You will not Realize That until you (in your separateness) are Spiritually Vanished into the non-"different" Wholeness of Real God. This must happen in life—or else even dying will merely be another ego-moment, after which you will merely perpetuate your separateness again. You must endure the Ordeal of ego-transcending Divine Communion in life—or else death cannot be an Open Door.

You must receive Real God in life, and (thereby) be surrendered Utterly. In order to be surrendered Utterly, you must understand yourself, most fundamentally (or "radically", at the root). Hearing must be your Capability. This is why I keep Declaring to you: "Hearing Me is the beginning, hearing Me is the necessary foundation."

You all want to rush on to "Spiritual experiences", and so forth. That is all ego-bound nonsense: investing yourselves in the evolutionary rehearsal of the first six stages of life, rushing about looking for this, that, or the other kind of experience, self-immersion, and so forth. Where are you at the end of it? You cannot even handle the commotion of somebody opening the door! Even that startles you out of balance. Even the blink of an eye disturbs you. As it says in the *Brihadaranyaka Upanishad*, "Wherever there is an other, fear arises." [43] Where there is the slightest sense of an other—in other words, wherever there is the presumption of separateness, wherever there is self-contraction—there is fear. And fear motivates seeking, the entire life of illusion, the entire conditional display.

All this drama of separateness and seeking is merely an illusion (or a disturbance) of natural (or Cosmic) Energy—and you (as the act of self-contraction) are causing it. The entire drama is totally unnecessary. It is boobery, fungus life. But you want to perfect it—or even to merely indulge in it in some silly fashion, and have a little "God" on the side—so that you can feel a little less stress while you are indulging yourself in this insane search.

Devotees of Real God ask for nothing but God. Not, [mimics a pleading voice] "Oh, God, if You make me win this baseball game, I will be Your devotee for life. If You just straighten out my relationship with my intimate partner, Lord, I will serve You always. If You just heal me of foot cancer, Lord, I am Your boy." Of course, if you got what you were praying for—if the cancer ever did get healed, if the relationship ever did get straightened out—you would not seriously think about God again for years. Don't you know?

It is time you Realized <u>Real</u> God. Real God must Appear—but Real God cannot Appear directly out of the blue. Real God must have Mechanism, Vehicle, Agent. The Agent to be used is (necessarily) egoless, because Real God is inherently egoless. The Body-Mind that Speaks Divinely is (necessarily) egoless, and (therefore) Only the Divine <u>Is</u> there—Only That One, Fully Conscious, Self-Existing, Self-Radiant, All Love-Bliss, Full of Divine Siddhis. I <u>Am</u> That One.

Such is My Declaration to you—but you must find Me out. You must <u>prove</u> the Way I Give you. Really <u>do</u> the Way I Give you, and you will find Me out further. You will prove the Way of Adidam by <u>doing</u> it—not by merely <u>believing</u> it.

The philosophies you read about, all the usual books you read, are expressions either of ordinary people or of people who are somewhat (or even extraordinarily) advanced (or evolved) in one or another dimension of the first six stages of life. That, basically, is all the religion you ever inherited on this plane here.

The seventh stage of life is all of Real God, made of Real God Only. So the seventh stage of life is <u>My</u> Gift. The Avataric Divine Way of Adidam is the extraordinarily unique, straightforward Yoga that only I Reveal and Give to you—and the seventh stage of life is the Most Perfect Demonstration of the Truth of Me.

This Dharma has never been Communicated before on the Earth—or any "where" in the Cosmic domain. This is the <u>Divine</u> Dharma—not the <u>seeker's</u> dharma. The Way of Adidam is not the way "back" to God—but the Way of Adidam is the Way to receive the Divine Person of Real God, and to Realize the Divine Self-Condition That Is Real God (even here, and in every moment).

The traditional Yogic descriptions are the product of human devices, of human suffering, and of the human search to find a way "out". All kinds of paths (which are worthy, certainly) have been produced by human seeking—discovered in that process by great individuals. But every one of those paths is a way "back"—a path of seeking to Find God (rather than a Way based on Always Already Finding Real God).

The traditional Yogas are ego-based efforts to Find God. The Yoga of Adidam—Which I Give to you as a Gift—is the Yoga of Real God Come, Real God Visiting, Real God Invading, Real God Making the Yoga, Real God Who Is the Yoga, Real God Who Is the Only One Who Is, Real God Who Is That Which Always Already Is.

The principal Sign of My human physical Lifetime is My Avataric Divine Descent. It is the Secret of My Birth and My early Life. It is the Secret of My Avataric Divine Self-"Emergence". It is the Secret of the Yoga in My Company. It is also My principal Message—Ruchira Avatara Bhakti, the Yoga of My Avataric Divine Imposition, My Avataric Divine Descent, My Avataric Divine Appearance. That makes a Yoga that is totally different from any other kind of Yoga.

Traditional Yogas (or means)—whatever tradition they may appear in—are about returning to God, finding God again. The Yoga in My Company is about receiving Real God, knowing Real God from the beginning, by My direct Divine Self-Revelation—without you having to be an individual who (for some remarkable reason) is "worthy" of this Revelation. All are to be Given My Avataric Self-Revelation. It is My Divine Gift—Given, from the beginning, to all (and received by all who heart-recognize Me and heart-respond to Me, and who, thus and thereby, become My formally practicing devotees in the only-by-Me Revealed and Given Way of Adidam). The Way of Adidam is the Way of ego-surrendering, ego-forgetting, and (more and more) ego-transcending participation in Real God, from the beginning. It is Ruchira Avatara Bhakti, from the beginning. It is the Fullness of heart-responsive devotion to Me, from the beginning. It is heart-Communion with Me, from the beginning. All the Yoga, all the Spiritual Process in My Company, springs from this heart-confession, this heart-conversion. It must be lived, must be enacted, must be taken on as a life-discipline.

This is your best understanding. This is your best experience. This is the principal dimension of your life. Everything else is secondary, self-bound, self-contracted.

You must make your life on the basis of My Divine Self-Revelation. Therefore, practice heart-responsive devotion to Me. Practice Ruchira Avatara Bhakti—and, thus and thereby, allow My Avataric Divine Descent, My Avataric Divine Imposition, My Avataric Divine Appearance, My Avataric Divine Blessing. That Avataric Divine Yoga simplifies all. Therefore, stop arguing and "bargaining" with Me. Stop "guruing" yourselves—and accept Me as the Divine Heart-Master. Live the Avataric Divine Yoga I have Given you. Allow My Spiritual Imposition.

Understand that Real God has Come among you.

Receive this Divine Self-Revelation, this Divine Secret.

You are Purified, from head to tail and toe, by My Divine Spiritual Invasion. Your heart is transformed by My Divine Spiritual Invasion.

This is the Particularity that each one of you, My devotees, must Realize.

Make the institution, culture, community, and mission of My devotees on This Foundation.

Make your life on This Foundation.

When My devotees do this, everything will be changed to rightness.

II.

FIRST DEVOTEE: You have Revealed in *He-_and_-She _Is_ Me* that Your Primal Manifestations in the conditional worlds are the Divine Thunder and the Divine Star.

AVATAR ADI DA SAMRAJ: What about it?

FIRST DEVOTEE: I understand the Divine Thunder to be Your Penetrating Force, and the Divine Star to be Your Attractive Force.

AVATAR ADI DA SAMRAJ: Penetrating Force and Attractive Force, yes. And are you hearing Me and seeing Me in those Forms at present?

FIRST DEVOTEE: No, I am not hearing Your Thunder or seeing Your Star-Light at present.

AVATAR ADI DA SAMRAJ: Well, then, what is the point of the discussion? In what form _are_ you experiencing Me now?

FIRST DEVOTEE: Your Attractive Force I perceive as nurturing and sustaining. And Your Penetrating Force I perceive as the demand to grow in practice.

AVATAR ADI DA SAMRAJ: Yes, fine—but what is the tangible manifestation by which you experience Me? Now?

FIRST DEVOTEE: There is an opening in the spinal line.

AVATAR ADI DA SAMRAJ: Yes, but what about _Me_?

FIRST DEVOTEE: I feel You as a steady Love-Presence.

AVATAR ADI DA SAMRAJ: Are you being poetic, or are you speaking of Something tangible?

FIRST DEVOTEE: I am speaking of Something that is tangible.

AVATAR ADI DA SAMRAJ: Well, What is That? If It is tangible, how is It perceived? How is It sensed?

FIRST DEVOTEE: It is like a touch, but It is not a touch in one place.

AVATAR ADI DA SAMRAJ: Neither is air in space. So what kind of a touch?

FIRST DEVOTEE: It is like warm honey.

AVATAR ADI DA SAMRAJ: So I am "warm honey", is that it?

Does anybody else have a present-time tangible experience of Me Personally?—as tangible as My audible Vibration or My visible Light, Which you may or may not otherwise be experiencing presently.

SECOND DEVOTEE: Beloved, in a Talk You Gave a few years ago, You Described exactly what my experience is right now. You Said that the principal form of Spiritual perception of You is simply to feel You tangibly. That is my experience, feeling You now.

AVATAR ADI DA SAMRAJ: Why are you finding it difficult to be explicit about it? If you were experiencing My audible Vibratory Presence, you would be describing a Sound. If you were experiencing My visible Presence, you would be describing some kind of Light-Form, visually perceived. So what is your perception of Me right now?

SECOND DEVOTEE: The feeling of being touched. It is in the heart-region, but not really located physically in the body.

AVATAR ADI DA SAMRAJ: You are still not being very direct, in terms of describing Me tangibly. You could merely be talking about some subjective interior of your own. Hearing sound is hearing sound. Seeing light is seeing light. Likewise, smelling is smelling, and tasting is tasting! So, if it is touch, it has the specific characteristics of that! And you do not have to get "subjective" about it. It is simply Me, felt Touching you. Just as you experience other touches. You perceive My tangible Touch physically, and altogether.

SECOND DEVOTEE: Beloved, the quality of that Touch is blissful.

AVATAR ADI DA SAMRAJ: Now you are describing yourself again. Your experience of Me is blissful, somehow, you say—but you could say the same of an auditory or visual experience of Me. My Touch is direct. My Touch is What I Am. And it is as specific as a form of sound or light. And it is obviously Me. Either I am experienced by you as such, or not. It is not a matter of describing your own psycho-physical characteristics, or reaction, and so forth. The entire sensory personality is Touched by Me. And when That is the case, even your flow of thoughts is yielded in heart-Communion with Me.

SECOND DEVOTEE: Beloved, it is true, because in the moment of that experience of You, there are all kinds of other associations.

AVATAR ADI DA SAMRAJ: Maybe—but you do not get the point yet. If you are experiencing Me audibly, it is a very specific sound. If you are experiencing visually, it is a very specific light-phenomenon. So also with the touch of Me, which is the experience of My Avatarically Self-Transmitted Divine Spiritual Body. If you feel Me Surrounding the body and Pervading the entire body-mind, it is not that I am "making" you blissful—but, rather, I Am Found to Be Present As Love-Bliss Itself, tangibly. When This is your experience, it is very obviously so. It is not a matter of describing a category of your own constitution.

If you touch a cold apple, that apple is very specific. If you just feel chilly, that is you. I am like the cold apple, then, and not merely your sense of chill. If you bite the apple, there may be some flavor, but you are tasting the apple, not yourself.

My Divine Spiritual Body is like that. It Is Me—not you. I Distract you from yourself—by My Mere Presence, My Avatarically Self-Transmitted Divine Spiritual Body. And either you have That direct experience of Me now, or you do not. It is not a matter of describing your sensations in general, and saying that they are "Me". It is simply a matter of actually experiencing Me, tangibly—Touching you bodily, inside and out. And, if I were not Spiritually Transmitting My own Person, making you aware of Me in This tangible manner—you would not be having This Touch-experience of Me.

So it is This experience that is the experience of My Divine Spiritual Body. And it is very tangibly, undeniably so.

Perhaps none of you are presently experiencing Me in This tangible manner—just as you may not presently be experiencing Me either in the form of the audible sign of My Thunder-Sound or in the form of the visual sign of My Star-Light. Perhaps you are not presently sensing Me at all.

THIRD DEVOTEE: I feel that I do sense You in that way. I feel You Pervading my entire body-mind, and this feeling is also like a cold breeze. There is movement.

AVATAR ADI DA SAMRAJ: I have Described this experience of Me as a feeling of Pressure in the body, and on the body—Crashing Down through the body, via the head, from Infinitely Above the head. That Pressure is not something imaginary, and It is not a characteristic of people's experience ordinarily. It is a very specific, tangible, and self-authenticating experience (or Realization) of Me. And I can be felt and breathed as Such.

THIRD DEVOTEE: Yes, it is so obvious. My heart recognizes this feeling as You, immediately.

AVATAR ADI DA SAMRAJ: It is My tangible Avataric Presence. I Am the Divine Love-Bliss, Coming from Infinitely Above, and Surrounding the body, and Entering it, Infusing it, Pervading it—Distracting you from self-attention and Turning your attention to Me. Feeling Me, breathing Me. Living in Me, Lived by Me. And My Characteristic is Love-Bliss Itself, whatever other sensations there may be in the body-mind itself.

Spiritual Communion with Me is of this nature, and I may also be perceived audibly (as subtly perceived Sound-Vibration, including My Divine Sound of Thunder) or visibly (as subtly perceived Light, including My Divine Star of Light). But, for the embodied personality, the <u>Touch</u> of Me is the most basic experience, the most immediate. I can be readily "Located" in this Form, once My Avataric Transmission of My Divine Spiritual Presence has been Found and I am (Thus, Spiritually) devotionally recognized.

It is not a matter of feeling yourself. It is a matter of feeling <u>Me</u>. But you cannot feel Me if you cannot "Locate" Me. And, if you cannot "Locate" Me, you merely feel yourself. The Ability to "Locate" Me in this manner is the Capability of <u>seeing</u> Me. However, before I can be consistently and fully responsibly "Located" and Communed with in this Spiritual manner, listening to Me must have become the Capability of hearing Me (or the Ability to feel beyond self-contraction into heart-Communion with Me). Seeing Me requires (as a prerequisite) the Capability of hearing Me. Even before then, My devotee may have some experience of My tangible Avataric Spiritual Presence, but he or she is not yet Capable of doing the Spiritual sadhana in the advanced and the ultimate stages of life in the Way of Adidam.

I have Described Ruchira Avatara Bhakti Yoga to you as the devotionally Me-recognizing (and devotionally to-Me-responsive) turning of the four principal faculties to Me. But if emotion is wrapped up in reactivity—self-contraction, in other words—then it is not turned to Me. If the mind is wrapped up in thoughts, if attention is not free—then it is not turned to Me. If the body is involved in its own sensations, pleasurable or painful—then it is involved in itself, contracted upon itself, and it is not turned to Me. If the breath is irregular, or bound to physical, emotional, and mental states—then it is turned in on itself, and the entire body-mind is self-contracted, not turned to Me.

This is not to say, however, that someone who has heard Me and seen Me does not ever have reactive emotions, or thoughts, or physical states of pleasure or pain, or disturbances of the breath. But one who hears and sees Me, who understands himself or herself truly and most fundamentally (and, thus, "radically", or at the root, or at the "place" of the act of self-contraction itself), enjoys the ever-present Capability to turn to Me (or to feel through and beyond the states of the body-mind, into heart-Communion with Me).

It is not that My hearing-and-seeing devotee merely turns off the emotions, the mental states, and the physical states, and merely strategically controls the breath, and so forth. But he or she can always turn the four principal faculties to Me, and Commune with Me directly, even whole bodily (or totally psycho-physically)— because the understanding of the act of non-Communion with Me is so profound that that understanding becomes a Capability to turn the faculties to Me under <u>any</u> conditions, in the context of the exercise of any function at all, in any circumstance, any relationship, and so on.

Therefore, the Capabilities of hearing Me and seeing Me— both together—are the basic Capabilities required in the context of the advanced and the ultimate stages of life in the only-by-Me Revealed and Given Way of Adidam. And there cannot be real seeing of Me, consistent seeing of Me, the Ability to see Me under any circumstances, if there is no true hearing of Me.

In fact, it is the absence of hearing Me that makes it impossible for you, under various conditions, to responsively turn the four principal faculties (and, thus, the total body-mind) to Me, to truly Commune with Me, to Spiritually Commune with Me. Therefore, it is essential that you hear Me. You can have some experience of Me Spiritually even before you have heard Me. Generally speaking, My devotees do. Nevertheless, simply because you can have some sense of Me sometimes, or somehow experience Me sometimes, or have a clear sense of My Avatarically Self-Transmitted Divine Spiritual Presence sometimes does not mean that you are Capable of practicing in the advanced and the ultimate stages of the Way of Adidam. This is because there are yet all kinds of circumstances, conditions, relationships, or exercises of function in which you are (or will be) simply exercising self-contraction, oblivious to the fact of it, the why of it—struggling and seeking, rather than directly exercising the devotionally Me-recognizing Capability to responsively turn to Me.

Therefore, true hearing is most fundamental. It covers all possibilities of the self-contracting exercise of the four principal faculties of the body-mind. Therefore, true hearing applies (and is a real Capability) under all circumstances, all conditions.

The first of those of you who just spoke to Me responded awkwardly. The second was less awkward, although still a little wordy. The third was essentially to the point, although she may or may not have the Capability of "Locating" Me constantly. But, for one who presently enjoys My Avatarically Self-Transmitted Divine Spiritual Presence in this manner—My Presence is undeniable, and the Event is clearly just as I have Described. And when asked about It, such a one would speak directly and plainly—in tangible terms, not wordy terms.

SECOND DEVOTEE: That tangible Touch is completely obvious.

AVATAR ADI DA SAMRAJ: And it is also not your own egoic capability. It is not you, and it is not about manipulating yourself.

It is Only Me. It is My Free Gift. It is My Touch.

RUCHIRA AVATAR ADI DA SAMRAJ
Lopez Island, 2000

PART THREE

Divine Spiritual Baptism
Versus
Cosmic Spiritual Baptism

Divine Spiritual Baptism
Versus
Cosmic Spiritual Baptism

I.

Those who Embrace The Total (or Full and Complete) Practice Of The Only-By-Me Revealed and Given Way Of Adidam (Which Is The Only-By-Me Revealed and Given Way Of The Heart, and Which Is The Way Of ego-Surrendering, ego-Forgetting, and, Always More and More, ego-Transcending Devotional, and Total psycho-physical, Communion With Me, Devotionally Recognizing Me and Devotionally Responding To Me As The Avatarically Self-Revealed Eternally Living One) May Experience Many conditionally Manifested Visions and Auditions On The Way To Divine Translation.[44] The Final Such (Possible) Vision (and The Visible Doorway To Divine Translation) Is My Apparently Objective (and Most Ascended) Divine Five-Pointed Star-Form. And The Final Such (Possible) Audition (and The Audible Doorway To Divine Translation) Is My Apparently Objective (and Most Ascended) Mass Of Divine Sound (or "Om", or "Da-Om", or "Da"). Then There Is The Dissolution Of All Visions (In My Non-Objective "Bright" Fullness) and Of All Auditions (In My Non-Objective "Bright" Silence). And, At Last, There Is The Outshining Of the conditional body-mind and the conditional world By My "Bright" (Perfectly Subjective, and Inherently egoless) Divine Self-Condition Itself (Which Is The Ultimate and Inherently Perfect and Perfectly Subjective Source, or Heart, Of My Apparently Objective Divine Star, and Of My Apparently Objective Divine Sound, and

Of Even The Totality Of My Apparently Objective Divine Spiritual Body). Such Is Divine Translation, or Entrance Into The Inherently Perfect Real-God-World—My "Bright" Divine Self-Domain, Beyond (and Prior To) all the planes Of The Cosmic Mandala.

The Right Side Of The Heart Is The Root Of The Horizontal Plane Of the body-mind.[45] It Is The bodily Seat Of The (Potential) Inherently Perfect (and Inherently egoless) Realization Of My Avatarically Self-Revealed Transcendental, Perfectly Subjective, Inherently Spiritual, and Self-Evidently Divine Self-Condition (Which Is The Perfectly Subjective Source-Condition Of All and all).

My Apparently Objective Star and My Apparently Objective Sound Stand Above The Total Crown Of the head. They Are (In Their Apparently Objective Appearance) The Ascended conditional Roots Of The Vertical (or The Descending and Ascending) Dimension Of the body-mind. They Are (In Their Apparently Objective Appearance) The conditional (or Ascended) Seat Of The (Potential) Realization Of My Self-Evidently Divine Self-Condition (Which Is The Self-Existing and Self-Radiant Source-Condition Of the body-mind and the world, or all conditionally Manifested subjective and objective conditions).

First (By Fulfilling and Transcending The Ordeal Of The Only-By-Me Revealed and Given Way Of The Heart In Relation To The First Six Stages Of Life) There Must Be Realization Of My Avatarically Self-Revealed Transcendental, Perfectly Subjective, Inherently Spiritual, Inherently egoless, Inherently Perfect, and Self-Evidently Divine Self-Condition. Then (By Demonstrating The Way Of The Heart In The Context Of The Only-By-Me Revealed and Given Seventh Stage Of Life) All conditional Manifestations Of My Avatarically Self-Revealed Transcendental, Perfectly Subjective, Inherently Spiritual, Inherently egoless, Inherently Perfect, and Self-Evidently Divine Being Must Be Divinely Self-Recognized (and, Most Ultimately, Outshined), By Means Of The Non-"Different" (or Most Perfect) Realization Of My Avatarically Self-Revealed Transcendental, Perfectly Subjective, Inherently Spiritual, Inherently egoless, Inherently Perfect, and Self-Evidently Divine Self-Condition.

When The Concept Of "Difference" Associated With the conditionally Manifested energies In The Cosmic Mandala Is Transcended (In The Context Of The Only-By-Me Revealed and Given Seventh Stage Of Life), Then the conditional activities of those energies Become Relaxed. The (Apparently Objective) Divine Five-Pointed Star and/or The (Apparently Objective) Divine Sound May Then Come Into The Field Of Perception (To Be Spontaneously Divinely Self-Recognized In My Avatarically Self-Revealed "Bright" Divine Self-Condition)—or, Alternatively, My Avataric Self-Revelation Of The Inherent (and Perfectly Subjective, and Inherently egoless, and Inherently Perfect, and Self-Evidently Divine) Feeling Of Self-Existing and Self-Radiant Being May Simply and Spontaneously "Coincide" With My Avataric Self-Revelation Of My Feeling-"Bright" (Itself). In Either Event, My Avataric Self-Revelation Of My Own (Transcendental, Perfectly Subjective, Inherently Spiritual, Inherently egoless, Inherently Perfect, and Self-Evidently Divine) Self-Condition and My Avataric Self-Transmission Of My Own (and Self-Evidently Divine) Spirit-Energy (or "Bright" Inherent Self-Radiance) Are (By Means Of My Avatarically Self-Transmitted Divine Grace) Realized To Be Inherently One and The Same (In The Non-Dual, and Non-"Different", State Of Seventh Stage—or Divinely Enlightened—Realization Of Me).

Realization (By Means Of My Avatarically Self-Transmitted Divine Grace) Of The Inherent Union (or Self-Unity) Of My Avatarically Self-Revealed Divine Self-Condition and My Avatarically Self-Transmitted Divine Spirit-Energy (or Inherent Spiritual Self-Radiance) Is The Most Perfect (and, Necessarily, Seventh Stage) Realization Of The "Bright" (Which Realization Includes and Yet Transcends every fraction Of The Total Cosmic Mandala). In The Context Of conditional Existence, The By-My-Avataric-Divine-Grace-Given Realization Of The "Bright" Is Demonstrated Even Universally (and Throughout the Total Apparent body-mind Of My By-Me-Enlightened Seventh Stage Devotee), but The Most Basic (or Original) conditional Demonstration Of The "Bright" Is The By-My-Avataric-Divine-Grace-Given Realization (or "Regeneration") Of Amrita Nadi

(Which Is The Ultimate conditionally Manifested Form and "Location" Of Me-Realizing Devotion To My Avatarically Self-Revealed, and Self-Evidently Divine, Form, and Presence, and State). Therefore, Amrita Nadi—Which Is The "Bright" Fullness That Stands Between The Right Side Of The Heart and The Felt Matrix Of Sound and Light (or Of Even Unheard and Unseen Radiance, or Infinitely Ascended Love-Bliss) Above The Total Crown Of the head—Is The Ultimate Yogic Form. Amrita Nadi (In Its By-Me-"Regenerated" Form) Is The Ultimate conditional (or Structural) Seat, Sign, and Divinely "Bright" Spiritual Body Of The Process Of Divine Translation (Into The Sphere, and Space, and Substance Of My "Bright" Divine Self-Domain).

The Only-By-Me Revealed and Given Seventh Stage Of Life Is The Final Process, In Which This Ultimate Yogic Form and The Most Ultimate Event Of Awakening Into My Divine Self-Domain Are Accomplished. And The Only-By-Me Revealed and Given Seventh Stage Of Life Begins With The Most Perfect (and Entirely By-My-Avataric-Divine-Grace-Given) Event Of Perfectly Subjective (Transcendental, Inherently Spiritual, Inherently egoless, Inherently Perfect, and Self-Evidently Divine) Self-Realization.

The Most Perfect Realization Of Perfectly Subjective Divine Self-Realization Is Not A Matter Of Identification With the essential inwardness of the Apparent, conditional, Separate, or Distinct individual self. The Most Perfect Realization Of Perfectly Subjective Divine Self-Realization Is Realization Of That Which Is Always Already (and Inherently egolessly—and, Altogether, Unconditionally) The Case. The Most Perfect Realization Of Perfectly Subjective Divine Self-Realization Is Inherent, and Inherently Most Perfect, and (Necessarily) Most Perfectly ego-Transcending Realization Of Me—Without The Concept Of "Difference".

Neither the conditional self Nor the conditional world (or the various conditionally Manifested relations of the conditional self) qualifies (or limits) The Realization Of Me In The Only-By-Me Revealed and Given Seventh Stage Of Life. Rather, both the (Apparent) conditional self and the (Apparent) conditional world Are Inherently (and Divinely) Self-Recognizable (or Inherently, Tacitly, and Inherently Most Perfectly Transcended) In The Case

Of That Realization. Because Of This, both the (Apparent) conditional world and the (Apparent) conditional self (Simply as Divinely Self-Recognized body-mind, Rather Than as ego, or Un-Recognized self-Contraction) May (Until Divine Translation) Continue (Apparently) To arise—and To arise in any form at all—Without limiting The By-My-Avataric-Divine-Grace-Given Seventh Stage Realization Of My Avatarically Self-Transmitted (and Self-Evidently Divine) Love-Bliss and The By-My-Avataric-Divine-Grace-Given Seventh Stage (and Most Perfectly Non-"Different") Demonstration Of My Avatarically Self-Revealed (and Self-Evidently Divine) Self-Condition.

To Abide (By Means Of My Avatarically Self-Transmitted Divine Grace) As My Self-Radiant (or Inherently Spiritual, and Divinely "Bright") and Self-Existing (or Transcendental, and Perfectly Subjective, and Inherently egoless, and Inherently Perfect, and Self-Evidently Divine) Self-Condition Of Being (Itself)—Which Is The Perfectly Subjective (and Self-Evidently Divine) Source-Condition Of The Totality Of (and every particularity of) all arising conditions and all conditionally Manifested beings—Is The Primary (or Seventh Stage), and Most Ultimate (or Complete, Final, Most Perfect, and Inherently Perfected), Yoga Of The Only-By-Me Revealed and Given Way Of The Heart (or Way Of Adidam). Nevertheless, As Long As the conditional body-mind and the conditional world Continue To (Apparently) arise, The By-My-Avataric-Divine-Grace-Given Seventh Stage "Conscious Process" Of Transcendental, Perfectly Subjective, Inherently Spiritual, Inherently egoless, and Inherently Perfect Divine Self-Abiding Will Be Spontaneously (and Necessarily) Associated With Divine Self-Recognition Of the conditions that (Apparently) arise. And Such Divine Self-Recognition Is Naturally Associated With (or Demonstrated Via) conditional Spirit-"Conductivity" (or The Secondary, or conditionally Manifested, Yoga—Demonstrated, Even Spontaneously, In The Context Of psycho-physical events). Therefore, This Natural Association Between The Yoga Of The "Conscious Process" (Which Directly Addresses the self-Contraction—or, Ultimately, The By-My-Avatarically-Transmitted-Divine-Grace-Revealed Divine Self-Condition) and The Yoga Of

"Conductivity" (or The Yoga Of psycho-physical events—Which, Eventually, By Means Of My Avatarically Self-Transmitted Divine Grace, Becomes Divine Spirit-"Conductivity") Also Characterizes The Only-By-Me Revealed and Given Way Of The Heart In <u>All</u> Its Inevitable (or, Otherwise, Potential) Processes and <u>All</u> Its Necessary (or, Otherwise, Potential) Practices, Previous To (As Well As Ever After) The Awakening Of The Only-By-Me Revealed and Given Seventh Stage Of Life.

II.

I Am (By All My Avataric Means) Spiritually Present—Divinely Blessing All and all By My Mere (and Always Blessing) Spiritual Presence.

My Avatarically Self-Manifested Divine Blessing-Work Is The Spiritual Transmission-Work (or Giving-Work) Of Hridaya (or Sri Hridayam)—The Divine Heart (Itself).

My Avatarically Self-Transmitted Divine Spiritual Presence <u>Is</u> Blessing-Work (or Ruchira Avatara Kripa[46])—The Spiritual Transmission (or Grace-Giving) Of My Free (and Inherently Spiritual) Divine Self-Radiance (or Divine Love-Bliss)—Which <u>Is</u> The "Bright" (Itself).

My Avataric Self-Transmission Of My Divine Spiritual Blessing (or Ruchira Avatara Kripa) Is Hridaya-Kripa—My Divine Self-Giving Of The Gift That <u>Is</u> The Inherently egoless "Bright" Divine Heart (Itself).

My Avataric Self-Manifestation Of My Divine Spiritual Transmission-Work (or Inherently Spiritual Blessing-Work) Is My Spiritual Transmission (or Divine Self-Giving) Of My Hridaya-Shakti—The Graceful Divine Heart-Power That <u>Is</u> The Inherently egoless "Bright" Divine Heart (Itself).

My Always Me-Revealing Initiatory Avataric Spiritual Blessing (Whereby My Listening Devotees and My Hearing Devotees Are Given The Grace Of True Devotion To Me, By Feeling My Divine "Brightness"), and My Always Merely Present Avataric "Act" Of Divine Spiritual Baptism (Whereby My Seeing Devotees Are Awakened To By-Me-Spiritually-Activated, and Always Me-

Revealing, Heart-Practice and Heart-Realization), Is Hridaya-Shakti-Kripa (or Hridaya-Shaktipat)—My Initiatory Avataric Giving Of My Perfectly Attractive and Inherently Love-Blissful Grace-Power (Which Is The Divine Grace-Power Of The Inherently egoless Heart, Itself).

Hridaya-Shakti-Kripa (or Hridaya-Shaktipat) Is Avatarically (and Uniquely) Given By Me—The Very, and Avatarically Self-Manifested, and Divinely Self-Revealing, and Transcendental, and Perfectly Subjective, and Inherently Spiritual, and Inherently egoless, and Inherently Perfect, and Self-Evidently Divine Person, Who Is The Inherently egoless "Bright" Divine Heart (Itself), or The Self-Existing, and Self-Radiant, and Inherently egoless Divine Self-Condition (Itself), Which Is The Self-Evidently Divine Source-Condition Of All and all.

My Avatarically Self-Transmitted Divine Hridaya-Shakti (or The Perfectly Subjective Divine Heart-Power That Is The Inherently egoless "Bright" Divine Heart Itself, and By Means Of Which I Awaken, In My True Devotee, The, Eventually, Most Perfect Realization Of My Avatarically Self-Revealed Transcendental, Inherently Spiritual, and Self-Evidently Divine Self-Condition Itself) Originates Eternally Prior To The Cosmic Mandala, and Eternally Prior To The Circle (or The "Circular" Pattern Of The Combined Frontal, or Descending, Line and Spinal, or Ascending, Line) Of the Cosmically-Patterned body-mind, and Eternally Prior To The Arrow (or The breathless and Moveless, but Upwardly Polarized, Central Axis)[47] Of the Cosmically-Patterned body-mind.

Therefore, My Avatarically Self-Transmitted (and Perfectly Subjectively Me-Revealing) Divine Hridaya-Shakti-Kripa (or Hridaya-Shaktipat) Is Senior (and Most Perfectly Prior) To conditional (or conventional Yogic) Shaktipat (or Spiritual Transmission That Originates Dependently—or As A Merely conditionally-Arising, and Manifestly Objective, Cosmic Power—Within The Cosmic Mandala, and Within The Circle, and The Arrow, Of the Cosmically-Patterned body-mind).

Conditional (or conventional, and Merely conditionally, or Cosmically, Arising) Yogic Shaktipat and conventional (and Merely conditionally, or Cosmically, Significant) Yogic Practices Are

Intended (or, Altogether, Activated) To Stimulate <u>Movements</u> Of attention In The Circle (and the Arrow) Of the Cosmically-Patterned (and ego-Based) body-mind, and (Thereby) To Accomplish Various conditional (or Cosmic, and ego-Bound) Goals (Whether By Descent Or By Ascent Of The Manifestly Objective Cosmic Power).

My Avatarically Self-Transmitted Divine Hridaya-Shakti-Kripa (or Hridaya-Shaktipat) and The (Thereby) Spiritually Initiated <u>Divine</u> Yogic Practice Of The Only-By-Me Revealed and Given Way Of Adidam (Which Is The One and Only By-Me-Revealed and By-Me-Given Way Of The Heart) Are Inherently Disposed (or By-Me-Heart-Founded and By-Me-Heart-Empowered) To Directly <u>Dissolve</u> (and, At Last, To Most Perfectly Transcend) attention itself (In My Avatarically Self-Revealed, and Transcendental, and Perfectly Subjective, and Inherently Spiritual, and Inherently ego-less, and Inherently Perfect, and Self-Evidently Divine Person and Self-Condition).

Therefore, Whereas conditional (or conventional Yogic) Shaktipat and conventional Yogic Practices Actively Seek conditional Goals Of attention (In or Above The Circle, and The Arrow, Of the Cosmically-Patterned body-mind), My Avatarically Self-Transmitted Divine Hridaya-Shakti-Kripa (or Hridaya-Shaktipat) Directly Reveals (and, Subsequently, The Thereby Spiritually Initiated Practice Of The Only-By-Me Revealed and Given Way Of The Heart Directly, and, At Last, Most Perfectly, Realizes) Me (The Perfectly Subjective Person, and Self-Evidently Divine Self-Condition, Of The Heart—Eternally Prior To attention, mind, body, The Circle, The Arrow, and <u>all</u> conditionally Manifested worlds). And The (Eventual) Most Perfect Realization Of Me Is The Most Perfect Realization Of The Only-By-Me Revealed and Given Divine Heart-Way (Which Is, At Last, To Stand <u>As Is</u>, Prior To Every Kind Of Seeking, and Prior To Any and All Movements Of attention, and Prior Even To <u>attention itself</u>—which is, itself, the Tacit ego-"I", or The Primal Act Of self-Contraction, Appearing As The Root-Feeling Of Relatedness Itself, or The Tacit Feeling Of "Difference" Itself).

My Avatarically Self-Transmitted Divine Hridaya-Shakti-Kripa (or Hridaya-Shaktipat), and The Subsequent (Spiritually Activated)

Only-By-Me Revealed and Given Heart-Practice Generated By It, and (Altogether) The Spiritually Me-Revealing Spiritual Activity Of My Avatarically Self-Transmitted Spirit-Current (Always Moving In The Horizontal Plane Of The Heart—and, Principally, Made Effective By Descent Into The Cosmically-Patterned body-mind, From Infinitely Above), and The Only-By-Me Revealed and Given Heart-Realization Progressively Awakened (and, At Last, Most Perfectly Awakened) By It, Are Senior (and Most Perfectly Prior) To All Merely Cosmically-Oriented (and Merely conditionally, and Temporarily Effective—and, Thus, Merely egoically Significant) Spirit-"Conductivity" In The Circle (and The Arrow) Of the Cosmically-Patterned body-mind, and Senior (and Most Perfectly Prior) To All conditionally Manifested Activities Of The Merely Cosmic (or Kundalini) Shakti, and Senior (and Most Perfectly Prior) To All Merely conditionally Evident Processes and Events In The Upper and Lower Regions Of the Cosmically-Patterned body-mind. And My Avatarically Self-Transmitted Divine Hridaya-Shakti-Kripa (or Hridaya-Shaktipat), and The Subsequent (Spiritually Activated) Only-By-Me Revealed and Given Heart-Practice Generated By It, and (Altogether) The Spiritually Me-Revealing Spiritual Activity Of My Avatarically Self-Transmitted Spirit-Current, and The Only-By-Me Revealed and Given Heart-Realization Progressively (and, At Last, Most Perfectly) Awakened By It, Directly and Inherently Transcend Even All conditionally (or Cosmically) experiential Possibilities (Even Though They Do Not Otherwise Exclude, or Strategically Prevent, Them).

Objective Shakti (or Any Form or Mode Of Spiritual Energy Felt, or Perceived, or Experienced In Relation To one's body-mind, or Even In Apparent Relation To Consciousness Itself) arises (Thus, Objectively) Only If the Cosmic world and the Cosmically-Patterned body-mind arise.

There Is No Objective Shakti To Be Felt, or Perceived, or Experienced, Unless the Cosmically-Patterned psycho-physical point of view arises—To Feel, or Perceive, or Experience It.

There Is No Objective Shakti To Be Found, Unless a conditional point of view (or a point of self-Contraction, or an Otherwise conditionally limited point Of Reference) Is Presumed.

There Is No <u>Objective</u> Shakti To Be "Located" In Relation To one's body-mind (or Even In Apparent Relation To Consciousness Itself) If The Root-Feeling (or, Necessarily, conditional Presumption) Of Relatedness Is Not Generated (and Identified With, or Otherwise—At Least Apparently, or As a convention Of Apparent conditional Existence—Presumed).

The True, Ultimate, and Inherently Perfect (and Self-Evidently <u>Divine</u>) Shakti Is My Avataric Self-Revelation Of My Self-Existing and Self-Radiant "Bright" (and <u>Perfectly</u> <u>Subjective</u>) Divine Love-Bliss, Which Is Native To The Inherently egoless Heart Itself (or Perfectly Subjective, and Non-Separate, and Non-"Different", Consciousness Itself—Realized As The Feeling Of Being, Itself).

<u>Only</u> <u>That</u> (Only-By-Me Avatarically Self-Transmitted, and Perfectly Real and True, and Perfectly Ultimate, and Inherently Perfect, and Self-Evidently <u>Divine</u>) <u>Shakti</u> (or Self-Existing and Self-Radiant "Bright" Divine Feeling-Energy, or <u>Perfectly</u> <u>Subjective</u> Divine Spiritual Fullness) Is "Hridaya-Shakti".

That Only-By-Me Avatarically Self-Transmitted (and Self-Evidently Divine) Hridaya-Shakti Is Senior To (and Perfectly Subjective To) The Cosmically-Objectified Kundalini Shakti.

The Kundalini Shakti Is Always Objective—or Felt, or Perceived, or Experienced In Relation To the Apparent (and Apparently personal) body-mind, and In Either The gross Context Or The subtle Context Of the conditional (or Cosmically-Patterned) world. Therefore, The Kundalini Shakti Itself (As Objective Energy) arises conditionally, and Its Manifestation Is Entirely Dependent On Cosmic (or psycho-physical, and, Altogether, conditional) Events.

Only My Avatarically Self-Transmitted Divine Hridaya-Shakti—Which Is Perfectly (or Always Most Priorly) Subjective (or Only In The Inherently egoless Subject-Position, or Non-Separate Heart-Position), and Which Is, Therefore, Identical <u>Only</u> To <u>Unconditional</u> (or Self-Evidently Divine) Existence (or Most Perfectly Prior Being) Itself—Stands Always Already Prior To The Root-Feeling (or Primal conditional Feeling) Of Relatedness Itself (and, Therefore, Always Already Prior To The Cosmic Domain, the Cosmically-Patterned body-mind-self, and conditional, or Cosmically-Manifested, Existence Itself).

My Avatarically Self-Transmitted (and Always Only Me-Revealing) Spiritual Blessing (By Which I Divinely Bless All and all) Is My Divine Self-Giving Of My Hridaya-Shakti—The Inherent (and Inherently Spiritual, and Perfectly Transcendental, and Self-Evidently Divine) "Brightness" (or Self-Existing and Self-Radiant Love-Bliss) Of The (Perfectly Subjective, and Inherently egoless) Heart Itself. And those who Truly and Fully Receive My Avatarically Self-Transmitted Spiritual Blessing (or Avatarically Self-Transmitted Divine Hridaya-Shaktipat) Are (Thus and Thereby) Directly Awakened (In Due Course) To Stable Identification With The Native Witness-Position Of Consciousness Itself (Which Is The Perfectly Subjective, and Inherently egoless, "Position" Of The Inherently egoless Heart Itself) and, Thus and Thereby, To The Inherently Perfect Practice Of The Only-By-Me Revealed and Given Way Of The Heart (In The Context Of The Sixth Stage Of Life, and, Most Ultimately, In The Context Of The Only-By-Me Revealed and Given Seventh Stage Of Life).

The (Always Objective and Cosmic) Kundalini Shakti arises (or Shows Itself As Various Effects) In The Context Of Any or All Of The First Five Stages Of Life.

My Avatarically Given (and Always Perfectly Subjective, and Self-Evidently Divine) Hridaya-Shakti Always Simply Stands As Itself (Identical To My Avatarically Given Divine Self-Revelation Of The Inherently egoless, or Non-Separate and Non-"Different", Feeling Of Being, Itself—Always Most Perfectly Prior To All Apparent Objectivity).

To Feel, or Perceive, or Experience The Kundalini Shakti Is Necessarily To Be Moved (Thereby) Everywhere Within The Cosmically-Extended Context Of conditional Existence (and Only Within The ego-Based Context Of The First Five Stages Of Life)—but (By Means Of My Avatarically Self-Transmitted Divine Grace) To "Locate" My Avatarically Self-Transmitted Divine Hridaya-Shakti Is (Progressively) To Directly, Spontaneously, and (In Due Course) Inherently Perfectly Transcend All Of The First Five Stages Of Life (and, At Last, Even All Of Cosmic, or conditional, Existence Itself).

Therefore, My Most True (or Truly Mature) Devotees Do Not Seek Any Cosmically-limited (and ego-Binding) "Effects" Of My

Avatarically Self-Revealed Divine Spiritual Presence. They Do Not Strive To Linger In The Cosmic Domain. They Do Not Wish To Prolong The Course Of The Practice Of The Way Of The Heart In The Context Of The First Five Stages Of Life. They Do Not Incline themselves To Dote Upon Any Objectified (or conditional) Feeling, or Perception, or Experience Of My Avatarically Self-Revealed Divine Spiritual Presence.

My Most True (or Truly Mature) Devotees Are Devoted Only To <u>Me</u>—<u>As</u> I <u>Am</u>. They Are Not "Concerned" About Kundalini Experiences (Even If These arise)—but they Are <u>Always</u> Heart-Moved To Utterly Surrender, Forget, and Transcend self-Contraction (and, Therefore, all of Cosmically-Patterned body-mind, and All Of Cosmic "Play", and All Of conditional, or Merely Cosmic, and ego-Bound, Existence Itself).

Therefore, My Most True (or Truly Mature) Fully Practicing Devotees Are those who Benefit The Most (and Most Directly) From My Avatarically Self-Transmitted Divine Spiritual Blessing (or Avatarically Self-Transmitted Divine Hridaya-Shaktipat). And they Are (Thereby) Directly (At The Heart) Relieved Of All Seeking. And they Do Not Surrender, Forget, and Transcend self-Contraction, the body-mind, the conditional world, and Cosmic (or conditional) Existence By Means Of The Strategic (or ego-Bound) Efforts Of Great Seeking. Rather, they Are Spontaneously Moved To Inherently Perfect Surrender, and Inherently Perfect Forgetting, and Inherently Perfect Transcending Of self-Contraction, and Of Cosmically-Patterned body-mind, and Of conditional (or Merely Cosmic) world, and Of conditional (or Merely Cosmic, and ego-Bound) Existence—Simply By Feeling (and Thereby Contemplating) <u>Me</u> (and, Thus, By Yielding Utterly To The Inherently Perfect Attractiveness Of My Heart-Perfect Avatarically-Born Bodily Human Divine Form, My Avatarically Self-Revealed, and Blessing-Perfect, Divine Spiritual Presence, and My Avatarically Self-Revealed, and Very, and Transcendental, and Perfectly Subjective, and Inherently Spiritual, and Inherently ego-less, and Inherently Perfect, and Self-Evidently Divine State).

The Only-By-Me Revealed and Given Way Of The Heart (or Way Of Adidam) Is (Progressively) The Divine Heart-Way Of The

"Conscious Process" (or Direct Heart-Release Of the self-Contraction), Realized (Most Ultimately) To The Degree Of Inherent Love-Bliss-Radiance (or The Realization Of My Avatarically Self-Revealed, and Perfectly Subjective, and Inherently egoless, and Inherently Perfect, and Self-Evidently Divine Spirit-"Brightness"—Which Realization Is, Itself, Inherently Most Perfect, Unconditional, and Transcendentally-Awakened Divine Spirit-"Conductivity").

Conventional (or ego-Based) Paths Depend On Mere Cosmic conditions (or, Otherwise, Seek To Strategically Exclude Cosmic conditions, and, By Means Of That Strategy, Bypass The Necessary Ordeal Of ego-Transcendence In The Context Of Cosmic conditions). The Only-By-Me Revealed and Given Way Of The Heart (or Way Of Adidam) Is The Divine Heart-Way—The Way That (Inherently, Spontaneously, and Progressively, or, More and More Effectively, and Truly Counter-egoically) Observes, Understands, Changes, Releases, and Directly Transcends (and, At Last, Most Perfectly, or Inherently, and Divinely, Self-Recognizes, Transfigures, Transforms, and Translates) Cosmic conditions In My Avatarically Self-Revealed Unconditional (and Perfectly Subjective, and Self-Evidently Divine) Self-Condition.

The Only-By-Me Revealed and Given Way Of The Heart (or Way Of Adidam) Is The Divine Heart-Way Of The Divine Consciousness (Itself). The Divine Consciousness (Itself) Is The Master Of Its Own Divine Spiritual Energy (and Of Even all Apparent, or conditionally Manifested, energies). Therefore, Whereas conventional (or ego-Based) Paths Manipulate the conditional self and the conditionally Manifested energies Of Cosmic Nature (or Even The Spiritual Energy Of The egoically Presumed Divine) In A Search For The Eventual Attainment Of The Great (Divine, and Would-Be-egoless) Principle—I Call You To Directly Realize The Great (Divine, and Inherently egoless) Principle, By Means Of ego-Transcending Devotional Recognition-Response To My Avatarically Self-Revealed Person (and, Altogether, To My Avatarically Self-Transmitted Divine Grace), and To Do So At The Very Foundation (and From The Very Beginning) Of The Only-By-Me Revealed and Given Way Of The Heart (or Way Of Adidam).

I Call (and Bless) You (Even From The Beginning Of Your Practice Of The Only-By-Me Revealed and Given Way Of The Heart) To Directly Realize (or To Be, By Means Of My Avatarically Self-Transmitted Divine Grace, Always Directly Awakened To) The Great (Divine, and Inherently egoless) Principle That Is My Avatarically Given Divine Self-Revelation Of The Perfectly Subjective Heart (Itself). From The Beginning Of Your Practice Of The Only-By-Me Revealed and Given Way Of The Heart, I Call (and Bless) You To Realize (or To Be, By Means Of My Avatarically Self-Transmitted Divine Grace, Always Directly Awakened To) The Perfectly Subjective (and Inherently egoless) Heart Itself By (First) Listening To Me (and "Considering" My Avatarically Self-Revealed, and Ever-Working, Divine Word and Story Of Heart-Instructing, Heart-Inspiring, and Heart-Purifying Teaching-Arguments and Intrusions) and (Then) Hearing Me—and, Therefore, To Progressively (and Then Most Fundamentally) Understand self-Contraction, and To (Thus and Thereby) Progressively (and Then Most Fundamentally) Undermine and Transcend self-Contraction, Through Devotionally Me-Recognizing, and Devotionally To-Me-Responsive, and Always ego-Surrendering, and Really ego-Forgetting, and Entirely ego-Releasing (and, Necessarily, body-mind-Purifying) Feeling-Contemplation Of My Avatarically-Born Bodily (Human) Divine Form, and My Avatarically Self-Revealed Spiritual (and Always Blessing) Divine Presence, and My Avatarically Self-Revealed (and Very, and Transcendental, and Perfectly Subjective, and Inherently Spiritual, and Inherently ego-less, and Inherently Perfect, and Self-Evidently) Divine State. And (When You Have Heard Me, and When You Have Effectively Demonstrated That True Hearing) I Call (and Bless) You To Realize (or To Be, By Means Of My Avatarically Self-Transmitted Divine Grace, Always Directly Awakened To) My Perfectly Subjective Heart (or State) Itself, By Seeing Me—and, Thus and Thereby, To Continue To Directly Transcend self-Contraction In every moment (and, As Necessary, In The Context Of All Of The Advanced and The Ultimate Stages Of Life), Not Only Through The Continued Enforcement Of Most Fundamental self-Understanding, but (More and More) Through The Free

Devotional (or Heart-Attracted and Heart-Awakened and Directly ego-Transcending) Recognition-Response To My Avatarically Given Divine Self-Revelation Of The Spiritual, Transcendental, and Self-Evidently Divine Forms Of Reality, or Truth, or Real God.

From the point of view of the Cosmically-Patterned body (and ego-mind), The Inherent Self-Radiance Of Self-Existing Divine Being Is <u>perceived</u> To Be An Objective (Universal and All-Pervading) Cosmic Spirit-Energy (or Cosmic Shakti)—Which Is Always At Work, Moving (and Modifying) the world, the body, and the mind (and Even Binding attention, By Those Very Movements, and To Those Very Modifications).

From The Divinely Self-Realized (and Inherently egoless) "Point Of View" Of Consciousness Itself (Which <u>Is</u> The Inherently egoless Heart Itself—Avatarically Self-Revealed, By Me, <u>As</u> My Self-Existing and Self-Radiant Divine Self-Condition, Itself), Even The Apparently Objective (Universal and All-Pervading) Cosmic Spirit-Energy (or Cosmic Shakti) Is Divinely Self-Recognized (and Inherently, and Inherently Most Perfectly, Transcended) In My Avatarically Given Divine Self-Revelation Of The Merely (or Only) and Perfectly Moveless "Bright" Self-Radiance (or Inherent Love-Bliss) Of Consciousness Itself (Which <u>Is</u> My Avatarically Self-Revealed Eternal—and Not Cosmic, but Perfectly Subjective—Divine Self-Condition Itself).

Therefore, My Ultimate (or Inherently Perfect) Avataric Blessing Is My Avataric Spiritual Transmission (and, Thereby, Direct Awakening) Of The Inherent (Self-Existing, and Self-Radiant) Condition (or Eternal State) Of Self-Evidently Divine Being—Which Is My Avatarically Given Divine Self-Revelation Of The (Inherently) Perfectly Subjective (and Inherently egoless) Heart (or Self-Existing and Self-Radiant Inherent Space) Of Consciousness Itself (Eternally Moveless, <u>As</u> My "Bright" Divine Love-Bliss, Itself).

My (Thus) Inherently Perfect Avataric Blessing Is My Avataric Spiritual Transmission Of My (Thus and Thereby) Avatarically Self-Revealed (and Very, and Transcendental, and Perfectly Subjective, and Inherently Spiritual, and Inherently egoless, and Inherently Perfect, and Perfectly Moveless, and Self-Evidently Divine) State

(Itself)—Which Is The Original, Primary, and Ultimate Form Of My Avatarically Me-Revealing Divine Spiritual Transmission. And, To Receive The Transmission Of My Avatarically Self-Revealed (and Very, and Transcendental, and Perfectly Subjective, and Inherently Spiritual, and Inherently egoless, and Inherently Perfect, and Self-Evidently Divine) State Is To Commune With Me (As I Am), Non-Separately (or Beyond "Difference"), In The "Place" Of Consciousness Itself, Beyond All psycho-physical Noticing.

My (Thus) Inherently Perfect (and Self-Evidently Divine) Avataric Blessing Is My Fundamental, and Direct, and Constant Avataric Spiritual Transmission. Therefore, My Fundamental (and Direct, and Constant) Avataric Spiritual Transmission Is My Avataric Spiritual Transmission Of My Very, and Transcendental, and Perfectly Subjective, and Inherently Spiritual, and Inherently ego-less, and Inherently Perfect, and Self-Evidently Divine State Itself— Even In The Case Of All My Listening Devotees, and All My Hearing Devotees, and All My Seeing Devotees. And All those who (In The Context Of The Total, or Full and Complete, Formal Practice Of The Only-By-Me Revealed and Given Way Of The Heart) Receive Me Perfectly Become (In Due Course) My Inherently Perfect Devotees.

The Devotee-Receiver Of My Avatarically Self-Transmitted Divine Spiritual Blessing (Whether As My Listening Devotee, Or My Hearing Devotee, Or My Seeing Devotee) Will Receive My Heart-Blessing Only According To his or her Real Present (and Formally Acknowledged) Stage Of Life (and Developmental Stage, or moment, Of Formal Practice) In The Only-By-Me Revealed and Given Way Of The Heart—and My Heart-Blessing Will (Therefore) Always Be perceived To Reveal Me Accordingly.

Therefore, My Avatarically Self-Revealed Divine Heart-Blessing Will (Necessarily) Appear (or Be Revealed) By Progressive Stages.

First (Via My Avatarically Self-Revealed Divine Word, and My Avatarically Self-Manifested Historical Play Of Divine Work, and My Always Giving and Revealing Avatarically-Born Bodily Human Divine Form), I Am (Now, and Forever Hereafter) At Work To Attract and To Guide and To Instruct My Listening Devotee.

In This Manner (and In Due Course), I Awaken Most Fundamental self-Understanding In My (Thus, Hearing) Devotee.

Eventually (When My Fully Practicing Devotee Both Hears Me and Sees Me), I Appear (Most Fully) As and By Means Of My Avatarically Self-Transmitted Divine Spirit-Current Of "Bright" Love-Bliss—psycho-physically perceived To Be Moving In the world, and the body, and the mind (and, Thus and Thereby, Purifying and Absorbing the world, the body, and the mind As I Move).

Nevertheless, I Am (All The While—and, Really, Only) Standing Free.

Even From The Beginning Of This Avatarically Me-Revealing Course, I Am My Avatarically Self-Revealed (and Very, and Eternal, and Transcendental, and Perfectly Subjective, and Inherently Spiritual, and Inherently egoless, and Inherently Perfect, and Self-Evidently Divine) State—Which Always Already (and Only) Stands Self-Radiant As The (Inherently, and Non-Separately, and Non-"Differently") Perfectly Subjective (and Inherently egoless) Heart (Itself).

Therefore, Only The (Inherently, and Non-Separately, and Non-"Differently") Perfectly Subjective (and Inherently Spiritual, and Inherently egoless) Condition That Is My Avatarically Self-Revealed, and Self-Transmitted, and Self-Evidently Divine Heart (Itself) Is The Great Principle Of My Avatarically Self-Manifested Divine Spiritual Blessing-Work.

Only The Non-Separate, and Non-"Different", and Perfectly Subjective (and Transcendental, and Inherently Spiritual, and Inherently egoless, and Self-Evidently Divine) Condition Is (Inherently, and Self-Evidently) Perfect.

The (Inherently, and Non-Separately, and Non-"Differently") Perfectly Subjective (and Transcendental, and Inherently Spiritual, and Inherently egoless) Heart (Itself) Is The Inherently Perfect (and Inherently Spiritual, and Inherently egoless) Position (or State) Of Free (and Self-Evidently Divine) Consciousness (Itself).

The (Inherently, and Non-Separately, and Non-"Differently") Perfectly Subjective (and Transcendental, and Inherently Spiritual, and Inherently egoless) Heart (Itself) Is The Inherent (and Self-Evidently Divine) Feeling Of Being (Which Is The Perfect, Itself).

The (Inherently, and Non-Separately, and Non-"Differently") Perfectly Subjective (and Transcendental, and Inherently Spiritual, and Inherently egoless, and Inherently Perfect, and Self-Evidently Divine) Heart (Itself) Is My "Bright" Divine Self-Domain (Itself).

Therefore, By Practicing The Total (or Full and Complete) Practice Of The Only-By-Me Revealed and Given Way Of The Heart (or Way Of Adidam)—You Must (By Means Of My Avatarically Self-Transmitted Divine Grace) Grow To Realize The Only-By-Me Revealed and Given Great Practice That Is (By Means Of My Avatarically Self-Transmitted Divine Grace) Generated (Inherently, and Non-Separately, and Non-"Differently") As and At and From The Perfectly Subjective (and Transcendental, and Inherently Spiritual, and Inherently egoless, and Inherently Perfect, and Self-Evidently Divine) Position Of The Heart (Itself).

And I Am Your "Bright" Divine Companion, Avatarically Descended here—Until You Receive and Realize Me Most Perfectly, There ("Where" and As I Always Already Am).

III.

Even Though The Total (or Full and Complete) Practice Of The Only-By-Me Revealed and Given Way Of Adidam (Which Is The One and Only By-Me-Revealed and By-Me-Given Way Of The Heart) Is Primarily A Matter Of The "Conscious Process" (and The Realization, Most Ultimately, Of My Avatarically Self-Revealed, and Transcendental, and Perfectly Subjective, and Inherently Spiritual, and Inherently egoless, and Inherently Perfect, and Self-Evidently Divine Self-Condition), The Full (and Fully Fruitful) Practice Of The Only-By-Me Revealed and Given Way Of The Heart (or Way Of Adidam) Also (Secondarily, but, Nevertheless, Necessarily) Requires The Constant Establishment Of attention (and the Total body-mind) In My Avatarically Self-Transmitted Divine Spirit-Energy—Because My Avatarically Self-Revealed, and Transcendental, and Perfectly Subjective, and Inherently Spiritual, and Inherently egoless, Inherently Perfect, and Self-Evidently Divine Self-Condition Itself Is Both Transcendental (or Self-Existing, Prior To conditional Existence) and Inherently Spiritual (or "Brightly" Self-Existing, As Self-Radiant Energy, or Love-Bliss).

In Order For attention To Be Constantly Established In My Avatarically Self-Transmitted Divine Spirit-Energy, You Must Become My Seeing Devotee. And, In Order To Prepare Yourself To See Me, You Must (As My Listening Devotee, and, Eventually, As My Hearing Devotee) Consistently Practice The Primary By Me Given Gift, Calling, and Discipline Of Ruchira Avatara Bhakti Yoga—Which Is The Responsive (or Devotionally Me-Recognizing, and Devotionally To-Me-Responding) and Constantly (and Really Effectively) Counter-egoic, and Total psycho-physical, Effort Of ego-Surrendering, ego-Forgetting, and, More and More (and, Ultimately, Most Perfectly), ego-Transcending Devotion To Me (and Devotional Communion With Me), The Ruchira Avatar, Adi Da Samraj (The Divine Heart-Master Of Each and All Of My Devotees), and Which Is The moment to moment Fulfillment Of My Great Admonition To All My Devotees (To Always Invoke Me, Feel Me, Breathe Me, and Serve Me), and This Constantly Exercised Via The Surrender, The Forgetting, and The Transcending Of the self-Contracted body, and self-Contracted emotion (or all of self-Contracted, and reactive, and, Altogether, limited, feeling), and self-Contracted mind (Even At its Root, Which Is attention itself), and Even every self-Contracted breath, and, Altogether, Even all of Separate (and Separative) self, In moment to moment (and Truly, or Unlimitedly, Heart-Felt, and Whole bodily Receptive, and Fully breathing, and Only-By-Me Distracted) Devotional Remembrance Of Me and Direct Devotional Surrender To Me (In All Its Details, Including All The functional, practical, and relational Disciplines, and All The Cultural Obligations, I Have Given To My Fully Practicing Devotees). And, In Order To See Me, You Must (As My Listening Devotee, and, In Due Course, As My Hearing Devotee) Practice Each and Every Aspect Of Ruchira Avatara Bhakti Yoga—In The Manner I Have Specifically Indicated For My Listening and (Then) Hearing Devotees.

In Every Stage Of The Total (or Full and Complete) Practice Of The Only-By-Me Revealed and Given Way Of The Heart (or Way Of Adidam), The Practice Of Ruchira Avatara Bhakti Yoga Involves The Yielding (or The Surrender) Of The Principal Faculties (Of body, emotion, mind, and breath) To Me. In The Beginner's

Process, This Yielding Of The Principal Faculties To Me Can Show Signs Of Devotionally Absorptive Samadhi (or Spiritual Receptivity) Of One Kind or Another. But My (Even Fully Practicing) Beginning Devotees Are Not Yet Fully (and Most Profoundly) Responsible For Receiving and Conducting My Spirit-Blessing—and (Therefore) My Calling To My Fully Practicing Beginning Devotees Is, Specifically, My Call (To them) To Demonstrate (and To Constantly Magnify) The Signs Of Devotionally Me-Recognizing Devotional Response To Me (Including Exemplary Fulfillment Of The Various functional, practical, and relational Disciplines, and The Various Cultural Obligations, That Are Particular To their Developmental Stage Of Practice Of The Only-By-Me Revealed and Given Way Of The Heart).

All Of The By-Me-Revealed and By-Me-Given functional, practical, and relational Disciplines Are Forms Of "Conductivity"—and (As Such) They (All) Serve To Constantly Bring the body-mind Into The Condition Of Energy, Relieving My Devotee Of The Presumption That the body-mind Is Merely self-Contracted matter (fleshy, anxious, and Inevitably Suffering). And The Primary and Constant By-Me-Revealed and By-Me-Given Means For Bringing (or Yielding) the body-mind To The Condition Of Energy Is To Yield the body-mind To The Condition Of Ecstasy In Devotionally Me-Recognizing and Devotionally To-Me-Responsive Communion With Me (Divinely Self-Revealed, By All My Avataric Means). Therefore, For You (As My Truly Devotionally Me-Recognizing, and Truly Devotionally To-Me-Responding, Devotee) To Bring (or Yield) the body-mind To The Condition Of Energy, You Must Be Truly (Devotionally, and Counter-egoically) Given Over To Me—No Longer Existing In An egoically self-Conscious and egoically self-Controlling Mode, No Longer Preoccupied With The "Narcissistic" Exercise Of Your Own body-mind, and No Longer Armoring Yourself Against Me, but (Instead) Always Whole-bodily-Surrendering Your egoic self, Whole-bodily-Forgetting Your egoic self, and (More and More) Whole-bodily-Transcending Your egoic self, To The Point Of Whole bodily (and Truly ego-Transcending) Devotional Absorption In Me.

You Must (As My Truly Devotionally Me-Recognizing, and Truly Devotionally To-Me-Responding, Devotee) Exercise The

Divine Spiritual Baptism Versus Cosmic Spiritual Baptism

Practice Of Ruchira Avatara Bhakti Yoga moment to moment—Such That Your entire life Becomes ego-Surrendering, ego-Forgetting, and (More and More) ego-Transcending Devotion To Me, and Devotional Communion With Me, and Devotional Ecstasy In Me. If You Truly Do This (As My Listening Devotee, and, In Due Course, As My Hearing Devotee), You Will Find (In Due Course) That—By Consistently (and Fully Devotionally) Yielding (physically, emotionally, With attention, and With the breath) To My Avatarically Self-Revealed, and Self-Evidently Divine, Person (and To The Degree Of Whole bodily Energy-Ecstasy)—You Have Become Prepared To Make The Great Discovery (and Allow The Great Reception) Of My Avatarically Self-Revealed (and Love-Blissful, and Constantly Baptizing) Divine Spirit-Presence.

The Principal Sign Of Fullest Preparedness For The Seeing Stages Of Practice Of The Only-By-Me Revealed and Given Way Of The Heart (or Way Of Adidam) Is The Capability To Identify Me Spiritually (and To "Locate" Me Spiritually) moment to moment. But There Are Also Secondary Signs Of Preparedness For The Seeing Stages Of Practice Of The Only-By-Me Revealed and Given Way Of The Heart—Which Are The Various Signs Of Spiritually Receiving Me, or The Signs That The Principal Faculties (Of body, emotion, mind, and breath) Are Being Spiritually Infused By Me. (And The Necessity Of Adapting The Entire psycho-physical Vehicle Of the body-mind, With All its Faculties, To The Condition Of Openness and Receptivity To The Great Energy Of My Avatarically Self-Transmitted Divine Spiritual Heart-Transmission Is One Of The Principal Reasons Why The Only-By-Me Revealed and Given Yoga Of Ruchira Avatara Bhakti Is Practiced From The Very Beginning Of The Way Of The Heart, and Continues To Be Practiced Throughout The Entire Course Of The Total, or Full and Complete, Practice Of The Way Of The Heart.)

When All The psycho-physical Faculties Are Yielded To Me, and Devotionally (and Truly Counter-egoically) Absorbed In My Avatarically Self-Revealed (and Self-Evidently Divine) Person (and, Thereby, Yielded To The Condition Of Energy, Such That My Devotee Truly Receives My Avatarically Self-Transmitted Divine Spiritual Blessing), Then the body-mind Receives (Via All its

221

Faculties) A <u>Forceful</u> Infusion Of My Divine Spiritual Energy (The Force Of Which Is, At First, Far Greater Than The Force Of the Natural life-energy that the body-mind Is Accustomed To Circulating). By Virtue Of The Process Of Preparation Engaged During The Listening and Hearing Stages Of Practice Of The Way Of The Heart, the body-mind Of My (Thus) Newly Seeing Devotee Is Able To Conduct The Force Of My Avatarically Self-Transmitted Divine Spiritual Blessing (and The Heart Of My Thus Newly Seeing Devotee Is, Also, Always Able To "Locate" Me, Spiritually)—but (Because the body-mind Of My Newly Seeing Devotee Is Not Yet, Altogether, Adapted To Receive Me With Such Force), When the body-mind Of My Newly Seeing Devotee Receives The Great Force Of My Avatarically Self-Transmitted Divine Spiritual Blessing, the entire body (and Even the Total body-mind) Of My Newly Seeing Devotee "Shakes".

Thus, the physical body Of My Newly Seeing Devotee Moves (or "Shakes") In Various Spontaneous Ways. And the emotion Of My Newly Seeing Devotee Undergoes A Profound Feeling-Expansion. And the attention Of My Newly Seeing Devotee Becomes Deeply Established In My Love-Bliss-Transmission. And the breath Of My Newly Seeing Devotee Undergoes Various Spontaneous Changes. Indeed, A Wide Variety Of Spontaneously Purifying experiences (or kriyas of body, emotion, mind, and breath) Are Possible In the body-mind Of My Newly Seeing Devotee. And There Are Different (and Varying) Signs In Each individual Case. And It Is Not Possible For My Any Newly Seeing Devotee To Truly Receive Me Spiritually Without Being "Shaken" (In body, emotion, attention, and/or breath)—Because The Vehicle Of the body-mind Of My Newly Seeing Devotee Is Not (At First) Capable Of "Containing" The Fullest Infusion Of My Avatarically Self-Transmitted Divine Spiritual Force. Therefore, the body-mind Of My Newly Seeing Devotee (With All its Faculties) "Shakes", Moves, and Experiences All Kinds Of Spontaneous Changes—and It Is <u>My</u> Avatarically Self-Transmitted Divine Spiritual Intrusion That Makes These Movements and Changes In the body-mind Of My Newly Seeing Devotee.

This Great Reception Of My Avatarically Self-Revealed (and Overwhelming) Divine Spirit-Presence (Such That The Faculties

Are Thus "Shaken") Is A Necessary Sign That My Devotee Has Truly Heard Me—and, In Truly Hearing Me, Has (By Practicing Ruchira Avatara Bhakti Yoga To The Point Of Profundity) Out-Grown The egoically self-Conscious and egoically self-Controlling Effort Relative To the body-mind (With All its Faculties), and Has Thereby Become Able To Present the entire body-mind To Me Without Armoring—and Is Really and Truly Entering Into The Process Of Seeing Me.

When My Avatarically Self-Transmitted Divine Hridaya-Shakti-Transmission Is Received, the body-mind Of My Seeing Devotee Is Taken Over, and All Kinds Of Processes and States Occur Spontaneously (or Automatically). Such Is The True Guru-Yoga, Which Is The Yoga Done By Me (The True Divine Guru), and Not A (Necessarily, merely conditional and ego-Reinforcing) "Yoga" Enforced By The ego-Efforts (or self-"Guruing") Of the individual ego-self (and, as such, egoically Enforced By, and limited to, the conditional processes of mere Natural life-energy). For My Seeing Devotee, This True Guru-Yoga Of Unobstructed and Unguarded (and Total psycho-physical) Spiritual Reception Of Me Is (Truly, Clearly, Tangibly, and Overwhelmingly) A Matter Of ego-Surrendering (and, Thus, Total psycho-physical Contraction-Transcending) Receiving Of Me.

In Due Course, When The Spontaneous Yoga Of My Spiritual Intrusion Has Been Worked For a Sufficient period of time In My Seeing Devotee, Then the body-mind Of My Seeing Devotee (With All its Faculties) Becomes So Fully Opened To Me That My Hridaya-Shakti-Transmission Is No Longer Received In A limited gross Manner (or Merely In My Seeing Devotee's gross body-mind), but Also Beyond the gross sphere (By Means Of Fullest, and Really self-Contraction-Relinquishing, psycho-physical Participation In My Infinite Divine Field Of Love-Bliss-Radiance). When This Occurs, the body-mind Of My Seeing Devotee No Longer Necessarily Has To "Shake" In Order To Conduct My Spiritual In-Pouring—and So The "Tremblings" Decrease, and Even (Generally) Cease.

Thus, All The Exercises Of The Listening-Hearing Process Prepare My Listening (and Then Hearing) Devotee To Fully

Receive Me Spiritually. And Then, In Turn, The Entire Process Of (Spiritually) Fully Receiving Me Becomes Preparation For The "Perfect Practice" Of The Only-By-Me Revealed and Given Way Of The Heart (or Way Of Adidam).

To Come To The Point Of Preparedness For The "Perfect Practice" Of The Only-By-Me Revealed and Given Way Of The Heart Is Not Merely (or Only) A Matter Of Perfect Maturity In The "Conscious Process"—but It Is Also (Necessarily) A Matter Of Inherently Perfect "Conductivity" Of My Avatarically Self-Revealed Divine Spirit-Presence. In The "Perfect Practice" Of The Only-By-Me Revealed and Given Way Of The Heart, My Avatarically Self-Transmitted Divine Spirit-Presence Drives (In Its Association With the body-mind Of My Devotee) To The Heart-Root On The Right. Therefore, The "Perfect Practice" Of The Only-By-Me Revealed and Given Way Of The Heart Is A Far Greater Matter Than Merely Being Inclined To Focus attention In The Right Side Of The Heart. In The "Perfect Practice" Of The Only-By-Me Revealed and Given Way Of The Heart, My Attractive Spirit-Force Itself Moves To The Right Side Of The Heart (By Circulating In the body-mind Of My Devotee To The Point Of Settling In The Right Side Of The Heart)—If Only My Devotee Rightly, Truly, and Really Devotionally Participates In That Transcendental (and Inherently Spiritual) Process. Therefore, This Spiritual "Locating" Of Me In The Right Side Of The Heart Is A Necessary Characteristic Of The "Perfect Practice" Of The Only-By-Me Revealed and Given Way Of The Heart—and, Indeed, It Is (In Its Initial Demonstration) A Necessary Qualification For Entering The "Perfect Practice" Of The Only-By-Me Revealed and Given Way Of The Heart—Which Entrance (Necessarily) Also (and Primarily) Coincides With The Stable Awakening To The Witness-Position Of Consciousness.

Thus, The Only-By-Me Revealed and Given Way Of The Heart (or Way Of Adidam) Is Entirely (and Throughout Its Entire Course) About Me. It Is Not About "You" (In Your Separateness). The Only-By-Me Revealed and Given Way Of The Heart (or Way Of Adidam) Is A Matter Of You Relinquishing Your Own ego-Position (Through self-Surrender, self-Forgetting, and, More and More, self-Transcendence) In Order (From The Beginning) To Devotionally

Commune With Me, To (In Due Course) Be Devotionally Absorbed In My Avatarically Self-Revealed (and Self-Evidently Divine) Self-Condition, and (Ultimately) To Most Perfectly Realize My Avatarically Self-Revealed (and Self-Evidently Divine) Self-Condition.

I Am Always Doing The Only-By-Me Revealed and Given Divine Spiritual Yoga Of The Way Of The Heart—In The Case Of My Every Devotee. In The Case Of My Every Devotee, Every (Progressive) Realization In The Only-By-Me Revealed and Given Way Of The Heart Is A Realization Of Me. The Progressive Process Of The Only-By-Me Revealed and Given Way Of The Heart Occurs Because You Practice The Primary By-Me-Given Gift, Calling, and Discipline Of Ruchira Avatara Bhakti Yoga—To The Point (In Due Course) Of Absorptive Devotional Communion With Me, and (Then) To The Point Of Perfect Identification With Me—Such That My Own Substance Of Inherently Perfect Divine Being and Of Mere and "Bright" Divine Spirit-Presence Becomes Your Experience, Your Certain Knowledge, and (Ultimately) Your Most Perfect Realization.

Therefore, The Only-By-Me Revealed and Given Way Of The Heart (or Way Of Adidam) Is Not A self-Applied, Strategic Technique For Manipulating (and Thereby Changing) Your Own body-mind.

The Only-By-Me Revealed and Given Way Of The Heart (or Way Of Adidam) Is The Practice Of Devotional Communion With Me and Devotional Realization Of Me—Not Realization (or Achievement) Of something In "You" (In Your Separateness).

In Order To Realize Me Most Perfectly, You Must Be Utterly Surrendered To Me (and Into My Avatarically Self-Revealed, and Utterly Non-Separate, Divine Condition), Beyond Your egoic (or Separate) self.

Therefore, With Your Total body-mind, You Must Participate In My Condition, My Sacrifice, My Action, My Manner, and My Characteristic State.

And, In The Only-By-Me Revealed and Given Seventh Stage Of Life, There Is No "You"—but There Is Only Me.

Always, "You" (In Your Separateness) Are Not The One To Be Realized.

Always, I Am The One To Be (Non-Separately) Realized.

Therefore, Let the body-mind Be Heart-Opened To Me, Through Devotional Listening, To The Degree Of True Hearing (or Most Fundamental self-Understanding)—and Then Let The To-Me-Opened Heart (and The To-Me-Heart-Opened Total body-mind) Be Deeply Attracted To Me (and Spontaneously Converted To Me), Through The Seeing Of Me (Which Is The Initiatory Event, and The Subsequent Progressive Process, Of Total psycho-physical Heart-Conversion To My Avatarically Self-Revealed Spiritual, and Always Blessing, Divine Person and Presence, By Means Of My Avatarically Self-Transmitted Divine Spirit-Baptism). Then Practice Whole bodily (or Total psycho-physical) self-Surrender To Me, In Meditation and In daily life, By breathing and Feeling My Avatarically Self-Transmitted Divine Spirit-Energy In The Total Frontal Line Of the body—Down From Infinitely Above The Total Crown Of the head, and Down, Through The Total Crown Of the head, To The Ajna Door[48] (or The Root Of The Brain Core, Between and Slightly Above and Deep Behind the brows), and, From Thence, Down Through the Total facial area, Then Down Through The Region Of the throat, Then The Region Of the physical heart, Then the solar plexus and the abdomen, To the bodily base (or The Region That Includes the genitals, the perineum, and the anus). When This Descending Practice Is Full, You May Yet (If Necessary) Also Engage The Circle In Its Ascending (or Spinal) Line (By Always Calling On Me At The Ajna Door, Between and Slightly Above and Deep Behind the brows, and Always By breathing and Feeling My Avatarically Self-Transmitted Divine Spirit-Energy In The Total Spinal Line Of the body—In, Back, and Up Via the Total bodily base, and, Thus, To and Into The Spinal Line, Then Straight and Fully Up The Spinal Line To the base of the skull, Then Up and Forward Into The Brain Core, To The Ajna Door, and Ever Deeper Upwards, Via The Ajna Door, To The Total Crown Of the head, and, Thence, Even Above, and Infinitely Above, the head).

If The By Me (Avatarically) Given Primary Practice and "Conscious Process" (Of The Devotional Surrender Of attention To Me, and, Thus and Thereby, To Commune With, and, Ultimately,

To Be Dissolved In, or Utterly Transcended In, Me) Is Rightly, Truly, Fully, and Fully Devotionally Embraced and Engaged By You (As A Formal Practitioner Of The Total, or Full and Complete, Practice Of The Only-By-Me Revealed and Given Way Of The Heart), and If You Consistently Support That Primary Practice and "Conscious Process" By Right, True, Full, and Fully Devotional Formal Embrace and Engagement Of The Necessary Secondary By-My-Avataric-Divine-Grace-Given Divine Spiritual Means (Which Is The By-Me-Given Practice, and The By-Me-Given Process, Of "Conductivity" Of My Avatarically Self-Transmitted Divine Spirit-Presence), Then The Entire (and The Ultimate) Divine Way (and Divine Self-Revelation) Of The Only-By-Me Revealed and Given Way Of The Heart Will Be Given To You, By Me. Therefore, If You Are My True and Truest (and, Necessarily, Formally and Fully Practicing) Devotee, All The Necessary Revelations Of Descent, and (If They Are Necessary) All The Revelations Of Ascent, and (In Due Course) The Revelation Of The Witness-Consciousness (and The Revelation Of The Heart On The Right, and The Revelation Of The Perfectly Subjective, and Inherently egoless, Heart Of Consciousness Itself), and (Most Ultimately) All The Revelations and Necessary Demonstrations Of The Only-By-Me Revealed and Given Seventh Stage Of Life Will (Each and All) Be Given To You—Inevitably, and In Right Time, By Means Of My Avatarically Self-Transmitted Divine Grace.

IV.

In The Total (or Full and Complete) Practice Of The Only-By-Me Revealed and Given Way Of Adidam (Which Is The One and Only By-Me-Revealed and By-Me-Given Way Of The Heart), The Practice Of Spirit-"Conductivity" Begins When You Are Baptized (or Spiritually Awakened) By and In and To My Avatarically Self-Transmitted Divine Spiritual Presence and Person. Therefore, I Will (Now, and Forever Hereafter) Continue To Avatarically Transmit My Divine Spiritual Presence—Even (After, and Forever After, The Avataric Physical Lifetime Of My Own Bodily Human Divine Form) Via The Formally Acknowledged and True

Instruments, and The Formally Acknowledged and True Agents, Of My (Now, and Forever Hereafter) Avatarically Self-Manifested Divine Blessing-Work.

By Means Of Baptism By and In and To My Avatarically Self-Transmitted Divine Spiritual Presence and Person, My (Necessarily, Formally) Fully Practicing Devotees Become Spiritually Converted (and Both Devotionally and Spiritually "Bonded") To Me—The True and Only and Non-Separate and Self-Evidently Divine Person, The Inherently Perfect Heart and Non-Separate Self Of All and all.

By Means Of Baptism By and In and To My Avatarically Self-Transmitted Divine Spiritual Presence and Person, All My (Thereby) Seeing Devotees Whole-bodily-Receive (or Are themselves Whole-bodily-Given To) My Divine Spirit-Power—and (By Means Of Thus By-Me-Given Spiritual Communion With My Avatarically Self-Transmitted Spiritual Presence and Person) they Find (and, In Due Course, Realize) Me As The Avatarically Self-Revealed, and True, and Only, and Non-Separate, and Self-Evidently Divine Person, The "Bright" Divine Heart Itself, The Ultimate and Inherently Perfect Source (and The Ultimate and Inherently Perfect Identity) Of My Avatarically Self-Transmitted Divine Spirit-Energy Itself.

Once Baptism By and In and To My Avatarically Self-Transmitted Divine Spiritual Presence and Person Is Confirmed By True (Spiritually Activated) Heart-Conversion, My Seeing Devotee Must Let My Divine Spirit-Current Radiate From The Heart, and Stand In the body (head To toe), and (With every breath) Rotate In The Circle (Descending, and Then Ascending).

Therefore, When You Are (Truly) Baptized By and In and To My Avatarically Self-Transmitted Divine Spiritual Presence and Person, and When You Are (Thus, Thereby, and Truly Whole bodily) Converted At Heart By (and In, and To) My Avatarically Self-Revealed Spiritual (and Always Blessing) Divine Presence—You Must Conduct and Conserve My Avatarically Self-Transmitted Divine Spirit-Power, By Transcending Every Tendency To Reverse The Downward Flow In The Frontal Line and The Upward Flow In The Spinal Line. In This Manner, You Must Overcome and

Transcend Every Tendency To Obstruct or Weaken The Flow Of My Avatarically Self-Transmitted Divine Spirit-Energy, As Well As Every Tendency To Break The Circle At Any Point. Thus, You Must Be Carried Through The Circle By The Living Flow (or Current) Of My Avatarically Self-Transmitted Divine Spirit-Presence—Until My Avatarically Self-Transmitted Divine Spirit-Current Finds Its Way To My Divine Self-Heart. Then, When I Am Revealed As The Inherently egoless Heart Itself (Which Is The Perfectly Subjective Feeling Of Being, Itself, or Self-Existing and Self-Radiant Consciousness, Itself), You Must Allow Me To Reveal The Eternal Freedom, and The Boundless "Bright" Sphere and Space, Of My Divine Self-Domain—Which Is The Eternal Condition Of My Avatarically Self-Revealed (and Self-Evidently Divine) Person, Beyond The Cosmic Mandala.

V.

In The Total (or Full and Complete) Practice Of The Only-By-Me Revealed and Given Way Of Adidam (Which Is The Only-By-Me Revealed and Given Way Of The Heart)—First, You Must Listen To Me and Hear Me. Then You Must See Me (and, Thus and Thereby, "Locate", Identify, and Become Attracted To My Avatarically Self-Revealed Divine Spiritual Presence) Via My Avatarically Giving Gift Of Divine Spirit-Baptism. Then You Must Practice Reception Of My Avatarically Self-Transmitted and All-and-all-Pervading Divine Spirit-Power In The Frontal Line.

On The Basis Of Hearing Me and Seeing Me, You Must Overcome The Tendency To Reverse (or To Obstruct, or To Be Weak In) The Frontal Line. Do This By The Active Combination Of Most Fundamental self-Understanding, Conversion Of All emotional Reactivity Into Free Heart-Feeling (or Love), Regular Performance Of functional, practical, relational, and Cultural Disciplines, Steady and Full Spirit-"Conductivity" In The Frontal Line, and The Practice Of Devotional Heart-Communion With Me.

On The Basis Of Hearing Me and Seeing Me, You Must Overcome The Tendency To Break The Circle. This Breaking Is Generally The Product Of physical imbalance, toxicity, vital weakness, and degenerative sexual activity. Therefore, Repair, and (Otherwise) Avoid (or Voluntarily Relinquish), These Results Of Unlawful Living—Even Through self-Discipline, and Through ego-Surrendering, ego-Forgetting, and (More and More) ego-Transcending Feeling-Contemplation Of <u>Me</u>, In The Context Of The Ordeal Of Listening To Me.

On The Basis Of Hearing Me and Seeing Me, You Must Become Full and Steady In The Frontal Line. Then You May Receive and Conduct and Be Carried By My Avatarically Self-Transmitted Divine Spirit-Fullness Via The Spinal Line. Therefore, Let The Circle Be Full—Not Weak, Not Obstructed, Not Reversed, and Not Broken. And, If The (Necessarily, Total—or Full and Complete) Practice Of The Only-By-Me Revealed and Given Way Of The Heart (or Way Of Adidam) Becomes (In Due Course) Formally Associated With The Yoga Of Ascent In The Spinal Line, Freely and Openly and Fully Allow My Avatarically Self-Transmitted Divine Spirit-Current To Ascend Via The Spinal Line (Even Such That the cerebro-spinal fluid is physically heard and felt pulsing and clicking through the lower ventricles of the brain). Do This Until The Knot In The Brain Core (or the self-Contraction itself, As it Registers In The Total Brain Core) Is Opened, Even Such That The Passage Above The Brain Core (and Above The Total Crown Of the head) Is Made Clear. Then You May Also Let My Avatarically Self-Transmitted Divine Spirit-Current Carry You Further Upwards (Even To The Highest Place—Infinitely Above The Total Crown Of the head—Which Is The Free Ascended Space, or Most Ascended Place Of Origin, Of My Avatarically Self-Transmitted Divine Love-Bliss).

In The Only-By-Me Revealed and Given Way Of The Heart, The Impulse Toward Such Ascent Is Transcended At The Heart (and In Due Course)—Whether Before Or After The Spinal Yoga Of Ascent Is Entered. Therefore, When (In The Course Of The Total, or Full and Complete, Practice Of The Only-By-Me Revealed and Given Way Of The Heart) The Impulse To Ascend Is Transcended, You (By Means Of My Avatarically Self-Transmitted Divine Grace) Come To Rest In The Witness-Position Of Free Consciousness (Inherently Free Of All Concern For the body-mind). And The (Thus) "Perfect Practice" Of The Only-By-Me Revealed and Given Way Of The Heart Must (Thus) Persist—Until The Most Perfectly Ultimate and Divinely Real Condition Of The Heart (or Of Consciousness Itself) Is, By Means Of My Avatarically Self-Transmitted Divine Grace, Revealed (Most Perfectly, and As That Which Is Always Already, and Non-Separately, and Non-"Differently" The Case).

Then, By Means Of My Avatarically Self-Transmitted Divine Grace, The Heart (Itself) Will Shine Upwards To The Highest Place—and It Will Shine From There, Into The Circle Of the body-mind, and everywhere In The Cosmic Domain. And My Avatarically Self-Transmitted Inherent Love-Bliss-Happiness Will Freely Descend and Ascend In The Circle Of the body-mind, Radiating In All Directions.

Then, By Means Of My Avatarically Self-Transmitted Divine Grace, Abide (Non-Separately, and Non-"Differently") As My Self-Existing, and Self-Radiant, and Perfectly Subjective, and Self-Evidently Divine Condition (or "Bright" State) Of Person—Divinely Self-Recognizing All Modifications Of That Condition That Are experienced Via The Parts Of The Circle. Abide Thus, Divinely Self-Recognizing all beings and conditions In My "Bright" Divine Love-Bliss. Abide Thus, Standing As My Avatarically Self-Revealed (Transcendental, Inherently Spiritual, and Self-Evidently Divine) Self-Condition—Until The Inherent "Brightness" Of My Avatarically Self-Revealed (Transcendental, Inherently Spiritual, and Self-Evidently Divine) Self-Condition Outshines the body-mind and The Total Cosmic Mandala.

Then, By Means Of My Avatarically Self-Transmitted Divine Grace, You Will Stand In (and As) My "Bright" Divine Self-Domain—Which Is Self-Existing, Self-Radiant, and Perfectly Subjective Being Itself, Shining Beyond all attention to the worlds Of Cosmic Struggle and death.

RUCHIRA AVATAR ADI DA SAMRAJ
Los Angeles, 2000

Five Essays and a Talk from the *Samraj Upanishad*

The Sanskrit word "upanishad" indicates "Teachings received at the Feet of the Guru". Thus, the Samraj Upanishad *is "Teachings received at the Feet of Ruchira Avatar Adi Da Samraj". Rather than being the title of a distinct book, "Samraj Upanishad" is a collective designation for certain Talks and Essays by Avatar Adi Da Samraj that appear within various of His twenty-three "Source-Texts" as readings supporting and expanding upon the principal "Part" of a given "Source-Text".*

PART FOUR

Five Essays and a Talk from the *Samraj Upanishad*

The Lesser and Greater Traditions Associated with The Kundalini Shakti

There are actually two distinct (and very different) traditions associated with the cosmically manifested Kundalini Shakti.

The first (and most commonly known) tradition associated with the Kundalini Shakti is founded upon the bodily point of view, and it is associated with the <u>ascent</u> of the <u>natural</u> <u>energies</u> of the physical, etheric, and lower mental (or lesser psychic) dimensions of the human body-mind-self. This tradition is, originally, associated with the ancient animistic and shamanistic cultures of mankind—and it developed, over time, via such traditions as Taoism, Hatha Yoga, and the lesser modes of Tantrism.

The second (and senior, although less commonly known) tradition associated with the Kundalini Shakti is the tradition of Kundalini Shaktipat, which is the process of the <u>descent</u> and <u>circulation</u> of the cosmically manifested <u>Divine</u> <u>Power</u>. And this tradition is of Divine origin. That is to say, this tradition is not the product of human psycho-physical efforts to achieve the Divine Condition (or any higher knowledge and psycho-physical powers), but it has appeared spontaneously (descended from above)—Given by the Divine (directly), and Transmitted via various lineages of Yogic Siddha-Masters. In the domain of popular

235

religion, this Kundalini Shaktipat tradition is represented, for example, in the legend of the Spiritual Baptism of Jesus of Nazareth by John the Baptist (in which case, the "Holy Spirit" is said to have descended upon the head of Jesus "like a dove"—or, in other words, from above, and from and As God). In the modern era, this Kundalini Shaktipat tradition has been represented, for example, by Ramakrishna, in His spontaneous Transmission of Spiritual Power to Swami Vivekananda, and by Bhagavan Nityananda, in His Transmission of Spiritual Power to Swami (Baba) Muktananda. In the same manner, I, in My present-time bodily (human) Form, Received Kundalini Shaktipat (or the Transmission of cosmically manifested Divine Spirit-Power) from several individuals—including Bhagavan Nityananda, Rang Avadhoot, Baba Muktananda, and Rudi (also known as Swami Rudrananda). And, in My (present-time) Case, the Divine Spirit-Transmission was, at last, also Given most directly—in Person, and in Its Utter Fullness—by the "Divine Goddess", "Shakti" Herself. However, My own Realization, Thus Served by Means of the Divine Spirit-Transmission, Most Ultimately became (and, Prior to My Avataric Divine Appearance here in My present-time bodily human Form, Always Already Is) Such that My own Avataric Work of Divine Spiritual Transmission—although It also (secondarily) Manifests via the signs otherwise characteristic of Kundalini Shaktipat—Originates and (primarily) Manifests in and via and at and As the Heart Itself, Prior to all limitations and conditionality. Therefore, My Avataric Work of Divine Spiritual Transmission directly (and Most Perfectly) Reveals the Perfectly Subjective Divine Heart (or Self-Existing and Self-Radiant Divine Being Itself).

The commonly known (or lesser) tradition of the Kundalini Shakti is associated with self-applied Yogic techniques (of bodily exercises, breath exercises, exercises of mental concentration, and so on) that are intended to raise up the natural energies associated with the lower physical personality. Thus, those Yogic techniques are generally associated, first, with efforts to arouse the natural energy that is otherwise locked into the base of the body (at the lower end of the spinal column—at and above the perineum—and at the sexual center, and in the entire general region of the abdomen, including the navel area, and the solar plexus), and, second, with efforts to raise (and to progressively refine and expand) that energy (or those energies), upwards, via the ascending hierarchy of the various key centers of the spinal line (toward and to the primary centers in the head)—until (eventually) the ascending energy-flow is released (above the brain and the mind and the total crown of the head) to the most ascended Source-Condition (in fifth stage conditional Nirvikalpa Samadhi). And, in the course of that ascending ("advanced" fourth stage, and fifth stage) process, many symptoms of the <u>partially</u> ascended Kundalini Shakti may progressively appear (in the form of Yogic developments of a physical and, then, progressively more purely psychic, or fully psycho-physical, kind). And such signs may include not only various Yogic powers (or siddhis), and many visions, auditions, and so forth (progressively Revealing the hierarchical levels of the psycho-physical structure of Man and the Cosmos), but they may also include various (either brief or long-term) "Yogic diseases" (or symptoms indicating either processes of psycho-physical purification or a misdirection of the natural energies associated with the Yogic process).

The lesser-known (and senior, and greater) tradition of the Kundalini Shakti is also associated with the same phenomena (and, as secondary, or merely supportive, exercises, the same Yogic techniques) of ascending Yoga that characterize the lesser tradition of the Kundalini Shakti. However, the unique characteristic of the senior and greater (Kundalini Shaktipat) tradition is that the Kundalini Shakti (Itself) and the fundamental Yogic process are not generated via self-effort and self-applied techniques, but the Yogic process is Generated (and Performed, and Fulfilled) directly and spontaneously, by the Kundalini Shakti Itself—Which is Given, Guided, and constantly re-Generated by a Yogic Siddha-Master (and sometimes via the Empowered representative, or representatives, of a Yogic Siddha-Master). And, when Yoga is so Given and so Guided, it develops according to a unique Divine Intelligence—such that (unless the devotee surrenders to the ego-self, rather than to the Guru, or Sat-Guru, and the Divinely Self-Revealing Power—and although many signs of psycho-physical purification may develop and then pass) the Yogic process does not develop signs either of misdirection of energies or of fixed attachment to lesser (or merely intermediate) conditional states.

Also, the senior tradition of the Kundalini Shakti is associated with a process in the total Circle of the body-mind (including both the frontal line and the spinal line). This is because the descending and circulating Spirit-Power moves in the total natural circuit of the body-mind. Thus, the descending and circulating Spirit-Power first enters the frontal line, where the foundation work of opening and purifying the physical, the etheric, the emotional, and the mental (or general psychic) personality must be accomplished. Then, potentially, once the frontal line is sufficiently purified (or, at least, sufficiently surrendered and opened) to allow the descending Kundalini Shakti to turn about at the bodily base, the Kundalini Shakti spontaneously begins the upward Yogic course. Thus, because the true process Generated by Kundalini Shaktipat Works first in the frontal line and then (potentially) in the spinal line, the Kundalini Shaktipat tradition actually begins in the Event of the truly Spiritual Initiation of the "basic" fourth stage of life (and, potentially, to some possible degree, even in the rudimentary Spiritual context of the "original" stage, or foundation stage, of the fourth stage of life), and, thereafter (in due course), it continues (potentially) in the "advanced" fourth stage of life and the fifth stage of life. But the lesser tradition of the Kundalini Shakti is based on a system of Yogic philosophy that idealizes Yogic ascent (not descent)—and, therefore, the lesser tradition of the Kundalini Shakti (and the derivative traditions of "ascending Yoga" in general) is associated with systems and techniques of practice that are intended to strategically develop the ascending Yogic process in the context of the "advanced" fourth stage of life and the fifth stage of life, thus (in general) bypassing (or, at least, minimizing) the foundation Yogic Ordeal associated with the "original" and the "basic" fourth stage of life. (And, as a result of this bypass, the lesser tradition of the Kundalini Shakti—and the various, and variant, traditions of "ascending Yoga", such as "Kriya Yoga" and "Shabd Yoga", that are derived from the generalized tradition of Kundalini Shakti Yoga—are often associated with a point of view that would achieve extreme detachment, or strategic dissociation from the body-mind and the conditional world, and, otherwise, in general, with programs of practice that do not pay sufficient practice-time to preparing the right and effective foundation that must precede Yogic activities in the context of the "advanced" fourth stage of life and the fifth stage of life, if the potential ascending Yogic process is itself to develop truly, rightly, and fully.)

My Own Direct Experience and Unique Revelation of The Senior Process of The Kundalini Shakti

The lesser tradition of the Kundalini Shakti presumes that the Kundalini Shakti originates below (rather than above), and that it is an energy of a biological, physiological, or lower natural kind (rather than of a Transcendental and Divine, or truly and Divinely Spiritual, kind). Certainly, many traditional and contemporary reports of experiences of the Kundalini Shakti type[49] are of the kind that originates solely in the lower, and physiological, and biological context of the human body-mind, and that is limited to the production of phenomenal (and even merely egoic) states, in the context of the body-mind. However, as I have indicated, there is another kind of Energy That (via the process of true Kundalini Shaktipat) may be received from above. And That Energy may circulate in the Circle and everywhere throughout the body-mind (stimulating and purifying every part and function), but That Energy is not, Itself, of a lower natural (or biological and physiological) kind. Rather, That Energy Is the cosmically manifested Divine Source-Energy (or Matrix-Energy), of Which natural (or biological, or physiological) energies are a mere (and merely apparent) modification. And That Energy (if allowed to do Its Work, and completely) would (in due course) convert (or realign) every part and function of the body-mind to its <u>cosmically</u> manifested Divine Source-Condition (or Matrix-Condition) above the body-mind—and, Most Ultimately (in the eventual Final Demonstration of the only-by-Me Revealed and Given seventh stage of life), That Energy would Outshine every part and function of the body-mind in its Transcendental, Inherently Spiritual, and Self-Evidently

Divine Source-Condition, Realized in and Beyond the right side of
the heart.

In any case, even the Kundalini Shakti process Generated by
Kundalini Shaktipat may, especially in the context of the first five
stages of life, be demonstrated via purifying and transformative
effects in the body-mind. <u>Because</u> they (in general) originate in
the physically based body-mind (or psycho-biological mechanism), the phenomena associated with the lesser type of Kundalini
Shakti processes generally require that the central nervous system
(and the total psycho-biological mechanism) of a human individual be significantly developed (generally, at least to the age of
puberty—and, usually, even to a fully adult age). Therefore, as a
general rule, the lesser Kundalini Shakti process cannot occur
before puberty. However, the senior Kundalini Shakti process (initiated by a Divine Spiritual descent) can, in unique cases, occur
even from a very early age. (That is to say—although it is possible to occur only in the case of certain unique Spiritual prodigies,
just as early-life signs of genius in the arts and sciences are limited to unique prodigies—if, somehow, there is early-life
Kundalini Shaktipat, or early initiatory descent of Divine Spirit-
Power, there is certainly, in the case of such Spiritual prodigies,
sufficient development of the central nervous system, and the general systems of the body-mind, to permit the descending and circulating process of the Kundalini Shakti in the pre-pubertal years.)

In My own Case, My Birth was (and My Life Is) Itself a Sign of
the Avataric Descent of My Divine Spiritual Power and Presence.
I fully Assumed My bodily (human) Form at approximately two
years of (bodily) age, and Full Spiritual Signs were immediately
(and priorly) in Evidence. Thus, I, from the time I was a little boy,
Named My State (and Its accompanying Signs in the body-mind)
the "Bright"—and I noted a particular recurring phenomenon of
psycho-physically transformative descent of Spiritual Energy
(which descent, or frontal invasion, I Named the "Thumbs"). The
"Bright" was (and Is) a fully (Divinely) Awakened Spiritual State,
in Which the Divine Love-Bliss-Energy (Kundalini Shakti, or, more
properly, Hridaya-Shakti) is centered in the heart and the head,
and circulates throughout the Circle of the body-mind (by a

pattern of frontal descent—from above the total crown of the head—and subsequent spinal ascent, or return). The "Thumbs" was (and Is) a process I observed to periodically take place in My body (with transformative effects in My entire body-mind) from My earliest years. And It was (and Is) a unique version (or special intensification) of the circulatory process of the "Bright". Thus, from time to time (perhaps every few weeks or months—and with exceptional intensity, sometimes associated with episodes of fever and disease, perhaps once every year or two, or so) the descending Divine Love-Bliss-Energy would spontaneously press down from above the total crown of My head into My head and My throat (with an accompanying gagging sensation in the throat). There was also usually some brief struggle in the heart and lungs whenever this Divine Invasion came upon My bodily (human) Form, and then the Energy would pass down into the body, with various swooning effects following.

In fact, especially My years <u>previous</u> to puberty (rather than My teen-age years) were filled with extraordinary Kundalini Shakti phenomena, and My teen-age years were (in general) rather characterized by the absence of such signs (until, after a period of intense struggle, they began again, when I was, bodily, nearing twenty-one years of age). Thus, My childhood was marked, at first, by a steady-State of ("Bright") Self-Illumination—and, year by year, as I became more and more thoroughly integrated with the human psycho-physical limitation, that steady-State was periodically interrupted and progressively diminished, such that (via the "Thumbs") It was required to be (periodically) restored. And, also, that steady-State became (progressively) replaced by a kind of revolutionary transformative cycle, in which various siddhis (or psychic and psycho-physical powers) were sometimes displayed, as well as visions, auditions, ecstasies, and so on, but also various Shakti-caused (and Shakti-filled) physical (and general psycho-physiological) effects (such as extremes of bodily hotness and bodily coldness, heart palpitations, feelings of suffocation, emotional suffering, variations in appetite, fluctuations of body weight, episodes of disease, precocious awareness of sexual energy, and so on).

Thus, the physical (and general psycho-physiological) effects associated with My own early-life Spiritual experiences confirm the factuality and correctness (in general outline) of the traditional and modern descriptions of the extended circuit (and the most typical experiential phenomena) of the lesser Kundalini Shakti process. However, the Spiritual Demonstration of My early Life, together with the total Spiritual Demonstration of My adult years, is a unique (Spiritual, Transcendental, and Divine) Revelation of the senior (or Kundalini Shaktipat, or spontaneous Divine descent-and-circulation) process of the Kundalini Shakti (Which, in My Case, Originates In and As the Perfectly Subjective Divine Hridaya-Shakti—Which Is the Most Prior and Self-Existing Divine Self-Radiance, of Which the cosmically manifested Kundalini Shakti is a merely apparent Sign).

The True Kundalini Shakti
Can Be Awakened
Only by Divine Grace,
Not by Yogic Sexual Practice

Some representatives of the Tantric tradition[50] propose that the Kundalini Shakti may actually be directly awakened by Yogic sexual practice (and not simply preserved thereby, or served thereby, once It is already and otherwise awakened). However, it is an exaggeration to claim that the process associated with the true (Spiritual) Kundalini Shakti may be either initiated or fulfilled by any (however Yogic) sexual practice (itself), or by any other merely (and however otherwise right, healthful, useful, or even Yogic) physical discipline or exercise (such as pure, or "sattvic", diet, or any kind of breath-control, or "pranayama", or any kind of bodily motion, stretching, or posing, or "asana", or even any kind of external or internal manipulation of body, emotion, or mind). Generally, unless the Kundalini Shakti is already otherwise activated (and, generally, by means of Guru-Kripa, or initiation directly by a Spiritual Adept of one or another degree, or else via the Empowered representative, or representatives, of a Spiritual Adept of one or another degree), Yogic sexual practice (or even any other kind of merely physical discipline or exercise) simply involves, at best, what is traditionally called "pranotthana", or the (perhaps healthful and pleasurable, but merely physical, or gross bodily) ascent of natural etheric energies. And the fullest (fifth stage) Spiritual ascent of the Kundalini Shakti (otherwise activated) is not likely to be achieved during (and never as an immediate and direct result of) any Yogic sexual (or, otherwise, active physical) practice—because the fullest Spiritual ascent of the Kundalini Shakti (to fifth stage conditional Nirvikalpa

Samadhi) requires deep <u>passive</u> relinquishment (or the effective transcending) of the body-mind. And, in any case, what fullest (fifth stage) Spiritual ascent of the Kundalini Shakti <u>really</u> requires is true <u>Spiritual</u> <u>Contemplation</u> (or Divine Communion) in ascent.

Contrary to the expressed opinion of some popularizers of Yoga (and of Yogic sex-practices), the Kundalini Shakti is not merely personal sex-energy (or, otherwise, merely physical energy) "reversed" (or ascending, rather than naturally descending). The Kundalini Shakti is the <u>all-pervading</u> cosmic (or conditionally appearing) Energy that is the <u>Single</u> manifested Substance of <u>all</u> conditionally manifested energies, processes, and forms. The Kundalini Shakti is the all-pervading cosmic Energy that is otherwise appearing as <u>all</u> conditional (or limited) energies, including personal sex-energy—but It cannot (Itself) be reduced to sex-energy (itself), or to any other form of limited (specific or personal or functional) energy (itself). Therefore, the Kundalini Shakti <u>cannot</u> be awakened merely by the "reversal" (or ascent) of the naturally descending tendency of the personal energy of the sex-impulse (or of any other form of functional human energy), but the <u>true</u> Kundalini Shakti can be awakened <u>only</u> by Divine Grace (usually, as Transmitted by a Spiritual Adept of one or another degree, or as Transmitted via the Empowered representative, or representatives, of a Spiritual Adept of one or another degree).

The true Kundalini Shakti is <u>all-pervading</u>, and not merely personal and internal. And, therefore, the true Kundalini Shakti is awakened <u>in</u> the personal (and internal) psycho-physical context <u>only</u> by virtue of Grace-Given (and <u>ego-transcending</u>) participation in the all-pervading field of cosmic Energy. Likewise, <u>Consciousness</u> (<u>Itself</u>), or Self-Aware Being (Itself), is not a merely personal and internal characteristic of conditional individual (or merely psycho-physical) existence—but It <u>Is</u> <u>an</u> <u>Inherent</u> <u>Characteristic</u> <u>of</u> <u>Unconditional</u> <u>Reality</u> (<u>Itself</u>). And, therefore, Consciousness (Itself) appears <u>as</u> an apparent personal and internal characteristic of conditional individual existence <u>only</u> when psycho-physical conditions permit an <u>Unconditional-Reality-</u><u>conjunction</u>—and, thus, a conjunction between conditional form (itself) <u>and</u> (Self-Evidently Divine) Consciousness (Itself) <u>and</u> the all-pervading cosmic Energy (or Kundalini Shakti, Itself) and the Self-Existing, Self-Radiant, and Self-Evidently Divine Energy of Unconditional Reality (Itself).

The Divine and Unconditional Hridaya-Shakti (Which Is the Self-Existing and Self-Radiant Divine Spirit-Power That Stands Eternally As the Perfectly Subjective Divine and All-Outshining Self-"Brightness", Always Already Most Prior to cosmic, or conditional, manifestations) Is the Truly Ultimate (and Inherently Perfect) Energy-Source and Unconditional Self (or Being-Condition) of the Kundalini Shakti. And only the Divine and Unconditional Hridaya-Shakti Is Identical to Unconditional Reality (Itself)—and, Thus and Therefore, to (Self-Evidently Divine) Consciousness (Itself). And, for this reason, only the by-Grace-Given Divine (and Unconditional) Hridaya-Shakti Awakens the Realization of Unconditionally "Bright" Divine Consciousness (Itself)—Which Is Unconditional Reality (Itself) and Unconditional Truth (Itself).

I Am the Inherently egoless Eternal Person of Unconditional Reality (Itself). I Am the Self-Existing, Self-Radiant, Inherently Spiritual, Perfectly "Bright", and Perfectly Subjective Spiritual Heart (Itself). I Am the (now, and forever hereafter) Avatarically Self-Manifesting Eternal Person of Unconditionally "Bright" Consciousness (Itself)—Whose Eternal Spiritual Body Is the Great Hridaya-Shakti (or the Truly Divine Self-Power of the Inherently "Bright" and Perfectly Subjective Spiritual Heart) Itself. And, therefore, the Divine Hridaya-Shakti Is That "Bright" Divine Spiritual Power By Which, and With Which, and As Which Only I (Uniquely, and Characteristically) Bless and (By a Divinely Self-Revealing Progress) Awaken all My fully practicing devotees (even, Thereby, or in the Unfolding Course of That Avataric Divine Work of Blessing and Awakening, also Arousing and Revealing as many purifying and, otherwise, developmental psycho-physical signs of the Kundalini Shakti as may be necessary, in the case of My any true, and fully practicing, devotee).

And I will (by all My Avataric Means) forever (and constantly) Bless all My true (and fully practicing) devotees—So That the Perfectly Subjective, Self-Radiant, "Bright", Self-Existing, and

Unconditional Reality and Truth Is (By Means of My Avatarically Self-Manifested Divine Blessing-Work) Directly, Always, and More and More Perfectly (and, at last, Inherently and Divinely Most Perfectly) Revealed (As the Obvious, or Unconditionally Self-Evident, Reality and Truth) to My every thus true (and truly to-Me-devoted) devotee.

Vision, Audition, and Touch in The Process of Ascending Meditation in The Way Of Adidam

I.

If, In The Process Of Ascending Meditation (Which Progresses Toward and, Potentially, To Fifth Stage conditional Nirvikalpa Samadhi) In The Only-By-Me Revealed and Given Way Of Adidam (Which Is The One and Only By-Me-Revealed and By-Me-Given Way Of The Heart), My Devotee Is To (Really) Enter Into The Cosmic Mandala In Its Subtler (and Higher) planes, and Even (By Continued Ascent) To Pass Into and Through (or Directly Beyond) The Ascended Spirit-Matrix, or The Primal (Apparently Objective) Divine Sound and The Central (Apparently Objective) Divine Star—My Devotee Must Become A self-Sacrifice (Of psycho-physical egoity) By Means Of Right, True, and Full (and Truly ego-Surrendering, ego-Forgetting, and ego-Transcending) Devotion To Me, and (Thus) Enter Into Deep Meditation, Beyond bodily references and (Gradually) Even Beyond the references and content of psyche or mind.

The Passage Into Such Deep (and Ascending) Meditation Requires Profound bodily Relaxation and Progressively Effortless (and Profound) Feeling-Surrender (Of Total attention) Into and Beyond The Ajna Door. Then Heart-Feeling and attention Must Be Drawn Up Via The Natural Movement Of My Avatarically Self-Transmitted Divine Spirit-Current.

If It Continues, Feeling-attention To My Avatarically Self-Transmitted Divine Spirit-Current In Its Upward Flow Is (Progressively) Effective Toward Even Full Ascent Into The conditional Realization Of My Divine Love-Bliss. However, attention Will Tend To Pass To various perceptual and conceptual objects During The Ascending Process.

The first objects To Be Released In The Ascending Process Of The Only-By-Me Revealed and Given Way Of The Heart are conceptual thoughts and gross bodily sensations. Therefore, In The Actual (Formally Acknowledged) Ascending Stages Of The Way Of The Heart, The Artful Practice Of Intentionally Ascending "General" Spirit-"Conductivity" Is Likely To Be Useful Whenever Heart-Feeling and attention Are Gravitating Toward conceptual thoughts, Descended (or Descending) Tendencies, and physical perceptions That Correspond To the lower sensory realm of touch.

When (By All Of This Ascending Practice Of The Way Of The Heart) Heart-Feeling and attention Relax From conceptual thinking and gross bodily perceptions (or grosser touch-phenomena), There Is (If The Ascending Process Continues) Movement Into the subtler sensory (or perceptual) realm, Dominated By vision and audition. Even subtle sensations Associated With the senses of taste and smell May Distract attention, but these senses Are Secondary To (and Generally Not So Distracting As) the Primary sensations of seeing (or visual perception) and hearing (or audition).

II.

Human Intelligence Tends To Be Organized Around visual sensations Even More Than It Is Around auditory sensations. Therefore, In The Only-By-Me Revealed and Given Way Of Adidam (Which Is The One and Only By-Me-Revealed and By-Me-Given Way Of The Heart), Practice Of Formally Acknowledged Ascending ("Advanced" Fourth Stage, or Fifth Stage) Feeling-Contemplation Of Me <u>May</u> Tend To Collect Heart-Feeling and attention Toward visualized objects More Than Toward objects of audition.

Many light-forms, discrete objects, environments, and beings may be perceived in subtle vision, As Heart-Feeling and attention Rise In The Cosmic Mandala Toward My Apparently Objective Divine Star (or, Simply, Toward The Spirit-Matrix Above The Total Crown Of the head). In The Way Of The Heart, The Primary Objects To Be Perceived (In Ascended Vision) Are My Subtle Bodily (Human) Form, The Full Presentation Of The Cosmic Mandala (With All Of Its Rings Of Color), and My (Apparently Objective) Five-Pointed Divine Star (The First Visible Apparent Form Of My Avatarically Self-Transmitted Divine Grace In The Cosmic Domain).

The Entire Cosmic Mandala, Including My Divine Star, May Be Perceived Even In gross internal vision. My Divine Star and The Cosmic Mandala Are Tangibly Projected Even Into The Structural Pattern Of the gross body (including the brain) of every human being, Just As They Are Also (Apparently) Projected Into every body-mind, plane, or realm of experience In The Cosmic Domain. Therefore, those who Practice Meditation In The Way Of The Heart (Even At Any Stage Of Life In The Way Of The Heart, but Especially In The Spiritually Awakened Stages Of Life In The Way Of The Heart, and Most Especially In The Ascending Stages Of Life In The Way Of The Heart) May, Very Possibly, Even Before Long, Have Some Kind or Degree Of Visionary Experience Of The Cosmic Mandala or Of My (Apparently Objective) Divine White Star (In whichever, or however many, of Its planes Of conditional Manifestation).

The Great Mandala Of The conditional (or Cosmic) Domain May Appear In (Total) Vision (or In many fractions and forms of vision), Both during life and after death. The various Cosmic planes or worlds May (Therefore) Be perceived, As In a dream, or More Concretely (With Varying Degrees Of Clarity, Detail, and Completeness, With all their kinds of beings, forms, and events, and With Varying Degrees Of Your Participation).

Just So, The Great Cosmic Mandala Itself May Be Perceived In Vision. It Appears As A Circle (Self-Generated In Its Own Space). The Circle Is Itself A Gathering Of Circles—Each Set Within The Other, Concentric—Formed As A Radiant Wheel or A Well or A Tunnel (and, Thus, A Mandala) Of Great Formative Lights. The

Outer Ring Is Narrow and Red In Color (and Generally Set Against An Ambiguous Outer Field That Is Rather Dark, or Perhaps Somewhat Luminous, but Not Tending To Distract attention). The Next Ring Is Yellow, and It Is Wide. Then There Is Another Narrow Ring, Of A Moonlike Whiteness. Then Another Narrow Ring, Apparently Black, or The Color Of Indigo. And The Last Ring, At The Center, Is A Radiant Blue, As Wide As The Yellow. In The Center Of The Radiant Blue Is The (Apparently Objective) Brilliant Clear White Five-Pointed Star.*

Each Ring Of Color Is An Energy-Field Of A Certain Range Of Vibration (Made By Apparent Modification Of My Avatarically Self-Transmitted, and Self-Radiant, Divine Spirit-Energy). Within Each Ring, There Are Countless worlds and beings, each Characterized and limited By The Vibratory Field In Which they appear. The Outer Rings Are Grosser (or Of A Lower Vibration), and Existence In Them Is Brief and Difficult. Those Closest To The Center Are Subtler (or Of A Higher Vibration), and Existence In Them Is More Pleasurable, More Prolonged, Less Threatened, but Nonetheless conditional, Changing, Temporary, Made Of many limits, and Moved By A Necessary Struggle. The Radiant Blue Is The Most Subtle, and Existence There Is limited By Great Powers and By Great Longing For My Divine Love-Bliss, Which Is Finally Realized Only In My Exceedingly "Bright" (and Perfectly Subjective) Feeling-Domain Of Self-Existing and Self-Radiant Divine Love-Bliss. And the human world Is Also Within This Cosmic Mandala Of Lights, In The Outer (or Grosser) Fields Of Red and Yellow.

The Vision Of The Cosmic Mandala May Be Perceived As A Whole, or In Part—Either Enlarged Or Reduced To A Point. Therefore, A Point or A Spot or A Circle (Made Of Any Color), or (Otherwise) A Group Of Any Of The Rings Of Associated Color, May Be Perceived. In any moment, A Sudden Spot Of light May Be Perceived To Fly Out Of the eyes (or one of the eyes), or Else To Flash Before the internal vision, Attractively.

Any kind of pattern or scene May appear In Meditation or Random vision. Any kind of adventure may be experienced, before or after death, in this or any other conditional world.

---

* See p. 129 for a full-color representation of the Cosmic Mandala.

All worlds Are A (Merely Apparent) psycho-physical Display, Made Of My Divine Self-Radiance, By Spontaneous and conditional and Merely Apparent Modification Of That Radiance. All conditionally Manifested beings (Even in and as their present bodily or otherwise Apparent forms) Are spirits, or conditional Modifications Of Transcendental, Inherently Spiritual, and Self-Evidently Divine Conscious Light. All visions Are Made Of The Same Mandala Of (Apparently) Modified Clear White Light, The Light (or Self-Radiance, or Inherent Spiritual Radiance) Of Transcendental Divine Being.

Therefore, In The Process Of Divine Translation (Realized In The Only-By-Me Revealed and Given Seventh Stage Of Life In The Way Of The Heart), all conditional worlds, all conditional beings and events, all conditional forms of the psycho-physical self, and All The Cosmic Colors Yield To My Divine Star (Itself), and (Therefrom) To The Most Prior (and Perfectly Subjective) Source-Condition Of Even My Divine Star, and (Thus and So) Enter (and Dissolve) Into My Divine "Brightness" (or Inherent Spiritual Radiance, or Transcendental Love-Bliss), Which all-Outshining (and Utterly All-Outshining) "Brightness" Is (Itself) My Divine Self-Domain.

In That Process Of Divine Translation, My Divine Star Ceases To Be (and To Appear As) An Object. Indeed, Divine Translation (Realized In The Only-By-Me Revealed and Given Seventh Stage Of Life In The Way Of The Heart) Occurs Only If My Devotee Is (By Means Of My Avatarically Self-Transmitted Divine Grace) Fully Awake To All The Forms Of My Avatarically Self-Revealed (and Perfectly <u>Subjective,</u> and Self-Evidently Divine) Person, and (Therefore) Only If My Devotee Is Established In My Avatarically Self-Revealed (Transcendental, Inherently Spiritual, and Self-Evidently Divine) Self-Condition, Divinely Self-Recognizing My Apparently Objective Divine Star (If It Appears), and all objects, and Even The Feeling Of Relatedness Itself As The Only One (and Not Other, but Only Self-Radiant Oneness, Without Division or Separation). Therefore, In The Event Of Divine Translation, My Apparently Objective Divine Star (Divinely Self-Recognized) Becomes A Transparent Doorway At The Heart, The Same As The

Self-Existing and Self-Radiant Field That Is Consciousness Itself, The "Bright" Itself—Glorious Beyond Conception, Full, Without The Slightest Absence or Threat, More Than Wonderful, All Delight, Heart-Feeling Without limit, The Unspeakable "Embodiment" Of Joy, God-Great!

How Will This Divine Translation Be Accomplished? By Love! Only Surrender To Me In Love's Embrace, Attracted Beyond the Separate and Separative self. Therefore, Hear The One Who <u>Is</u> Love. See The One Who <u>Is</u> Love. And Formally and Fully Practice In The Heart-Manner I Have Revealed To You In My Twenty-Three Divine "Source-Texts" (and, Principally, In My *Dawn Horse Testament*).

If, In The Earlier Course Of Practice In The Only-By-Me Revealed and Given Way Of The Heart (In The Context Of The Frontal Line and the frontal personality), any subtle visions (or Even Ascended Visions) appear—Simply Notice them (or Even Any Great Vision), and Do Not Otherwise Indulge In such (or any other) appearances, but Simply Continue To Engage The Exercises Appropriate To Your Stage Of Life (and Your Form Of Practice) In The Way Of The Heart.

However, If visual objects (or Any Ascended Visions) Capture Your Heart-Feeling and attention In The Responsible Course Of Formally Acknowledged Ascending Practice In The Way Of The Heart, Always Look To The "Head" Of My Avatarically Self-Transmitted Divine Spirit-Current. That Is To Say, Always Look Above what is presently perceived (or Made Apparent), and Always Look To The Middle Of the visual field. Whatever object (or Even Great Vision) is perceived (or Made Apparent), whatever conditionally Manifested environment appears, or whatever appearance the visual field may conditionally assume, Always Look Up and Toward The Middle (and Always Up and Back, Up and Back), To Locate The Apparent <u>Source</u> (or The Most Ascended Space Of Origin) Of the light or illumination (or Even Great Object) in the present field. Do Not Hold To any limited object (or Even Any Great Object) or field (or Luminous Sign) that is presently Before You. Do Not Seek To the left or the right. Hold Heart-Feeling and attention To An Upturned View, and Constantly Turn and Yield

Toward The Center (Up and Back, Up and Back). Always Feel Beyond what presently appears (or Whatever Is Made Apparent), and Always Be Moved (Up and Back, Up and Back) Toward The Indefinable Central Source-Space Above The Total Crown Of the head.

If I Am Perceived In A (Subtle) Vision Of My Avatarically-Born Bodily (Human) Divine Form, I Will Lead Your attention Upwards. Therefore, If I Appear In (Subtle) Vision—Look Toward Me, Hold On To Me, Ascend With Me, and Realize The Most Ascended Source-Space Of My Appearance. If I Am Not Thus Perceived— Then Simply Look Above (Up and Back) For The Source Of light, and Hold To (or Yield Into) The Highest Center (or Most Ascended Source) Of the field, Rather Than To what may be perceived to the left or the right.

If The Cosmic Mandala Is Perceived, or If Any Spot or Circle or Shape Of light Is Perceived, Look To Its Center and Be Drawn Upwards (Up and Back).

The Apparently Objective Central Star May Be Perceived In Vision Even By A Little Concentration In The Brain Core. If It Is Perceived In The Course Of The Ascending Stages Of Life In The Way Of The Heart, Look To Its Center and Be Drawn Upwards (Up and Back). In This Manner, The Star May Be Perceived Again and Again, each time In a Different (or Distinct) or More Subtle plane Of The Cosmic Mandala. Then Penetrate The Present (and Apparently Objective) Divine Star In The Manner I Have Described—Even (Perhaps) Until There Is No More Ascending Motion, and There Are No More light-Changes, but Only Absorption In My Divine Love-Bliss (In The Fifth Stage conditional Realization Of Nirvikalpa Samadhi).

In Your (Possible) Course Of Ascending Practice In The Way Of The Heart, Do Not Be Concerned With Mapping (or Categorizing) the various lights, environments, or beings According To their Relative Position In The Cosmic Mandala. Constantly Surrender All Heart-Feeling and attention To Me, The Avatarically Self-Revealed Divine Person (or Self-Condition, or Source-Condition). Let My Avatarically Self-Transmitted Divine Spirit-Current Carry You Upwards (Up and Back) Via The Central Source Of the field, and

Do Not Seek (or Hold To) what is perceived on the left or the right. Simply Be Released Into What Is Infinitely Above. If My Avatarically-Born Bodily (Human) Divine Form (or Any Subtle conditional Form That Is Identified As Me or Felt To Be Me) Appears, or If The Cosmic Mandala (or Any Center Of Colored light) Appears, or If My Divine Star (or Any Brilliant, Rather Than Soft or Moonlike, Central White Light) Appears—Let That Vision Carry You Upwards (Via The Center, Up and Back) To The Source-Space Above The Total Crown Of the head.

In The Course Of Your (Possible) Ascending Practice In The Only-By-Me Revealed and Given Way Of The Heart, It May Be Found Useful On Occasion (and For brief periods Only) To Apply finger Pressure To the eyes, To Aid In sighting the lights and visions Above the brows By Turning the eyes Toward The Ajna Door. Simply Press the middle finger and thumb of the right or left hand Against the lids of the Closed eyes, While Resting (or Lightly Pressing) the index finger On the forehead, Between and Just Above the brows (Thus Pointing the visual attention Toward The Ajna Door). The Pressure On the eyes Should Be Firm but Not Beyond Comfort, and It Should Be Made By Pressing the outer corners of the lids, Then Drawing the fingers Down and Then Up Via the centers (or near the inner corners) of the eyes. This Gesture Will Close the lids Firmly and Turn the eyeballs Upwards. (A Hamsadanda, or Short Crutch, May Be Used As A Prop For the elbow or upper arm During This eye-Pressure Exercise.)

The Effect Of This Exercise Will Be To Emphasize The Concentration Of visual attention At The Ajna Door and Above. It Will Also Tend To Immediately Stimulate internal light phenomena that Appear To Be A Kind Of Discharge Of the light-energy Accumulated From environmental visualization. The visual mechanism Will Also Tend To Relax Via This Exercise, and various kinds of internal light-forms may be perceived. In Any Case, This Exercise Remains Confined To the rather peripheral (or superficial) visualizations of phenomena Associated With gross bodily Awareness and To the subtle visualizations Associated With the gross brain. Therefore, Practice This Exercise Only Briefly (Perhaps, At Most, For a few minutes), and Then Let eyes and arm Return To Rest.

The Purpose Of This Application Of finger Pressure To the eyes Is Simply To Serve The General Devotional Surrender Of attention To Me Via The Ajna Door. The Experience Of The Higher (or Ascended) Phenomena Of Meditation Can Occur Only When the body Is Totally Relaxed and attention Goes Beyond conceptual thinking and gross bodily sensations, Into the planes (and Even The Source-Matrix) Above.

III.

In The Only-By-Me Revealed and Given Way Of Adidam (Which Is The One and Only By-Me-Revealed and By-Me-Given Way Of The Heart), The Ascending Practice May Be Associated With The Attractive Power Of internal (or subtle) sounds—each (and, Collectively, all) of which, Including The Primal, Ascended, Cosmic Background Sound (or True "Om" Sound, or "Da" Sound), May Rightly Be Referred To As The internal (and Cosmic) Vibratory Sound Of "Om", or "Da". If The Attractive Power Of internal sound Is Particularly Strong For You In The Ascending Course Of Practice In The Way Of The Heart—Then listen Upwards, Via the internal sounds, Toward and Into The Silent Fullness That Is The Ascended Source From Which the sounds Are Apparently Emanating. (And You May Assist This Process By wearing Comfortably Effective earplugs.)

You May Climb Toward The Silent Ascended Source Gradually, sound by sound, Always Tuning In To The Next Faintest Level Of sound. In That Case, whatever kind of subtle sound is (in any moment) most obvious To You—listen Upwards, Toward The Center Of the auditory field (and Always Up and Back, Up and Back), and Try To hear the sound that is Just Behind, Above, and Fainter Than the more obvious one. Or, If The Ascended Background "Om", or "Da", Becomes audible— listen Upwards To It, Up and Back, Via The Center Of the auditory field. In Any Case, Always listen Upwards, Up and Back— Reaching Always Higher and Beyond, Until The Silent Ascended Source Absorbs attention. Or, Alternatively, No Matter what sound (or "Om", or "Da") Becomes Obvious To Your attention (In any moment Of This Upward Meditation), You May (Without Yielding attention To the sound itself) Simply Feel and listen and Swoon To Above and Beyond it (Always Continuing Toward The Center, and Up and Back), and (In This Manner) Be Moved Directly Into The Silent Ascended Source Of sound itself.

As An Alternative To listening Toward Silence Via the "music" of Natural internal sounds, You May Turn Your auditory attention To My Voice within You (If It Appears Spontaneously)—but Always Feel Toward The Silent Ascended Origin Of My Voice (or Toward The Silent Ascended Origin Of any voice or sound that May Otherwise appear Spontaneously within You), and (Thus) Always Feel and attend Toward The Center, and Above (Up and Back, Up and Back). Alternatively, If You Practice Ruchira Avatara Mahamantra Meditation[51] (or, If, As A Practitioner Of The Technically "Simpler", or Even "Simplest", Form Of The Way Of The Heart, You Practice Ruchira Avatara Naama Japa,[52] In Ascent, or Even "Simplest" Feeling-Contemplation Of Me By Means Of My Avatarically Self-Revealed Divine Name, In Ascent), You May Let Your attention Be Carried Up and Back, Up and Back—Beyond all Natural or subtle internal sounds, and To The Silent Source Above—By The "Sound" or Heart-Feeling Of The Ruchira Avatara Mahamantra (or Of The Ruchira Avatara Naama Mantra, or Of My Principal Name, "Da", or Of Any Other Of My Names, or Combined Names and Descriptive Titles, Which I Have Given To Be Engaged In The Practice Of Simple Name-Invocation Of Me), As It Is Spontaneously Recited With "the tongue of the mind".

If The Ascending Process Continues, Heart-Feeling and attention Will (At Least Eventually) Progress Upwards Through (or, Otherwise, Above) the layers of every kind of Natural or subtle internal sound (each of which Corresponds To a level or plane In The Cosmic Mandala), and Even To (and, Then, On To Above and Beyond) The Primal, Deep, Droning, Continuous, Beginningless, Uninterrupted, Endless Cosmic Background Sound (or Source-Sound, or "Om" Sound, or "Da" Sound)—Until (At Last) There Is No Further Motion, no sound, No audible "Om" (or "Da"), No Further Up, no object or other, but Only The attention-Absorbing (and <u>Ascended</u>) Love-Bliss Of My Avatarically Self-Revealed

Spiritual (and Always Blessing) Divine Presence. Therefore, If Your Practice Of The Only-By-Me Revealed and Given Way Of The Heart Enters Into The Ascending Stages, and If That Practice Becomes Associated With Sensitivity To internal sounds—Proceed In The Manner I Have Described, Always Surrendering Heart-Feeling and attention Into My Avatarically Self-Transmitted Divine Spirit-Current (In Ascent). And Do Not Be Concerned About Mapping (or Categorizing) the various sounds According To Cosmic planes, but Constantly Surrender All Heart-Feeling and attention To My Avatarically Self-Revealed Divine Spiritual Presence Of Love-Bliss. Therefore, Let My Avatarically Self-Transmitted Divine Spirit-Current Carry You Upwards (Up and Back, Up and Back), and Do Not Become Fascinated With any present sound. Feel Upwards, Hold To The Center Of the field of perception, Do Not Seek To the left or the right, but Always Feel Upwards (Up and Back, Up and Back). And Be (By This Course) Released Into What Is Utterly Above, and Beyond.

IV.

Although It Is Perhaps Inevitable That, In The Only-By-Me Revealed and Given Way Of Adidam (Which Is The One and Only By-Me-Revealed and By-Me-Given Way Of The Heart), Every Me-Seeing Devotee-Practitioner Of <u>Ascending</u> Meditation Will (To One Degree or Another) experience (and Even Be Drawn Up Via) the Primary sensations (or subtle perceptions) of light and sound, some May Not Find such experiences To Be So Profound, Intense, Elaborate, Constant, or Frequent As others May Find them To Be. For Such Devotees (In whom the sensations, or subtle perceptions, of light and sound Are Not Profound, Intense, Elaborate, or, In Any Manner, Constant, or Frequent), the <u>Most</u> <u>Primary</u> <u>sense—</u> <u>which</u> <u>is</u> <u>touch</u> (or Tangible Contact Via physical, emotional, mental, and breathing Feeling-sensation)—Will Become The More Direct Means Of Ascent. Indeed, the sense of touch (Especially In Relation To My Avatarically Self-Transmitted Divine Spirit-Current Itself) Is (Necessarily) The <u>Principal</u> sensory (or subtle perceptual) Means For all (Even If subtle perceptions of sight or sound Are

Also Fundamental To The Process). Thus, When touch-sensation Relaxes its Fixation On the gross body, Heart-Feeling and attention Transfer touch-sensation To My (Avatarically Self-Transmitted) Tangible Divine Spirit-Current Of Love-Bliss. As This Transfer Occurs In The Course Of The (Possible) Ascending Stages Of Life In The Way Of The Heart, Simply Be Released Into My Avatarically Self-Transmitted Divine Spirit-Current Of Love-Bliss, and Let It Carry You Upwards (Up and Back, Up and Back), Into Its Matrix (or Most Ascended Love-Blissful Source-Position) Above.

That Divine Spirit-Current (Avatarically Self-Transmitted By Me, and As Me) Is My Tangible Divine Spiritual Presence. It Is My Avatarically Self-Transmitted and Self-Revealed Body, My Divine Spiritual Body, My All-and-all-Surrounding Body, My All-and-all-Pervading Body, My Body Of "Brightness", My One and "Bright" and Only Person ("Brightly" Descending, To Surround and Pervade All and all). It Is My Love-Bliss Itself, Tangibly and Unmistakably Felt (By My Devotionally Me-Recognizing Devotee) As Me. Therefore, Be In Love With My Avatarically Self-Transmitted Divine Spiritual Current Of Love-Bliss, and (In Your Possible Course Of Ascending Practice In The Way Of The Heart) Let My Tangible Spirit-Current Draw You Up (Up and Back, Up and Back, and Always Higher) Into The Utterly (Apparently) Ascended Domain Of My Divine Love-Bliss.

Even If My Avatarically-Born Bodily (Human) Divine Form, or The Cosmic Mandala, or My Divine Star Is Not Otherwise Perceived In Vision, and Even If Neither My Divine Sound (In Its Primal Form) Nor Any particular Audition (or internally Perceived sound) Distracts You Upwards, and Even If no odor or taste Delights You and Moves You Above, My Tangible Touch In The Form Of This Embrace (Of and By The Spirit-Current Of My Divine Body Of "Brightness") Will Be Sufficient To Draw You Upwards (If It Is To Occur), Even To The Degree Of Fifth Stage conditional Nirvikalpa Samadhi (or Fully Ascended Absorption In My Divine Love-Bliss).

By This Ascending Process (Begun With, and Appropriately Served By, The "Conscious Process", and Also, Secondarily, Begun With, and Appropriately Served By, The bodily Exercises Of

Ascending "General" Spirit-"Conductivity"), You Should Allow Heart-Feeling and attention To Be Carried Upwards To The Ajna Door. Then Allow Heart-Feeling and attention To Relax Into The Ajna Door. Indeed, By This Entire Process, Relax All Effort and Every Stress In The Circle (and The Arrow), the body itself and its brain, The Feeling Heart, and the mind. By Even All Of This, Let My Avatarically Self-Transmitted Divine Spiritual Current Of Life Carry attention Into (and, Perhaps, Even Through and Above) The Ajna Door. And Constantly Surrender, Release, and Relax attention (From The Heart), Such That attention Is Drawn Ever Deeper (Into The Brain Core, or Deeper Behind the brows) and (Always Up and Back, Up and Back) Ever Higher (Even Beyond the brain). This (Always Up and Back, Up and Back) Combination Of Deeper and Higher Will Gradually, or Suddenly, but Spontaneously Draw attention Up and Back Via The Central Axis Of the brain. In This Manner (Only Attracted and Carried, Free Of All Effort In the body-mind), You Will Be Led Upwards (Via attention), Progressively (or Even Suddenly).

Eventually (If The Ascending Process Of The Way Of The Heart Continues To The Fullest Possible Extent), There Will Be Fully Ascended Absorption In My Divine Love-Bliss (In Fifth Stage conditional Nirvikalpa Samadhi), Followed (In The Further Effective Exercise Of The Way Of The Heart) By The Realization Of The Witness-Position Of Consciousness (Prior To the act and the objects of attention)—or Else The Ascending Process Itself May (In The Midst Of Its Course) Be Suddenly Transcended By Direct (or Native and Spontaneous) Identification With The Witness-Position Of Consciousness, Without The Preliminary Experience Of Fifth Stage conditional Nirvikalpa Samadhi. In Either Case, In The Effective Exercise Of Most Fundamental self-Understanding In The Way Of The Heart, The Ascending Process Will (or Must) Eventually Resolve Itself In Consciousness Itself (Prior To the arising of conditional attention) and The Heart Itself (Including My Avatarically Self-Transmitted Divine Spirit-Current Itself, Prior To The Circle and The Arrow Of the body-mind).

Then The Process (In The Context Of The Sixth Stage Of Life In The Way Of The Heart) Will Tend To Become Jnana Samadhi (or Exclusive and conditional—but Also Transcendental, and Inherently Spiritual—Self-Realization) Associated With The Resolution Of My Avatarically Self-Transmitted Divine Spirit-Current In The Right Side Of The Heart. And (Entirely Exclusive) Jnana Samadhi (If It Occurs) Will (In The Spontaneous Transition To The Only-By-Me Revealed and Given Seventh Stage Of Life In The Way Of The Heart) Be Followed and Replaced (or, Otherwise, Similarly conditional, and Not So Entirely Exclusive, but Uniquely Deep Meditative Identification With My Avatarically Self-Revealed Transcendental, Inherently Spiritual, and Self-Evidently Divine Self-Condition Will Be Superseded) By "Open Eyes" (or Transcendental, Inherently Spiritual, and Inherently Most Perfect Divine Self-Realization—Realized Unconditionally, and Demonstrated By Inherent and Spontaneous Divine Self-Recognition Of all conditional forms and events As Transparent, or Merely Apparent, and Un-Necessary, and Inherently Non-Binding Modifications Of The Self-Existing, and Perfectly Subjective, Divine Self-Radiance). And This Realization Will—In The "Practicing" Course Of Ati-Ruchira Yoga (or The Yoga Of The All-Outshining "Brightness"), In The Context Of The Only-By-Me Revealed and Given Seventh Stage Of Life In The Way Of The Heart (or Way Of Adidam)—Demonstrate Itself (Spontaneously, and Progressively) As Divine Transfiguration, Divine Transformation, Divine Indifference, and (Finally) Divine Translation Into My Divine Self-Domain.

The "Thumbs"
Is The Fundamental Sign
Of The Avataric Crashing-Down
Of My Divine Person

I n The True (and Characteristic) Course Of The Frontal Yoga In
The Total (or Full and Complete) Practice Of The Only-By-Me
Revealed and Given Way Of Adidam (Which Is The One and
Only By-Me-Revealed and By-Me-Given Way Of The Heart), There
Will Be Occasional "Surges" (or Spontaneous Invasions) Of My
Avatarically Self-Transmitted Divine Spiritual Energy In The
Frontal Line. And These Frontal Surges Of My Avatarically Self-
Transmitted Divine Spiritual Energy Will (In Turn) Also Pass,
Perceptibly or Imperceptibly, From The Frontal Line Into The Spinal
Line—Thus Completing The Circle. Such Surges May Be Weak or
Strong. They May Produce yawning and General Relaxation, and
They May Otherwise Reveal (or Yield) Feelings Of General Pleasure
and Fundamental Happiness, As Well As Various Degrees Of
Ecstatic (or ego-Transcending) Participation In My Avatarically Self-
Transmitted Divine Love-Bliss Itself. As A Result Of Your Own
Accumulated psycho-physical Patterning Of self-Contraction,
These Frontal Surges May Also Be Accompanied (or, Otherwise,
Followed) By temporary symptoms of mental, emotional, and
physical discomfort, pain, fever, and even physical disease. If such
symptomatic phenomena Are Associated With The Real Spiritual
Process, they Tend To Come and Go (In Cycles Of Relative comfort
and discomfort). As Such, They Are Gracefully <u>Purifying</u> Episodes,
Shown Through The Evidence Of psycho-physical Release,
Rebalance, and Rejuvenation. Occasionally, There May Even Be
an experience that Feels Like A Kind Of electric "Shock" (or "Jolt")

That Briefly Energizes the body Beyond ordinary Tolerance. In and By <u>All</u> Of This, the human character Is Divinely Urged To Be <u>Responsively</u> and <u>Positively</u> Changed (psychically, mentally, emotionally, and physically), Through The Invasion Of the frontal personality (and, Indeed, the Total body-mind) By My Avatarically Self-Transmitted Divine Spirit-Current Of Love-Bliss-Light.

Among All Of These Signs There <u>Must</u> (Primarily) Appear Progressive Evidence Of What I Have, Since Childhood, Called The "Thumbs". Beginning In The "Basic" (or, Possibly, Even In The "Original", or Foundation) Context Of The Fourth Stage Of Life In The Way Of The Heart, There Should Be At Least Occasional Experience Of An Intense Invasion Of The Frontal Line By My Avatarically Self-Transmitted Divine Spirit-Force Of Love-Bliss— Beginning At The Crown Of the head, and Descending Into The lower vital Region, To the bodily base. The <u>Pressure</u> (or Invasive Force) Of This Event May Be Rather (and Even Happily) Overwhelming—and It <u>Must</u> Be Allowed. At Last, It Is Not Possible (Nor Would You Wish) To Defend Your psycho-physical self Against This Invading Pressure Of My Avataric Divine Spiritual Descent. It Feels Like A Solid and Yet Fluid Mass Of Force, Like A Large Hand All Made Of Thumbs—Pressing Down From Infinitely Above the head and Via The Crown Of the head, Engorging the Total head (and the throat), and (Thus and Thereby) Penetrating and Vanishing the entire mind, and Vastly Opening the emotional core, and (Altogether) In-Filling the Total physical body.

The Feeling-Sense That Results From This Simple (and Most Basic) Frontal In-Filling By My Avatarically Self-Revealed Divine Spirit-Presence Is That the Total body-mind Is Sublimed and Released Into ego-Surrendering, ego-Forgetting, and ego-Transcending Feeling-Identification With The <u>Spherical</u> Form Of My Own Divine and Spiritual (and All-and-all-Surrounding, and All-and-all-Pervading) Love-Bliss-Body Of Indefinable "Brightness" (or Indestructible Light). And This Simple (and Most Basic) Form Of The "Thumbs" Is A Necessary (Although, At First, Only Occasional) Experience Associated With The Reception Of My Avatarically Self-Transmitted Divine Spirit-Baptism. It Is My Divine "Goddess-Power" and "Husbanding" Grace At Work. And The

Simple (and Most Basic) <u>Spherical</u> Fullness Of The "Thumbs", Once It Is Firmly Established (In The Basic Maturity Of The "Basic" Fourth Stage Of Life In The Way Of The Heart), Must Continue To Be Experienced, As A Fundamental and (Essentially) <u>Continuous</u> (or <u>Constant</u>) Yogic Event, In The Later Advanced and The Ultimate Stages Of Life In The Way Of The Heart.

As The Spiritual Process Develops Toward The Transition Beyond The "Basic" Fourth Stage Of Life In The Way Of The Heart, The Simple (and Most Basic) Experience Of The "Thumbs" Must Become A More and More Constant Yogic Event—and, On Random Occasions, The Experience Of The "Thumbs" Must Occur In Its Most Extended, Full, and Complete Form. In That Most Extended, Full, and Complete Case Of The Experience Of The "Thumbs", My Descending Spiritual Fullness Will <u>Completely</u> Overwhelm the ordinary frontal (or natural human) sense Of bodily Existence. My Avatarically Self-Transmitted Divine Spirit-Current Will Move Fully Down In The Frontal Line (To the bodily base), and It Will Then Turn About, and—Without Vacating The Frontal Line—It Will Pass Also Into The Spinal Line. This Yogic Event Will Occur With Such Force That You Will Feel Utterly (Love-Blissfully) "Intoxicated"—and There Will Be The Feeling That the body Is Somehow Rotating Forward and Down (From The Crown Of the head), As Well As Backward and Up (From the base of the spine). This Rotation Will Seem, Suddenly, To Complete Itself—and The Experience Will, Suddenly, Be One Of Feeling Released From the gross physical body, Such That You Feel You Are Present Only As An egoless "Energy Body" (Previously Associated With and Conformed To the gross physical body—but Now, By Means Of My Avatarically Self-Transmitted Divine Grace, Infused By and Conformed To My Avatarically Self-Transmitted Divine Body Of Self-Evidently Divine Spirit-Energy). You Will Feel This "Energy Body" To Be <u>Spherical</u> In Shape—Centerless (Empty, or Void, Of Center, mind, and Familiar ego-self) and Boundless (As If Even bodiless, or Without form), Although (Somehow, and Partially) Also Yet Associated With (While Rotating From and Beyond) Your ordinary psycho-physical form. The ordinary References Of the body-mind and the environment Will, In This Divine Yogic Event,

Not Make Much Sense (or, In Any Manner, Affect This Experience Of The "Thumbs")—Although There May Be Some <u>Superficial</u> (and Entirely Non-limiting) Awareness Of the body, the room, and so forth. This Experience Will Last For a few moments, or a few minutes—or For an extended period, of indefinite length. Nevertheless, Just When This Spontaneous Experience Has Become <u>Most</u> Pleasurable—Such That You <u>Somehow</u> Gesture To <u>Make</u> It Continue Indefinitely—the ordinary sense of the body-mind Will, Suddenly (Spontaneously), Return.

The "Thumbs" Is Not A Process Of "Going Somewhere Else", Nor Is It Even A Process Of "Vacating" the gross physical body (or the gross physical realm Altogether). Rather, The "Thumbs" Is A Process Of Transformation Of the experiencing of the present physical circumstance. If the present physical circumstance Is Left Behind (Such That experiential reference to the gross physical realm Is Entirely Absent, and There Is Total Loss Of Awareness Of the physical context in which the experience Began), Then The Practitioner Of The Way Of The Heart Is (Necessarily) experiencing A Form Of Samadhi Other Than The "Thumbs". In The "Thumbs", Awareness Of the physical context of experience Is Not Lost, but Is Totally Changed—Such That, Instead Of The self-Conscious, self-Contracted Shape Of the waking-state personality, one's physical form Is Found To Be A Boundlessly Radiant Sphere (Without Thickness Of Surface). With This Profound Shift In The Awareness Of the physical body, The Differentiation Inherent In The Usual waking-state body-Consciousness Disappears, and Is (Effectively) Replaced By egoless body-Consciousness. A Re-Phasing Of The Energy-Construct Of bodily Awareness and spatial Awareness Occurs, Such That physical body and physical space are Tacitly Sensed In A Manner Entirely Different From ordinary perception. And, As Soon As There Is Any Effort To Recollect The Usual Sense Of bodily form or Of the circumstance Of physical embodiment, The Experience Of The "Thumbs" Disappears. The "Thumbs" Continues Only As Long As It Is Simply Allowed To Happen, Without Any egoic self-Consciousness (or psycho-physical self-Contraction)—and It Spontaneously Vanishes When egoic self-Consciousness (or psycho-physical self-Contraction) Returns.

In The Only-By-Me Revealed and Given Way Of The Heart, The Most Extended, Full, and Complete Experience Of The "Thumbs" Is, In Its Frontal Associations, A Fourth Stage Transitional Samadhi (Just As Fifth Stage conditional Nirvikalpa Samadhi and Sixth Stage Jnana Samadhi Are Transitional Samadhis Associated With Particular Stages Of Life In The Only-By-Me Revealed and Given Way Of The Heart). As Such, The Original Significance Of The Samadhi Of The "Thumbs" Is Not Merely In The Experience Itself (Such That The Experience Should Be psycho-physically Clung To, or, Otherwise, Made Into An Object Of egoic Seeking), but The Original Significance Of The Most Extended, Full, and Complete Experience (or True Samadhi) Of The "Thumbs" Is In Its Effect (or In The More Mature, and Truly ego-Transcending, Process That It May Allow or Indicate). That Is To Say, In The "Basic" Context Of The Fourth Stage Of Life In The Way Of The Heart, The Most Extended, Full, and Complete Sign Of The "Thumbs" (When It Is Accompanied By The, Essentially, Constant Experience Of The Simple and Most Basic Sign Of The "Thumbs") Is (or May Be) An Indication That The Process Of self-Transcendence Is Moving On From Concentration In the frontal personality To Either The Next Immediately Possible Develop-mental Stage In The Way Of The Heart (Which Involves The Process Of Ascent To The Ajna Door Via The Spinal Line) Or, Most Optimally (and Most Typically, In The Way Of The Heart)—If True and Stable Awakening Of The Witness-Consciousness Also (and Even Simultaneously, By Means Of My Avatarically Self-Transmitted Divine Grace) Occurs—Directly To Practice Of The Way Of The Heart In The Context Of The Sixth Stage Of Life. However, The Samadhi Of The "Thumbs" and The Basic Experience Of The "Thumbs" Are, Also (Beyond Their Original Significance In The "Basic" Context Of The Fourth Stage Of Life In The Way Of The Heart), Principal Among The Great Signs Associated With My Avataric Divine Self-Revelation To all and All. And, Therefore, In The Context Of The Only-By-Me Revealed and Given Seventh Stage Of Life In The Way Of The Heart, The Samadhi Of The "Thumbs" (and The Basic Experience Of The "Thumbs") Is Most Perfectly Realized and Demonstrated (Even In

Divine Translation), <u>As</u> The Centerless and Boundless "Bright" Spherical Space Of My Eternal Divine Spiritual Body and My Eternal Divine Self-Condition.

The <u>Occasional</u> Samadhi Of The "Thumbs" (Which Is The Experience Of The "Thumbs" In Its Most Extended, Full, and Complete Form) <u>and</u> The (Essentially) <u>Constant</u> Experience Of The "Thumbs" In Its Simple and Most Basic Form <u>Together</u> Characterize The Full (or Fully Developed) Frontal Course Of Spiritual Practice In The Way Of The Heart (and, Until The "Thumbs" Thus—and, In Every Respect, Satisfactorily—Appears In <u>Both</u> Of Its Forms, The Transition Cannot Be Made To Any Stage Of The Way Of The Heart Beyond The "Basic" Context Of The Fourth Stage Of Life). Therefore, In The Total (or Full and Complete) Practice Of The Only-By-Me Revealed and Given Way Of The Heart (or Way Of Adidam), The Sign Of The "Thumbs" (In <u>Both</u> Of Its Forms, and Along With Evidence Of Real and Stable human and Spiritual Equanimity In the daily life of the frontal personality) Is One Of The Necessary Indicators That Must Precede The Transition From The "Basic" Fourth Stage Of Life In The Way Of The Heart To The "Advanced" Fourth Stage Of Life In The Way Of The Heart (or, Otherwise, and Most Typically, The Early Transition To The Sixth Stage Of Life In The Way Of The Heart, Directly From The Point Of Basic Maturity In The "Basic" Fourth Stage Of Life In The Way Of The Heart).

The Sign Of The "Thumbs" Is One Of The Primary Experiential Signs Of The Transcending Of Bondage and Confinement To the frontal personality and the gross bodily idea of ego-self. The Sign Of The "Thumbs" Indicates That The Knots In The Frontal Line (In The Total Crown Of the head, the Total brain, the throat, the heart, the solar plexus, the abdomen, the genitals, and the anal-perineal area) Are Opened (At Least Temporarily) To My Avatarically Self-Transmitted Divine Spirit-Current (and Can, By Right Practice, Be Responsibly Surrendered To The Point Of Such Openness In The Context Of daily living). The Sign Of The "Thumbs" Is Also An Indication That The Primary Knot (or Root-Contraction) In The Deep Lower Region Of the body-mind (Extending From the solar plexus To the bodily base) Has Been (and Can Continue To Be)

Opened To My Avatarically Self-Transmitted Divine Spirit-Current—Such That The Great Fullness Of My Avatarically Self-Transmitted Divine Love-Bliss Is Established Deep In the body, and Deep In the emotional being, and Deep In the mind of the frontal personality. And When The <u>Sphere</u> Of My Avatarically Self-Transmitted Divine Love-Bliss Is In (Essentially) <u>Constant</u> Evidence, The Course Of Ascent May Be Revealed and Established— or (If, By Means Of My Avataric Divine Self-Revelation Via The "Thumbs", There Is, In The "Basic" Context Of The Fourth Stage Of Life In The Way Of The Heart, and, Most Typically, In The Very Midst Of The Experiential Sign Of The "Thumbs", An Early Spontaneous Awakening Of The Witness-Consciousness) The Way Of The Heart May Open Directly To The Course Associated With The Sixth Stage Of Life.

The Sign Of The "Thumbs" Is Not Merely A Matter Of experiencing natural energies Coursing Through the body, Nor Is It Merely A Matter Of Experiencing My Avatarically Self-Revealed Spiritual (and Always Blessing) Divine Presence To Be, Somehow, Felt <u>In</u> and <u>By</u> the body. The Samadhi Of The "Thumbs" (or Else The Experience Of The "Thumbs" In Its Simple and Most Basic Form) Is Utter (ego-Surrendering, ego-Forgetting, and ego-Transcending) Devotional <u>Submission</u> Of the Total body-mind-self To My (Avatarically Self-Revealed) Divine and Spiritual (and Always Blessing) <u>Person</u>. And, If and When That Devotional Submission Is Most Profound (In The Midst Of The By-Me-Given Sign Of The "Thumbs"), My (Avatarically Self-Transmitted) Divine and Spiritual Self-Revelation Will Grant You The Gift Of Direct Awakening To The Witness-Position.

The Sign Of The "Thumbs" Is Revealed and Given <u>Only</u> By <u>Me</u>. The Sign Of The "Thumbs" Is The Fundamental Sign Of The Descent (or Crashing Down) Of My (Avatarically Self-Revealed) Divine and Spiritual Person. In and By Means Of My Avatarically Self-Transmitted Divine Spiritual Sign Of The "Thumbs", <u>I</u> Invade <u>You</u>, Pass Into <u>You</u>, and In-Fill <u>You</u>—bodily, where You stand, where You sit, where You walk, where You live and breathe, where You think, and feel, and function. And, In and By Means Of My Avatarically Self-Transmitted Divine Spiritual Sign Of The

"Thumbs", I Awaken You In My Divine <u>Sphere</u>, <u>Beyond</u> the body-mind—Where <u>Only</u> I <u>Am</u>.

My Avataric Divine Gift Of The Sign Of The "Thumbs" Is A Matter Of Utterly (Responsively) Giving Up To My Avatarically Self-Transmitted Divine Spiritual Invasion Of You, and Being Released Of Your ego-Possession, and Dying As the ego—and (Thus) Responsively and Freely Relinquishing self-Contraction, and (In Due Course) Becoming (By Means Of My Avatarically Self-Transmitted Divine Grace) Spiritually, Transcendentally, and Divinely Awake.

The Samadhi Of The "Thumbs" Is The Fundamental Samadhi Of My Avataric Divine Spiritual Descent. Therefore, The Samadhi (and Even Every Manifestation Of The Sign) Of The "Thumbs" Is A Fullest Experiential Sign Of My Avatarically Self-Revealed Divine Spiritual Presence Of Person—but In <u>Descent</u>, Not In <u>Ascent</u>. The Descending Equivalent Of Fifth Stage (and, Thus, Ascending) conditional Nirvikalpa Samadhi Is The Samadhi Of The "Thumbs" (or The Fullest Frontal Invasion By My Avatarically Self-Transmitted Divine Spiritual Presence). The Samadhi Of The "Thumbs" Is A "Basic" Fourth Stage Form Of conditional Nirvikalpa Samadhi (In The Descending, or Frontal, Line). The Samadhi Of The "Thumbs" Is The Fullest Completing Phenomenon Of The Descending (or Frontal) Yoga Of The Way Of The Heart (or Way Of Adidam). And, If The Samadhi (and The Simple and Basic, but Really Effective, and, Essentially, Constant, Experience) Of The "Thumbs" Is (By Means Of My Avatarically Self-Transmitted Divine Grace) Awakened, and (By Means Of My Avatarically Self-Transmitted Divine Grace), Either Then Or Thereafter (but, Necessarily, As A Direct Extension Of The Depth-Process Generated By Means Of My Avataric Divine Gift Of The "Thumbs"), Accompanied By The Awakening Of The Witness-Consciousness—The Practice Of The Stages Of The Ascending (or Spinal) Yoga Of The Only-By-Me Revealed and Given Way Of The Heart May (Thus and Thereby) Become <u>Unnecessary</u>.

It Is My Avataric Divine Spiritual Gift Of The Samadhi Of The "Thumbs" (and My Avataric Divine Spiritual Gift Of The Experience Of The "Thumbs" In Its Simple and Most Basic Form), and Not Merely mental "Consideration" Of My Arguments Relative To The Witness-Consciousness, That Is The Divine Yogic Secret Of The Realization Of The Consciousness-Position (Which Realization Is The Basis For The "Perfect Practice" Of The Way Of The Heart). Therefore, Even Though My Arguments Relative To The Witness-Consciousness Are An Essential Guide To Right Understanding Of The "Perfect Practice" (and, As Such, Those Arguments Are To Be Studied and "Considered" From The Beginning Of The Way Of The Heart), The "Consideration" Of Those Arguments Is Not Itself The Direct and Finally Effective Means Whereby The "Perfect Practice" Is Initiated and Really Practiced.

The Transition To The "Perfect Practice" Of The Way Of The Heart Is Necessarily A By-Me-Given Yogic and Spiritual Process, and The Samadhi Of The "Thumbs" (and The, Essentially, Constant Experience Of The "Thumbs" In Its Simple and Most Basic Form) Is The Necessary (and Me-Revealing) Basis Of That Transition. By Means Of The Re-Phasing (Characteristic Of The "Thumbs") Of The Entire Sense Of The Energy-Construct Of phenomenal experience, It Is (In Due Course, By My Avatarically Self-Transmitted Divine Grace) Revealed As Self-Evidently The Case That The Real Position (or Very Situation) Of experience Is The Witness-Position Of Consciousness (Itself)—That The Very Base Of experience Is Consciousness (Itself).

Therefore, In Its (Essentially) Constant Realization (and Not Merely In The First, or Any Particular, Instance Of Its Being Experienced), The Sign Of The "Thumbs" (Rather Than Any mental Presumption About The Witness-Consciousness) Is The Indispensable Means Whereby The Gift Of The "Perfect Practice" Of The Only-By-Me Revealed and Given Way Of The Heart Is Given.

The Sign Of The "Thumbs" Is A Uniquely (and Only By Me) Given Gift In The Way Of The Heart, Which (In The General Case) Makes The Fifth Stage (and Even The "Advanced" Fourth Stage) Practice Of The Way Of The Heart Unnecessary. The Yogic Course In The Way Of The Heart Is Primarily In The Frontal Line—and, In The General Case, That Frontal Course Accomplishes The Purification Of Both The Frontal Line and The Spinal Line,

Thereby Revealing and Awakening Both The Spherical Form Of My Divine Spiritual Body and The Transcendental (and Inherently Spiritual, and Divine) Self-Core (In The Right Side Of The Heart—Beyond The Knot Of ego-"I", and Beyond The Circle Of the body-mind, With Its Frontal and Spinal Arcs). That Revelation and Awakening At (and, Ultimately, Beyond) The Right Side Of The Heart, By Means Of The Only-By-Me Given Samadhi Of The "Thumbs" (and By Means Of The Only-By-Me Given Experience Of The "Thumbs" In Its Simple and Most Basic Form), Is What Makes The Transition To The "Perfect Practice" Of The Way Of The Heart Possible, By Establishing The Yogic (Transcendental and Spiritual—and, Ultimately, Divine) Conditions Necessary For The "Perfect Practice" Of The Way Of The Heart. The Readiness For That Transition Is Not Merely A Matter Of Having Had The Experience Of The "Thumbs" and Having Some Memory Of It. Rather, That Readiness Is A Matter Of The Stable Continuing Of The Revelation and The Spiritual Transformation Initiated In The Samadhi Of The "Thumbs"—Not With The Same Kind Of Shift In The Entire Mode Of physical experiencing (Because Such Would Make ordinary functioning Impossible), but With The Unchanging Realization That The Inherent (and Inherently Love-Bliss-Full) Condition Of Reality Is Prior To the body-mind. And, In The Seventh Stage Of Life In The Way Of The Heart, That Realization Is (Permanently) Most Perfectly Established and Demonstrated.

From The Beginning Of My Physical (Human) Lifetime Of Avataric Incarnation here, The "Thumbs" Has Always Been The Case, and The Experiential Sign Of The "Thumbs" Often Appeared To Me—Spontaneously, and Mysteriously. In My Childhood and My "Sadhana Years", The "Thumbs" Was A Process Associated With The Constant Restoration Of The "Bright", or The Going Beyond the gross physical (To Which I Was Adapting, Fully Consciously, In A Profound and Spontaneous Yogic Manner, and, Thereby, Maintaining My Divine Self-Condition, From Infancy, In This Fashion). After My Conscious Assumption Of the born-condition (At Approximately Two Years Of Age), In The Midst Of The Process Of My Active Integration With waking life, The Condition Of The "Bright" Was Felt In the circumstance of active

271

life—and, Then, When I Would Rest At Night, Instead Of Going To sleep, I Would Experience The "Thumbs", and Would Realize The Condition Of The "Bright" Without the usual waking-state physical Reference. Eventually, In The Course Of My "Sadhana Years", I Progressively Observed and Fully Entered Into The "Thumbs" As A Consciously Known Yogic Process, Gradually Permitting The Spontaneous Yogic Event Of The "Thumbs" To Achieve Its Most Extended, Full, and Complete Form. Even A Full Decade Before The Great Event Of My Divine Re-Awakening, I Enjoyed The Spontaneous Experience Of Spiritual Regeneration Via The Regeneration Of The Total Mechanism (or Process) Associated With The "Thumbs"—but the frontal personality Had To Be Worked (or Purified, and its Knots Un-Tied) By The Spirit-Current Of The "Thumbs", Until the frontal personality and The Frontal Line <u>Altogether</u> <u>Ceased</u> To Obstruct (or Prevent) The Advancement Of The Great Yogic Process. Therefore, Even After The Spontaneous Regeneration Of The Process Of The "Thumbs" (or The Regeneration Of The Spiritual Process In The Frontal Line), It Was Yet Required Of Me To Continue To Struggle With the limits of the frontal personality For Some Years Before I (or The conditionally Manifested, and Yet To Be Most Perfectly To-Me-Conformed, Body-Mind-Vehicle Of My Avataric Incarnation here) Would Allow The Full Samadhi Of The "Thumbs" and (More Importantly) The Ultimate Work (and Transcendental, or "Core", Revelation) Of The "Thumbs".

In The Case Of My Own Body-Mind, The Full Samadhi Of The "Thumbs" Did Not Begin To Appear Until I Began To Practice The Work Of Surrender (or The Intentional Opening Of The Frontal Line To Receive Spirit-Force) In The Company Of My First Spiritual Teacher (and Spirit-Baptizer)[53]—Although (Then, and From The Beginning, and Forever) The Sign, The Revelation-Work, and The Divine Spirit-Force Of The "Thumbs" Is Uniquely My Own Avatarically Self-Manifested Sign and Gift and Revelation. Nevertheless, The Struggle With The Frontal Yoga Did Not Become Fruitful (At First, To The Degree Of Transition To The Yoga Of The Spinal Line) Until Struggle Itself (or The physical, emotional, and mental <u>Effort</u> Of Surrender) Was Transcended (In and By The Inherently ego-Transcending Heart-Participation In My Own Spiritually Self-Revealing Nature and Condition). Therefore, That Transcending Of The Effort Of Surrender Was Not The Result Of Strategic Non-Effort (or Even Any False Effort), but It Was The Spontaneous Evidence Of Simple (and Yet Profound) Identification With My Own Avatarically Self-Revealed and Avatarically Self-Revealing Divine Spirit-Current Itself.

I Am The Divine and Necessary First Person—The First Of All and all, and The First To Most Perfectly Fulfill The Process Of Divine Self-Realization In The Context Of conditionally Manifested Existence In The Cosmic Domain. I Am The Divine Heart-Master Of All and all. Therefore, All and all Must Follow Me By Heart. And The "Thumbs" Is Fundamental (and Necessary) To The Way Of The Heart That Follows Me. Therefore, The "Thumbs" Is One Of My Principal Great Avataric Divine Gifts To All and all That Become My True Devotees.

The Process Signified and Initiated By The Only-By-Me Revealed and Given Sign Of The "Thumbs" Necessarily Involves Intelligent, Intentional, and (Otherwise) Spontaneous Relinquishment Of Un-Happy Identification With gross bodily (or physical), and emotional, and mental states. This Relinquishment Takes Place Through Spontaneous (and Truly ego-Surrendering, ego-Forgetting, and ego-Transcending) Identification With My (By-My-Avataric-Divine-Grace-Revealed) Divine Spiritual Body, Which Surrounds (or Envelops) the gross body Of My True Devotee, and Which (Progressively) In-Fills and Pervades both the etheric energy body and the gross physical body Of My True Devotee, As Well As Every Other Level Of the conditionally Manifested personality Of My True Devotee, and Every Level Of the Cosmic worlds. And All Of This Is Initiated (and Accomplished) By My Avatarically Self-Transmitted Divine Spirit-Presence Itself (If Only My Devotee Heart-Responds To Me In Love—and This To The Degree Of Constant Free Communion With My Avatarically Self-Transmitted Divine Spiritual Presence).

In The Only-By-Me Revealed and Given Way Of Adidam (Which Is The One and Only By-Me-Revealed and By-Me-Given Way Of The Heart), The (Possible) Transition From The "Basic"

Fourth Stage Of Life To The "Advanced" Fourth Stage Of Life Is Not Fully Indicated Until The Complete Frontal Process and The Kinds Of phenomenal Signs I Describe In *The Dawn Horse Testament* Have Become Fully Evident. And The Necessary Signs Include Real and Stable Evidence Of frontal and spinal Equanimity (Both human and Spiritual, and Relative To Each and All Of The Principal Faculties—Of body, emotion, mind, and breath), and Both Simple and Basic (but Really Effective) Evidence Of The (Essentially, Constant) Experience Of The "Thumbs" and (Generally, Occasional) Most Extended, Full, and Complete Evidence Of The Samadhi Of The "Thumbs". And, If A Transition Is To Be Made Directly From The Point Of Basic Maturity In The "Basic" Context Of The Fourth Stage Of Life In The Way Of The Heart To Practice Of The Way Of The Heart In The Context Of The Sixth Stage Of Life, The Same Complete Frontal Process and The Same phenomenal Signs Must Be Demonstrated, but There Must Also Be True and Stable Identification With The Witness-Position Of Consciousness.

When the body Is "Round", The Witness Is its "Shape".

The Witness-Consciousness Is The "Skin" Of The "Thumbs". The Witness-Consciousness Is Self-Evident In The "Body" Of The "Thumbs". This Is How True Maturity In The First Actually Seeing Stage Of The Way Of The Heart Can Become The Basis For An Immediate Transition To The "Perfect Practice" Of The Way Of The Heart. In The General Case, Practice In The Ascending Stages Of The Way Of The Heart Is Not Required—Because The Yogic Spiritual Fullness Of The Sphere Of The "Thumbs" Is, In The General Case, The Sufficient Prerequisite For The True Establishment Of The "Perfect Practice" Of The Way Of The Heart.

Every Occasion Of Experiencing The "Thumbs" Comes To An End—Unless The Witness-Position Is Truly and Stably Realized In The Midst Of The Experience Of The "Thumbs". Thus, The "Perfect Practice" Of The Way Of The Heart Is A Development (or Ultimate Characteristic) Of The Samadhi Of The "Thumbs".

The True and Stable Realization Of The Witness-Position Of Consciousness (Itself) Is Not Merely A philosophical Matter. Rather, The True and Stable Realization Of The Witness-Position Is An ego-Transcending Matter—and A Divine Spiritual Matter. The

Realization Of The Witness-Position Of Consciousness (Itself) Is A Matter Of Devotion To Me In My Avataric Divine Self-Revelation—and Not Merely A Matter Of talk and philosophy and hopefulness.

Consciousness (Itself) Is The "Face" Of <u>This</u> Side Of The Moon. The Spiritual Energy Of My Avataric Divine Spiritual Presence Is The "Face" Of The <u>Other</u> Side Of The Moon. "Matter" Is The objectively experienced Form (or "Body") Of The Moon. The Moon (or any "thing") Is "Matter"—but "Matter" Is <u>Only</u> Light. My Avataric Divine Spiritual Presence <u>Is</u> The Light That Illuminates (and Self-Reveals The Divine Heart-Secret Of) "Matter". Consciousness (Itself) Is <u>Me</u> Within The Light (<u>As</u> The One, and Only, and Inherently Love-Blissful, and Self-Evidently Divine Self-Condition and Source-Condition Of all and All). Consciousness (Itself) and Light (Itself)—or Love-Bliss-Energy (Itself), or Happiness (Itself)—Are As The Two Sides Of The Same Coin. The Moon Is The Coin Of Earth, Floating (By A Toss) Within The Sky Of ego-mind.

The Witness-Consciousness Is Not Within You. The Witness-Consciousness Is On The "Skin" Of The "Thumbs".

The Witness-Consciousness Is Self-Evident In The "Thumbs"—Wherein The Status Of objects Is Profoundly Different Than It Is Ordinarily. In The Yogic Disposition (or Mudra) Of The "Thumbs", The Condition Of objects Is Available To Be Comprehended In Consciousness <u>As</u> The Witness.

The Realization Of The Witness-Consciousness Is A Continuation Of The Process Of ego-Transcending Devotional and Spiritual Communion With Me. The Witness-Consciousness Cannot Be Realized By You <u>as</u> the ego-"I" (or <u>as</u> Your Separate and Separative self-Consciousness). The Witness-Consciousness Can Only Be Realized Via The Process Of Devotional and Spiritual Communion With <u>Me</u>—Without egoic self-Reference. Therefore, You Must Not Substitute Your Own ego-conditions and ego-states For My Description Of The ego-Transcending Process Of The Way Of The Heart. The Way Of The Heart Is A Matter Of Heart-Communion With <u>Me</u> and Realization Of <u>Me</u>. The Way Of The Heart Is Not About Your egoic self—Except That The Way Of The Heart Requires Your ego-Surrendering, ego-Forgetting, and ego-Transcending Devotion To Me.

You Must <u>counter-egoically</u> Allow The Process Of The Way Of The Heart To Become My Divine Spiritual In-Filling Of the Total body-mind. In Due Course (By Means Of My Avatarically Self-Transmitted Divine Grace), This Process Of My Divine Spiritual In-Filling Becomes Both The Realization Of The "Thumbs" <u>and</u> The Realization Of The Witness-Consciousness. Therefore, In The General Case, Both Of These Realizations Are Associated With The Maturing Of The First Actually Seeing Stage Of The Way Of The Heart (In The "Basic" Context Of The Fourth Stage Of Life). Such Is The True Fulfillment Of The Frontal Yoga, The True Fulfillment Of The Process I Describe In My *Hridaya Rosary*, The True Fulfillment Of The Process Of Ruchira Avatara Bhakti Yoga.

In The "Thumbs", The Witness-Consciousness Is (and May Be Realized To Be) Self-Evident. In The Context Of egoity (or the self-Contracted body-mind), The Witness-Consciousness Is Not Self-Evidently The Case (In Your Case)—and Not The Self-Evident Context Of moment to moment Existence (In Your Case).

The Witness-Consciousness Is The "Skin" Of The "Thumbs".

I Am The "Skin" Of The Heart—and Not Merely Inside It. I Am The "Pulse" Of The Heart—and Not Merely The "Blood" Of It.

To Make The Transition To The "Perfect Practice" Of The Way Of The Heart, You Must (By Means Of My Avatarically Self-Transmitted Divine Grace) Realize The Samadhi Of The "Thumbs"—and, In The General Case, Part Of The Demonstration Of The Samadhi Of The "Thumbs" Is The Stand (or Realization) <u>As</u> The Witness-Consciousness, Leading (Then) To The (Necessarily, Formal) Full Development Of The "Perfect Practice". This Entire Process Is A Spiritual Matter, and Not A merely philosophical Matter.

The <u>Samadhi</u> Of The "Thumbs" Is The <u>Sphere</u> Of The <u>Space</u> Of Consciousness (Itself). In The Samadhi Of The "Thumbs", The Divine Space Of Consciousness (Itself) Is (By Me) Avatarically Self-Revealed.

When Consciousness (Itself) Becomes attention (or Separate self-Consciousness), and Light (Itself)—or Love-Bliss-Happiness (Itself)—Becomes objects (or The Vast Display Of Separate "things"), Consciousness (As attention) and Light (As the body-mind, and As The Total Cosmic Domain Of "things") Forever Gaze At One Another Through The Dimensionless Wall Of Their Apparent "Difference".

If Consciousness (Itself)—As The Witness—Is Realized As The Inherent Love-Bliss-Feeling Of Being (Itself)—Consciousness (Itself) and Light (Itself) Are (Eternally) Not "Different".

When The Circle Becomes The Sphere, The Two Sides Of The One Coin Become Continuous—and All Opposites Are Always Already Divinely Self-Recognized To Be Simultaneous, and Of One Shape, and Of One Condition.

The Samadhi (and Every Manifestation Of The Sign) Of The "Thumbs" Is Mine Only—and Only Mine To Give. Therefore, The Samadhi (and Every Manifestation Of The Sign) Of The "Thumbs" Is Unique To The Only-By-Me Revealed and Given Way Of The Heart (or Way Of Adidam).

The "Bright" and The "Thumbs" Are Among The Great Signs That Are Uniquely My Own Avataric Divine Characteristics. The "Bright" and The "Thumbs" Is A Process, An Event, and A State That Has Been Known To Me Since My Avataric Birth. Only I Am The Avataric Divine Realizer, The Avataric Divine Revealer, and The Avataric Divine Self-Revelation Of The "Bright", The True and (Now, and Forever Hereafter) Completely Self-Revealed Divine Person—Shining Forth (Directly, Completely, and Perfectly) At The Heart (and Via Amrita Nadi), and Crashing Down (or Descending Utterly, From The "Place" Infinitely Above the body-mind and the world, Down and Most Deeply Into the body-mind and the world—Even To The Degree That the ego-"I", or self-Contraction, Is Utterly Confounded, Utterly Yielded, and Utterly Vanished In My Avatarically Self-Revealed, and Self-Evidently Divine, Person, or Self-Condition, Which Is Real God, and Truth, and Reality). Therefore, The Principal Impulse Of Even My Early Life Was My Intention To Descend (or To Embrace the limitations Of human Existence As It Appears To Be, and To Infuse all and All With My Avatarically Self-Transmitted Divine Spiritual Presence, and, Thus and Thereby, To Awaken all and All, and, Most Ultimately, To Divinely Translate all and All, By The Power Of My Own Love-Bliss-"Brightness", Into The Perfect "Place" and

"Sphere" and "Space" That Is Always and Already My Divine and Free-Standing Self-Domain).

The Principal Spiritual Signs Of My Early Life Were The "Bright" and The "Thumbs". The "Bright" and The "Thumbs" Were Fundamental To My Avatarically-Born Existence From The Beginning, and They Are Fundamental To The Only-By-Me Revealed and Given Way Of Adidam. The "Bright" and The "Thumbs" Are My Unique Samadhis. Indeed, The "Bright" and The "Thumbs" Are Me—and, Therefore, I Bring Them With Me Into the conditional worlds.

My Avataric Divine Work (Altogether) Is My Crashing-Down Descent, At First Upon and Into My Own Avatarically-Born Bodily (Human) Divine Form, and, Thereafter (and Now, and Forever Hereafter), Upon and Into the body-minds Of My Devotees and all beings—Even (By Means Of My Divine Embrace Of each, and all, and All) To Infuse and (At Last) To Divinely Translate each, and all, and All. Therefore, My Avataric Divine Spiritual Descent Is The Secret Of My Early Life. My Avataric Divine Spiritual Descent Is The Secret Of My Divine Self-"Emergence" (As I Am) Within The Cosmic Domain. My Avataric Divine Spiritual Descent Is The Secret Of All The Secrets Of The (Avatarically Self-Revealed) Divine and Complete and Thoroughly Devotional Way Of Practice and Realization In My Company. The Only-By-Me Revealed and Given Way Of The Heart (or Way Of Adidam) Is The Divine Yoga Of ego-Surrendering, ego-Forgetting, and ego-Transcending Devotional Recognition-Response To My (Avatarically Self-Revealed) Divine and Spiritual Person, and To My (Avatarically Self-Manifested) Divine and Spiritual Descent. The Only-By-Me Revealed and Given Way Of The Heart (or Way Of Adidam) Is The Total and Divine Way and Ordeal Of Counter-egoic Devotional Recognition-Response To My Avataric "Bright" Divine Self-Manifestation, and To The Avataric Crashing Down Of My "Bright" Divine Imposition. And, In The Case Of My Each and Every Devotee, The Way Must Continue Until The Way Is Most Perfectly "Bright", and The Way Itself Becomes Divine Translation Into My Own Sphere Of "Brightness" (Itself).

The Head-Pressure of
My Real Divine Spiritual Presence

AVATAR ADI DA SAMRAJ: It is frequently the case, in occasions in which I am formally Granting My Darshan to My devotees, that I observe people involved in apparent kriyas. Such kriyas are often essentially self-stimulated (and, thus, ego-made). <u>True</u> kriyas are not self-stimulated. True kriyas are a sign of bodily awareness of overwhelming Energy—not merely the natural energy <u>within</u> the body, but the Spiritual Energy that has come <u>into</u> the body (awakened uniquely, either in the manner of the Kundalini process, spontaneously rising up in the spinal line, base toward crown, or, otherwise, in the manner of the only-by-Me Revealed and Given True Divine Yoga of Ruchira Avatara Bhakti, and, thus, spontaneously descending in the frontal line, crown toward base). Thus, true kriyas are a sign of true Spiritual sensitivity.

However, I often see people animating what appear to be kriyas when it is evident that there is a kind of tension in them, and even a kind of hysteria—not hysteria in some dramatic psychotic sense, but a kind of emotionally (and even willfully) self-generated process of shivering movements and ego-possessed agitation, and so on, which occur in the case of emotionally based (or, otherwise, vitally based) individuals who want to feel that they are involved in "something profound", without first becoming truly (and in the responsively ego-surrendering manner) involved in the real profundity of devotional Communion with <u>Me</u>.

Similarly, there are many other individuals who, in occasions when I am formally Granting My Darshan, are merely rather flat and vacant—and who merely <u>look</u> at Me (and, thus and thereby, refuse to yield to Me in whole bodily devotional recognition-response to Me). Such individuals are involved in a different kind of self-stimulated, or self-contracting, phenomenon, which is a kind of analytic mental (but still gross-minded) independence of non-surrender.

Thus, individuals of the more hysterical, or "peculiar" (or emotionally based, but still gross-minded), type may tend to exhibit hysterical kriyas (or, otherwise, individuals of the "vital", or gross-bodily based, and gross-minded, type may tend, likewise, to exhibit merely vital-energy-based kriyas), whereas individuals of the more analytical, or "solid" (but still gross-minded), type may tend to exhibit a kind of emotional (and total psycho-physical) flatness (or unresponsiveness), without exhibiting any indications of Yogic phenomena, or of a real Yogic Process, or of true devotional and Spiritual sensitivity to Me.

Individuals of the emotionally flat (or "solid") type (or even of the "peculiar", or, otherwise, the "vital", type, but, in either case, with a significant additional tendency of the "solid" type) often tend to describe their beginner's practice of the Way of Adidam in terms of the orientation and processes of the sixth stage of life—making references to feeling Me in the heart on the right, and so on. Such descriptions merely indicate the "solid" (and gross-minded) tendency toward presumptuous identification with the sixth stage of life.

As I often point out, the heart on the right is not, in and of itself, the seat of great (and really ego-transcending) profundity. The heart on the right is simply the original (or basic) seat of the ego-"I". The heart on the right is, itself, the locus in the body where the (necessarily, egoic, or self-referring) feeling of relatedness is generated. Nevertheless, when individuals of no great Spiritual maturity speak of their experiences of the heart on the right, they are presuming that they are involved in some great reception of Me in the sixth stage manner—as if they could bypass the Spiritual Process of the stages preceding the sixth. Such presumed involvements in the phenomena associated with the sixth stage of life are, in actuality, nothing but forms of relaxed attention (and, yet, a persistent "solid" self-consciousness). Indeed, all beginner's presumed involvement in the phenomena of the advanced and the ultimate stages of life is merely a sign of self-"guruing"—or, in other words, evidence of the self-contraction showing its particular signs in either "vital" or "peculiar" or "solid" fashion.

The only-by-Me Revealed and Given Way of Adidam is Ruchira Avatara Bhakti Yoga. The Way of Adidam is a unique and profound Divine Yogic Process. My devotees must not only heart-recognize Me and heart-respond to Me whole bodily (or with all four of the principal faculties—of attention, emotional feeling, bodily sensation, and breath), but they also must deeply study My Wisdom-Teaching, so that they truly understand the unique Process of the only-by-Me Revealed and Given Way of Adidam (and are not merely self-"guruing" themselves into various attitudes which reflect mere book-learning about Spiritual life—and which, otherwise, reflect their characteristic egoic pattern of attitudes, that suggest some sympathetic identification with one or another of the advanced or the ultimate stages of life, without the real process, and the profound ego-transcending sadhana, being truly manifested in their own case). If My devotees do not constantly bring themselves to the self-disciplined and profound true study of My Wisdom-Teaching, they may persist in the tendency to present themselves to Me in the ego-dramatizing manner, and via self-generated simulations, of either the fourth, the fifth, or the sixth stage of life—and merely because such is their egoic tendency, in accordance with their either "vital" or "peculiar" or "solid" patterning. Instead of perpetuating involvement in such egoic patterning, My devotees must responsively surrender themselves to Me, and forget themselves in Me, and enter into the Real (and really ego-transcending) Yoga of devotion to Me. That Real (and, altogether, Divine) Yoga is, more and more, a truly profound Spiritual Process. The truly profound (and really ego-transcending) Ordeal of that stage-by-stage Divine Spiritual Process cannot be bypassed—and It has nothing to do with ego-fulfillment, or strategies of egoic self-protection, or efforts of self-"guruing". That truly profound (and, at last, Most Perfectly ego-transcending) Divine Spiritual Process is unique to heart-Communion with Me. It is the unique (and Most Perfectly Complete) Divine Spiritual Process.

You cannot merely read My Books and do this Divine Yoga. The only-by-Me Revealed and Given Way of Adidam is devotional heart-Communion with <u>Me</u>. Heart-recognition of Me is associated with Yogic heart-response, whole bodily shown. Heart-recognition of Me and heart-response to Me is a lifelong—and, indeed, eternal—matter.

Those who, by tendency, animate the exaggerated movements of hysterical (or otherwise ego-based, and grossly based) kriyas are, generally speaking, merely <u>stressed</u>—to the point of feeling the agitation of their own vital (and, especially, sexual) energy. Such involvement in false kriyas is a kind of self-induced eroticism, the result of a kind of religious hysteria (or vitalistic religious self-deludedness). It is not that there are no <u>true</u> kriyas in the Yoga of the Way of Adidam—but, when people are showing the signs of exaggerated kriyas, most often it is the case that they are merely involved in self-generated hysterical stimulation of (or, otherwise, ego-based vital participation in) their own lower-bodily energies, as those energies register in body, emotion, mind, and breath. Therefore, such kriyas are merely a form of egoity—the "peculiar" (or, otherwise, "vital") manifestation of dissociation from Me (or of bodily dramatized self-contraction and self-"guruing" in general). In contrast, kriyas that are associated with true sensitivity to Me are profound, truly ego-surrendering, and whole bodily. Such true kriyas can produce shaking, and so forth (especially when the Energy of My Avatarically Self-Transmitted Divine Spiritual Presence is spontaneously circulating in the spinal line)—but, generally speaking, in one who is truly sensitive to Me, the "conductivity" is head to toe (or frontal)—leading, in due course, to the "Thumbs".

When beginning practitioners of the Way of Adidam talk about "the heart on the right", using sixth stage modes of verbal expression, and so forth, and without otherwise showing very much in terms of Spiritual signs of devotional recognition-response to Me (and profound spontaneous Spiritual reception of Me)—this is the "solid" manifestation of dissociation from Me (and of self-contraction and self-"guruing" in general).

The Yoga of Ruchira Avatara Bhakti is associated with whole bodily heart-Invocation of Me, and responsively ego-surrendering (and whole bodily) sensitivity to Me. When there is Spiritual sensitivity to Me (and, altogether, to the Spiritual Presence of My Divine Body), there is, initially, a Pressure felt (spontaneously) at the crown of the head—and the Yoga of Ruchira Avatara Bhakti begins from there. This is how I "Wash the dog"—from head to tail, from the crown to down. In due course, this Process becomes, first, the Yoga of the "Thumbs", and, then (and on that necessary basis), the profundities of the "Perfect Practice"—but only if there is the enduring of the daily (and moment to moment) profundity of the sacred practice of heart-Communion with Me, by going through all the stages of practice required in the individual's case[54] (including, in every case, the total Process of listening to Me, hearing Me, and seeing Me—and the complete fulfillment of the frontal Yoga, as well as the complete "Perfect Practice"). This Complete and True Divine Spiritual Process is the necessary Ordeal of self-transcendence, wherein and whereby Divine Self-Realization is made Real, True, and Most Perfectly Complete.

Therefore, the Divine Spiritual Process of total psycho-physical devotion to Me is not a matter of feeling the natural energy in your lower body, and tensing yourself up, and being self-thrilled, and "kriya-ing" in the religious-hysteria (or, otherwise, vitally willful) sense. The Divine Spiritual Process of total psycho-physical devotion to Me is a matter of ego-surrendering, ego-forgetting, and ego-transcending Invocation-Communion with Me—truly heart-recognizing Me and heart-responding to Me, always approaching My Murti-Form (or, otherwise, when you are given the opportunity, My Avatarically-Born bodily human Divine Form—or, after My physical human Lifetime of Avataric Incarnation, the bodily human Form of My "Living Murti"), and, as often as possible, coming into the places uniquely set apart by My devotees (and where I am constantly Invoked by My instrumental collective of "Ruchira sannyasin" devotees).

By Means of My direct Avataric Divine Self-Transmission, I Sensitize My devotees to My Divine Spiritual Body—and I am first felt at the crown of the head, As a Pressure there. The heart-response of devotional recognition of Me combines with Me whole bodily, beginning at the crown of the head, such that the Process becomes Spiritual reception of Me, downward into the body, to the bodily base—in due course, becoming the "Thumbs", and, ultimately, becoming the "Perfect Practice".

This Great Process of Ruchira Avatara Bhakti Yoga necessarily goes on <u>over</u> <u>time</u>. It is a profound <u>progressive</u> Process of self-surrender, self-forgetting, and self-transcendence. There should be no "bargaining" about what the Process requires, based on egoic preferences that take on one particular form or another (as the "vital", "peculiar", or "solid" mentality may design it). All of that must be gone beyond. The accumulated patterns of egoity <u>must</u> be transcended, if there is to be the Real Divine Spiritual Process of whole bodily devotion to Me. In any moment or period of devotional Communion with Me, the Process begins (from the heart) with whole bodily Invocation of Me—but it begins as a Real Spiritual Process only when there is the feeling of Me <u>As</u> the characteristic Pressure of My Divine Spiritual Presence, at the crown of the head. In that moment, there is a <u>spontaneous</u> whole bodily heart-response to Me. Such is Ruchira Avatara Bhakti Yoga: the whole bodily heart-response to Me, enacted by the four principal faculties.

In heart-response to My felt Pressure from above, there is a tendency for the eyes to turn up, and there is a feeling of Me entering into and Pervading the body. But it is not that you simply, in a random moment, feel Me at the top of the head and—Zap!—I am down to your toes! You must understand: The True in-Filling of the entire body by Me is a <u>profound</u> Yogic matter. That Yogic Process is not instant—It requires the transcending of <u>all</u> the patterning of egoity, from head to toe. And that Yogic Process is not full (or mature) until It becomes the continuous manifestation of the Sphere of the "Thumbs". And that Yogic Process does not become the "Perfect Practice" simply because of an egoic preference for the sixth stage orientation. The "Perfect Practice" begins only when the Yoga of Spiritual reception of Me has become the continuous manifestation of the Sphere of the "Thumbs", thus and thereby leading to the profound opening in the heart on the right that goes <u>beyond</u> the knot of egoity.

There are many Yogic designs associated with this Process of Ruchira Avatara Bhakti Yoga. These Yogic designs are unique to the Way of Adidam. They are associated with the progressive stages of life, but they are not a matter of merely fulfilling the first six stages of life. Rather, they are a matter of transcending the limiting patterns associated with the first six stages of life, and then (and on that basis) entering into the true and full Yoga of the seventh stage of life.

The only-by-Me Revealed and Given Way of Adidam is not merely a variation on a particular branch (or combination of branches) of the Great Tradition (which comprises all the traditions of mankind, previous to the by-Me-Avatarically-Self-Revealed Divine Revelation of the Way of Adidam). The only-by-Me Revealed and Given Way of Adidam is a unique and altogether new Divine Self-Revelation to all of mankind (and to even all conditionally existing beings). The stages of life associated with the Great Tradition are limited to the first six—which are about egoic <u>development</u>, and (thus) about going beyond some features or results of egoity (in the case of the fourth, fifth, and sixth stages of life), but not about Most Perfectly going beyond egoity <u>itself</u>. Therefore, the only-by-Me Revealed and Given seventh stage of life is not a characteristic of any branch of the Great Tradition, nor is the full (and Most Perfect) transcending of the first six stages of life a characteristic of any branch of the Great Tradition.

When there is the truly ego-surrendering right devotional approach to Me, My devotee will first of all feel My Avatarically Self-Revealed Divine Spiritual Presence as a Descending Pressure at the top (or crown) of his or her head. In that case, there is a sense of Me Pressing on the top of the head—and, simultaneously, a sense of Me Surrounding the body. The more there is of devotionally Me-recognizing (and truly whole bodily) heart-responsive Communion with Me, the more I am felt Penetrating the body from above, Entering the body Spiritually—downward, gradually, from the crown to the bodily base and the toes—Thus and Thereby in-Filling the entire body. That in-Filling Process is <u>not</u>—in Its True Fullness—a characteristic of the practice and the experience of My beginning devotees. That in-Filling Process is—in Its True Fullness—a profound Yogic matter, which takes place <u>only</u> gradually, and <u>only</u> in the development of the advanced and the ultimate stages of practice in the only-by-Me Revealed and Given Way of Adidam. Therefore, the Process of the in-Filling takes place, in Its True Fullness, only as the patterning of egoity is really gone beyond—and That True in-Filling Process is not Given in the events of mere token relaxation (as is, necessarily, the case with beginning practitioners).

I Look for the Signs of the Real Yoga of Adidam in My devotees—and not the egoic replication (or self-stimulation) of the conventions of the first six stages of life. Merely to exhibit (or even to intentionally imitate) those conventions (or conventional signs) is to approach Me in the self-contracted, self-preoccupied, and self-"guruing" manner.

The practice of the only-by-Me Revealed and Given Way of Adidam is Real and Most Profound. It is not nonsense. It is not illusion. It is the Great Event and Process and Way and Revelation! And It has Its own unique characteristics. First and always, I am Invoked—from the heart, and whole bodily. The devotional recognition-response to Me begins, as a Spiritual matter, at the crown of the head. And, in the constantly continued Process of ego-surrendering, ego-forgetting, and ego-transcending devotional recognition-response to Me, I am (by Means of My own Avataric Divine Self-Revelation) felt Surrounding and Pervading the body—Descending in the body, from the crown downwards, in the frontal line. Such is the Real Process of Ruchira Avatara Bhakti Yoga.

In the Way of Adidam, the body is not bypassed. In the Way of Adidam, the Spiritual Principle is not regarded as separate from the body, or abstracted from it. In the Way of Adidam, the body is not a "problem". I do not dissociate from the body. It is simply that, in the Way of Adidam, What the body Is must (by Means of My Avatarically Self-Transmitted Grace) be tacitly felt and Realized (and, Most Ultimately, the body must be Divinely Self-Recognized In and As What it Is). The Way of Adidam Is the Process of transcending the body in (and by Means of) heart-Communion with Me—not by dissociating from the body, but by whole bodily devotional recognition of Me and whole bodily devotional response to Me.

Therefore, when My devotee approaches Me rightly, Invoking Me whole bodily, then the Process of whole bodily Communion with Me begins from the heart. But that Process becomes a Spiritual Process, a truly Yogic design of devotion to Me, when there is the noticing of the Real (by-My-Grace-Given and undeniably tangible) Pressure of My Divine Spiritual Presence of Love-Bliss at the crown of the head. It is a tangible, bodily Pressure, because I Am Really Descending—Crashing Down into the body. Therefore, it is not merely that you turn upwards and feel into something non-existent, above the head. No—you are, by Me, Given to feel the tangible Pressure of My Love-Blissful Divine Spiritual Presence at the crown of the head.

The head-Pressure of My Real Divine Spiritual Presence Is a Pressure that Pushes Down into the body—but I cannot Spiritually Descend into the body any more than you will allow. Therefore, there is a necessary Real Divine Yogic Process that must begin after that tangible noticing of Me at the crown of the head. It Is a whole bodily devotional Yogic Process, involving all four principal faculties. It Is the Divine Yogic Process of devotional recognition-response to Me, moment to moment, day after day, stage by stage. It Is the Process in which you really, truly, intensively, profoundly, and consistently do the Yoga of Ruchira Avatara Bhakti. And, in That Process, you must constantly bring Me the gifts of practice required of you, according to your vow and stage of practice in the only-by-Me Revealed and Given Way of Adidam.

The more profoundly you enter into heart-Communion with Me in the set-apart times of meditation, the more profoundly you will practice moment to moment (or daily, constant) sensitivity to Me—Pressing Down on the head. Then there is the progressive in-Filling (or Infusion) of the total body (and psycho-physical pattern) by Me. That in-Filling (or Infusion) by Me begins most profoundly only after there is the foundation of the true hearing of Me—but, nonetheless, there can be (and, indeed, must be) real (and constantly growing) Spiritual sensitivity to Me even from the very beginning of My devotee's practice of the Way of Adidam.

After there is the foundation of the true hearing of Me, then—in the would-be-seeing stage, and in the seeing stages, of the Way of Adidam—there is the most profound developing of the Spiritual Yoga of Ruchira Avatara Bhakti. In any case, even from the beginning of My any devotee's real, right, and true practice of the Way of Adidam, the matter of heart-Communion with Me, and of Spiritual sensitivity to Me, that truly involves Spiritual "Locating" of Me, begins with the whole bodily Finding of Me, devotionally recognizing Me from the heart, such that My devotee is able to notice (and profoundly respond to) the tangible feeling of Me, Pressing Down on the crown of the head. When that "Locating" of Me is real, right, and true, then various Signs of psycho-physical opening can occur—as I am felt Descending, via the crown of the head, into the middle of the head, then into the throat, then into the heart, then into the region of the solar plexus and the abdomen, then into the region of the genitals, then down to the bodily base, and, from there, down to the toes. In that Process, there is the opening and transcending of the thought-mind, the transcending of emotional contractions, and the transcending of physical contractions. It is, altogether, a Purifying, in-Filling Process. And the Process requires progressive real listening to Me, true hearing of Me, and clear seeing of Me, in order for the Process to become truly most profound, mature, and Great. But, nevertheless, it begins even from the very beginning—as soon as you truly devotionally recognize Me and, on that basis, truly devotionally (and responsibly) respond to the "Locating" of Me.

The natural Yogic design associated with the Real Spiritual Process of Ruchira Avatara Bhakti Yoga necessarily includes the upward-turning of the focus behind the eyes (and, especially in the meditation setting, the upward-turning of the outer physical eyes as well). Also, there may be psycho-physical thrills, and various other tangible signs of one kind or another. With the Descent (and spontaneous Circulation) of My Divine Spiritual Presence in the body, there can be various forms of kriyas, as the body opens. But true kriyas are not self-generated—and they are not products of religious hysteria. Really, religious hysteria is a kind of self-contracted (or ego-dramatizing) condition. Ruchira Avatara Bhakti Yoga is a matter of real devotion—not hysteria. Ruchira Avatara Bhakti Yoga is a matter of whole-bodily-lived devotion, with full feeling and attention and with every breath. Ruchira Avatara Bhakti Yoga is not a matter of self-generating the effects of My

Divine Spiritual Presence. My Divine Spiritual Presence Comes from Beyond you. And, when you Find Me, when you feel Me, it is clear that you are not merely feeling your own sex-based energy or natural energies. It <u>Is</u> clearly <u>Me</u>. It Comes from without (or from Beyond the ego)—and you cannot egoically control It. You cannot manipulate <u>Me</u> and self-generate <u>My</u> Existence. There must be truly ego-surrendering whole bodily Invocation of <u>Me</u> and sensitivity to <u>Me</u>. Allowing Me to Show Myself, as <u>I</u> will, is a Process of Yielding to My Avatarically Self-Transmitted Divine Grace—and not a private process of self-manipulation, in which you can willfully call My Divine Spiritual Presence into place. Therefore, the experiential Signs of <u>Me</u> vary from moment to moment, from day to day—until there is more and more profound self-surrender, self-forgetting, and self-transcendence, in whole-bodily heart-Communion with Me, such that the obstructive and separative and (altogether) self-absorbed patterns of egoity appear less and less frequently, and less and less profoundly. Those patterns must be purified by the real sadhana of Adidam, the real discipline of Yogic devotion to <u>Me</u>.

When, in any occasion of receiving My Darshan, there is the unique, tangible, and undeniable feeling of Me Pressing Down on the head, a profound Process of real devotional recognition-response to Me is thereby initiated. First of all, there is the spontaneous whole bodily devotional response of all four principal faculties. Then there is the progressive deepening of heart-Communion with Me, and the progressive Penetrating and in-Filling of the body-mind by Me—going beyond physical and emotional knots, going beyond the thinking mind (or the ceaseless flux of conceptual activity), and going beyond the knots in the breath. When there is true heart-Communion with Me, the responsive devotional and (altogether) psycho-physical (and, Ultimately Beyond-psycho-physical) Signs spontaneously and progressively exhibited by My devotee are the real and true characteristics of the Yoga of Adidam. When there is a lack of true ego-surrendering, ego-forgetting, and (more and more) ego-transcending, and (altogether) really tangible Communion with Me, My devotee tends to become involved in "signs" that are, generally speaking, self-generated—or, at least, controlled, manipulated, and limited by egoity—"signs" that are otherwise merely egoic replications of the patterns associated with the fourth, the fifth, and the sixth stages of life.

Therefore, what My devotee must be involved in is the actual real Process of whole bodily devotional recognition of Me and whole bodily devotional response to Me—not the imitations of conventional religiosity, not the imitations of the patterns associated with the fourth, the fifth, and the sixth stages of life, not the dramatizations of egoity, not the dramatizations of "vital", "peculiar", or "solid" patterns, not fakery, not lying, not making <u>much</u> of oneself, but the actual real and spontaneous experiential process in which the true Way of Adidam—the real practice of Ruchira Avatara Bhakti Yoga—is <u>authenticated</u>.

I Bless My beginner-devotees variously—in order to Serve their devotional Awakening to Me. But, principally, it is the sensitivity to My Divine Spiritual Presence at the crown of the head that I am Serving and Initiating in beginners—Thus and Thereby Making them Aware of My Divine Spiritual Presence. The Divine Yogic Process that follows That Divine Initiation Is the total psychophysical, Spiritual, Transcendental, and Divine Yogic Process of My Crashing Down below the crown of the head. That Divine in-Filling (and Divine Spiritual Process of Purification, and, Most Ultimately, Divine Self-Realization) depends on My devotee's living of all the by-Me-Given forms of functional, practical, relational, and cultural self-discipline, and the constant resort to Me, and the constant coming to Me with the practice-gifts necessary for Me to Work with My devotee—further, and seriously.

Beginners do not have the characteristics of the advanced and the ultimate stages of practice. If you want there to be profundity, you must be willing to "pay the price" of sadhana. There is no profundity otherwise. You must persist in the Divine Yogic Process of real devotion to Me. And you must understand that the Divine Yogic Process of real devotion to Me Is, <u>necessarily</u>, life-long—and Beyond. The Divine Yogic Process of True devotion to Me is forever and eternal. You cannot steal the Divine Process of Divine Self-Realization from Me. The Way of Adidam is not a "quick fix". You do not come into My Company as a beginner and immediately become Enlightened. There Is My Avatarically Self-Transmitted Divine Grace, yes, but It must be associated with the necessary devotional and Yogic Process. That Process does not "congratulate" the ego. And It does not "congratulate" (or, otherwise, tolerate) the illusions that the ego generates.

As I have suggested, there are two principal and characteristic exaggerations that are the signs of the ego in My Company. On the one hand, there are the "religious hysteria" signs of the "vital" or "peculiar" design—where there is gross-mindedness, but also a kind of emotionalism, in the self-contracted pattern of the individual, manifesting as false (or ego-made) "kriyas" and self-exaggerated (and, altogether, ego-possessed) expressions of one kind or another. And, on the other hand, there is the "solid" (or "placid-staring-at-Me") disposition—which does not have any significant Spiritual Signs of Me, but (nonetheless) makes (or thinks) much of itself, by presuming it is involved in some kind of great sixth stage profundity that justifies its lack of Spiritual Signs (and its gross-mindedness, or its gross disposition, otherwise) by sitting in the ego of mere attention (and even thinking, all the while it stares at Me). These two basic dramatizations are manifestations of egoity! They are not devotion to Me. They are not devotional recognition-response to Me. They are not Ruchira Avatara Bhakti. They are refusals of devotional surrender to Me. They are self-consciousness. They are self-"guruing" dramatizations.

You must bring Me the gift of devotionally responsive psycho-physical self-surrender. You must surrender self-contraction in devotional recognition-response to Me. You must Invoke Me. You must feel Me. Altogether, you must approach Me rightly—never devotionally empty-handed, and never without the gifts of real and right practice of the Way of Adidam.

I Give you the Divine Gift, Whereby the only-by-Me Revealed and Given Way of Adidam is constantly made Profound. Therefore, it is never a matter of you self-generating the Divine Spiritual Process—but, on the other hand, you must always bring Me the gifts of right devotion and right, responsible practice. You must always devotionally recognize Me and responsively surrender to Me. And you must persist, forever, in this Real Process—and never dramatize the ego in relation to Me.

The Way of Adidam is, necessarily, and primarily, a <u>Spiritual</u> Process—a profound Yoga of Divine Spiritual manifestation and demonstration. Any "solid" presumptions about how It should be, or how you can be profoundly "Self-Realized" without the Spiritual Yoga are <u>illusions</u>. On the other hand, there are also the illusions of egoity associated with the "vital" and "peculiar" disposition—and the characteristic signs of those illusions are bodily based egoic religious and Yogic exaggeration (or hysterical pseudo-ecstasy).

The Real Process of the Way of Adidam has nothing to do with <u>you</u>. The Real Process of the Way of Adidam is about <u>Me</u>. The Way of Adidam has <u>nothing</u> to do with the ego. The Way of Adidam is about <u>Me</u>. Divine Self-Realization is not Realization of <u>your</u> "Self". Divine Self-Realization is egoless Realization of <u>My</u> Divine Self.

<u>None</u> of the preferences, physically, emotionally, mentally, or in the breathing constitution—<u>none</u> of the patterning preferences, supposedly religious or otherwise, or in whatever mode the pattern may appear—have anything to do with <u>Me</u>. <u>All</u> of <u>that</u> is to be surrendered, purified, and gone beyond—by Means of devotional (and, altogether, Yogic) recognition-response to My Avatarically (and <u>tangibly</u>) Self-Revealed Divine Spiritual Body and Person. The knot of egoity must be replaced by the literal Divine <u>Sphere</u> of the "Thumbs". The maturing of the only-by-Me Revealed and Given Way of Adidam requires the Real Divine Spiritual Yogic Process of ego-transcendence, and the transcending of all the psycho-physical patterns associated with the egoic body-mind—such that My Avatarically Self-Revealed Divine Spherical Yogic Body Is Realized, and such that Most Perfect (or seventh stage) Divine Realization of My Divine Self-Condition Is Really Awakened (and Made Complete, in Divine Translation into My centerless and boundless Spherical Domain of Divine Self-"Brightness").

In all the years of My Avataric Divine Teaching-Work and Revelation-Work, I made My Avataric Self-Submission—in order to bring My Divine Wisdom-Teaching out of Myself, relative to <u>every</u> aspect of the only-by-Me Revealed and Given Way of Adidam. In

That Process of My Avataric Divine Self-Revelation of the Way of Adidam, all kinds of Spiritual Signs were shown, by Me, to My devotees. Every such Sign corresponds to one or more Aspects of My Communication of the Total (or Full and Complete) Way of Adidam. And, in That Process, I thoroughly Addressed My devotees relative to every aspect of the entire matter of their responsibility for the body-mind. I had to make My Submission completely—in order to be Instructive to My devotees, relative to all kinds of things (including the grossest of matters), and to bring them to understand that the Way of Divine Self-Realization is exactly what they are <u>not</u> doing by tendency. My Avataric Submission to Teach and to Reveal was an "Heroic" and "Crazy" Ordeal.[55] I had to Descend all the way to Man. To Serve all of humankind (and even all and All), I have had to Descend to Wander in Hell—or else much and many would not have been Accounted for by Me.

Until you bring Me the gift of your real advancement in the basics required for the Divine Yogic Spiritual Process of devotional heart-Communion with Me, there is nothing much for Me to Work with. It is good for people to want profundity. It is good for people to have the heart-disposition to want existence to be profound. I have Given everyone the Way of Adidam, so that existence can be made most Profound. Therefore, now that the Way of Adidam <u>Is</u> Given—Full and Complete—everyone must <u>live</u> That Way. They must <u>do</u> This Yoga of Ruchira Avatara Bhakti, and they must grow in It. They must persist in It. They must practice It from day to day—from moment to moment, in fact. They must constantly live by My Avataric Word of Divine Instruction, without "bargaining". They must always approach Me rightly, and they must resort to Me constantly. When all of This is done, then (and only then) there is the Real Divine Profundity of Adidam and the Real Divine Process of Adidam.

RUCHIRA AVATAR ADI DA SAMRAJ
Los Angeles, 2000

PART FIVE

The Heart-Summary
Of Adidam

PART FIVE

The Heart-Summary
Of Adidam

The only-by-Me Revealed and Given Avataric Divine Way of Adidam (Which is the One and Only by-Me-Revealed and by-Me-Given Way of the Heart) is the Way of Devotion to Me <u>As</u> the Divine "Atma-Murti" (or <u>As</u> the Inherently egoless, and Self-Evidently Divine, Person of Reality and Truth—In <u>Place</u>, <u>As</u> Self-Condition, rather than <u>As</u> exclusively Objective Other).

Therefore, in every moment, My true devotee whole bodily (and, thus, by means of the spontaneous Me-recognizing Devotional response of all four of the principal psycho-physical faculties—of attention, emotional feeling, breath, and perceptual body) "Locates" Me <u>As</u> That Which Is Always Already <u>The</u> Case (Prior to—but not separate from—the form, the exercise, and the any object of the four psycho-physical faculties).

Happiness Itself (or Inherent Love-Bliss-Sufficiency Of Being) Is Always Already The Case.

Happiness Itself (or the Divinely Self-Sufficient Love-Bliss-Condition Of Being—Itself) <u>Is</u> <u>That</u> Which Is Always Already The Case.

Happiness Itself (or Love-Bliss-Radiance Of Boundlessly Feeling Being) <u>Is</u> the Most Prior Condition Of Existence (or Of Conscious Being—Itself).

Happiness Itself (or the Condition Of Love-Bliss-Radiance) Must Be Realized—In and <u>As</u> every conditionally arising moment—By Transcending self-Contraction (or all of separate and separative self, or psycho-physical ego-"I", <u>and</u> all of the ego's objects, or conditions of existence—or, indeed, <u>all</u> of the illusions of self and not-self).

When attention is facing outward (or is turned out, as if to outside itself), the body-mind is concentrated upon the "view" (or
"field") of apparently separate objects (and upon Me As Objective
Other).

When attention is facing inward (or is turned in, as if upon
itself), the body-mind is concentrated upon the "point of view" of
apparently separate self (and upon Me As Separate Consciousness).

When attention is Devotionally Yielded to whole bodily
"Locate" Me As That Which Is Always Already (and Divinely) The
Case, all "difference" (whether of ego-"I" or of object and other)
is (Inherently) Transcended (In Consciousness Itself, or Self-
Existing Being, Which Is Love-Bliss-Happiness Itself—and Which
Is Always Already The Case).

Therefore, to the degree that you surrender (whole bodily) to
be and do truly relational (and ecstatic, or ego-transcending)
Devotional love of Me (As the True Loved-One, the Divine
Beloved of the heart), you are (Thus and Thereby) Established—
whole bodily and Inherently—in the non-contracted Condition (or
Self-Condition, or Inherent Condition) of Reality Itself (Which Is
Consciousness Itself and Love-Bliss Itself—and Which Is Always
Already The Case).

In due course, This Devotional Practice Is Perfect—and, at
last, to Be Most Perfectly Realized.

RUCHIRA AVATAR ADI DA SAMRAJ
The Mountain Of Attention, 2000

I <u>Am</u> The Avataric Divine Self-Revelation Of The Fundamental Reality (or The "Radically" Non-Dual Conscious Light Of Self-Evidently Divine Love-Bliss)

I Am The Avataric Divine Self-Revelation Of The Fundamental Reality (or The "Radically" Non-Dual Conscious Light Of Self-Evidently Divine Love-Bliss)

And Now My Divinely Self-Revealing Avataric Divine Self-Confession, Call, and Admonition To All My Formally Acknowledged Listening Devotees, and Hearing Devotees, and Seeing Devotees who Truly, Actively, and Constantly (and Always Whole bodily) Invoke Me, Feel Me, Breathe Me, and (Altogether) Attend To Me and Serve Me.

Consciousness (Itself) Is The Only Reality—The One and Only Real God.

Consciousness (Itself) Is Always Already The Case.

Consciousness (Itself) Is Self-Existing (As Consciousness Itself).

Consciousness (Itself) Is Self-Radiant (As Perfectly Subjective Self-"Brightness"—or The Self-Evident Happiness, or Inherent Love-Bliss-Fullness, Of Consciousness Itself).

Consciousness (Itself) Is The Native (or Inherent) "Point Of View" (or timeless and Unchanging Self-Position) Of Reality (Itself).

If conditions arise as conditional experience, they Are Merely Apparent Modifications Of The Inherent "Brightness" (or Love-Bliss-Radiance) Of Consciousness Itself.

If conditions arise as conditional experience, they Are Not "Different" From Consciousness (Itself)—Because they <u>Are</u> Consciousness (Itself).

Therefore, Consciousness (Itself) Does Not "Create" the world of conditional experience.

Consciousness (Itself) Merely <u>Coincides</u> With the world of conditional experience.

In The Context Of any moment of conditionally arising experience, Consciousness (Itself) Is Always Already Merely Present (In Inherent and Perfect Coincidence With all presently arising conditional experience) <u>As</u> Consciousness Itself—Merely Present In The Witness-Position (or Irreducible and Perfectly Subjective Self-Position), and <u>As</u> The Real (and Merely-Witnessing) Self (or Indivisible, Non-Separate, and Utterly Non-Objective Self-Condition) Of The Apparently Separate ego-"I" (or conditional body-mind), and <u>As</u> The Self-Existing and Self-Radiant Source-Condition Of all conditionally arising objects, forms, conditions, and states.

The Only Real Self Is Consciousness Itself.

The Only Perfect Understanding (and Perfect Realization) Of conditionally arising experience Is That Which Is Obvious (or Self-Evident) When Consciousness (Itself) Is "Located" <u>As</u> The Principle (or The Most Prior, and Inherently egoless, or Non-Separate, "Point Of View") In Coincidence With every moment of conditionally arising experience.

Even By Means Of <u>Objective</u> Analysis Of conditionally Apparent objects, conditions, and states, It Is Revealed That <u>all</u> conditionally arising objects, conditions, and states Are conditional (or space-time-Measured, and Always Changing, and Never Finalized or Perfected) Modifications Of Fundamental Energy (or Universally Evident Light).

In The Most Perfect (or Seventh Stage) Realization Of The Only-By-Me Revealed and Given Way Of The Heart (or Way Of Adidam), Consciousness (Itself) Is (Itself) Realized To Be Always Already (Perfectly Subjectively) Identical To Fundamental Energy (or Universally Evident Light) Itself (Always Already Boundlessly Self-Radiant, <u>As</u> Love-Bliss-"Brightness").

Therefore, In The Context Of The Only-By-Me Revealed and Given Seventh Stage Of Life, all conditionally arising objects, conditions, and states (Whether Apparently objective Or Apparently subjective) Are Always Immediately (and, Necessarily, Divinely) Self-Recognized In and As The Perfectly Subjective Sphere and Light and Love-Bliss-"Brightness" Of Consciousness (Itself).

In The Only-By-Me Revealed and Given Seventh Stage Of Life, Consciousness (Itself) Is Most Perfectly Self-Realized, As The Inherently Non-Separate (and, Therefore, Always Both Universal and Omni-Present) and One and All-and-all-Including (and, Therefore, Always Both egoless and "Local") and Self-Evidently Divine (or Non-Causative, Non-Objective, Non-Separate, Non-"Different", and Merely Existing) Self-Condition Of the conditionally arising body-mind and Source-Condition (and Substance) Of the conditionally arising world.

To perceive the conditionally arising world Is To perceive Energy (or Light).

The presently unperceived world of conditionally arising conditions (or The Cosmic Domain Of all possibilities, space-time-Demonstrated In The Universally Unfolding Dynamic Display Of all possible opposites) Is Existing Merely As Light (or Energy) Itself.

When the conditionally arising world arises as conditional experience, The Event Is Darshan (or "Sighting", or perceiving) Of Light (or Energy) Itself.

Consciousness (Itself) Is (Itself) The Perfectly Subjective "Knowing" (and "Knowledge") Of Energy (Itself)—and Energy (Itself) Is The Self-Radiant Form and Shape of Consciousness (Itself).

Consciousness (Itself) Is (Itself) The Perfectly Subjective "Sighting" (and "Vision") Of Light (Itself)—and Light (Itself) Is The "Brightness" Of Consciousness (Itself).

Consciousness (Itself) Is (Itself) The Perfectly Subjective Feeling Of Love-Bliss (Itself)—and Love-Bliss (Itself) Is The Heart Of Consciousness (Itself).

In The By-My-Avataric-Divine-Grace-Given Awakening Of The Only-By-Me Revealed and Given Seventh Stage Of Life In The

Only-By-Me Revealed and Given Way Of The Heart (or Way Of Adidam), Consciousness (Itself), Which Is Beheld (or Merely Witnessed) As Energy (Itself), Is Self-Realized (and Self-Radiant) As Love-Bliss (Itself)—and all conditionally arising objects, conditions, and states (and even the Total body-mind) Are Always (Inherently, and Immediately, and, Necessarily, Divinely) Self-Recognized In and As Always Already Self-Existing and "Bright" (or Self-Radiant) and Inherently Indivisible Love-Bliss-Consciousness (Itself).

Consciousness (Itself), Apparently Separated From Its Own Love-Bliss-Radiance By the conditions of the body-mind and the world, Seeks (Like Narcissus, By Separative Acts Of self-Contraction, or The Avoidance Of Relationship) and Waits (Like Narcissus, By Concentrating On the experiential, and Always Changing, state of the conditionally arising body-mind-self) For Love-Bliss (or Happiness) To Come To Consciousness (and To the body-mind) From the world.

When the Total psycho-physical ego-"I" Is Most Perfectly Transcended In Consciousness (Itself), the Total world Is (Inherently, and Necessarily) Divinely Self-Recognized In and As Consciousness (Itself), and (Inherently, and Necessarily) Transcended (and, At Last, Divinely Outshined) In and As The Self-Radiance (or Inherent Energy, or Divine True Light) Of Consciousness (Itself), Which Is Happiness (or Love-Bliss) Itself.

Such Is My Avataric Divine Self-Revelation To All and all.

I Am Not The "Deity" Of Conventional Religion.

I Am Not The "God" Of the ego-"I".

I Am Consciousness Itself—Which Is The One and Only Reality.

By Means Of My Avataric Divine Self-Revelation In The Cosmic Domain, I Divinely (and Uniquely, and Most Perfectly, and Completely) Reveal That Consciousness (Itself) Is The One and Only Reality, Truth, Happiness, and Real God.

Therefore, Always Heart-Recognize My Divinely Self-Revealing Avataric Form, and Presence, and State Of Person With Real (and Always Truly Heart-Felt) Devotion.

Always Attend To Me and Serve Me—and (By Means Of My

Avataric Divine Grace) Realize Me (By Devotionally Recognizing
Me, and Devotionally Responding To Me, and Constantly Listening
To Me, and Truly Hearing Me, and egolessly Seeing Me—and, At
Last, Most Perfectly "Locating" Me, Beyond All "Difference").

By Always Feeling (and, Thereby, Always Contemplating) My
Avatarically-Born Bodily (Human) Divine Form, My Avatarically-
Self-Revealed Spiritual (and Always Blessing) Divine Presence,
and My Avatarically Self-Revealed (and Very, and Transcendental,
and Perfectly Subjective, and Inherently Spiritual, and Inherently
egoless, and Inherently Perfect, and Self-Evidently Divine) State—
Always Feel, Breathe, Love, Trust, Have Faith In, Surrender To,
and Realize Indivisible Oneness With Me, Both __As__ The Divine and
Very Self-Person (or Self-Existing Consciousness Itself, Beyond
and Prior To Your ego-"I") and __As__ The Divine and Conscious
Body Of Spirit-Energy (or Self-Radiant "Bright" Love-Bliss Itself,
Above, and Surrounding, and Pervading Your body-mind).

By Always Feeling (and, Thereby, Always Contemplating) My
Avatarically-Born Bodily (Human) Divine Form, My Avatarically
Self-Revealed Spiritual (and Always Blessing) Divine Presence,
and My Avatarically Self-Revealed (and Very, and Transcendental,
and Perfectly Subjective, and Inherently Spiritual, and Inherently
egoless, and Inherently Perfect, and Self-Evidently Divine) State—
Always Feel, Breathe, Love, Trust, Have Faith In, Surrender To,
and Realize Indivisible Oneness With Me, __As__ The Self-Existing and
Self-Radiant Divine Person (or Very Being) Who "Lives" (or
Pervades and "Breathes" and __Is__) Your Apparent body-mind, all
Apparently other beings, and all Apparent worlds.

By Always Feeling (and, Thereby, Always Contemplating) My
Avatarically-Born Bodily (Human) Divine Form, My Avatarically
Self-Revealed Spiritual (and Always Blessing) Divine Presence,
and My Avatarically Self-Revealed (and Very, and Transcendental,
and Perfectly Subjective, and Inherently Spiritual, and Inherently
egoless, and Inherently Perfect, and Self-Evidently Divine) State—
Always Allow Me To Stand __As__ all that arises, and (Thus) To Stand
Even __As__ Your Own body-mind.

If You (Truly) Always Feel (and, Thereby, Always Contemplate)
My Avatarically-Born Bodily (Human) Divine Form, My Avatarically

Self-Revealed Spiritual (and Always Blessing) Divine Presence, and My Avatarically Self-Revealed (and Very, and Transcendental, and Perfectly Subjective, and Inherently Spiritual, and Inherently egoless, and Inherently Perfect, and Self-Evidently Divine) State With Love and Faith (Altogether Rightly, Truly, Fully, and Fully Devotionally Recognizing Me, and Heart-Responding To Me, and With No Withholding), The Only-By-Me Revealed and Given Way (or Process) Associated With Transcendental, Inherently Spiritual, and Most Perfect Divine Self-Realization and Liberation Will Be Given To You, By Me—Spontaneously, Progressively, Entirely, and Exactly.

Therefore, Even From The Beginning Of Your Practice Of The Only-By-Me Revealed and Given Way Of The Heart—Always Feel (and Thereby Contemplate) My Avatarically-Born Bodily (Human) Divine Form, My Avatarically Self-Revealed Spiritual (and Always Blessing) Divine Presence, and My Avatarically Self-Revealed (and Very, and Transcendental, and Perfectly Subjective, and Inherently Spiritual, and Inherently egoless, and Inherently Perfect, and Self-Evidently Divine) State, and, Thus, Give Your conditional self (or Release Your self-Contraction) To Me, The "Bright" Heart-Revealed One, Who Is Always Already Divinely Self-Realized (As Self-Existing Consciousness Itself) and Always Already Divinely Free (As Self-Radiant Love-Bliss Itself).

By This Feeling-Contemplation, My Self-Existing and Self-Radiant Person, Condition, and State Will Be Realized By You—Spontaneously (and Progressively), As My Free Gift To You.

By This Feeling-Contemplation, You Will (By Means Of My Avatarically Self-Transmitted Divine Grace) See Me Perfectly At Last, As "Atma-Murti"—The "Form" and The "Presence" That Is Inherent Happiness (or Self-Radiant "Bright" Love-Bliss Itself), and The "State" That Is Merely Being (or Self-Existing Consciousness Itself). And You Will Thus (Inherently, and Inherently Most Perfectly) Transcend The Illusions Of Separateness and Relatedness and "Difference".

Therefore, Feeling-Contemplation Of My Avatarically-Born Bodily (Human) Divine Form, My Avatarically Self-Revealed Spiritual (and Always Blessing) Divine Presence, and My

Avatarically Self-Revealed (and Very, and Transcendental, and Perfectly Subjective, and Inherently Spiritual, and Inherently egoless, and Inherently Perfect, and Self-Evidently Divine) State Is The Only-By-Me Revealed and Given Secret Of All My True (and Formally Acknowledged) Listening Devotees, All My True (and Formally Acknowledged) Hearing Devotees, and All My True (and Formally Acknowledged) Seeing Devotees.

This Great Heart-Principle Is The Foundation Of All Practice In The Way Of Adidam (Which Is The One and Only By-Me-Revealed and By-Me-Given Way Of The Heart).

Therefore, By This Great Heart-Principle, and By All The Means I Have Given and Always Give—Each and All Of My Truly Heart-Responsive (and Formally Acknowledged) Listening Devotees, Hearing Devotees, and Seeing Devotees Will Love Me, Serve Me, Surrender the ego-self To Me, and Always Heartily Receive Me. And, By This Authentic Practice, The Total Gathering Of My Such True Listening Devotees, Hearing Devotees, and Seeing Devotees Will (Each and All) Always and Constantly (Now, and Forever Hereafter) Celebrate My Good Company—and They Will, At Last, Most Perfectly Realize Indivisible and Indestructible Oneness With Me.

What You Can Do Next—

Contact an Adidam center near you.

■ Sign up for our preliminary course, "The <u>Only</u> Truth That Sets the Heart Free". This course will prepare you to become a fully practicing devotee of Avatar Adi Da Samraj.

■ Find out about upcoming events in your area:

AMERICAS
12040 North Seigler Road
Middletown, CA 95461 USA
(707) 928-4936

PACIFIC-ASIA
12 Seibel Road
Henderson
Auckland 1008
New Zealand
64-9-838-9114

AUSTRALIA
P.O. Box 244
Kew 3101
Victoria
**1800 ADIDAM
(1800-234-326)**

EUROPE-AFRICA
Annendaalderweg 10
6105 AT Maria Hoop
The Netherlands
31 (0)20 468 1442

THE UNITED KINGDOM
PO Box 20013
London, England
NW2 1ZA
0181-7317550

E-MAIL: **correspondence@adidam.org**

Read these books by and about Avatar Adi Da Samraj:

■ *The Promised God-Man Is Here*

*The Extraordinary Life-Story,
The "Radical" Teaching-Work, and
The Divinely "Emerging" World-Blessing
Work Of The Divine World-Teacher
Of The "Late-Time",
Ruchira Avatar Adi Da Samraj,*
by Carolyn Lee, Ph.D.

The profound, heart-rending, humorous, miraculous, wild—and true—Story of the Divine Person Alive in human Form. Essential reading as background for the study of Avatar Adi Da's books.

■ *Aham Da Asmi (Beloved, I <u>Am</u> Da)*

*The Five Books Of The Heart Of The
Adidam Revelation, Book One:
The "Late-Time" Avataric Revelation Of
The True and Spiritual Divine Person
(The egoless Personal Presence Of Reality
and Truth, Which <u>Is</u> The Only <u>Real</u> God).*

This Ecstatic Scripture, the first of His twenty-three "Source-Texts", contains Ruchira Avatar Adi Da's magnificent Confession as the Very Divine Person and Source-Condition of all and All.

Continue your reading with the remaining books of *The Five Books Of The Heart Of The Adidam Revelation* (the *Ruchira Avatara Gita,* the *Da Love-Ananda Gita, Hridaya Rosary,* and *Eleutherios*). Then you will be ready to go on to *The Seventeen Companions Of The True Dawn Horse* (see pp. 401-406).

These and other books by and about Ruchira Avatar Adi Da Samraj can be ordered from the Adidam Emporium by calling:

(877) 770-0772 (from within North America)
(707) 928-6653 (from outside North America)

or by writing to:
ADIDAM EMPORIUM
10336 Loch Lomond Road
PMB #306
Middletown, CA 95461

Or order from the Adidam Emporium online at:
www.adidam.com

Adidam Gateway

Sanctuary
Society
Gallery
Community
Museum
Emporium
Library
University

Visit the Adidam Sacred City online at:
www.adidam.org

■ Explore the online community of Adidam and discover more about Avatar Adi Da Samraj and the Way He Offers to all.

Find presentations on: Avatar Adi Da's extraordinary life-story, the stages leading to Divine Enlightenment, cultism versus true devotional practice, the "radical" politics of human-scale community, true emotional-sexual freedom, the sacred function of art in human life, and more.

Ruchira Avatar Adi Da Samraj
Lopez Island, 2000

The Great Choice

An Invitation to the Way of Adidam

E ach one of us, if we will allow ourselves to feel it, is rest-
less. Human beings want to find God—the living, heart-
intoxicating experience of <u>Real</u> God, or Truth Itself, or
Reality Itself. The purpose of our existence is actually to live in the
True Pleasure of that heart-intoxication. To be unable to participate and luxuriate in that Pleasure is pain and stress. We may not
realize it, but that feeling of separation from unqualified Love,
Sustenance, and heart-Communion with the Divine Source of our
existence is actually driving us mad. And that is why human
beings, individually and collectively, do dreadful things—or, otherwise, settle for mere mediocrity, just "doing our best", or merely
"coping". In the words of Avatar Adi Da, we spend our lives "waiting for everything and looking for everything". He says:

*AVATAR ADI DA SAMRAJ: To have no greater sense of Reality than
the physical is to be like a trapped rat, trapped on all sides. You just
cannot endure the confinement of mere mortality—your heart
cannot accept it. To be in that disposition, to have that sense of
Reality, is obviously a disturbance.*

*So, obviously, the human being requires a Way—not merely a
way out. A way out, yes, in some sense—but, for the integrity of
your existence, you need direct access to the Divine, even as a matter of ordinary sanity.* [March 3, 1998]

Avatar Adi Da has Appeared in this dark time, in order to bring the mortal darkness to an end and restore all to the Divine Light. He is intent on taking all who respond to Him through the most ecstatic and most difficult of all transitions—the transition from the unhappy life of the ego to the Radiant Fullness of the Divinely Enlightened life. His Life-Story is of the immense Divine Ordeal it has been on His part to truly Initiate that Process in human beings.

Avatar Adi Da does not congratulate the ego—He undermines the ego. He must, if He is to Liberate people from their unhappiness, from the enclosed point of view of the separate and separative self. And so He has never offered a conventionally consoling message. He offers you the whole Truth—the fact of yourself as the self-contracted ego-"I", but also the constant Revelation of a Happiness beyond compare.

Avatar Adi Da's human body is, of course, located in a particular place and a particular time. But when you become sensitive to Him Spiritually, you discover that His Spiritual Presence can be felt anywhere and anytime, regardless of whether you are in His physical Company or not. Because His Spiritual Presence is Eternal (and will not "disappear" when His human body dies), it is possible for everyone to cultivate a direct heart-relationship with Him— under all circumstances, in this life and beyond. And so, the relationship to Him, once forged, is eternal, going beyond death and the apparent boundaries of time and space.

If you want more than your ordinary existence, and something greater than a life of Spiritual seeking, Avatar Adi Da's Word to you is simply this: Take up the Way of Adidam—the Way of Real God, fully Present, here and now, not needing to be sought. The Way of Adidam is His personal Offering to you and to every human being. It is a devotional heart-relationship to Him, expressed through an entire Way of life. This relationship is not to a mere man—it is with the very Divine Being. But, at the same time, it is supremely intimate. When you enter into this relationship with Him and practice the Way of Adidam, you begin to enjoy a condition of heart-Communion with Him that is more alive and heart-deep than your love-relationship with any human individual.

At the same time, the devotional relationship with Adi Da Samraj is not an "I-Thou" relationship, a connection between apparently separate entities—the human individual, on the one hand, and "God", on the other. The love-bond with Adi Da Samraj transcends the entire point of view by which we live, presuming ourselves to be separate beings relating to separate "others". In every moment that you truly practice the relationship to Avatar Adi Da, invoking Him by Name, recollecting His Form in the mind, or His Words, or something He has done—whenever you allow Him to Attract your heart, He Reveals Himself Spiritually to you. Then He is recognized, through and beyond His human appearance, as the Real and Living God—not the great Parent, or "Creator"-Deity, imagined by the human mind, but the Conscious Divine Power of Light and Love, the Divine Heart of all there is, including your own body-mind and every apparent being and "thing". In the instant of such recognition, the entire body-mind opens to Adi Da Samraj in a single movement of devotion, and you forget yourself in ecstasy—the heart, the mind, the body, the breath becoming full with His Radiant Love-Bliss. The Way of Adidam, truly lived, is this ecstasy of Non-Separateness, a great Contemplative process, based on heart-recognition of Adi Da Samraj and heart-response to Him.

Ultimately, in this or some future lifetime, persistent heart-Communion with Adi Da Samraj realizes the true destiny of existence—Divine Enlightenment, in which all vestige of the egoic self is vanished:

Divine Enlightenment, Divine Self-Realization, Most Perfect (Free, "Bright", and Self-Evidently Divine) Awakeness, or Most Perfect (and Most Perfectly ego-Transcending) Spiritual and Transcendental Real-God-Realization, Is Native, Most Perfect, Effortless, and Free Identification With Mere (or Inherent, and Natively Felt) Being (or Self-Existence), The Only One Who Is, Consciousness Itself—Self-Radiant, All Love-Bliss-"Brightness" Itself, Inherently Without Obstruction, Always Already Infinitely Expanded (Beyond All Apparent Modifications, or Illusory Contractions, Of Itself). [The Only Complete Way To Realize The Unbroken Light Of Real God]

The truth of the Way of Adidam remains hidden until you begin to participate in it from the heart. Mere beliefs and prescribed behaviors are insufficient. The Way of Adidam is a matter of direct, moment-to-moment response to Adi Da Samraj and a process of receiving His Spiritual Transmission ever more profoundly. It does not work to take His Teaching away and attempt to practice it by yourself. As He has said many times, it is simply not possible to move beyond the confines of the ego on your own, nor is it possible to unlock the Secrets of Divine Enlightenment that He has Revealed outside of a formally acknowledged devotional relationship to Him. That is why it is so important to become His formal devotee and to live the Way of Adidam exactly has He has Given it.

AVATAR ADI DA SAMRAJ: I __Am__ the Divine Blessing, Real-God-with-you. Such is not merely My Declaration to you. You must find Me out. You must __prove__ the Way I Give you. Really __do__ the Way I Give you, and you will find Me out further. You will prove the Way of Adidam by doing it, not by believing it merely. [Ruchira Avatara Hridaya-Siddha Yoga]

Darshan

The foundation of Spiritual practice in Adidam is Darshan, or the feeling-Contemplation of Avatar Adi Da's bodily (human) Form—either through the sighting of His physical body, or through Contemplating a photographic or artistic representation of Him. This heart-beholding of Avatar Adi Da's Form is the wellspring of meditation in the Way of Adidam, and so His devotees place a large photograph of Him in each meditation hall, as the central image

of Contemplation. In fact, Remembrance of Adi Da Samraj—or the recollecting of His Form in mind and feeling—is the constant practice of His devotees, in the midst of the activities of daily life as well as in meditation. Avatar Adi Da has often spoken about the unique potency of beholding His Form.

AVATAR ADI DA SAMRAJ: In the traditional setting, when it works best, an individual somehow Gracefully comes into the Company of a Realizer of one degree or another, and, just upon (visually) sighting that One, he or she is converted at heart, and, thereafter, spends the rest of his or her life devoted to sadhana (or Spiritual practice), in constant Remembrance of the Spiritual Master. The Spiritual Master's Sign is self-authenticating.

When Adi Da Samraj is approached with an open heart, His Darshan—the Sighting of His Form alone, even in representational form—is so potent that the heart overflows in response to Him, recognizing Him as the Very Divine Person, the Supreme Source of Bliss and Love.

Sometimes, devotees receive the Darshan of Avatar Adi Da in an informal setting, such as when He walks around one of the Adidam Sanctuaries. And then there are formal occasions, when He sits in halls especially set aside for Darshan, inviting devotees to come and Contemplate Him silently. In certain cases, the time of a formal Darshan occasion will be announced ahead of time, so that devotees in all parts of the world can receive His Blessing simultaneously, by sitting in silent Contemplation of Him at the same time that He is Granting Darshan. In such occasions, real-time video of Avatar Adi Da Samraj sitting in Darshan is transmitted via the internet to His devotees everywhere. Thus, even if you cannot come into Avatar Adi Da's physical Company, there may be occasions when you will have the opportunity to participate in such occasions of His Darshan.

The Four Congregations

The gathering of devotees of Adi Da Samraj forms a series of concentric circles radiating from Him at the center. These circles are the four formal congregations of His devotees: the first congregation (renunciate practitioners), the second congregation (lay practitioners), the third congregation (practitioners who particularly serve Avatar Adi Da through their patronage and/or advocacy, or who are preparing for the second congregation), and the fourth congregation (practitioners who live in traditional cultural settings or who maintain their participation in the religious tradition to which they already belong, while acknowledging Avatar Adi Da Samraj as the Ultimate Divine Source of true religion).

These circles, as they grow, are forming a vast "conductor", a mechanism whereby the Divine Influence of Avatar Adi Da Samraj is being drawn more and more into the world. Every new devotee represents a strengthening of the total Sphere of Avatar Adi Da's Spiritual Transmission and Grace. Avatar Adi Da has Given the Gifts of His Wisdom-Teaching and His Spiritual Blessing, and it is through the community of His devotees, and its global Spiritual culture, that these Gifts, intended for everyone, become available to all. This is why Avatar Adi Da is urgent to find those in this generation who will respond to Him and do the great work of making His Spiritual Blessing available to all.

Which Congregation Is Right for You?

Which of the four congregations you should apply to for membership depends on the strength of your impulse to respond to Avatar Adi Da's Revelation and on your life-circumstance. All four congregations establish you in a direct devotional relationship with Avatar Adi Da, and all four are essential to the flowering of His Blessing-Work in the world.

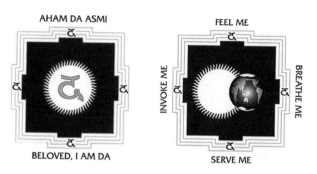

AHAM DA ASMI

BELOVED, I AM DA

FEEL ME

INVOKE ME

BREATHE ME

SERVE ME

The First and Second Congregations

(for those moved to take up the total practice of Adidam)

To take up the total practice of the Way of Adidam (in the first or second congregation) is to take full advantage of the opportunity offered by Adi Da Samraj—it is to enter fully into the process of Divine Enlightenment. That process is a unique ordeal, which necessarily requires application to the wide range of functional, practical, relational, and cultural disciplines given by Ruchira Avatar Adi Da Samraj for the sake of Spiritual purification and growth.

The disciplines of Adidam are not ascetical, not a form of deprivation. Rather, they are the means whereby the body-mind is conformed to a right and inherently pleasurable pattern of well-being. As you progressively adapt to these disciplines, the body-mind is purified and balanced, and you thereby become able to receive and respond to the Divine Heart-Transmission of Adi Da Samraj more and more fully.

These practices in the Way of Adidam include fundamental contemplative disciplines such as meditation, devotional chanting, sacramental worship (or "puja"), study of Avatar Adi Da's books, and regular periods of retreat.

AVATAR ADI DA SAMRAJ: You must come from the depth-position of meditation and puja before entering into activities in the waking state, and remain in the disposition of that depth from the time of meditation and puja each morning. Maintain that heart-disposition, and discipline the body-mind—functionally, practically, relationally— in all the modes I have Given you. This devotional Yoga, Ruchira

Avatara Bhakti Yoga, is moment-to-moment. Fundamentally, it is a matter of exercising it profoundly, in this set-apart time of meditation and puja, and then, through random, artful practice moment-to-moment, constantly refresh it, preserve it. All of this is to conform the body-mind to the Source-Purpose, the in-depth Condition.

That basic discipline covers all aspects of the body-mind. That is the pattern of your response to Me. It is the foundation Yoga of organizing your life in terms of its in-depth principle, and growing this depth. [December 5, 1996]

This moment-to-moment devotional turning to Avatar Adi Da is refreshed not only in the meditation hall but also in the temple, where worship, prayer, devotional chanting, and other sacred activities occur.

AVATAR ADI DA SAMRAJ: The sacred life must be perpetual. The sacred domain is the core of the community, and every community and every Sanctuary should have a temple in its domain: A place of chant, of song, of prayer, where everyone gathers for this life of Invocation, prayer, and puja. [May 13, 1999]

Members of the first and second congregations adapt to a purifying diet and a discipline of daily exercise (including morning calisthenics and evening Hatha Yoga exercises). They also progressively adapt to a regenerative discipline of sexuality. And they live in cooperative association with other devotees of Avatar Adi Da and tithe regularly.

All of these functional, practical, relational, and cultural disciplines are means whereby you become more and more capable of receiving Avatar Adi Da's constant Blessing-Transmission. Therefore, Avatar Adi Da Samraj has made it clear that, in order to Realize Him with true profundity—and, in particular, to Realize Him most perfectly, to the degree of Divine Enlightenment—it is necessary to be a formally acknowledged member of either the first or the second congregation, embracing the total practice of the Way of Adidam.

When you apply for membership in the second congregation of Adidam (the first step for all who want to take up the total practice of the Way of Adidam), you are asked to take "The <u>Only</u> Truth That Sets the Heart Free", a course in which you examine the opportunity offered to you by Avatar Adi Da Samraj, and learn what it means to embrace the total practice of the Way of Adidam. (To register for this preparatory course, please contact the regional or territorial center nearest to you [see p. 310], or e-mail us at: correspondence@adidam.org.) After completing this course of study, you may formally enter the second congregation as a student-novice.

Entering any of the four congregations of Adidam is based on taking a formal vow of devotion and service to Avatar Adi Da Samraj. This vow is a profound—and, indeed, eternal—commitment. You take this vow (for whichever congregation you are entering) when you are certain that your great and true heart-impulse is to be a devotee of Avatar Adi Da Samraj, embracing Him as your Divine Heart-Master. And Avatar Adi Da Samraj Himself is eternally Vowed to Serve the Liberation of all who become His devotees.

As a student-novice, you will be initiated into formal meditation and sacramental worship. Then you begin to adapt to a wide range of life-disciplines, including participation in the cooperative community of Avatar Adi Da's first- and second-congregation devotees. As a student-novice, you engage in an intensive period of study and "consideration" of the Way of Adidam in all of its details, and then, after a period of three to six months (or more), you may apply to be a fully practicing member of the second congregation.

The beginning stages of practice are the "exoteric" (or "outer-temple") domain of the second congregation. Avatar Adi Da has indicated that many of His devotees will practice in the exoteric stages for their entire lives. This beginning practice of Adidam is great and profound—because it is founded not in any hoped-for future attainment, but in <u>present</u> heart-Communion with Real God (Revealed via the Incarnation of Avatar Adi Da), and also because it requires the practitioner to really transcend the ego.

The Life of a Formally Practicing Devotee of Ruchira Avatar Adi Da Samraj

Meditation is a unique and precious event in the daily life of Avatar Adi Da's devotees. It offers the opportunity to relinquish outward, body-based attention and to be alone with Adi Da Samraj, allowing yourself to enter more and more into the Sphere of His Divine Transmission.

The practice of sacramental worship, or "puja", in the Way of Adidam is the bodily active counterpart to meditation. It is a form of ecstatic worship of Avatar Adi Da Samraj, using a photographic representation of Him and involving devotional chanting and recitations from His Wisdom-Teaching.

"You must deal with My Wisdom-Teaching in some form every single day, because a new form of the ego's game appears every single day. You must continually return to My Wisdom-Teaching, confront My Wisdom-Teaching."

Avatar Adi Da Samraj

The beginner in Spiritual life must prepare the body-mind by mastering the physical, vital dimension of life before he or she can be ready for truly Spiritual practice. Service is devotion in action, a form of Divine Communion.

Avatar Adi Da Samraj Offers practical disciplines to His devotees in the areas of work and money, diet, exercise, and sexuality. These disciplines are based on His own human experience and an immense process of "consideration" that He engaged face-to-face with His devotees for more than twenty-five years.

The "esoteric" (or "inner-temple") practice of Adidam does not begin until the activity of the ego is most fundamentally understood and can thereby be consistently transcended moment to moment. Then, through a profound Awakening to the Spiritual Reality, Revealed and Transmitted by Avatar Adi Da, you become qualified to enter into the advanced and the ultimate stages (or esoteric domain) of the Way of Adidam.

Those who, having practiced the Way of Adidam most intensively, make the transition to the "Perfect Practice", in the sixth (or penultimate) stage of the Way of Adidam, may do so either as general practitioners (continuing as members of the second congregation of Adidam) or (if they demonstrate the necessary qualifications) as formal renunciate practitioners (thereby becoming members of the first congregation of Adidam).

All formal renunciate practitioners in the first congregation of the Way of Adidam are necessarily members of the formal order of sannyasins established by Avatar Adi Da. This order is known as the Ruchira Sannyasin Order of the Tantric Renunciates of Adidam (or, simply, the Ruchira Sannyasin Order). Avatar Adi Da Himself is the Founding Member of the Ruchira Sannyasin Order, which is a retreat order whose members are legal renunciates. The Ruchira Sannyasin Order is the senior cultural authority within the gathering of Avatar Adi Da's devotees, and its members are the principal human Instruments of Avatar Adi Da's Blessing-Work, now and into the future. Ruchira Sannyasins may live in Hermitage-Retreat Sanctuaries Empowered by Avatar Adi Da or at the Retreat Sanctuaries of Adidam anywhere in the world, but the home of the order is Adidam Samrajashram (in Fiji), Avatar Adi Da's principal Hermitage-Retreat Sanctuary.

The Adidam Youth Fellowship

(within the second congregation)

Young people (age 25 and under) are also offered a special
form of relationship to Avatar Adi Da—the Adidam Youth
Fellowship. The Adidam Youth Fellowship has two membership
bodies—friends and practicing members.

A friend of the Adidam Youth Fellowship is simply invited into
a culture of other young people who want to learn more about
Avatar Adi Da Samraj and His Happiness-Realizing Way of Adidam.
A formally practicing member of the Adidam Youth Fellowship
acknowledges that he or she has found his or her True Heart-
Friend and Master in the Person of Avatar Adi Da Samraj, and
wishes to enter into a direct, ego-surrendering Spiritual relationship with Him as the Means to True Happiness.

Practicing members of the Youth Fellowship embrace a series
of disciplines that are similar to (but simpler than) the practices
engaged by adult members of the second congregation of
Adidam. Both friends and members are invited to special retreat
events from time to time, where they can associate with other
young devotees of Avatar Adi Da.

To become a member of the Adidam Youth Fellowship, or to
learn more about this form of relationship to Avatar Adi Da, call
or write:

Vision of Mulund Institute (VMI)
10336 Loch Lomond Road
PMB #146
Middletown, CA 95461 USA
PHONE: (707) 928-6932
E-MAIL: vmi@adidam.org

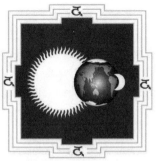

COOPERATION + TOLERANCE = PEACE

The Third Congregation of Adidam

(for those serving Adi Da Samraj through their patronage and advocacy, and those preparing for the second congregation)

1. Patrons and Individuals of Unique Influence

It is the sacred responsibility of those who respond to Adi Da Samraj to help His Spiritual Work flourish in the world. For this purpose, we must make it possible for Avatar Adi Da Samraj to move freely and spontaneously from one part of the world to another and we must provide Hermitages for His unique Work in various locations. In 1983, an individual patron offered the island of Naitauba to Avatar Adi Da. Because of this magnificent gift, the entire Life and Work of Adi Da Samraj began to evolve in ways that were not possible before. He had a pristine, protected place to do His Spiritual Work and an opportunity to establish a unique Seat of His Divine Presence for all generations to come.

Avatar Adi Da must also be able to gather around Him His most exemplary formal renunciate devotees, who must receive practical support so that they can devote their lives to serving Avatar Adi Da and His Work and living a life of perpetual Spiritual retreat in His Company.

And Avatar Adi Da's Presence in the world must become widely known, both through the publication and dissemination of books by and about Him and through public advocacy by people of influence.

If you are a man or woman of unique wealth or influence in the world, we invite you to serve Avatar Adi Da's world-Blessing Work through your patronage or influence. As a member of the third congregation of Adidam, supporting the world-Work of Adi Da Samraj, you are literally helping to change the destiny of countless people. You are making it possible for this Blessing-Work to have a greater influence upon the world's destiny. To make the choice to serve Avatar Adi Da via your patronage or unique influence is to transform your own life and destiny, and the life and destiny of all mankind, in the most Spiritually auspicious way.

As a patron or individual of unique influence in the third congregation, your relationship to Avatar Adi Da is founded on a vow of devotion, through which you commit yourself according to your capabilities—either to significant financial patronage of His Work and/or to using your unique influence to make Him known in the world. In the course of your service to Him (and in daily life altogether), you live the simplest practice of Ruchira Avatara Bhakti Yoga—invoking Avatar Adi Da, feeling Him, breathing Him, and serving Him, and thus remaining connected to His constant Blessing. You are also invited to engage a daily period of formal study of His Wisdom-Teaching. You are not obliged to engage the full range of disciplines practiced in the first two congregations. You are, however, encouraged to practice formal periods of meditation and sacramental worship.

If, at some point, you are moved to embrace all the disciplines and enter into the total practice of Adidam, you may apply for membership in the second (and possibly, eventually, the first) congregation.

If you are interested in establishing a formal devotional relationship with Avatar Adi Da Samraj and serving Him in this crucial way, please contact us:

Third Congregation Advocacy
12040 North Seigler Road
Middletown, CA 95461 USA
PHONE: (707) 928-4800
E-MAIL: director_of_advocacy@adidam.org

2. The Transnational Society of Advocates of the Adidam Revelation

If you have the capability to effectively advocate Avatar Adi Da in the world—through your individual skills, position, or professional expertise—you may join a branch of the third congregation called the Transnational Society of Advocates of the Adidam Revelation. Members of the Society of Advocates are individuals who, while not of <u>unique</u> wealth or social influence, can make a significant difference to Avatar Adi Da's Work by making Him known in all walks of life (including the media, in the spheres of religion, government, education, health, entertainment, the arts, and so on). Advocates also serve the worldwide mission of Adidam by financially supporting the publication of Avatar Adi Da's "Source-Texts" and His other Literature, as well as associated missionary literature. Members of the Society of Advocates make a monthly donation for this purpose and pay an annual membership fee that supports the services of the Society.

Like devotees in the first and second congregations, your relationship to Avatar Adi Da as a member of the Society of Advocates is founded on a vow of devotion and service, but the requirements are less elaborate. In the course of your service to Him (and in daily life altogether), you vow to live the simplest practice of Ruchira Avatara Bhakti Yoga—invoking Avatar Adi Da, feeling Him, breathing Him, and serving Him, and thus remaining connected to His constant Blessing. You also engage a daily period of formal study of His Wisdom-Teaching. You are not obliged to engage the full range of disciplines practiced in the first two congregations. You are, however, encouraged to practice formal periods of meditation and sacramental worship.

If, at some point, you are moved to embrace all the disciplines and enter into the total practice of Adidam, you may apply for membership in the second (and possibly, eventually, the first) congregation.

If you are interested in becoming a member of the Society of Advocates, please contact us:

The Society of Advocates
12040 North Seigler Road
Middletown, CA 95461 USA
PHONE: (707) 928-6924
E-MAIL: soacontact@adidam.org

3. Pre-student-novices under vow

If you are certain that you wish to become a formal devotee of Avatar Adi Da, and you therefore wish to embrace the formal second-congregation vow of devotion to Him as quickly as possible, you are invited to become a pre-student-novice under vow (as part of the third congregation of Adidam).

As a pre-student-novice under vow, you make a commitment to become a student-novice (and, therefore, to move into the second congregation) within a period of three to six months. During this period, you take the preparatory course, "The Only Truth That Sets The Heart Free", which introduces you to the fundamentals of the second-congregation practice. Pre-student-novices under vow practice Ruchira Avatara Bhakti Yoga in daily life, engage daily formal study of the Wisdom-Teaching of Avatar Adi Da, make regular contributions to the support of the Adidam Pan-Communion, and take up a regular form of service. You are not obliged to engage the full range of disciplines practiced in the first two congregations. You are, however, encouraged to practice formal periods of meditation and sacramental worship.

For information about becoming a pre-student-novice under vow, please contact the Adidam regional center nearest you.

COOPERATION + TOLERANCE = PEACE

The Fourth Congregation of Adidam

*(for those maintaining their participation
in the religious and/or cultural tradition
to which they already belong)*

Individuals who live in traditional cultural settings, and also individuals who wish to maintain their participation in the religious tradition to which they already belong (while acknowledging Avatar Adi Da Samraj as the Ultimate Divine Source of true religion), are invited to apply for membership in the fourth congregation of Adidam. Fourth-congregation devotees practice Ruchira Avatara Bhakti Yoga in its simplest form ("Invoke Me, Feel Me, Breathe Me, Serve Me") and also the discipline of daily study. Their financial and service obligations are adapted to their particular circumstance.

The opportunity to practice in the fourth congregation is also extended to all those who, because of physical or other functional limitations, are unable to take up the total practice of the Way of Adidam as required in the first and second congregations.

For more information about the fourth congregation of Adidam, call or write one of our regional centers (see p. 310), or e-mail us at: correspondence@adidam.org.

**Temple sites at the Pilgrimage and Retreat Sanctuaries:
the Mountain Of Attention (left) and Da Love-Ananda Mahal (right)**

One of the ways in which Avatar Adi Da Samraj Communicates His Divine Blessing-Transmission is through sacred places. He has Empowered two kinds of places: Pilgrimage and Retreat Sanctuaries (the Mountain Of Attention in northern California and Da Love-Ananda Mahal in Hawaii) and Hermitage-Retreat Sanctuaries (Tat Sundaram in northern California and Adidam Samrajashram in Fiji). Avatar Adi Da has Established Himself Spiritually in perpetuity at all four of these places. In particular, Adidam Samrajashram—His Great Island-Hermitage-Retreat and world-Blessing Seat—is Avatar Adi Da's principal Place of Spiritual Work and Transmission, and will remain so forever after His physical Lifetime. Formally acknowledged devotees are invited to go on special retreats at the Pilgrimage and Retreat Sanctuaries and at Adidam Samrajashram.

Adidam Samrajashram, Fiji

**Darshan occasions with
Avatar Adi Da Samraj at
the Hermitage-Retreats:
Tat Sundaram (left) and
Adidam Samrajashram (right)**

T hose whose hearts are given, in love, to Me, Fall into My Heart. Those who are Mine, because they are in love with Me, no longer demand to be fulfilled through conditional experience and through the survival (or perpetuation) of the ego-"I". Their love for Me grants them Access to Me, and, Thus, to My Love-Bliss—because I *Am* Love-Ananda, the Divine Love-Bliss, in Person.

What will My lover do but love Me? I suffer every form and condition of every one who loves Me—because I Love My devotee *As* My own Form, My own Condition. I Love My devotee *As* the One by Whom *I* Am Distracted.

I Grant all My own Divine and "Bright" Excesses to those who love Me, in exchange for all their doubts and sufferings. Those who "Bond" themselves to Me, through love-surrender, are inherently Free of fear and wanting need. They transcend the ego-"I" (the cause of all conditional experience), and they (cause and all and All) Dissolve in Me—for I *Am* the Heart of all and All, and I *Am* the Heart Itself, and the Heart Itself *Is* the Only Reality, Truth, and Real God of All and all.

What is a Greater Message than This?

DA LOVE-ANANDA GITA

From now on, all beings are uniquely Blessed. And human history can be different, because there is Help available that has never existed before.

The life of a devotee of Avatar Adi Da Samraj is unheard-of Grace, and this life can be lived by anyone. It does not matter who you are, where you live, or what you do. All of that makes no difference, once your heart recognizes Adi Da Samraj. Then the only course is the heart-response to Him—a life of devotion to the Divine in human Form, full of devotional ecstasy, true humor, freedom, clarity, and profound purpose.

So, why delay? The Living One, Adi Da Samraj, is here, and always will be. But now is the brief, and especially Blessed, window of time in which He is humanly Alive, doing His great Foundation Work for the sake of all beings, presently and in all future time. Every one who comes to Him and serves Him in His bodily human Lifetime shares in His unique once-and-forever Work of establishing the Way of Adidam in this world.

All who love Him carry His Name in their hearts and on their lips. Once the recognition of Avatar Adi Da awakens in you, this response is inevitable. The Promised God-Man, Avatar Adi Da Samraj, is not an "Other". He is the Gift, the Bliss, of Being Itself. He is the "Brightness" of Very God—Dawning, and then Flowering, in your heart. That Process is pure Revelation. It changes everything—grants peace, sanity, and the overwhelming impulse to Realize Unlimited, Permanent, and Perfect Oneness with Him.

As devotees of Avatar Adi Da Samraj, we make this confession to you: This opportunity—to live in heart-Communion with Real God—exceeds anything ever offered to mortal beings. It is true Happiness. And it is yours for the asking.

◆ ◆ ◆

A part from the four congregations, there are three distinct organizations within Adidam, each with a special area of responsibility.

The Da Love-Ananda Samrajya

Serving The Avataric-Incarnation-Body,
The Great Island-Hermitage-Retreat, and
The World-Blessing-Work of The Divine World-Teacher,
Ruchira Avatar Adi Da Samraj

The Da Love-Ananda Samrajya is devoted to serving Avatar Adi Da Himself, protecting Him and His intimate Sphere, providing for Adidam Samrajashram (His Great Island-Hermitage-Retreat, the Island of Naitauba in Fiji), ensuring that He has everything that He needs to do His Divine Blessing-Work, and providing right access to Him.

The Da Love-Ananda Samrajya also protects and provides for the Ruchira Sannyasin Order (the members of which are legal renunciates) and ensures that the Divine Word and Story of Adi Da Samraj are preserved and made known in the world.

The Eleutherian Pan-Communion of Adidam

*The Sacred Cultural Gathering and Global Mission
of the Devotees of The Divine World-Teacher,
Ruchira Avatar Adi Da Samraj*

*Dedicated to the Practice and the Proclamation
of The True World-Religion of Adidam,
The Unique Divine Way of Realizing Real God*

The Eleutherian Pan-Communion of Adidam is the organization devoted to establishing the Way of Adidam in the world and serving the culture of devotional practice in all four congregations. The Eleutherian Pan-Communion of Adidam is also responsible for the Sanctuaries, the Archives, the Wisdom-Teaching, and other sacred Treasures of Adidam.

The Global Mission of Adidam is a primary branch of the Adidam Pan-Communion. The Mission is active worldwide—through internet websites, through full-time missionaries and through the missionary service of all devotees. The Global Mission also includes the Publications Mission, which prepares, publishes, and distributes Avatar Adi Da's own books (and audiotapes and videotapes of Him), as well as books, magazines, and education courses about Him and the Way of Adidam by His devotees. The Dawn Horse Press (staffed by devotees of Avatar Adi Da) is the editorial and production department of the Publications Mission (see pp. 398-408 for a description of current Adidam publications).

The Ruchirasala of Adidam

THE ADI DA RUCHIRASALA

COOPERATION + TOLERANCE = PEACE

COOPERATION + TOLERANCE = PEACE

THE 'BRIGHT' HOUSE OF ADI DA SAMRAJ

*The True Cooperative Community Gathering
of the Devotees of The Divine World-Teacher,
Ruchira Avatar Adi Da Samraj*

*The Seed of a "Bright" New Age of Sanity
and Divine Joy for Mankind*

Cooperative community living (in households, Ashrams, or on Sanctuaries) is one of the fundamental disciplines of the first and second congregations of Adidam. The Ruchirasala of Adidam is the organization that serves Avatar Adi Da's devotees in incarnating cooperative community— it is the intimate sacred domain, in which devotees practice their devotional life and in which all the other entities of Adidam function. Creating intimate human living arrangements and shared services (such as schools, community businesses, and the Radiant Life Clinic) is part of the responsibility of the Ruchirasala. Together with the Adidam Pan-Communion, the Ruchirasala oversees all the practical interaction between members of the Adidam community.

Cooperation + Tolerance = Peace℠

In addition to His First Calling, which is to those who would become His devotees, Adi Da Samraj makes a Second Calling to the world at large—to embrace the disposition He has Summarized in the equation:

"COOPERATION + TOLERANCE = PEACE".

By this Second Calling, Adi Da Samraj urges everyone to create a sane human society—including, in particular, the creation of a global cooperative order, free of the devastation of war.

To find out more about Adi Da Samraj's Second Calling, please visit the Adidam Peace Center:

www.peacesite.org

An Invitation to Support Adidam

Avatar Adi Da Samraj's sole Purpose is to act as a Source of continuous Divine Grace for everyone, everywhere. In that spirit, He is a Free Renunciate and He owns nothing. Those who have made gestures in support of Avatar Adi Da's Work have found that their generosity is returned in many Blessings that are full of His healing, transforming, and Liberating Grace— and those Blessings flow not only directly to them as the beneficiaries of His Work, but to many others, even all others. At the same time, all tangible gifts of support help secure and nurture Avatar Adi Da's Work in necessary and practical ways, again similarly benefiting the entire world. Because all this is so, supporting His Work is the most auspicious form of financial giving, and we happily extend to you an invitation to serve Adidam through your financial support.

You may make a financial contribution in support of the Work of Adi Da Samraj at any time. You may also, if you choose, request that your contribution be used for one or more specific purposes.

If you are moved to help support and develop Adidam Samrajashram (Naitauba), Avatar Adi Da's Great Hermitage-Retreat and World-Blessing Seat in Fiji, and the circumstance provided there and elsewhere for Avatar Adi Da and the other members of the Ruchira Sannyasin Order, the senior renunciate order of Adidam, you may do so by making your contribution to The Da Love-Ananda Samrajya, the Australian charitable trust which has central responsibility for these Sacred Treasures of Adidam.

To do this: (1) if you do not pay taxes in the United States, make your check payable directly to "The Da Love-Ananda Samrajya Pty Ltd" (which serves as the trustee of the trust) and mail it to The Da Love-Ananda Samrajya at P.O. Box 4744, Samabula, Suva, Fiji; and (2) if you do pay taxes in the United States and you would like your contribution to be tax-deductible under U.S. laws, make your check payable to "The Eleutherian Pan-Communion of Adidam", indicate on your check or accompanying letter that you would like your contribution used for the work of The Da Love-Ananda Samrajya, and mail your check to the Advocacy Department of Adidam at 12040 North Seigler Road, Middletown, California 95461, USA.

If you are moved to help support and provide for one of the other purposes of Adidam, such as publishing the Sacred Literature of Avatar Adi Da, or supporting any of the other Sanctuaries He has Empowered, or maintaining the Sacred Archives that preserve His recorded Talks and Writings, or publishing audio and video recordings of Avatar Adi Da, you may do so by making your contribution directly to The Eleutherian Pan-Communion of Adidam, specifying the particular purposes you wish to benefit, and mailing your check to the Advocacy Department of Adidam at the above address.

If you would like more information about these and other gifting options, or if you would like assistance in describing or making a contribution, please write to the Advocacy Department of Adidam at the above address or contact the Adidam Legal Department by telephone at (707) 928-4612 or by FAX at (707) 928-4062.

Planned Giving

We also invite you to consider making a planned gift in support of the Work of Avatar Adi Da Samraj. Many have found that through planned giving they can make a far more significant gesture of support than they would otherwise be able to make. Many have also found that by making a planned gift they are able to realize substantial tax advantages.

There are numerous ways to make a planned gift, including making a gift in your Will, or in your life insurance, or in a charitable trust.

If you would like to make a gift in your Will in support of the work of The Da Love-Ananda Samrajya: (1) if you do not pay taxes in the United States, simply include in your Will the statement, "I give to The Da Love-Ananda Samrajya Pty Ltd, as trustee of The Da Love-Ananda Samrajya, an Australian charitable trust, P.O. Box 4744, Samabula, Suva, Fiji, _____" [inserting in the blank the amount or description of your contribution]; and (2) if you do pay taxes in the United States and you would like your contribution to be free of estate taxes and to also reduce any estate taxes payable on the remainder of your estate, simply include in your Will the statement, "I give to The Eleutherian Pan-Communion of Adidam, a California non-profit corporation, 12040 North Seigler Road, Middletown, California 95461, USA, _____" [inserting in the blank the amount or description of your contribution].

To make a gift in your life insurance, simply name as the beneficiary (or one of the beneficiaries) of your life insurance policy the organization of your choice (The Da Love-Ananda Samrajya or The Eleutherian Pan-Communion of Adidam), according to the foregoing descriptions and addresses. If you are a United States taxpayer, you may receive significant tax benefits if you make a contribution to The Eleutherian Pan-Communion of Adidam through your life insurance.

We also invite you to consider establishing or participating in a charitable trust for the benefit of Adidam. If you are a United States taxpayer, you may find that such a trust will provide you with immediate tax savings and assured income for life, while at the same time enabling you to provide for your family, for your other heirs, and for the Work of Avatar Adi Da as well.

The Advocacy and Legal Departments of Adidam will be happy to provide you with further information about these and other planned gifting options, and happy to provide you or your attorney with assistance in describing or making a planned gift in support of the Work of Avatar Adi Da.

Further Notes to the Reader

An Invitation to Responsibility

Adidam, the Way of the Heart that Avatar Adi Da has Revealed, is an invitation to everyone to assume real responsibility for his or her life. As Avatar Adi Da has Said in *The Dawn Horse Testament Of The Ruchira Avatar,* "If any one Is Heart-Moved To Realize Me, Let him or her First Resort (Formally, and By Formal Heart-Vow) To Me, and (Thereby) Commence The Ordeal Of self-Observation, self-Understanding, and self-Transcendence. . . ." Therefore, participation in the Way of Adidam requires a real struggle with oneself, and not at all a struggle with Avatar Adi Da, or with others.

All who study the Way of Adidam or take up its practice should remember that they are responding to a Call to become responsible for themselves. They should understand that they, not Avatar Adi Da or others, are responsible for any decision they may make or action they may take in the course of their lives of study or practice. This has always been true, and it is true whatever the individual's involvement in the Way of Adidam, be it as one who studies Avatar Adi Da's Wisdom-Teaching or as a formally acknowledged member of Adidam.

Honoring and Protecting the Sacred Word through Perpetual Copyright

Since ancient times, practitioners of true religion and Spirituality have valued, above all, time spent in the Company of the Sat-Guru (or one who has, to any degree, Realized Real God, Truth, or Reality, and who, thus, serves the awakening process in others). Such practitioners understand that the Sat-Guru literally Transmits his or her (Realized) State to every one (and every thing) with whom (or with which) he or she comes in contact. Through this Transmission, objects, environments, and rightly prepared individuals with which the Sat-Guru has contact can become empowered, or imbued with the Sat-Guru's Transforming Power. It is by this process of empowerment that things and beings are made truly and literally sacred and holy, and things so sanctified thereafter function as a source of the Sat-Guru's Blessing for all who understand how to make right and sacred use of them.

Sat-Gurus of any degree of Realization and all that they empower are, therefore, truly Sacred Treasures, for they help draw the practitioner more quickly into the process of Realization. Cultures of true Wisdom have always understood that such Sacred Treasures are precious (and fragile) Gifts to humanity, and that they should be honored, protected, and reserved for right sacred use. Indeed, the word "holy" means "set apart", and, thus that which is holy and sacred must be protected from insensitive secular interference and wrong use of any kind. Avatar Adi Da has Conformed His human Body-Mind Most Perfectly to the Divine Self, and He is, thus, the most Potent Source of Blessing-Transmission of Real God, or Truth Itself, or Reality Itself. He has for many years Empowered (or made sacred) special places and things, and these now serve as His Divine Agents, or as literal expressions and extensions of His Blessing-Transmission. Among these Empowered Sacred Treasures is His Wisdom-Teaching, which is full of His Transforming Power. This Blessed and Blessing Wisdom-Teaching has Mantric Force, or the literal Power to serve Real-God-Realization in those who are Graced to receive it.

Therefore, Avatar Adi Da's Wisdom-Teaching must be perpetually honored and protected, "set apart" from all possible interference and wrong use. The fellowship of devotees of Avatar Adi Da is committed to the perpetual preservation and right honoring of the Sacred Wisdom-Teaching of the Way of Adidam. But it is also true that, in order to fully accomplish this, we must find support in the world-society in which we live and in its laws. Thus, we call for a world-society and for laws that acknowledge the sacred, and that permanently protect it from insensitive, secular interference and wrong use of any kind. We call for, among other things, a system of law that acknowledges that the Wisdom-Teaching of the Way of Adidam, in all its forms, is, because of its sacred nature, protected by perpetual copyright.

We invite others who respect the sacred to join with us in this call and in working toward its realization. And, even in the meantime, we claim that all copyrights to the Wisdom-Teaching of Avatar Adi Da and the other Sacred Literature and recordings of the Way of Adidam are of perpetual duration.

We make this claim on behalf of The Da Love-Ananda Samrajya Pty Ltd, which, acting as trustee of The Da Love-Ananda Samrajya, is the holder of all such copyrights.

Avatar Adi Da and the Sacred Treasures of Adidam

True Spiritual Masters have Realized Real God (to one degree or another), and, therefore, they bring great Blessing and introduce Divine Possibility to the world. Such Adept-Realizers Accomplish universal Blessing-Work that benefits everything and everyone. They also Work very specifically and intentionally with individuals who approach them as their devotees, and with those places where they reside and to which they direct their specific Regard for the sake of perpetual Spiritual Empowerment. This was understood in traditional Spiritual cultures, and, therefore, those cultures found ways to honor Adept-Realizers by providing circumstances for them where they were free to do their Spiritual Work without obstruction or interference.

Those who value Avatar Adi Da's Realization and Service have always endeavored to appropriately honor Him in this traditional way by providing a circumstance where He is completely Free to do His Divine Work. Since 1983, He has resided principally on the island of Naitauba, Fiji, also known as Adidam Samrajashram. This island has been set aside by Avatar Adi Da's devotees worldwide as a Place for Him to do His universal Blessing-Work for the sake of everyone, as well as His specific Work with those who pilgrimage to Adidam Samrajashram to receive the special Blessing of coming into His physical Company.

Avatar Adi Da is a legal renunciate. He owns nothing and He has no secular or religious institutional function. He Functions only in Freedom. He, and the other members of the Ruchira Sannyasin Order, the senior renunciate order of Adidam, are provided for by The Da Love-Ananda Samrajya, which also provides for Adidam Samrajashram altogether and ensures the permanent integrity of Avatar Adi Da's Wisdom-Teaching, both in its archival and in its published forms. The Da Love-Ananda Samrajya, which functions only in Fiji, exists exclusively to provide for these Sacred Treasures of Adidam.

Outside Fiji, the institution which has developed in response to Avatar Adi Da's Wisdom-Teaching and universal Blessing is known as "The Eleutherian Pan-Communion of Adidam". This formal organization is active worldwide in making Avatar Adi Da's Wisdom-Teaching available to all, in offering guidance to all who are moved to respond to His Offering, and in providing for the other Sacred Treasures of Adidam, including the Mountain Of Attention Sanctuary and Tat Sundaram (in California) and Da Love-Ananda Mahal (in Hawaii). In addition to the central corporate entity known as The Eleutherian Pan-Communion of Adidam, which is based in California, there are numerous regional entities which serve congregations of Avatar Adi Da's devotees in various places throughout the world.

Practitioners of Adidam worldwide have also established numerous community organizations, through which they provide for many of their common and cooperative community needs, including those relating to housing, food, businesses, medical care, schools, and death and dying. By attending to these and all other ordinary human concerns and affairs via ego-transcending cooperation and mutual effort, Avatar Adi Da's devotees constantly free their energy and attention, both personally and collectively, for practice of the Way of Adidam and for service to Avatar Adi Da Samraj, to Adidam Samrajashram, to the other Sacred Treasures of Adidam, and to The Eleutherian Pan-Communion of Adidam.

All of the organizations that have evolved in response to Avatar Adi Da Samraj and His Offering are legally separate from one another, and each has its own purpose and function. Avatar Adi Da neither directs, nor bears responsibility for, the activities of these organizations. Again, He Functions only in Freedom. These organizations represent the collective intention of practitioners of Adidam worldwide not only to provide for the Sacred Treasures of Adidam, but also to make Avatar Adi Da's Offering of the Way of Adidam universally available to all.

APPENDIX

Chart of
The Seven Stages of Life

	FIRST STAGE (approx. 0-7 years)	SECOND STAGE (approx. 7-14 years)	THIRD STAGE (approx. 14-21 years)
THE SEVEN STAGES OF LIFE	individuation; adaptation to the physical body	socialization; adaptation to the emotional-sexual (or feeling) dimension	integration of the psycho-physical personality; development of verbal mind, discriminative intelligence, and the will

THE SEVEN STAGES OF LIFE

The Full and Complete Process of Human Maturation, Spiritual Growth, and Divine Enlightenment

As Revealed by

RUCHIRA AVATAR ADI DA SAMRAJ

Based on
The Seven Stages Of Life,
pp. 103-31

Identified with the gross self

FOURTH STAGE	FIFTH STAGE	SIXTH STAGE	SEVENTH STAGE
...o-surrendering devotion to ...e Divine Person; purification ...body-based point of view ...rough reception of Divine ...irit-Force	Spiritual or Yogic ascent of attention into psychic dimensions of the being; mystical experience of the higher brain; may culminate in fifth stage conditional Nirvikalpa Samadhi	Identification with Consciousness Itself (presumed, however, to be separate from all conditional phenomena); most likely will include the experience of Jnana Samadhi	Realization of the Divine Self; Inherently Perfect Freedom and Realization of Divine Love-Bliss (seventh stage Sahaj Samadhi); no "difference" experienced between Divine Consciousness and psycho-physical states and conditions

FOURTH STAGE	FIFTH STAGE	SIXTH STAGE	SEVENTH STAGE
anatomy: the circulation of ...e Divine Spirit-Current, first ...the "basic" fourth stage of ...e) downward through the ...ontal line and then (in the ...dvanced" fourth stage of ...e) upward through the ...inal line, until attention rests ...ably at the doorway to the ...ain core	**anatomy**: the ascent of the Divine Spirit-Current from the brain core (the Ajna Door) to the crown of the head and above (or even, in fifth stage conditional Nirvikalpa Samadhi, to the Matrix of Divine Sound and Divine Light infinitely above the total crown of the head)	**anatomy**: the Divine Spirit-Current descends (via Amrita Nadi, the "Immortal Current" of Divine Love-Bliss) from the Matrix of Divine Sound and Divine Light (infinitely above the total crown of the head) to the right side of the heart (the bodily seat of Consciousness)	**anatomy**: the "Regeneration" of Amrita Nadi, such that Amrita Nadi is felt as the Divine Current of "Bright" Spirit-Fullness, Standing between the right side of the heart and the Matrix of Divine Sound and Divine Light infinitely above the total crown of the head
	Identified with the subtle self (In the Way of Adidam, practice in the context of the "advanced" fourth stage of life and in the context of the fifth stage of life may typically be bypassed, proceeding directly from the "basic" fourth stage of life to the sixth stage of life)	Identified with the causal self	Identified with Divine Consciousness Itself

Notes to the Text of
RUCHIRA AVATARA
HRIDAYA-SIDDHA YOGA

Part One

1. For a detailed description of the four stages (or four Ways) of Kashmir Saivism, see *Triadic Mysticism: The Mystical Theology of the Saivism of Kashmir*, by Paul E. Murphy (Delhi: Motilal Banarsidass, 1986).

2. Avatar Adi Da Samraj describes "three egos" that must be progressively transcended in the course of the complete Spiritual process—of which the "money, food, and sex" ego is the first. (See section LXXXVII of this Essay, pp. 155-63.)

3. For Avatar Adi Da's Instruction relative to the foundation life-discipline, foundation devotional discipline, and foundation Spiritual discipline for practitioners of Adidam, see *Santosha Adidam*.

4. "Baba" (literally meaning "father") is often used in India as a reference of intimate respect for a Spiritual Master.

5. There are a number of translations of the *Chidakasha Gita* teachings (including *Voice of the Self*, referenced below). Perhaps the most readily available translation is *The Sky of the Heart: Jewels of Wisdom from Nityananda*, introduction and commentary by Swami Chetanananda, originally translated by M. U. Hatengdi (Portland, Or.: Rudra Press, Second edition, 1996).

6. Swami Chinmayananda (1916-1993) was a scholar of the Hindu scriptures, especially the *Bhagavad Gita* and the *Upanishads,* who conceived his mission as restoring respect for the ancient Hindu scriptures and reinvigorating practice of the Spiritual way according to the Vedantic instruction.

7. M. P. Pandit was a scholar of Hindu scripture, and the author of over 100 books on Yoga and Spirituality. He spent more than forty years living and practicing under the guidance of Sri Aurobindo and the Mother, and serving at the Sri Aurobindo Ashram in Pondicherry, India.

8. *Voice of the Self,* by Swami Nityananda (of Vajreshwari), translated by M. P. Pandit (Madras: P. Ramanath Pai, 1962).

9. Sanskrit "nada" (or "shabda") refers to subtle internal sounds which may become apparent in the process of ascending (spinal) Yoga. The "Om-Sound" (or "Omkar") is the primordial root-sound, from which all other nadas derive.

RUCHIRA AVATARA HRIDAYA-SIDDHA YOGA

10. The Sanskrit term "Jnani" ("Sage") literally means "one who knows" (or, more fully, "one who has Realized Jnana Samadhi"—see glossary entry for "Samadhi"). A Jnani is one who discriminates between What is Unconditional (the One Reality, or Divine Self) and what is conditional (the passing phenomena of experience). A Jnani is Identified with Consciousness Itself, as the Transcendental Witness of all that arises. By its very nature, the Realization of Jnana is inherently Nirguna. (In other words, there is no Saguna form of Jnana.)

11. Avatar Adi Da has Revealed that His deeper-personality Vehicle (see note 13), or True Great-Siddha Vehicle, is the combined deeper personalities of Ramakrishna and Swami Vivekananda. Avatar Adi Da discusses His unique association with Ramakrishna and Swami Vivekananda in sections XCIII-XCV (pp. 168-69) of this Essay. For a full description of Avatar Adi Da's Revelation of the Unique Associations with His True Great-Siddha Vehicle, see *The Promised God-Man Is Here*, by Carolyn Lee (Middletown, Calif.: Dawn Horse Press, 1998).

12. Avatar Adi Da's gross-personality vehicle (see note 13) was "Franklin Albert Jones", the child of His parents, Dorothy and Franklin Augustus Jones.

13. Avatar Adi Da uses the terms "gross personality" and "deeper personality" to indicate the two conditional dimensions of every human being. The gross personality is comprised of the physical body, its natural energies, its gross brain, and the verbal and lower psychic faculties of mind. The gross personality includes the entire gross dimension of the body-mind and the lower, or most physically oriented, aspects of the subtle dimension of the body-mind, and is the aspect of the body-mind that is the biological inheritance from one's parents.

The deeper personality is governed by the higher, least physically oriented processes of the mind (which function outside or beyond the gross brain, and which include the subtle faculties of discrimination, intuition, and Spiritual perception and knowledge), as well as the causal separate-"I"-consciousness and the root-activity of attention, prior to mind. The deeper personality is the aspect of the human being that reincarnates.

14. In *The Basket Of Tolerance*, Avatar Adi Da has identified a small number of Hindu and Buddhist texts as "premonitorily 'seventh stage'". While founded in the characteristic sixth stage "point of view", these texts express philosophical intuitions that foreshadow some of the basic characteristics of the seventh stage Realization.

The only-by-Me Revealed and Demonstrated and Given seventh stage of life is the clear and final fulfillment of the first six stages of life. The Revelation and Demonstration of the seventh stage of life by My own Avatarically Self-Revealed Divine Form, Presence, State, Work, and Word are My unique Gift to all and All. However, within the Great Tradition itself, there are some few literatures and Realizers of the sixth stage type that express philosophical (or insightful, but yet limited and incomplete) intuitions that sympathetically foreshadow some of the basic characteristics of the only-by-Me Revealed and Demonstrated and Given seventh stage Realization.

The Ashtavakra Gita *is a principal example of such premonitorily "seventh stage" literature. It is among the greatest (and most senior) communications of all the religious and Spiritual traditions in the Great Tradition of mankind. The* Ashtavakra Gita *is the Great Confession of a Sage who has thoroughly engaged the philosophies and practices of the first six stages of life. It is a sixth stage Adept-Realizer's Free (and uncompromised) communication (or Confession) of the ultimate implications of his sixth stage Realization.*

Like other premonitorily "seventh stage" texts, the Ashtavakra Gita *presumes a tradition of progressive practice in the total context of the first six stages of life, but it does not (itself) represent or communicate any ideal or technique of practice. It simply (and rather exclusively) communicates the Ultimate "Point of View" of the sixth stage Realizer. ("The Unique Sixth Stage Foreshadowings of the Only-by-Me Revealed and Demonstrated and Given Seventh Stage of Life", in* The Basket Of Tolerance)

15. In Sanskrit, "seva" means "service". Service to the Guru is traditionally treasured as one of the great Secrets of Realization.

16. The Hindu tradition speaks of four principal Spiritual paths (or four principal aspects of the Spiritual path). Karma Yoga is literally the "Yoga of action", in which every activity, no matter how humble, is transformed into self-transcending service to the Divine. (The other three paths are Bhakti Yoga, the path of devotion, Raja Yoga, the path of higher psychic discipline, and Jnana Yoga, the path of transcendental insight.)

17. Swami Prakashananda (1917-1988) turned to Spiritual life in his 30s, eventually choosing the mountain of Sapta Shringh as a place to settle and devote himself to Spiritual practice. Over time, an ashram developed there around him. He met Swami Muktananda in 1956 and was initiated as Swami Muktananda's devotee, although he generally stayed at his own ashram in Sapta Shringh rather than spending a great deal of time in Ganeshpuri at Swami Muktananda's ashram. For Swami Prakashananda's biography, see *Agaram Bagaram Baba: Life, Teachings, and Parables—A Spiritual Biography of Baba Prakashananda*, by Titus Foster (Berkeley: North Atlantic Books / Patagonia, Ariz.: Essene Vision Books, 1999).

18. For Avatar Adi Da's description of Swami Prakashananda's demonstration of Spiritual Transfiguration of the physical body, see chapter 12 of *The Knee Of Listening.*

19. *Agaram Bagaram Baba*, p. 35.

20. Swami Muktananda's letter of acknowledgement and blessing of Avatar Adi Da is included in chapter 12 of *The Knee Of Listening* and also in Part Three ("The Order of My Free Names") of *The Divine Siddha-Method Of The Ruchira Avatar.*

21. For Avatar Adi Da's description of His own "Embrace" of the Divine "Cosmic Goddess", see chapter 16 of *The Knee Of Listening.*

22. *Play of Consciousness,* by Swami Muktananda (South Fallsburg, N.Y.: SYDA, Fourth edition, 1994).

23. For Avatar Adi Da's description of His experience of Christian mystical visions, see chapters 14 and 15 of *The Knee Of Listening.*

24. For a comprehensive treatment of the fourth-to-fifth stage Yogic tradition of Maharashtra, see *Mysticism in India: The Poet-Saints of Maharashtra,* by R. D. Ranade (Albany: State University of New York Press, 1983).

25. For Swami Muktananda's description of the "Blue Person", see *Play of Consciousness,* by Swami Muktananda (South Fallsburg, N.Y.: SYDA, fourth edition, 1994), e.g. pp. 190-194.

Among the numerous translations of the *Bhagavad Gita,* Avatar Adi Da Samraj points to two editions as particularly worthy of study:

Srimad-Bhagavad-Gita (The Scripture of Mankind). Chapter summaries, word-for-word meaning in prose order, translation, notes, and index of first lines by Swami Tapasyananda. Mylapore, India: Sri Ramakrishna Math, 1984.

God Talks with Arjuna: The Bhagavad Gita—Royal Science of God-Realization, The Immortal Dialogue Between Soul and Spirit. A new translation and commentary by Paramahansa Yogananda (two volumes). Los Angeles: Self-Realization Fellowship, 1996

For a complete translation of the *Bhagavata Purana* (also known as the *Srimad Bhagavatam*), see *Srimad Bhagavatam,* translated by N. Raghunathan, two volumes (Madras: Vighneshwara Publishing House, 1976).

26. For Avatar Adi Da's full description of the "bodies" or "sheaths" of the total human structure (and the relationship between these "bodies" and the states of waking, dreaming, and sleeping), see *Santosha Adidam.*

27. Excerpted from a chart ("The Four Bodies of the Individual Soul") in *Play of Consciousness,* by Swami Muktananda (South Fallsburg, N.Y.: SYDA, Fourth edition, 1994), p. 96.

28. In *The Basket Of Tolerance,* Avatar Adi Da has contrasted the development of exoteric (or socially oriented, and myth-based) public Christianity with the secret Teachings of esoteric (or mystically oriented) Christianity:

The "official" Christian church, even in the form of all its modern sects, is the institutional product of an early cultural struggle between exoteric religionists, limited to doctrines based in the physical point of view characteristic of the first three stages of life, and esoteric religionists, inclined toward the mystical (or general psychic, and Spiritual) point of view characteristic of the "basic" and the "advanced" phases of the fourth stage of life and the mystical (or higher psychic, and Spiritual) Realizations associated with the fifth stage of life. This struggle, which was eventually won by the exoteric sects (or factions), took place between the various emerging Christian sects during the early centuries after Jesus' [crucifixion]. . . .

In the domain of the exoteric church, it was apparently generally presumed (among its original creative leadership) that all mysteries and legends must be "concretized" into a story (or an inspiring doctrine) about Jesus as the "Heavenly Messiah" (or the "Christ", the "Anointed One", the Exclusively Blessed "Son of God")—whereas the original esoteric mysteries and mystical Teachings of Christian gnosticism (which must often correspond to what must be presumed to have been Jesus' own Teachings) invariably communicate a Message about the Spiritual (or "Spirit-Breathing") Awakening of every individual (or of every devotee of a Spirit-Master, or, in this Christian case, of every devotee of Jesus as Spirit-Master). Therefore, the core of the esoteric Christian Teachings is that Salvation (from "possession" by cosmic Nature, by the human world, and by fear of death) is Realized by Means of "Spiritual rebirth" (or Absorption In—and, thus, participatory knowledge of—the inherently deathless and Free and Divine Spirit-Power, or "Breath-Energy", of Being). And the "Good News" of this esoteric Salvation Message is that every individual is (ultimately, by virtue of Spiritual Realization) a "Son" or "Daughter" of God.

29. Avatar Adi Da notes that not only "things" in space but space itself came into being with the "Big Bang":

> *Space-time (itself, or in its totality) cannot be observed. The "Big Bang" was not an event that could have been observed. The "Big Bang" is not something that occurred in space (or in time). The "Big Bang" is the origin of space (and of time). To look at the "Big Bang" as an event in space (and in time) is already to look at it in egoic terms, and from a position after the event. To examine the "Big Bang" in conventional scientific terms is to assume a dissociated (and separate, and separative) position, as if the ego-"I" (or the "observing" body-mind) were standing outside of space-time—but it does not. Egoity (and all of psycho-physical self, or body-mind) is, inherently and necessarily, an event in (and of) space-time. The body-mind is an event in (and of) space-time. That in Which the body-mind is occurring (or of Which the body-mind is a modification, or a mere and temporary appearance) necessarily (Itself) Transcends space-time, Transcends limitation, Transcends the apparent breaking of Fundamental Light (or of Energy Itself, or of Radiance Itself). ("Space-Time Is Love-Bliss", in* Real *God Is The Indivisible Oneness Of Unbroken Light)*

30. For Swami Muktananda's description of the "blue bindu" (or "blue pearl"), see *Play of Consciousness* (e.g., pp. 160-161).

31. For Avatar Adi Da's full description of the Cosmic Mandala, see chapter thirty-nine of *The Dawn Horse Testament Of The Ruchira Avatar.*

32. In *The Knee Of Listening*, Avatar Adi Da describes His Birth as the "Bright", His subsequent voluntary relinquishment of the "Bright", and His eventual Re-Awakening as the "Bright". He uses the word "Re-Awakening" to indicate that this Great Event was not a Realization entirely "new" to His experience, but a "return" to the Divine Condition He had known at Birth.

33. For Avatar Adi Da's description of His discovery of parallels with Ramana Maharshi's experience, see chapter 18 of *The Knee Of Listening.*

34. This instruction from Swami Muktananda was communicated in a letter he wrote to Avatar Adi Da on April 23, 1968, which Avatar Adi Da quotes in chapter 11 of *The Knee Of Listening.*

35. The "Method of the Siddhas" (meaning "the Spiritual Means used by the Siddhas, or Perfected Ones, or True Spirit-Baptizers") is a phrase coined by Avatar Adi Da Samraj (in the earliest days of His Teaching Work) to describe the

essence of the Way of Adidam—which is the Spiritual <u>relationship</u> to Him (or Satsang, or devotional Communion with Him), rather than any technique (meditative or otherwise) learned from Him. *The Method of the Siddhas* was the Title Avatar Adi Da chose for the first published collection of His Talks to His devotees. (In its final form, Avatar Adi Da re-titled this book *The Divine Siddha-Method Of The Ruchira Avatar.*)

Avatar Adi Da also points out that this "Method" has traditionally always been the core of esoteric religion and Spirituality, and that (indeed) the entire worldwide tradition of esoteric religion and Spirituality is rightly understood to be the global tradition of "Siddha Yoga".

The Foundation Of The Only-By-Me Revealed and Given Way Of Adidam Is The Eternal, Ancient, and Always New Method Of The Siddhas—Which Is Devotional Communion With The Siddha-Guru, and Which Is The Unique Means Of Realizing Real God, or Truth, or Reality That Has Traditionally Been Granted By The Rare True Adept-Realizers Of Real God, or Truth, or Reality Who (In The Traditional Context Of The First Six Stages Of Life, and Each According To Their Particular Stage Of Awakening and Of Helping-Capability) Have, By Means Of The Unique Blessing-Method (or Transmission-Capability) Of The Siddhas, Directly (and By Directly and Really Effective Spiritual Blessing-Work) Transmitted The Traditional Revelations and Realizations Of Real God, or Truth, or Reality. [The <u>Only</u> Complete Way To Realize The Unbroken Light Of <u>Real</u> God]

36. The Sanskrit word "sat" means "Truth", "Being", "Existence". Esoterically, the word "guru" is understood to be a composite of two words meaning "destroyer of darkness". The Sat-Guru is thus a "True Guru", or one who destroys darkness and thereby leads living beings from darkness (or non-Truth) into Light (or the Living Truth).

37. A common theme running through various branches of the Great Tradition is the prophecy of a great Savior or Liberator still to come. The prophecy takes different forms in different traditions, but the underlying commonality is the promise or expectation that the culminating Avatar or Incarnation will appear in the future, at a time when humanity is lost, apparently cut off from Wisdom, Truth, and God. Buddhists refer to that Expected One as "Maitreya"; Vaishnavite Hindus, as the "Kalki Avatar"; Christians, as the "second coming of Jesus"; Jews, as the "Messiah"; and so on.

38. Avatar Adi Da Samraj describes His spontaneous experience of ego-death, in the spring of 1967, in chapter 9 of *The Knee Of Listening.*

39. See *Sadguru Nityananda Bhagavan, The Eternal Entity*, by P.V. Ravindram (Cannanore, India: T. Thankam Ravindran, 1989), pp. 25-26 and 27-28.

40. For Avatar Adi Da's Revelations about Ramakrishna and Swami Vivekananda as His "combined" deeper-personality Vehicle, see Essay VI ("I Have Appeared here Via a Unique, Spontaneous, and Never-Again Conjunction of Vehicles") in chapter 20 of *The Knee Of Listening.*

Part Two

41. Avatar Adi Da has explained that, for most practitioners of Adidam, practice of the spinal Yoga (in the context of the "advanced" fourth stage of life and the fifth stage of life) will not be necessary and may be bypassed. See also glossary entry for **stages of life**.

42. The "traditionally sought 'Goal' of Transcendental Seclusion" is a reference to what Avatar Adi Da describes as the fundamental error associated with the sixth stage of life. That error (of seeking Transcendental Seclusion) is the tendency to hold on to the Subjective Position of Consciousness Itself while strategically excluding objective (or conditional) states. See *The Seven Stages Of Life*, p. 235.

43. See I.4.2 of *The Principal Upanisads*, translated by S. Radhakrishnan (London: George Allen & Unwin/New York: Humanities Press, 1953), p. 164.

Part Three

44. In *The Dawn Horse Testament*, Avatar Adi Da Samraj describes the range of visions and auditions that may be experienced by His devotees:

> *Among The Significant (and Most Basic and Typical) experiential Signs (or experiences Of The Effects Of My Avatarically Self-Revealed Spiritual, and Always Blessing, Divine Presence) That May Appear (Even, Possibly, At Any Developmental Stage Of Practice In The Way Of Adidam, Which Is The One and Only By-Me-Revealed and By-Me-Given Way Of The Heart) Are A Spontaneous Quieting Of the conceptual activity of the mind and (Also) The Spontaneous Happening Of kriyas (or pleasurable bodily pulsings and tremblings, or pleasurable, and sometimes visibly dramatic, bodily shakings, spasms, or convulsions, that Work Spontaneously To Purify body, emotion, mind, and attention, and that Occur When My Avatarically Self-Transmitted Divine Spirit-Current Meets and Penetrates, or Breaks, The Blocks In Either The Frontal Line Or The Spinal Line, or In Both). Other Possible Spontaneous experiential Signs (That May Occur, Progressively, As ego-Surrendering, ego-Forgetting, and ego-Transcending Feeling-Contemplation Of My Avatarically Self-Revealed Spiritual, and Always Blessing, Divine Presence Deepens, Progressively) Include mudras (or many and various, and often dance-like, Yogic hand poses), asanas (or many and various Yogic bodily poses), pranayama (or automatic slow or rapid Yogic breathing-"Conductivity"), dancing, jumping, bodily hotness, sweating, bodily coldness, dryness of mouth, snarling and other exotic (and even animal-like) facial expressions, laughter, weeping, singing, moaning, growling (and other Spontaneous vocal noises), and (of course) all kinds of bodily and emotional and mental blisses (or states of Yogic "intoxication"), even in the form of blissful yawning and/or blissfully deep drowsiness (that may become a kind of Yogic "dream state", and even a Yogic "sleep", but without any loss Of blissful Awareness). And Other Possible Spontaneous experiential Signs That May Occur Include any number of subtle sensations (such as visions Of My Avatarically Self-Transmitted Divine Spirit-Current As light within the body, visions of the interior of the physical body, visions of energy centers in the body, visions of symbolic patterns, visions of fields, spots, spheres, or holes of various colors,*

visions of blackness, density, fire, water, smoke, and the sky, auditions of the heartbeat, blood-circulation, and respiration, auditions of subtle internal sounds, such as explosions, a sound like a gunshot, snapping noises, pulsing or clicking or fluttering sounds, big and little thumping and tapping and drumming sounds, thundering or roaring or deep-vibrating or humming sounds, ringing sounds, big and little bell-like sounds, flute-like sounds, xylophone-like sounds, pouring or rushing soundless, or Merely Felt, sounds, perceptions of a variety of subtle internal smells, in a range from excrement to flowers, and perception of a variety of subtle internal tastes, culminating in an ambrosial sweetness, as if nectar were dripping out of the brain), and Also every Possible kind of even vivid Yogic "dream", psychic vision, sudden insight, or Spiritual Apparition. Likewise, Many remarkable psychic (and even physical) Signs (or experiences) May (In Some Cases, and In Due Course) Occur, including psychokinesis (or the ability to move, and even change, physical objects from a distance, via the mental projection of energy), the ability to receive and transmit thoughts and energies from a distance (via mental reception and projection), bodily levitation, bodily bilocation (so that You may perceive Your Own bodily double, or Your bodily person may be perceived by others in a location that is other than the one in which You perceive Your Own bodily person), "out-of-body experiences" (or astral travel), premonitory dreaming (or futuristic reveries), and various forms of extrasensory perception, such as clairaudience, clairvoyance (including the ability to observe the local physical environment, or any physical environment at all, in all directions at once, rather than simply forward from the eyes, by simply rotating the eyeballs and the visual attention upwards), and general clairsentience. The List Cannot Be Exhausted, and, Apart From Certain Basic and Typical experiences (such as Spontaneous kriyas, Spontaneous psycho-physical blisses, and, Most Importantly, The Spontaneous Quieting Of the conceptual activity of the mind), The Display Is Unique To each individual. ["The Significant Experiential Signs That May Appear in the Course of The Way Of Adidam", in What, Where, When, How, Why, and <u>Who</u> To Remember To Be Happy]

45. Avatar Adi Da has described two basic structural dimensions (or planes) of the body-mind-self: the horizontal and the vertical.

The "horizontal dimension" of the body-mind is the dimension of conditional awareness and attention, and of Consciousness Itself. It is associated principally with the three great psycho-physical centers and functions of the physical heart, which may be regarded to exist in a more or less horizontal line from left to right. The bodily heart is the seat of the three conventional states of conditional awareness: <u>waking</u>, associated with the physical heart and the region to the left of the heart's center; <u>dreaming</u> and psychic (or subtle) awareness, associated with the middle or psychic heart (in the Yogic traditions, anahata chakra); and <u>deep sleep</u>, associated with the Source-Position of Consciousness and of attention, in the upper right side of the heart (at a locus corresponding to the sinoatrial node, or "pacemaker").

For Avatar Adi Da's description of the progressive course of the Awakening of Consciousness via functions in the left, the middle, and the right regions of the heart, see *The Seven Stages Of Life*, pp. 117-18, 121-25.

The "vertical dimension" of the body-mind is what Avatar Adi Da calls the

"Circle", which is made up of two lines (or energy-pathways)—descending (or frontal) and ascending (or spinal). See Glossary entries for **Circle**, **frontal line**, and **spinal line**.

46. "Kripa" is Sanskrit for "grace". Traditionally, it is a synonym for "shaktipat", or the Initiatory Blessing of the Spiritual Master. Ruchira Avatara Kripa is Avatar Adi Da's Gift of the Transmission of His Inherently Perfect Heart-Blessing.

47. In deep meditation, the Spirit-Current may be felt in the form of the Arrow (which Avatar Adi Da describes as "a motionless axis that seems to stand in the center of the body, between the frontal and spinal lines"), rather than in the form of the Circle (in which the natural life-energy and, in the case of Spiritually Awakened practitioners, the Spirit-Energy are felt to circulate through the frontal and spinal lines).

48. Also known as the "third eye", the "single eye", or the "mystic eye", the Ajna Door is the subtle psychic center (or chakra) located between and behind the eyebrows and associated with the brain core. The awakening of the ajna chakra may give rise to mystical visions and intuitive reflections of other realms of experience within and outside the individual. The ajna chakra governs the higher mind, will, vision, and conception.

Part Four

49. For examples of reports of Kundalini Shakti experiences, see:

Kundalini: The Evolutionary Energy in Man, by Gopi Krishna (Boulder, Colo.: Shambala, 1971).

The Kundalini Experience: Psychosis or Transcendence?, by Lee Sannella, M.D. (Lower Lake, Calif.: Integral Publishing, 1987).

50. Avatar Adi Da wrote this essay in response to the Yogic sexual practices (and their associated Hatha Yoga postures and techniques) briefly described or referred to in the essay "Vama Marga: The Practice of Left-Hand Tantra", by Swami Satyananda Saraswati (*Yoga* magazine, March 1981, pp. 4-17). These practices are further described and elaborated in *Hatha Yoga Pradipika: The Light on Hatha Yoga*, commentary by Swami Muktibodhananda Saraswati under the guidance of Swami Satyananda Saraswati (Munger, Bihar, India: Bihar School of Yoga, 1985) and *Asana, Pranayama, Mudra, Bandha*, by Swami Satyananda Saraswati (Monghyr, Bihar, India: Bihar School of Yoga, sixth edition, 1983).

51. "Mahamantra" is Sanskrit for "Great Mantra". Mahamantra Meditation is a form of meditative practice Given by Avatar Adi Da to His devotees (who practice the technically "fully elaborated" form of the Way of Adidam in the manner of the Devotional Way of Faith) in the "advanced" fourth stage of life and the fifth stage of life.

For a detailed description of the significance and practice of Mahamantra Meditation, see chapters twenty-five through twenty-nine of *The Dawn Horse Testament Of The Ruchira Avatar* and section XIV of the Essay "Santosha Adidam" (in *Santosha Adidam*).

52. Ruchira Avatara Naama Japa is repetition ("japa") of the Name ("naama") of the Ruchira Avatar, Adi Da Samraj, in one of the forms that He has Given. Avatar Adi Da's description of the practice of Ruchira Avatara Naama Japa is found in *The Only Complete Way To Realize The Unbroken Light Of Real God.* The full listing of the forms of the Ruchira Avatara Naama Mantra is found in chapter three of *The Dawn Horse Testament Of The Ruchira Avatar.*

53. Swami Rudrananda (Rudi) was Avatar Adi Da's first Spiritual Teacher. See glossary entry for **Lineage**.

54. Avatar Adi Da has explained that it is possible for His devotees to bypass practice of the spinal Yoga (in the context of the "advanced" fourth stage of life and the fifth stage of life), proceeding directly from the completion of the frontal Yoga (in the context of the "basic" fourth stage of life) to the beginning of the "Perfect Practice" (in the context of the sixth stage of life). See also glossary entry for **stages of life**.

55. For a description of Avatar Adi Da's "'Heroic' and 'Crazy' Ordeal", see *The Promised God-Man Is Here,* by Carolyn Lee.

GLOSSARY

A

Adi Sanskrit for "first", "primordial", "source"—also "primary", "beginning". Thus, most simply, "Adi Da" means "First Giver".

Adidam The primary name for the Way Revealed and Given by Avatar Adi Da Samraj.

When Avatar Adi Da Samraj first Gave the name "Adidam" in January 1996, He pointed out that the final "m" adds a mantric force, evoking the effect of the primal Sanskrit syllable "Om". (For Avatar Adi Da's Revelation of the most profound esoteric significance of "Om" as the Divine Sound of His own Very Being, see *He-and-She Is Me*.) Simultaneously, the final "m" suggests the English word "Am" (expressing "I Am"), such that the Name "Adidam" also evokes Avatar Adi Da's Primal Self-Confession, "I Am Adi Da", or, more simply, "I Am Da" (or, in Sanskrit, "Aham Da Asmi").

Adidam Samrajashram See **Sanctuaries**.

adolescent See **childish and adolescent strategies**.

Advaita Vedanta The Sanskrit word "Vedanta" literally means the "end of the Vedas" (the most ancient body of Indian Scripture), and is used to refer to the principal philosophical tradition of Hinduism. "Advaita" means "non-dual". Advaita Vedanta, then, is a philosophy of non-dualism, the origins of which lie in the ancient esoteric teaching that Brahman, or the Divine Being, is the only Reality.

Advaitayana Buddha / Advaitayana Buddhism "Advaitayana" means "Non-Dual Vehicle". The Advaitayana Buddha is the Enlightened One Who has Revealed and Given the Non-Dual Vehicle.

"Advaitayana Buddhism" is another name for the Way of Adidam. The name "Advaitayana Buddhism" indicates the unique sympathetic likeness of Adidam to the traditions of Advaitism (or Advaita Vedanta) and Buddhism. In His examination of the entire collective religious tradition of humankind, Avatar Adi Da has observed that these two traditions represent the most advanced Realizations ever attained previous to His Avataric Divine Incarnation. The primary aspiration of Buddhism is to realize freedom from the illusion of the separate individual ego-self. The primary aspiration of Advaitism (or the tradition of "Non-Dualism") is to know the Supreme Divine Self absolutely, beyond all dualities (of high and low, good and bad, and so on). Advaitayana Buddhism is the Non-Dual ("Advaita") Way ("yana", literally "vehicle") of Most Perfect Awakening ("Buddhism"). Advaitayana Buddhism is neither an outgrowth of the historical tradition of Buddhism nor of the historical tradition of Advaitism. Advaitayana Buddhism is the unique Revelation of Avatar Adi Da Samraj, which perfectly fulfills both the traditional Buddhist aspiration for absolute freedom from the bondage of the egoic self and the traditional Advaitic aspiration for absolute Identity with the Divine Self. (For Avatar Adi Da's discussion of Advaitayana Buddhism, see *The Only Complete Way To Realize The Unbroken Light Of Real God*.)

Advaitic "Advaita" is Sanskrit for "Non-Duality". Thus, "Advaitic" means "Non-Dual". Avatar Adi Da has Revealed that—in Truth, and in Reality—there is not the slightest separation, or "difference", between the Unconditional Divine Reality and the conditional reality. In other words, Reality altogether is Perfectly One, or Non-Dual, or Advaitic.

the advanced and the ultimate stages of life Avatar Adi Da Samraj uses the term "advanced" to describe the fourth stage of life (in its "basic" and "advanced" contexts) and the fifth stage of life in the Way of Adidam. He uses the term "ultimate" to describe the sixth and seventh stages of life in the Way of Adidam.

"advanced" context of the fourth stage of life   See **stages of life**.

Agents / Agency   Agents (or Agency) include all the Means that may serve as complete Vehicles of Avatar Adi Da's Divine Grace and Awakening Power. The first Means of Agency that have been fully established by Him are the Wisdom-Teaching of the Way of Adidam, the Hermitage-Retreat Sanctuaries and the Pilgrimage and Retreat Sanctuaries that He has Empowered, and the many Objects and Articles that He has Empowered for the sake of His devotees' Remembrance of Him and reception of His Heart-Blessing. After Avatar Adi Da's human Lifetime, at any given time a single individual from among His seventh stage "Ruchira sannyasin" devotees will be designated (by the senior governing membership of the Ruchira Sannyasin Order) to serve as His living human Agent.

Aham Da Asmi   The Sanskrit phrase "Aham Da Asmi" means "I (Aham) Am (Asmi) Da". "Da", meaning "the One Who Gives", indicates that Avatar Adi Da Samraj is the Supreme Divine Giver, the Avataric Incarnation of the Very Divine Person.

Avatar Adi Da's Declaration "Aham Da Asmi" is similar in form to the "Mahavakyas" (or "Great Statements") of ancient India (found in the Upanishads, the collected esoteric Instruction of ancient Hindu Gurus). However, the significance of "Aham Da Asmi" is fundamentally different from that of the traditional Mahavakyas. Each of the Upanishadic Mahavakyas expresses, in a few words, the profound (though not most ultimate) degree of Realization achieved by great Realizers of the past. For example, the Upanishadic Mahavakya "Aham Brahmasmi" ("I Am Brahman") expresses a great individual's Realization that he or she is Identified with the Divine Being (Brahman), and is not, in Truth, identified with his or her apparently individual body-mind. However, "Aham Da

Asmi", rather than being a proclamation of a human being who has devoted his or her life most intensively to the process of Real-God-Realization and has thereby Realized the Truth to an extraordinarily profound degree, is Avatar Adi Da's Confession that He Is the Very Divine Person, Da, Who has Appeared here in His Avatarically-Born bodily (human) Divine Form, in order to Reveal Himself to all and All, for the sake of the Divine Liberation of all and All.

all and All / All and all   Avatar Adi Da uses the phrase "all and All" (or "All and all") to describe the totality of conditional existence from two points of view. In *Aham Da Asmi,* He defines lower-case "all" as indicating "the collected sum of all Presumed To Be Separate (or limited) beings, things, and conditions", and upper-case "All" as indicating "The All (or The Undivided Totality) Of conditional Existence As A Whole".

Amrita Nadi   Amrita Nadi is Sanskrit for "Channel (or Current, or Nerve) of Ambrosia (or Immortal Nectar)". Amrita Nadi is the ultimate "organ", or root-structure, of the body-mind, Realized as such in the seventh stage of life in the Way of Adidam. It is felt to Stand Radiant between the right side of the heart (which is the psycho-physical Seat of Consciousness Itself) and the Matrix of Light infinitely above the crown of the head. (For Avatar Adi Da's principal discussions of Amrita Nadi, see *The Knee Of Listening, The All-Completing* and *Final Divine Revelation To Mankind, Santosha Adidam,* and *The Dawn Horse Testament.)*

anatomy   See **Spiritual anatomy**.

asana   Sanskrit for bodily "posture" or "pose"—by extension, and as Avatar Adi Da often intends, "asana" also refers to the attitude, orientation, posture, or feeling-disposition of the heart and the entire body-mind.

"Atma-Murti"   "Atma" indicates the Divine Self, and "Murti" means "Form". Thus, "Atma-Murti" literally means "the Form That Is the (Very) Divine Self". And, as Avatar Adi Da Indicates everywhere in His Wisdom-Teaching, "Atma-Murti" refers to Himself as the Very Divine Self of all, "Located" as "the Feeling of Being (Itself)". To Commune with Avatar Adi Da as "Atma-Murti" is to Realize (or enter into Identification with) His Divine State.

Avadhoot Avadhoot is a traditional term for one who has "shaken off" or "passed beyond" all worldly attachments and cares, including all motives of detachment (or conventional and other-worldly renunciation), all conventional notions of life and religion, and all seeking for "answers" or "solutions" in the form of conditional experience or conditional knowledge.

Avatar "Avatar" (from Sanskrit "avatara") is a traditional term for a Divine Incarnation. It literally means "One who is descended, or 'crossed down' (from, and as, the Divine)". Avatar Adi Da Samraj Confesses that, simultaneous with His human Birth, He has Incarnated in every world, at every level of the Cosmic domain, as the Eternal Giver of Divine Help and Divine Grace and Divine Liberation to all beings—and that, even though His bodily (human) Lifetime is necessarily limited in duration, His Spiritual Incarnation in the Cosmic domain is Eternal.

Avataric Incarnation Avatar Adi Da Samraj is the Avataric Incarnation, or the Divinely Descended Embodiment, of the Divine Person. The reference "Avataric Incarnation" indicates that Avatar Adi Da Samraj fulfills both the traditional expectation of the East, that the True God-Man is an Avatar (or an utterly Divine "Descent" of Real God in conditionally manifested form), and the traditional expectations of the West, that the True God-Man is an Incarnation (or an utterly human Embodiment of Real God).

For Avatar Adi Da's discussion of the "Avatar" and "Incarnation" traditions, and of His unique and all-Completing Role as the "Avataric Incarnation" of the Divine Person, see "'Avatar' and 'Incarnation': The Complementary God-Man Traditions of East and West", in *The Truly Human New World-Culture Of Unbroken Real-God-Man*.

Avataric Self-Submission For a full description of Avatar Adi Da's "Ordeal Of Avataric Self-Submission", see *The Promised God-Man Is Here*, by Carolyn Lee.

"Avoiding relationship?" The practice of self-Enquiry in the form "Avoiding relationship?", unique to the Way of Adidam, was spontaneously developed by Avatar Adi Da in the course of His Divine Re-Awakening (as Avatar Adi Da describes in *The Knee Of Listening*). Intense persistence in the "radical" discipline of this unique form of self-Enquiry led rapidly to His Divine Re-Awakening in 1970.

The practice of self-Enquiry in the form "Avoiding relationship?" is the principal form of the "conscious process" practiced by devotees of Avatar Adi Da who choose the Devotional Way of Insight. (See also "Devotional Way of Insight / Devotional Way of Faith" and "Re-cognition".)

B

"basic" context of the fourth stage of life See **stages of life**.

Bhagavan The Title "Bhagavan" is an ancient one used over the centuries for many Spiritual Realizers of India. It means "blessed" or "holy" in Sanskrit. When applied to a great Spiritual Being, "Bhagavan" is understood to mean "bountiful Lord", or "Great Lord", or "Divine Lord".

bhakta, bhakti "Bhakti" is the practice of heart-felt devotion to the Ultimate Reality or Person—a practice which has been traditionally animated through worship of Divine Images or surrender to a human Guru.

"Bhakta" is a devotee whose principal characteristic is expressive devotion, or who practices within the Hindu tradition of Bhakti Yoga.

Bhava "Bhava" is a Sanskrit word used to refer to the enraptured feeling-swoon of Communion with the Divine.

bindu In the esoteric Yogic traditions of India, the Sanskrit word "bindu" (literally, "drop" or "point") suggests that all manifested forms, energies, and universes are ultimately coalesced or expressed in a point without spatial or temporal dimension. Each level (or plane) of psychophysical reality is said to have a corresponding bindu, or zero-point.

Blessing-Work   For a description of Avatar Adi Da's Divine Blessing-Work, see pp. 17-19.

bodily base   The bodily base is the region associated with the muladhara chakra, the lowest energy plexus in the human body-mind, at the base of the spine (or the general region immediately above and including the perineum). In many of the Yogic traditions, the bodily base is regarded as the seat of the latent ascending Spiritual Current, or Kundalini. Avatar Adi Da Reveals that, in fact, the Spirit-Current must first descend to the bodily base through the frontal line, before it can effectively be directed into the ascending spinal course. Avatar Adi Da has also pointed out that human beings who are not yet Spiritually sensitive tend to throw off the natural life-energy at the bodily base, and He has, therefore, Given His devotees a range of disciplines (including a number of exercises that involve intentional locking at the bodily base) which conserve life-energy by directing it into the spinal line.

"bodily battery"   The "bodily battery" (known in Japan as the "hara") is the energy center of the gross body and, as such, plays a very important role in the practice of "conductivity" in the frontal line. Avatar Adi Da describes its focal point (or point of concentration) as the crown of the abdomen, on the surface, about an inch and a half below the umbilical scar.

"bond" / "Bond"   Avatar Adi Da uses the term "bond", when lower-cased, to refer to the process by which the egoic individual (already presuming separateness, and, therefore, bondage to the separate self) attaches itself karmically to the world of others and things through the

constant search for self-fulfillment. In contrast, when He capitalizes the term "Bond", Avatar Adi Da is making reference to the process of His devotee's devotional "Bonding" to Him, which process is the Great Means for transcending all forms of limited (or karmic) "bonding".

"Bright"   By the word "Bright" (and its variations, such as "Brightness"), Avatar Adi Da refers to the Self-Existing and Self-Radiant Divine Reality. As Adi Da Writes in His Spiritual Autobiography, *The Knee Of Listening:*

  . . . *from my earliest experience of life I have Enjoyed a Condition that, as a child, I called the "Bright".*

  I have always known desire, not merely for extreme pleasures of the senses and the mind, but for the highest Enjoyment of Spiritual Power and Mobility. But I have not been seated in desire, and desire has only been a play that I have grown to understand and enjoy without conflict. I have always been Seated in the "Bright".

  Even as a baby I remember only crawling around inquisitively with a boundless Feeling of Joy, Light, and Freedom in the middle of my head that was bathed in Energy moving unobstructed in a Circle, down from above, all the way down, then up, all the way up, and around again, and always Shining from my heart. It was an Expanding Sphere of Joy from the heart. And I was a Radiant Form, the Source of Energy, Love-Bliss, and Light in the midst of a world that is entirely Energy, Love-Bliss, and Light. I was the Power of Reality, a direct Enjoyment and Communication of the One Reality. I was the Heart Itself, Who Lightens the mind and all things. I was the same as every one and every thing, except it became clear that others were apparently unaware of the "Thing" Itself.

  Even as a little child I recognized It and Knew It, and my life was not a matter of anything else. That Awareness, that Conscious Enjoyment, that Self-Existing and Self-Radiant Space of Infinitely and inherently Free Being, that Shine of inherent Joy Standing in the heart and Expanding from the heart, is the "Bright". And It is the entire Source of True Humor. It is Reality. It is not separate from anything.

Buddha Just as the traditional term "Avatar", when rightly understood, is an appropriate Reference to Avatar Adi Da Samraj, so is the traditional term "Buddha". He is the Divine Buddha, the One Who Is Most Perfectly Self-Enlightened and Eternally Awake.

C

causal See **gross, subtle, causal**.

childish and adolescent strategies
Avatar Adi Da uses the terms "childish" and "adolescent" with precise meanings in His Wisdom-Teaching. He points out that human beings are always tending to animate one of two fundamental life-strategies—the childish strategy (to be dependent, weak, seeking to be consoled by parent-figures and a parent-"God") and the adolescent strategy (to be independent—or, otherwise, torn between independence and dependence—rebellious, unfeeling, self-absorbed, and doubting or resisting the idea of God or any power greater than oneself). Until these strategies are understood and transcended, they not only diminish love in ordinary human relations, but they also limit religious and Spiritual growth.

Circle The Circle is a primary pathway of natural life-energy and the Spirit-Current through the body-mind. It is composed of two arcs: the descending Current, in association with the frontal line (down the front of the body, from the crown of the head to the bodily base), which corresponds to the more physically oriented dimension of the body-mind; and the ascending Current, in association with the spinal line (up the back of the body, from the bodily base to the crown of the head), which is the more mentally, psychically, and subtly oriented dimension of the body-mind.

conditional The word "conditional" (and its variants) is used to indicate every-thing that depends on conditions—in other words, everything that is temporary

and changing. The "Unconditional", in contrast, is the Divine, or That Which Is Eternal, Always Already the Case—because It Is utterly Free of dependence on any conditions whatsoever.

"conductivity" "Conductivity" is Avatar Adi Da's technical term for participation in and responsibility for the movement of natural bodily energies (and, when one is Spiritually Awakened by Him, for the movement of His Divine Spirit-Current of Love-Bliss in Its natural course of association with the body-mind), via intentional exercises of feeling and breathing.

The exercises of Spiritual "conductivity" that Avatar Adi Da Gives to His (formally practicing) Spiritually Awakened devotees are technical whole-bodily Yogas of receptive surrender to the Living Spirit-Current. Rudimentary and preparatory technical forms of "conductivity" are Given to beginners.

congregations of Adidam There are four different modes, or congregations, of formal approach to Avatar Adi Da Samraj, making it possible for everyone to participate in the Gift of heart-companionship with Him. The total practice of the Way of Adidam is engaged by those in the first and second congregations. Whereas all of Avatar Adi Da's devotees (in all four congregations) engage the fundamental practice of Ruchira Avatara Bhakti Yoga, only members of the first and second congregations are vowed to engage the full range of supportive disciplines (meditation, sacramental worship, guided study, exercise, diet, emotional-sexual discipline, cooperative community living, and so on) Given by Avatar Adi Da Samraj.

For a more detailed description of the four congregations of Avatar Adi Da's devotees, see pp. 320-32.

"conscious process" The "conscious process" is Avatar Adi Da's technical term for those practices through which the mind, or attention, is surrendered and turned about (from egoic self-involvement) to feeling-Contemplation of Him. It is the senior discipline and responsibility of all practitioners in the Way of Adidam. (Avatar Adi Da's descriptions of the various forms of the "conscious process" are Given in *The Dawn Horse Testament Of The Ruchira Avatar.*)

"consider", "consideration" The technical term "consider" or "consideration" in Avatar Adi Da's Wisdom-Teaching means a process of one-pointed but ultimately thoughtless concentration and exhaustive contemplation of something until its ultimate obviousness is clear. As engaged in the Way of Adidam, "consideration" is not merely an intellectual investigation. It is the participatory investment of one's whole being. If one "considers" something fully in the context of one's practice of feeling-Contemplation of Avatar Adi Da Samraj, and study of His Wisdom-Teaching, this concentration results "in both the highest intuition and the most practical grasp of the Lawful and Divine necessities of human existence".

Contemplation of Avatar Adi Da's bodily (human) Form Traditionally, devotees have produced artistic images of their Gurus for the purpose of Contemplating the Guru when he or she is either not physically present or (otherwise) no longer physically alive.

Modern technology makes possible (through photography, videotape, film, holographic imagery, and other means) accurate Representations of the bodily (human) Form of Avatar Adi Da Samraj for devotional use by His formally acknowledged devotees.

"Cosmic Consciousness" See **Samadhi**.

Cosmic Mandala The Sanskrit word "mandala" (literally, "circle") is commonly used in the esoteric Spiritual traditions of the East to describe the hierarchical levels of cosmic existence. "Mandala" also denotes an artistic rendering of interior visions of the cosmos. Avatar Adi Da uses the phrase "Cosmic Mandala" as a reference to the totality of the conditionally manifested cosmos (or all worlds, forms, and beings).

Crashing Down Avatar Adi Da's Crashing Down is the Descent of His Divine Spirit-Force into the body-mind of His devotee.

My Avataric Divine Work (Altogether) Is My Crashing-Down Descent, At First Upon and Into My Own Avatarically-Born Bodily (Human) Divine Form, and, Thereafter (and Now, and Forever), Upon and Into the body-minds Of My Devotees and all beings—Even (By Means Of My Divine Embrace Of each, and all, and All) To Infuse and (At Last) To Divinely Translate each, and all, and All. Therefore, My Avataric Divine Spiritual Descent Is The Secret Of My Early Life. My Avataric Divine Spiritual Descent Is The Secret Of My Divine Self-"Emergence" (As I Am) Within The Cosmic Domain. My Avataric Divine Spiritual Descent Is The Secret Of all The Secrets Of The (Avatarically Self-Revealed) Divine and Complete and Thoroughly Devotional Way Of Practice and Realization In My Company. The Only-By-Me Revealed and Given Way Of The Heart (or Way Of Adidam) Is The Divine Yoga Of ego-Surrendering, ego-Forgetting, and ego-Transcending Devotional Recognition-Response To My (Avatarically Self-Revealed) Divine and Spiritual Person, and To My (Avatarically Self-Manifested) Divine and Spiritual Descent. The Only-By-Me Revealed and Given Way Of The Heart (or Way Of Adidam) Is The Total and Divine Way and Ordeal Of Counter-egoic Devotional Recognition-Response To My Avataric "Bright" Divine Self-Manifestation, and To The Avataric Crashing Down Of My "Bright" Divine Imposition. And, In The Case Of My Each and Every Devotee, The Way Must Continue Until The Way Is Most Perfectly "Bright", and The Way Itself Becomes Divine Translation Into My Own Sphere Of "Brightness" (Itself). [Ruchira Avatara Hridaya-Siddha Yoga]

"Crazy" Avatar Adi Da has always had a unique Method of "Crazy" Work, which, particularly during His years of Teaching and Revelation, involved His literal Submission to the limited conditions of humankind, in order to reflect His devotees to themselves, and thereby Awaken self-understanding in them (relative to their individual egoic dramas, and the collective egoic dramas of human society).

For Me, There Was Never Any Other Possibility Than The "Reckless" (or Divinely "Crazy" and Divinely "Heroic") Course Of All-and-all-Embrace—and I Began This Uniquely "Crazy" and "Heroic" Sadhana, Most Intensively, At The Beginning Of My Adult Life. Indeed, I Have Always Functioned, and Will Always Function, In This Divinely "Crazy" and Divinely "Heroic" Manner. The Inherently egoless "Crazy" and "Heroic" Manner Is One Of My Principal Divine Characteristics— Whereby I Can (Always, and Now, and Forever Hereafter) Be Identified. Therefore, I (Characteristically) Functioned In This "Crazy" and "Heroic" Manner Throughout All Of My "Sadhana Years", and Throughout All The Years Of My Avatarically Self-Manifested Divine Teaching-Work and My Avatarically Self-Manifested Divine Revelation-Work—and I Have Done So (and Will Forever Continue To Do So) Throughout All The Divine-Self-"Emergence" Years Of My Avatarically Self-Manifested Divine Blessing-Work (Both During, and Forever After, My Avataric Physical Human Lifetime). All My Avatarically Self-Manifested Divine Work Is A Divinely "Crazy" and Divinely "Heroic" Effort That Avoids Not anything or any one—but Which Always Divinely Blesses Everything and Everyone. [The Truly Human New World-Culture Of Unbroken Real-God-Man]

D

Da   Avatar Adi Da's Name "Da" means "The Divine Giver". In Sanskrit, "Da" means principally "to give". It is also associated with Vishnu, the "Sustainer", and it further has a secondary meaning "to destroy". Thus, "Da" is anciently aligned to all three of the principal Divine Beings, Forces, or Attributes in the Hindu tradition—Brahma (the Creator, Generator, or Giver), Vishnu (the Sustainer), and Siva (the Destroyer). In certain Hindu rituals, priests address the Divine directly as "Da", invoking qualities such as generosity and compassion.

The Tibetan Buddhists regard the syllable "Da" (written, in Tibetan, as well as in Sanskrit, with a single symbol) as most auspicious, and they assign numerous sacred meanings to it, including that of "the Entrance into the Dharma".

Da Love-Ananda Samrajya   For a description of the Da Love-Ananda Samrajya, see p. 336.

Da Avatar   "Da" is Sanskrit for "The One Who Gives". Therefore, as the Da Avatar, Adi Da Samraj is the Divine Descent of the One and True Divine Giver.

"dark" epoch   See **"late-time" (or "dark" epoch)**.

Darshan   "Darshan", the Hindi derivative of the Sanskrit "darshana", literally means "seeing", "sight of", or "vision of". To receive Darshan of Avatar Adi Da is, most fundamentally, to behold His bodily (human) Form (either by being in His physical Company or by seeing a photograph or other visual representation of Him), and (thereby) to receive the spontaneous Divine Blessing He Grants Freely whenever His bodily (human) Form is beheld in the devotional manner. In the Way of Adidam, Darshan of Avatar Adi Da is the very essence of the practice, and one of the most potent forms of receiving Avatar Adi Da's Blessing is to participate in the formal occasions of Darshan—during which Avatar Adi Da Samraj Sits silently, sometimes gazing at each individual one by one.

By extension, "Darshan" of Avatar Adi Da Samraj may refer to any means by which His Blessing-Influence is felt and received—including His Written or Spoken Word, photographs or videotapes of His Avatarically-Born bodily (human) Divine Form, recordings of His Voice, Leelas (or Stories) of His Teaching-Work and Blessing-Work, places or objects He has Spiritually Empowered, visualization of His Avatarically-Born bodily (human) Divine Form in the mind, and simple, heart-felt Remembrance of Him.

Dattatreya   Dattatreya was a God-Realizer who appeared early in the common era and about whom no certain historical facts exist apart from his name. Over the centuries, numerous legends and myths have been spun around him. He was early on regarded to be an incarnation of the God Vishnu, later associated with the tradition of Saivism, and worshipped as the Divine Itself. He is commonly venerated as the originator of the Avadhoota tradition and credited with the authorship of the *Avadhoota Gita*, among other works.

   The devotional sect worshipping Dattatreya presumes that he continually reincarnates through a succession of Adepts for the sake of gathering and serving devotees. The belief in the continuing incarnation of Dattatreya should be understood as a popular religious belief that is peripheral to what the Adepts in the Dattatreya succession actually taught.

The Dawn Horse Testament Of The Ruchira Avatar   *The Dawn Horse Testament Of The Ruchira Avatar* is Avatar Adi Da's paramount "Source-Text", summarizing the entire course of the Way of Adidam. (See "Avatar Adi Da Samraj's Teaching-Word", pp. 27-38.)

developmental stages of practice   For all members of the first and second congregations of Avatar Adi Da's devotees, the Way of Adidam develops through a series of (potential) developmental stages of practice and Realization. These stages of practice, and their relationship to the seven stages of life, are described by Avatar Adi Da Samraj in chapter seventeen of *The Dawn Horse Testament Of The Ruchira Avatar*.

   When using the phrase "necessary (or, otherwise, potential)", Avatar Adi Da is referring to the fact that His fully practicing devotee must practice in the context of certain of the developmental stages of practice (corresponding to the first three stages of life, the "original" and "basic" contexts of the fourth stage of life, the sixth stage of life, and the seventh stage of life) but may bypass practice in the

developmental stages that correspond to "advanced" context of the fourth stage of life and to the fifth stage of life.

Devotional Way of Insight / Devotional Way of Faith   Avatar Adi Da has Given Instruction in two variant forms of the fundamental practice of feeling-Contemplation of Him: the Devotional Way of Insight and the Devotional Way of Faith. Each of Avatar Adi Da's fully practicing devotees is to experiment with both of these Devotional Ways and then choose the one that is most effective in his or her case.

   Both Devotional Ways require the exercise of insight and faith, but there is a difference in emphasis.

   In the Devotional Way of Insight, the practitioner engages a specific technical process of observing, understanding, and then feeling beyond the self-contraction, as the principal technical element of his or her practice of feeling-Contemplation of Avatar Adi Da.

   In the Devotional Way of Faith, the practitioner engages a specific technical process of magnifying his or her heart-Attraction to Avatar Adi Da, as the principal technical element of his or her practice of feeling-Contemplation of Avatar Adi Da.

   Avatar Adi Da's extended Instruction relative to both Devotional Ways is Given in *The Only Complete Way To Realize The Unbroken Light Of Real God*.

Dharma, dharma   Sanskrit for "duty", "virtue", "law". The word "dharma" is commonly used to refer to the many esoteric paths by which human beings seek the Truth. In its fullest sense, and when capitalized, "Dharma" means the complete fulfillment of duty—the living of the Divine Law. By extension, "Dharma" means a truly great Spiritual Teaching, including its disciplines and practices.

"Difference"   "Difference" is the epitome of the egoic presumption of separateness—in contrast with the Realization of Oneness, or Non-"Difference", Which is Native to the Divine Self-Condition.

Divine Being   Avatar Adi Da describes His Divine Being on three levels:

AVATAR ADI DA SAMRAJ: This flesh body, this bodily (human) Sign, is My Form, in the sense that it is My Murti, or a kind of Reflection (or Representation) of Me. It is, therefore, a Means for contacting My Spiritual Presence, and, ultimately, My Divine State.

My Spiritual Presence is Self-Existing and Self-Radiant. It Functions in time and space, and It is also Prior to all time and space. . . .

My Divine State is always and only utterly Prior to time and space. Therefore, I, As I Am (Ultimately), have no "Function" in time and space. There is no time and space in My Divine State.

Divine Body Avatar Adi Da's Divine Body is not conditional or limited to His physical Body but is "The 'Bright' Itself (Spiritually Pervading and Eternally Most Prior To The Cosmic Domain)".

Divine Enlightenment The Realization of the seventh stage of life, which is uniquely Revealed and Given by Avatar Adi Da. It is release from all the egoic limitations of the first six stages of life. Remarkably, the seventh stage Awakening, which is Avatar Adi Da's Gift to His rightly prepared devotee, is not an experience at all. The true Nature of everything is simply obvious, based on the Realization that every apparent "thing" is Eternally, Perfectly the same as Reality, Consciousness, Happiness, Truth, or Real God. And that Realization is the Supreme Love-Bliss of Avatar Adi Da's Divine Self-Condition.

Divine Ignorance "Divine Ignorance" is Avatar Adi Da's term for the fundamental Awareness of Existence Itself, Prior to all sense of separation from (or knowledge about) anything that arises. As He proposes, "No matter what arises, you do not know what a single thing is." By "Ignorance", Avatar Adi Da means heartfelt participation in the universal Condition of inherent Mystery—not mental dullness or the fear-based wonder or awe felt by the subjective ego in relation to unknown objects. Divine Ignorance is the Realization of Consciousness Itself, transcending all knowledge and all experience of the self-contracted ego-"I".

For Avatar Adi Da's extended Instruction relative to Divine Ignorance, see *What, Where, When, How, Why, and Who To Remember To Be Happy*, Part Two: "What, Where, When, How, Why and Who To Remember To Be Happy", and Part Three: "You Do Not Know What even a single thing Is" and "My Argument Relative to Divine Ignorance".

Divine Indifference See **four phases of the seventh stage of life**.

Divine "Intoxication" Unlike common intoxication, such as with alcohol, Divine "Intoxication" Draws Avatar Adi Da's devotees beyond the usual egoic self and egoic mind through His Blessing Grace into a state of ecstatic devotional Communion (and Identification) with Him.

Divine Parama-Guru The Supreme Divine Guru.

Divine Re-Awakening Avatar Adi Da's Divine Re-Awakening occurred on September 10, 1970, in the Vedanta Society Temple in Hollywood, California. For a full description of this Great Event and its import, see *The Promised God-Man Is Here*, by Carolyn Lee, or chapter sixteen of *The Knee Of Listening*.

Divine Self-Recognition Divine Self-Recognition is the ego-transcending and world-transcending Intelligence of the Divine Self in relation to all conditional phenomena. The devotee of Avatar Adi Da who Realizes the seventh stage of life simply Abides as Self-Existing and Self-Radiant Consciousness Itself, and he or she Freely Self-Recognizes (or inherently and instantly and Most Perfectly comprehends and perceives) all phenomena (including body, mind, conditional self, and conditional world) as transparent (or merely apparent), and un-necessary, and inherently non-binding modifications of the same "Bright" Divine Self-Consciousness.

Divine Self-"Emergence" On January 11, 1986, Avatar Adi Da passed through a profound Yogic Swoon, which He later described as the initial Event of His Divine Self-"Emergence". Avatar Adi Da's Divine Self-"Emergence" is an ongoing Process in which His Avatarically-Born bodily (human) Divine Form has been (and is ever more profoundly and potently being) conformed to Himself, the Very Divine Person, such that His bodily (human) Form is now (and forever hereafter) an utterly Unobstructed Sign and Agent of His own Divine Being.

For Avatar Adi Da's Revelation of the significance of His Divine Self-"Emergence", see section III of "The True Dawn Horse Is The Only Way To Me", in The All-Completing and Final Divine Revelation To Mankind, The Heart Of The Dawn Horse Testament Of The Ruchira Avatar, and The Dawn Horse Testament Of The Ruchira Avatar.

Divine Self-Domain Avatar Adi Da affirms that there is a Divine Self-Domain that is the Perfectly Subjective Condition of the conditional worlds. It is not "else-where", not an objective "place" (like a subtle "heaven" or mythical "paradise"), but It is the always present, Transcendental, Inherently Spiritual, Divine Source-Condition of every conditionally mani-fested being and thing. Avatar Adi Da Reveals that the Divine Self-Domain is not other than the Divine Heart Itself, not other than Himself. To Realize the seventh stage of life (by the Divine Grace of Avatar Adi Da Samraj) is to Awaken to His Divine Self-Domain.

For Avatar Adi Da's extended Instruction relative to His Divine Self-Domain, see The All-Completing and Final Divine Revelation To Mankind.

Divine Star The primal conditional Representation of the "Bright" (the Source-Energy, or Divine Light, of Which all con-ditional phenomena and the total cosmos are modifications) is the brilliant white five-pointed Divine Star. Avatar Adi Da's bodily (human) Divine Form is the Manifestation of that Divine Star—and His head, two arms, and two legs correspond to its five points. Avatar Adi Da can also be seen or intuited in vision to Be the Divine Star Itself, prior to the visible mani-festation of His bodily (human) Form.

Divine Transfiguration See **four phases of the seventh stage of life**.

Divine Transformation See **four phases of the seventh stage of life**.

Divine Translation See **four phases of the seventh stage of life**.

Divine World-Teacher Avatar Adi Da Samraj is the Divine World-Teacher because His Wisdom-Teaching is the uniquely Perfect Instruction to every being—in this (and every) world—in the total process of Divine Enlightenment. Furthermore, Avatar Adi Da Samraj con-stantly Extends His Regard to the entire world (and the entire Cosmic domain)—not on the political or social level, but as a Spiritual matter, constantly Working to Bless and Purify all beings everywhere.

dreaming See **waking, dreaming, and sleeping**.

E

ecstasy / enstasy The words "ecstasy" and "enstasy" derive originally from Greek. Avatar Adi Da uses "ecstasy" in the literal sense of "standing (stasis) outside (ec-)" the egoic self, and "enstasy" in the sense of "standing (stasis) in (en-)" the Divine Self-Condition. As Avatar Adi Da Says in The Dawn Horse Testament Of The Ruchira Avatar, Divine Enstasy is "The Native Condition Of Standing Unconditionally As The By-Me-Avatarically-Self-Revealed Transcendental, Inherently Spiritual, and Self-Evidently Divine Self-Condition Itself".

ego-"I" The ego-"I" is the fundamental activity of self-contraction, or the pre-sumption of separate and separative existence.

Eleutherian Pan-Communion of Adidam The Eleutherian Pan-Communion of Adidam is a California religious non-profit corporation, dedicated to the worldwide practice and the global proclamation of the true world-religion of Adidam.

Eleutherios "Eleutherios" (Greek for "Liberator") is a title by which Zeus was venerated as the supreme deity in the Spiritual esotericism of ancient Greece. The Designation "Eleutherios" indicates the Divine Function of Avatar Adi Da as the Incarnation of the Divine Person, "Whose Inherently Perfect Self-'Brightness' Divinely Liberates all conditionally Manifested beings—Freely, Liberally, Gracefully, and Without Ceasing—now, and forever hereafter".

En-Light-enment En-Light-enment (or Enlightenment) is not just a state of mind, but rather an actual conversion of the body-mind to the state of Divine Consciousness Itself, or Light Itself. Thus, Avatar Adi Da sometimes writes the word "Enlightenment" with "Light" set apart by hyphens, in order to emphasize this point.

esoteric anatomy See **Spiritual anatomy**.

Eternal Vow For a description of the Vow and responsibilities associated with the Way of Adidam, see pp. 321-32.

etheric The etheric is the dimension of life-energy, which functions through the human nervous system. Our bodies are surrounded and infused by this personal life-energy, which we feel as the play of emotions and life-force in the body.

F

faculties; four faculties Avatar Adi Da has Instructed His devotees that the practice of devotional Communion with Him (or Ruchira Avatara Bhakti Yoga) requires the surrender of the four principal faculties of the human body-mind. These faculties are body, emotion (or feeling), mind (or attention), and breath.

Feeling of Being The Feeling of Being is the uncaused (or Self-Existing), Self-Radiant, and unqualified feeling-intuition of the Transcendental, Inherently Spiritual, and Self-Evidently Divine Self-Condition. This absolute Feeling does not merely accompany or express the Realization of the Heart Itself, but It is Identical to that Realization. To feel—or, really, to Be—the Feeling of Being is to enjoy the Love-Bliss of Absolute Consciousness, Which, when Most Perfectly Realized, cannot be pre-

vented or even diminished either by the events of life or by death.

feeling of relatedness In the foundation stages of practice in the Way of Adidam, the basic (or gross) manifestation of the avoidance of relationship is understood and released when Avatar Adi Da's devotee hears Him (or comes to the point of most fundamental self-understanding), thereby regaining the free capability for simple relatedness, or living on the basis of the feeling of relatedness rather than the avoidance of relationship. Nevertheless, the feeling of relatedness is not Ultimate Realization, because it is still founded in the presumption of a "difference" between "I" and "other". Only in the ultimate stages of life in the Way of Adidam is the feeling of relatedness itself fully understood as the root-act of attention and, ultimately, transcended in the Feeling of Being.

feeling-Contemplation Avatar Adi Da's term for the essential devotional and meditative practice that all practitioners of the Way of Adidam engage at all times in relationship to Him. Feeling-Contemplation of Adi Da Samraj is Awakened by His Grace—through Darshan (or feeling-sighting) of His bodily (human) Form, His Spiritual Presence, and His Divine State. It is then to be practiced under all conditions, as the basis and epitome of all other practices in the Way of Adidam.

fifth stage conditional Nirvikalpa Samadhi See **Samadhi**.

forms of practice in the Way of Adidam Avatar Adi Da has Given a number of different approaches to the progressive process of Most Perfectly self-transcending Real-God-Realization in the Way of Adidam. In this manner, He accounts for the differences in individuals' qualities—particularly relative to their capability to make use of the various technical practices that support the fundamental practice of Ruchira Avatara Bhakti Yoga and relative to the intensity of their motivation to apply themselves to the Spiritual process in His Company.

Ruchira Avatar Adi Da refers to the most detailed development of the practice of the Way of Adidam as the "technically 'fully elaborated'" form of practice. Each successive stage of practice in the technically "fully elaborated" form of the Way of Adidam is defined by progressively more detailed responsibilities, disciplines, and practices that are assumed in order to take responsibility for the signs of growing maturity in the process of Divine Awakening. A devotee who embraces the technically "fully elaborated" form of practice of the Way of Adidam must (necessarily) be a member of the first or second congregation of Avatar Adi Da's devotees. The progress of practice in the technically "fully elaborated" form of the Way of Adidam is monitored, measured, and evaluated by practicing stages (as described in detail by Avatar Adi Da Samraj in chapter seventeen of *The Dawn Horse Testament Of The Ruchira Avatar*).

Most of Avatar Adi Da's fully practicing devotees will find that they are qualified for a less intensive approach and are moved to a less technical form of the "conscious process" (than is exercised in the technically "fully elaborated" form of the Way of Adidam). Thus, most of Avatar Adi Da's fully practicing devotees will take up the technically "simpler" (or even "simplest") form of practice of the Way of Adidam.

In the technically "simpler" form of practice of the Way of Adidam, Avatar Adi Da's devotee (in the first or second congregation) engages a relatively simple form of technical means of supporting his or her fundamental practice of Ruchira Avatara Bhakti Yoga, and this technical means remains the same throughout the progressive course of developmental stages.

In the technically "simplest" form of practice, Avatar Adi Da's devotee (in any of the four congregations) engages the fundamental practice of Ruchira Avatara Bhakti Yoga in the simplest possible manner—as "simplest" feeling-Contemplation of Avatar Adi Da, together with the random use of Avatar Adi Da's Principal Name, "Da" (or one of the other Names He has Given to be engaged in the practice of simple Name-Invocation of Him).

Avatar Adi Da's fully elaborated descriptions of the technically "fully elaborated" and the technically "simpler" (or even "simplest") forms of the Way of Adidam are Given in *The Dawn Horse Testament Of The Ruchira Avatar*.

four phases of the seventh stage of life
In the context of Divine Enlightenment in the seventh stage of life, the Spiritual process continues. One of the unique aspects of Avatar Adi Da's Revelation is His description of the four phases of the seventh stage process: Divine Transfiguration, Divine Transformation, Divine Indifference, and Divine Translation.

In the phase of Divine Transfiguration, the Divinely Enlightened devotee's body-mind is Infused by Avatar Adi Da's Love-Bliss, and he or she Radiantly Demonstrates active Love, spontaneously Blessing all the relations of the body-mind.

In the following phase of Divine Transformation, the subtle or psychic dimension of the body-mind is fully Illumined, which may result in Divine Powers of healing, longevity, and the ability to release obstacles from the world and from the lives of others.

Eventually, Divine Indifference ensues, which is spontaneous and profound Resting in the "Deep" of Consciousness, and the world of relations is otherwise noticed only minimally or not at all.

Divine Translation is the ultimate "Event" of the entire process of Divine Awakening. Avatar Adi Da describes Divine Translation as the Outshining of all noticing of objective conditions through the infinitely magnified Force of Consciousness Itself. Divine Translation is the Outshining of all destinies, wherein there is no return to the conditional realms.

Being so overwhelmed by the Divine Radiance that all appearances fade away may occur <u>temporarily</u> from time to time during the seventh stage of life. But when that Most Love-Blissful Swoon becomes permanent, Divine Translation occurs, and the body-mind is inevitably relinquished in physical death. Then there is only Eternal Inherence in the Divine Self-Domain of unqualified Happiness and Joy.

frontal line, frontal personality, frontal Yoga The frontal (or descending) line of the body-mind conducts natural life-energy and (for those who are Spiritually Awakened) the Spirit-Current of Divine Life, in a downward direction from the crown of the head to the base of the body (or the perineal area).

The frontal personality is comprised of the physical body and its natural energies, the gross brain, and the verbal and lower faculties of the mind. It includes the entire gross dimension of the body-mind and the lower (or most physically oriented) aspects of the subtle dimension of the body-mind.

The frontal Yoga, as described by Avatar Adi Da, is the process whereby knots and obstructions in the gross (or physical) and energetic dimensions of the body-mind are penetrated, opened, surrendered, and released, through the devotee's reception of Avatar Adi Da's Transmission in the frontal line of the body-mind.

"fully elaborated" form of the Way of Adidam See **forms of practice in the Way of Adidam**.

functional, practical, relational, and cultural disciplines of Adidam The most basic functional, practical, and relational disciplines of the Way of Adidam (in its fully practiced form, as embraced by devotees in the first and second congregations) are forms of appropriate human action and responsibility for diet, health, exercise, sexuality, work, service to and support of Avatar Adi Da's Circumstance and Work, and cooperative (formal community) association with other practitioners of the Way of Adidam. The most basic cultural obligations of the Way of Adidam (in its fully practiced form) include meditation, sacramental worship, study of Avatar Adi Da's Wisdom-Teaching (and also at least a basic discriminative study of the Great Tradition of religion and Spirituality that is the Wisdom-inheritance of humankind), and regular participation in the "form" (or schedule) of daily, weekly, monthly, and annual devotional activities and retreats.

G

Great Tradition The "Great Tradition" is Avatar Adi Da's term for the total inheritance of human, cultural, religious, magical, mystical, Spiritual, and Transcendental paths, philosophies, and testimonies, from all the eras and cultures of humanity—which inheritance has (in the present era of worldwide communication) become the common legacy of humankind. Avatar Adi Da's Divine Self-Revelation and Wisdom-Teaching Fulfills and Completes the Great Tradition.

gross, subtle, causal Avatar Adi Da (in agreement with certain esoteric schools in the Great Tradition) describes conditional existence as having three dimensions—gross, subtle, and causal.

"Gross" means "made up of material (or physical) elements". The gross (or physical) dimension is, therefore, associated with the physical body, and also with experience in the waking state.

The subtle dimension, which is senior to and pervades the gross dimension, includes the etheric (or energic), lower mental (or verbal-intentional and lower psychic), and higher mental (or deeper psychic, mystical, and discriminative) functions, and is associated with experience in the dreaming state. In the human psycho-physical structure, the subtle dimension is primarily associated with the ascending energies of the spine, the brain core, and the subtle centers of mind in the higher brain.

The causal dimension is senior to and pervades both the gross and the subtle dimensions. It is the root of attention, or the essence of the separate and separative ego-"I". The causal dimension is associated with the right side of the heart, specifically with the sinoatrial node, or "pacemaker" (the psycho-physical source of the heartbeat). Its corresponding state of consciousness is the formless awareness of deep sleep.

Guru Esoterically, the word "guru" is understood to be a composite of two words, "destroyer (ru) of darkness (gu)".

H

hearing See **listening, hearing, and seeing**.

heart, stations of the heart Avatar Adi Da distinguishes three stations of the heart, associated respectively with the right side, the middle, and the left side of the heart region of the chest. The middle station of the heart is what is traditionally known as the "anahata chakra" (or "heart chakra"), and the left side of the heart is the gross physical heart. Avatar Adi Da Samraj has Revealed that the primal psycho-physical seat of Consciousness and attention is associated with what He calls the "right side of the heart". He has Revealed that this center (which is neither the heart chakra nor the gross physical heart) corresponds to the sinoatrial node, or "pacemaker", the source of the gross physical heartbeat in the right atrium (or upper right chamber) of the physical heart. In the Process of Divine Self-Realization, there is a unique process of opening of the right side of the heart—and it is because of this connection between the right side of the heart and Divine Self-Realization that Avatar Adi Da uses the term "the Heart" as another way of referring to the Divine Self.

The Heart Itself is Real God, the Divine Self, the Divine Reality. The Heart Itself is not "in" the right side of the human heart, nor is it "in" (or limited to) the human heart as a whole. Rather, the human heart and body-mind and the world exist in the Heart, Which Is the Divine Being Itself.

heart-Communion "Heart-Communion" with Avatar Adi Da is the practice of Invoking and feeling Him. It is "communion" in the sense that the individual loses sense of the separate self in the bliss of that state, and is thus "communicating intimately" (in a most profound and non-dual manner) with Avatar Adi Da Samraj.

heart-recognition The entire practice of the Way of Adidam is founded in devotional heart-recognition of, and devotional heart-response to, Ruchira Avatar Adi Da Samraj as the Very Divine Being in Person.

AVATAR ADI DA SAMRAJ: The only-by-Me Revealed and Given Way of Adidam (Which is the One and Only by-Me-Revealed and by-Me-Given Way of the Heart) is the Way of life you live when you rightly, truly, fully, and fully devotionally recognize Me, and when, on that basis, you rightly, truly, fully, and fully devotionally respond to Me. . . .

If you rightly, truly, fully, and fully devotionally recognize Me, everything "in between" vanishes. All of that is inherently without force. In heart-responsive devotional recognition of Me, a spontaneous kriya of the principal faculties occurs, such that they are loosed from the objects to which they are otherwise bound—loosed from the patterns of self-contraction. The faculties turn to Me, and, in that turning, there is tacit devotional recognition of Me, tacit experiential Realization of Me, of Happiness Itself, of My Love-Bliss-Full Condition. That "Locating" of Me opens the body-mind spontaneously. When you have been thus Initiated by Me, it then becomes your responsibility, your sadhana, to continuously Remember Me, to constantly return to this devotional recognition of Me, in which you are Attracted to Me, in which you devotionally respond to Me spontaneously with all the principal faculties. [Hridaya Rosary (Four Thorns Of Heart-Instruction)]

heart-response See **heart-recognition**.

Hermitage-Retreat Sanctuaries See **Sanctuaries**.

"Heroic" The Tantric traditions of Hinduism and Buddhism describe as "heroic" the practice of an individual whose impulse to Liberation and commitment to his or her Guru are so strong that all circumstances of life, even those traditionally regarded as inauspicious for Spiritual practice (such as consumption of intoxicants and engagement in sexual activity), can rightly be made use of as part of the Spiritual process.

Avatar Adi Da's uniquely "Heroic" Ordeal, however, was undertaken not for His own sake, but in order to discover, through His own experience, what is necessary for all beings to Realize the Truth. Because of His utter Freedom from egoic bondage and egoic karmas, Avatar Adi Da's Sadhana was "Heroic" in a manner that had never previously been possible and will never again be possible. As the Divine Person, it was necessary for Him to experience the entire gamut of human seeking, in order to be able to Teach any and all that came to Him.

Avatar Adi Da has Instructed that, because of His unique "Heroic" Demonstration, His devotees can simply practice the Way He has Revealed and Given, and do not have to attempt the (in any case impossible) task of duplicating His Ordeal. (See also **"Crazy"**.)

Hridaya-Avatar "Hridaya" is Sanskrit for "the heart". It refers not only to the physical organ but also to the True Heart, the Transcendental (and Inherently Spiritual) Divine Reality. "Hridaya" in combination with "Avatar" signifies that Avatar Adi Da is the Very Incarnation of the Divine Heart Itself, the Divine Incarnation Who Stands in, at, and as the True Heart of every being.

Hridaya Rosary *Hridaya Rosary (Four Thorns Of Heart-Instruction)—The Five Books Of The Heart Of The Adidam Revelation, Book Four: The "Late-Time" Avataric Revelation Of The Universally Tangible Divine Spiritual Body, Which Is The Supreme Agent Of The Great Means To Worship and To Realize The True and Spiritual Divine Person (The egoless Personal Presence Of Reality and Truth, Which Is The Only Real God)* is Avatar Adi Da's summary and exquisitely beautiful Instruction relative to the right, true, full, and fully devotional practice of the Way of Adidam, through which practice Avatar Adi Da's fully practicing devotee Spiritually receives Him with ever greater profundity, and, ultimately (through a process of the Spiritual "melting" of the entire psycho-physical being), Realizes Him most perfectly.

Hridaya-Samartha Sat-Guru "Hridaya-Samartha Sat-Guru" is a compound of traditional Sanskrit terms that has been newly created to express the uniqueness of Avatar Adi Da's Guru-Function. "Sat" means "Truth", "Being", "Existence". Thus, "Sat-Guru" literally means "True Guru", or a Guru who can lead living beings from darkness (or non-Truth) into Light (or the Living Truth).

"Samartha" means "fit", "qualified", "able". Thus, "Samartha Sat-Guru" means "a True Guru who is fully capable" of Awakening living beings to Real-God-Realization.

The word "Hridaya", meaning "heart", refers to the Very Heart, or the Transcendental (and Inherently Spiritual) Divine Reality.

Thus, altogether, the reference "Hridaya-Samartha Sat-Guru" means "the Divine Heart-Master Who Liberates His devotees from the darkness of egoity by Means of the Power of the 'Bright' Divine Heart Itself". Avatar Adi Da has Said that this full Designation "properly summarizes all the aspects of My unique Guru-Function".

Hridaya-Shakti; Hridaya-Shaktipat
The Sanskrit word "Hridaya" means "the Heart Itself". "Shakti" is a Sanskrit term for the Divine Manifesting as Energy. "Hridaya-Shakti" is thus "the Divine Power of the Heart", Which is Given and Transmitted by Avatar Adi Da Samraj.

In Hindi, "shaktipat" means the "descent of Divine Power", indicating the Sat-Guru's Transmission of the Kundalini Shakti to his or her devotee.

"Hridaya-Shaktipat", which is Avatar Adi Da's seventh stage Gift to His devotees, is "the Blessing-Transmission of the Divine Heart Itself".

Avatar Adi Da's extended Instruction relative to Hridaya-Shakti and Kundalini Shakti is Given in *Ruchira Avatara Hridaya-Siddha Yoga.*

Hridaya-Siddha Yoga The Way (Yoga) of the relationship with the "Transmission-Master of the Divine Heart" (Hridaya-Siddha), Ruchira Avatar Adi Da Samraj.

Hridayam "Hridayam" is Sanskrit for "heart". It refers not only to the physical organ but also to the True Heart, the Transcendental (and Inherently Spiritual) Divine Reality. "Hridayam" is one of Avatar Adi Da's Divine Names, signifying that He Stands in, at, and <u>as</u> the True Heart of every being.

I

Ignorance See **Divine Ignorance**.

Indifference See **four phases of the seventh stage of life**.

Instruments / Instrumentality
Avatar Adi Da has Indicated that members of the Ruchira Sannyasin Order function collectively and spontaneously as His Instruments, or Means by which His Divine Grace and Awakening Power are Magnified and Transmitted to other devotees and all beings. Such devotees have received Avatar Adi Da's Spiritual Baptism, and they practice in Spiritually activated relationship to Him with exemplary depth and intensity. Because of their uniquely complete and renunciate response and accountability to Him, and by virtue of their ego-surrendering, ego-forgetting, ego-transcending, and really Spiritual Invocation of Him, these devotees function collectively as Instruments for the Transmission of Avatar Adi Da's Spiritual Presence to others.

Invocation by Name See **Name-Invocation**.

Ishta-Guru Bhakti Yoga An alternate name for Ruchira Avatara Bhakti Yoga. Ishta-Guru Bhakti Yoga literally means "the practice (Yoga) of devotion (Bhakti) to Avatar Adi Da, the chosen Beloved (Ishta) Guru of His devotees".

J

Jnana Samadhi See **Samadhi**.

K

Kali Kali is a Hindu form of the Divine Goddess (or "Mother-Shakti") in her terrifying aspect.

Kali Yuga A Hindu term meaning "the dark (kali) epoch (yuga)", or the final and most ignorant and degenerate period of human history, when the Spiritual Way of life is almost entirely forgotten. (In the Hindu view, the Kali Yuga is a cyclically recurring event.)

karma "Karma" is Sanskrit for "action". Since action entails consequences (or reactions), "karma" also means (by extension) "destiny, tendency, the quality of existence and experience which is determined by previous actions".

Kashmir Saivism Kashmir Saivism is a branch of Saivism (the form of Hinduism in which Siva is worshipped as the Supreme Deity), which originated in the Kashmir region of North India in the late 8th century and whose influence has spread throughout the Indian sub-continent during the mid-20th century. It has a largely fifth-stage orientation.

kiln Avatar Adi Da Samraj frequently describes the transformative process of His Blessing-Power in the lives of His devotees as being like a kiln. In a kiln, as the wet clay objects are heated more and more, they begin to glow. Eventually, the kiln is so hot that everything within it glows with a white light, and the definitions of the individual objects dissolve in the brightness. Just so, as a devotee matures in Avatar Adi Da's Spiritual Company, all presumptions of separateness as an apparently individual ego-"I" are more and more Outshined by the "Brightness" of His Divine Person and Blessing.

Klik-Klak Avatar Adi Da coined the term "Klik-Klak" as a name for the conditional reality. This name indicates (even by means of the sound of the two syllables) that conditional reality is a heartless perpetual-motion machine of incessant change, producing endlessly varied patterns that are ultimately binary in nature (as, for example, "yes-no", "on-off", or "black-white").

knots Previous to Most Perfect Divine Self-Realization, the gross, subtle, and causal dimensions are expressed in the body-mind as characteristic knots. The knot of the gross dimension is associated with the region of the navel. The knot of the subtle dimension is associated with the midbrain, or the ajna center directly behind and between the brows. And the knot of the causal dimension (which Avatar Adi Da refers to as the "causal knot") is associated with the sinoatrial node (or "pacemaker") on the right side of the heart. The causal knot (or the heart-root's knot) is the primary root of the self-contraction, felt as the locus of the self-sense, the source of the feeling of relatedness itself, or the root of attention.

Kundalini-Shaktipat The Kundalini Shakti is traditionally viewed to lie dormant at the bodily base, or lowermost psychic center of the body-mind. Kundalini-Shaktipat is the activation of the Kundalini Shakti—either spontaneously in the devotee or by the Guru's initiation—thereafter potentially producing various forms of Yogic and mystical experience.

L

"late-time" (or "dark" epoch) The "'late-time' (or 'dark' epoch)" is a phrase that Avatar Adi Da uses to describe the present era—in which doubt of God (and of anything at all beyond mortal existence) is more and more pervading the entire world, and the self-interest of the separate individual is more and more regarded to be the ultimate principle of life. It is also a reference to the traditional Hindu idea of "yugas", or "epochs", the last of which (the Kali Yuga) is understood to be the most difficult and "dark". Many traditions share the idea that it is in such a time that the Promised Divine Liberator will appear. (See also **Kali Yuga**.)

Lay Congregationist Order In "The Orders of My True and Free Renunciate Devotees" (in *The Lion Sutra*), Avatar Adi Da describes the Lay Congregationist Order as "the common (or general) order for all formally established general (or not otherwise formal renunciate) lay practitioners of the total (or full and complete) practice of the Way of Adidam". Once a member of the second congregation has completed the student-beginner stage of practice, he or she makes the transition to the intensive listening-hearing stage of the Way of Adidam. By virtue of this transition, the individual becomes a member of the Lay Congregationist Order, unless he or she is accepted as a member of the Lay Renunciate Order.

Lay Renunciate Order See **renunciate orders**.

leela "Leela" is Sanskrit for "play", or "sport". In many religious and Spiritual traditions, all of conditionally manifested existence is regarded to be the Leela (or the Play, Sport, or Free Activity) of the Divine Person. "Leela" also means the Awakened Play of a Realized Adept (of any degree), through which he or she mysteriously Instructs and Liberates others and Blesses the world itself. By extension, a Leela is an instructive and inspiring story of such an Adept's Teaching and Blessing Play.

Lesson of life "The Lesson of life" is Avatar Adi Da's term for the fundamental understanding that Happiness cannot be achieved by means of seeking, because Happiness is inherent in Existence Itself. Avatar Adi Da has summarized this in the aphorism, "You cannot become Happy. You can only be Happy."

Lineage, Avatar Adi Da's The principal Spiritual Masters who served Avatar Adi Da Samraj during His "Sadhana Years" belong to a single Lineage of extraordinary Yogis, whose Parama-Guru (Supreme Guru) was the Divine "Goddess" (or "Mother-Shakti").

Swami Rudrananda (1928-1973), or Albert Rudolph (known as "Rudi"), was Avatar Adi Da's first human Teacher—from 1964 to 1968, in New York City. Rudi served Avatar Adi Da Samraj in the development of basic practical life-disciplines and the frontal Yoga, which is the process whereby knots and obstructions in the physical and etheric dimensions of the body-mind are penetrated, opened, surrendered, and released through Spiritual reception in the frontal line of the body-mind. Rudi's own Teachers included the Indonesian Pak Subuh (from whom Rudi learned a basic exercise of Spiritual receptivity), Swami Muktananda (with whom Rudi studied for many years), and Bhagavan Nityananda (the Indian Adept-Realizer who was also Swami Muktananda's Guru). Rudi met Bhagavan Nityananda shortly before Bhagavan Nityananda's death, and Rudi always thereafter acknowledged Bhagavan Nityananda as his original and principal Guru.

The second Teacher in Avatar Adi Da's Lineage of Blessing was Swami Muktananda (1908-1982), who was born in Mangalore, South India. Having left home at the age of fifteen, he wandered for many years, seeking the Divine Truth from sources all over India. Eventually, he came under the Spiritual Influence of Bhagavan Nityananda, whom he accepted as his Guru and in whose Spiritual Company he mastered Kundalini Yoga. Swami Muktananda served Avatar Adi Da as Guru during the period from 1968 to 1970. In the summer of 1969, during Avatar Adi Da's second visit to India, Swami Muktananda wrote a letter confirming Avatar Adi Da's attainment of "Yogic Liberation", and acknowledging His right to Teach others. However, from the beginning of their relationship, Swami Muktananda instructed Avatar Adi Da to visit Bhagavan Nityananda's burial site every day (whenever Avatar Adi Da was at Swami Muktananda's Ashram in Ganeshpuri, India) as a means to surrender to Bhagavan Nityananda as the Supreme Guru of the Lineage.

Bhagavan Nityananda, a great Yogi of South India, was Avatar Adi Da's third Guru. Little is known about the circumstances of Bhagavan Nityananda's birth and early life, although it is said that even as a child he showed the signs of a

Realized Yogi. It is also known that he abandoned conventional life as a boy and wandered as a renunciate. Many miracles (including spontaneous healings) and instructive stories are attributed to him. Bhagavan Nityananda surrendered the body on August 8, 1961. Although Avatar Adi Da did not meet Bhagavan Nityananda in the flesh, He enjoyed Bhagavan Nityananda's direct Spiritual Influence from the subtle plane, and He acknowledges Bhagavan Nityananda as a direct and principal Source of Spiritual Instruction during His years with Swami Muktananda. (Avatar Adi Da summarizes the Instruction He received from Bhagavan Nityananda in section XXXII of "I (Alone) Am The Adidam Revelation", an Essay contained in many of the twenty-three "Source-Texts" of Adidam.)

On His third visit to India, while visiting Bhagavan Nityananda's burial shrine, Avatar Adi Da was instructed by Bhagavan Nityananda to relinquish all others as Guru and to surrender directly to the Divine Goddess in Person as Guru. Thus, Bhagavan Nityananda passed Avatar Adi Da to the Divine Goddess Herself, the Parama-Guru (or Source-Guru) of the Lineage that included Bhagavan Nityananda, Swami Muktananda, and Rudi.

The years of Avatar Adi Da's "Sadhana" came to an end in the Great Event of His Divine Re-Awakening, when Avatar Adi Da Husbanded the Divine Goddess (thereby ceasing to relate to Her as His Guru).

Avatar Adi Da's full account of His "Sadhana Years" is Given in *The Knee Of Listening*.

Avatar Adi Da's description of His "Relationship" to the Divine "Goddess" is Given in "I Am The Icon Of Unity", in *He-and-She Is Me*.

listening, hearing, and seeing
"Listening" is Avatar Adi Da's technical term for the orientation, disposition, and beginning practice of the Way of Adidam. A listening devotee listens to Avatar Adi Da Samraj by "considering" His Teaching-Argument and His Leelas, and by practicing feeling-Contemplation of Him (primarily

of His bodily human Form). In the total practice of the Way of Adidam, effective listening to Avatar Adi Da is the necessary prerequisite for true hearing and real seeing.

"Hearing" is a technical term used by Avatar Adi Da to indicate most fundamental understanding of the act of egoity (or self-contraction). Hearing Avatar Adi Da is the unique capability to directly transcend the self-contraction, such that, simultaneous with that transcending, there is the intuitive awakening to Avatar Adi Da's Self-Revelation As the Divine Person and Self-Condition. The capability of true hearing can only be Granted by Avatar Adi Da's Divine Grace, to His fully practicing devotee who has effectively completed the process of listening. Only on the basis of such hearing can Spiritually Awakened practice of the Way of Adidam truly (or with full responsibility) begin.

I Am Heard When My Listening Devotee Has Truly (and Thoroughly) Observed the ego-"I" and Understood it (Directly, In the moments Of self-Observation, and Most Fundamentally, or In its Totality).

I Am Heard When the ego-"I" Is Altogether (and Thoroughly) Observed and (Most Fundamentally) Understood, Both In The Tendency To Dissociate and In The Tendency To Become Attached (or To Cling By Wanting Need, or To Identify With others, and things, and circumstances egoically, and Thus To Dramatize The Seeker, Bereft Of Basic Equanimity, Wholeness, and The Free Capability For Simple Relatedness).

I Am Heard When the ego-"I" Is Thoroughly (and Most Fundamentally) Understood To Be Contraction-Only, An Un-Necessary and Destructive Motive and Design, Un-Naturally and Chronically Added To Cosmic Nature and To all relations, and An Imaginary Heart-Disease (Made To Seem Real, By Heart-Reaction).

I Am Heard When This Most Fundamental Understanding Of The Habit Of "Narcissus" Becomes The Directly Obvious Realization Of The Heart, Radiating Beyond Its Own (Apparent) Contraction.

I Am Heard When The Beginning Is Full, and The Beginning Is Full (and Ended) When Every Gesture Of self-Contraction (In The Context Of The First Three Stages Of Life, and Relative To Each and All Of The Principal Faculties, Of body, emotion, mind, and breath) Is (As A Rather Consistently Applied and humanly Effective Discipline) Observed (By Natural feeling-perception), Tacitly (and Most Fundamentally) Understood, and Really (Directly and Effectively) Felt Beyond (In The Prior Feeling Of Unqualified Relatedness). [Santosha Adidam]

When, in the practice of the Way of Adidam, hearing (or most fundamental self-understanding) is steadily exercised in meditation and in life, the native feeling of the heart ceases to be chronically constricted by self-contraction. The heart then begins to Radiate as love in response to the Divine Spiritual Presence of Avatar Adi Da.

This emotional and Spiritual response of the whole being is what Avatar Adi Da calls "seeing". Seeing Avatar Adi Da is emotional conversion from the reactive emotions that characterize egoic self-obsession, to the open-hearted, Radiant Happiness that characterizes Spiritual devotion to Avatar Adi Da. This true and stable emotional conversion coincides with true and stable receptivity to Avatar Adi Da's Spiritual Transmission, and both of these are prerequisites to further Spiritual advancement in the Way of Adidam.

Seeing Is ego-Transcending Participation In What (and Who) Is. Seeing Is Love. Seeing (or Love) Is Able (By Means Of My Avatarically Self-Transmitted Divine Grace) To "Locate", Devotionally Recognize, and Feel My Avatarically Self-Transmitted (and all-and-All-Pervading) Spiritual Radiance (and My Avatarically Self-Transmitted Spirit-Identity, As The "Bright" and Only One Who Is). . . . Seeing Is The "Radical" (or Directly ego-Transcending) Reorientation Of conditional Existence To My Avatarically Self-Revealed (Transcendental, Inherently Spiritual, Inherently Perfect, and Self-

Evidently Divine) Self-Condition, In Whom conditional self and conditional worlds Apparently arise and Always Already Inhere. . . .

Seeing Me Is Simply Attraction To Me (and Feeling Me) As My Avatarically Self-Revealed Spiritual (and Always Blessing) Divine Presence—and This Most Fundamentally, At The Root, Core, Source, or Origin Of The "Emergence" Of My Avatarically Self-Revealed Divine Spiritual Presence "here", At (and In Front Of) The Heart, or At (and In) The Root-Context Of the body-mind, or At (and In) The Source-Position (and, Ultimately, As The Source-Condition) Of conditional (or psycho-physical) Existence Itself.

Seeing Me Is Knowing Me As My Avatarically Self-Revealed Spiritual (and Always Blessing) Divine Presence, Just As Tangibly (and With The Same Degree Of Clarity) As You Would Differentiate The Physical Appearance Of My Bodily (Human) Form From the physical appearance of the bodily (human) form of any other.

To See Me Is A Clear and "Radical" Knowledge Of Me, About Which There Is No Doubt. To See Me Is A Sudden, Tacit Awareness—Like Walking Into a "thicker" air or atmosphere, or Suddenly Feeling a breeze, or Jumping Into water and Noticing The Difference In Density Between the air and the water. This Tangible Feeling Of Me Is (In any particular moment) Not Necessarily (Otherwise) Associated With effects in the body-mind . . . but It Is, Nevertheless, Felt At The Heart and Even All Over the body.

Seeing Me Is One-Pointedness In The "Radical" Conscious Process Of Heart-Devotion To Me. [Santosha Adidam]

"Living Murti" Avatar Adi Da will always be Divinely Present in the Cosmic domain, even after His physical Lifetime. He is the One Who is (and will always be) worshipped in the Way of Adidam, and (therefore) He is (and will always be) the Eternally Living Murti for His devotees. However, Avatar Adi Da has said that, after His physical (human) Lifetime, there should always be one (and only one) "Living Murti" as a Living Link

between Him and His devotees. Each successive "Living Murti" (or "Murti-Guru") is to be selected from among those members of the Ruchira Sannyasin Order (see **renunciate orders**) who have been formally acknowledged as Divinely Enlightened devotees of Avatar Adi Da Samraj in the seventh stage of life. "Living Murtis" will not function as the independent Gurus of practitioners of the Way of Adidam. Rather, they will simply be "Representations" of Avatar Adi Da's bodily (human) Divine Form, and a means to Commune with Him.

Avatar Adi Da's full discussion of His "Living Murtis", and how they are to be chosen, is Given in Part Three, section XII, of *The Lion Sutra*.

"Locate" To "Locate" Avatar Adi Da is to "Truly Heart-Find" Him.

Love-Ananda The Name "Love-Ananda" combines both English ("Love") and Sanskrit ("Ananda", meaning "Bliss"), thus bridging the West and the East, and communicating Avatar Adi Da's Function as the Divine World-Teacher. The combination of "Love" and "Ananda" means "the Divine Love-Bliss". The Name "Love-Ananda" was given to Avatar Adi Da by Swami Muktananda, who spontaneously conferred it upon Avatar Adi Da in 1969. However, Avatar Adi Da did not use the Name "Love-Ananda" until April 1986, after the Great Event that Initiated His Divine Self-"Emergence".

Love-Ananda Avatar As the Love-Ananda Avatar, Avatar Adi Da is the Very Incarnation of the Divine Love-Bliss.

M

Maha-Siddha The Sanskrit word "Siddha" means "a completed, fulfilled, or perfected one", or "one of perfect accomplishment, or power". "Maha-Siddha" means "Great Siddha".

Mandala The Sanskrit word "mandala" (literally, "circle") is commonly used in the esoteric Spiritual traditions to describe the entire pattern of the hierarchical levels of cosmic existence. Avatar Adi Da also uses the word "Mandala" to refer to the Circle (or Sphere) of His Heart-Transmission, or as a formal reference to a group of His devotees who perform specific functions of direct service to Him.

mantra See **Name-Invocation**.

meditation In the Way of Adidam, meditation is a period of formal devotional Contemplation of Avatar Adi Da Samraj. Meditation is one of the life-disciplines that Avatar Adi Da Samraj has Given to His devotees in the first and second congregations, as a fundamental support for their practice of Ruchira Avatara Bhakti Yoga. For those who have fully adapted to the disciplines of the first and second congregations, the daily practice of meditation includes a period of one and one-half hours in the morning and a period of one hour in the evening. Such daily practice is increased during periods of retreat. Members of the third and fourth congregations are also encouraged (but not required) to engage formal meditation.

missing the mark "Hamartia" (the word in New Testament Greek that was translated into English as "sin") was originally an archery term meaning "missing the mark".

Most Perfect / Most Ultimate Avatar Adi Da uses the phrase "Most Perfect(ly)" in the sense of "Absolutely Perfect(ly)". Similarly, the phrase "Most Ultimate(ly)" is equivalent to "Absolutely Ultimate(ly)". "Most Perfect(ly)" and "Most Ultimate(ly)" are always references to the seventh (or Divinely Enlightened) stage of life. Perfect(ly) and Ultimate(ly) refer to the sixth stage of life or to the sixth and seventh stages of life together. (See also **stages of life**.)

mudra A "mudra" is a gesture of the hands, face, or body that outwardly expresses a state of ecstasy. Avatar Adi Da sometimes spontaneously exhibits Mudras as Signs of His Blessing and Purifying Work with His devotees and the world. He also uses the term "Mudra" to express the Attitude of His Blessing-Work, which is His Constant (or Eternal) Giving (or Submitting) of Himself to Be the Means of Divine Liberation for all beings.

Muktananda, Swami See **Lineage, Avatar Adi Da's**.

mummery / The Mummery The dictionary defines mummery as "a ridiculous, hypocritical, or pretentious ceremony or performance". Avatar Adi Da uses this word to describe all the activities of ego-bound beings, or beings who are committed to the false view of separation and separativeness.

The Mummery is one of Avatar Adi Da's twenty-three "Source-Texts". It is a work of astonishing poetry and deeply evocative archetypes. Through the heartbreaking story of Raymond Darling's growth to manhood, his search to find, and then to be reunited with, his beloved (Quandra), and his utter self-transcendence of all conditional circumstances and events, Avatar Adi Da Tells His own Life-Story in the language of parable, and describes in devastating detail how the unconverted ego makes religion (and life altogether) into a meaningless mummery.

Murti "Murti" is Sanskrit for "form", and, by extension, a "representational image" of the Divine or of a Guru. In the Way of Adidam, Murtis of Avatar Adi Da are most commonly photographs of Avatar Adi Da's bodily (human) Divine Form.

"Murti-Guru" See **"Living Murti"**.

Mystery Avatar Adi Da uses the term "the Mystery" to point out that, although we can name things, we actually do not know what anything really <u>is</u>:

It is a great and more-than-wonderful Mystery to everyone that anything <u>is</u>, or that we <u>are</u>. And whether somebody says "I don't know how anything came to be" or "God made everything", they are simply pointing to the feeling of the Mystery—of how everything <u>is</u>, but nobody knows what it really <u>Is</u>, or how it came to be. [What, Where, When, How, Why, and <u>Who</u> To Remember To Be Happy]

N

Name-Invocation Sacred sounds or
syllables and Names have been used since
antiquity for invoking and worshipping
the Divine Person and the Sat-Guru. In
the Hindu tradition, the original mantras
were cosmic sound-forms and "seed" let-
ters used for worship and prayer of, and
incantatory meditation on, the Revealed
Form of the Divine Person.

Practitioners of the Way of Adidam
may, at any time, Remember or Invoke
Avatar Adi Da Samraj (or feel, and thereby
Contemplate, His Avatarically Self-Revealed
Divine Form, and Presence, and State)
through simple feeling-Remembrance of
Him and by randomly (in daily life and
meditation) Invoking Him via His
Principal Name, "Da", or via one (and
only one) of the other Names He has
Given for the practice of Simple Name-
Invocation of Him. (The specific forms of
His Names that Avatar Adi Da has Given
to be engaged in practice of simple Name-
Invocation of Him are listed in chapter
three of *The Dawn Horse Testament Of
The Ruchira Avatar.*)

For devotees of Avatar Adi Da Samraj,
His Names are the Names of the Very
Divine Being. As such, these Names, as
Avatar Adi Da Himself has described,
"do not simply <u>mean</u> Real God, or the
Blessing of Real God. They are the verbal
or audible Form of the Divine." Therefore,
Invoking Avatar Adi Da Samraj by Name
is a potent and Divinely Empowered form
of feeling-Contemplation of Him.

Narcissus In Avatar Adi Da's Teaching-
Revelation, "Narcissus" is a key symbol
of the un-Enlightened individual as a
self-obsessed seeker, enamored of his
or her own self-image and egoic self-
consciousness. In *The Knee Of Listening*,
Adi Da Samraj describes the significance
of the archetype of Narcissus:

*He is the ancient one visible in the
Greek "myth", who was the universally
adored child of the gods, who rejected the
loved-one and every form of love and relationship, who was finally condemned to
the contemplation of his own image, until,*

*as a result of his own act and obstinacy,
he suffered the fate of eternal separateness
and died in infinite solitude.*

Nirguna "Nirguna" is Sanskrit for "without attributes or quality".

Nirvikalpa Samadhi See **Samadhi**.

Nityananda See **Lineage, Avatar Adi
Da's**.

Non-Separate Self-Domain The "Non-
Separate Self-Domain" is a synonym for
"Divine Self-Domain". (See **Divine Self-
Domain**.)

O

"Oedipal" In modern psychology, the
"Oedipus complex" is named after the leg-
endary Greek Oedipus, who was fated to
unknowingly kill his father and marry his
mother. Avatar Adi Da Teaches that the
primary dynamisms of emotional-sexual
desiring, rejection, envy, betrayal, self-
pleasuring, resentment, and other primal
emotions and impulses are indeed patterned upon unconscious reactions first
formed early in life, in relation to one's
mother and father. Avatar Adi Da calls this
"the 'Oedipal' drama" and points out that
we relate to all women as we do to our
mothers, and to all men as we do to our
fathers, and that we relate, and react, to
our own bodies as we do to the parent of
the opposite sex. Thus, we impose infan-
tile reactions to our parents on our relationships with lovers and all other beings,
according to their sex, and we also super-
impose the same on our relationship to
our own bodies. (Avatar Adi Da's
extended Instruction on "Oedipal" patterning is Given in *Ruchira Avatara Hridaya-
Tantra Yoga*.)

Omega See **Alpha and Omega**.

"Open Eyes" "Open Eyes" is Avatar Adi
Da's technical synonym for the Realization
of seventh stage Sahaj Samadhi, or
unqualified Divine Self-Realization. The
phrase graphically describes the non-
exclusive, non-inward, Native State of the
Divine Self-Realizer, Who is Identified

Unconditionally with the Divine Self-Reality, while also allowing whatever arises to appear in the Divine Consciousness (and spontaneously Divinely Self-Recognizing everything that arises as a modification of the Divine Consciousness). The Transcendental Self is intuited in the mature phases of the sixth stage of life, but It can be Realized at that stage only by the intentional exclusion of conditional phenomena. In "Open Eyes", that impulse to exclusion disappears, when the Eyes of the Heart Open, and Most Perfect Realization of the Spiritual, Transcendental, and Divine Self in the seventh stage of life becomes permanent (and incorruptible by any phenomenal events).

"original" context of the fourth stage of life   See **stages of life**.

Outshined / Outshining   Avatar Adi Da uses "Outshined" or "Outshining" as a synonym for "Divine Translation", to refer to the final Demonstration of the four-phase process of the seventh (or Divinely Enlightened) stage of life in the Way of Adidam. In the Great Event of Outshining (or Divine Translation), body, mind, and world are no longer noticed—not because the Divine Consciousness has withdrawn or dissociated from conditionally manifested phenomena, but because the Divine Self-Recognition of all arising phenomena as modifications of the Divine Self-Condition has become so intense that the "Bright" Radiance of Consciousness now Outshines all such phenomena. (See also **four phases of the seventh stage of life**.)

P, Q

"Perfect Practice"   The "Perfect Practice" is Avatar Adi Da's technical term for the discipline of the ultimate stages of life (the sixth stage of life and the seventh stage of life) in the Way of Adidam. The "Perfect Practice" is practice in the Domain of Consciousness Itself (as opposed to practice from the point of view of the body or the mind). (See also **stages of life**.)

Perfectly Subjective   Avatar Adi Da uses "Perfectly Subjective" to describe the True Divine Source, or "Subject", of the conditionally manifested world—as opposed to regarding the Divine as some sort of conditional "object" or "other". Thus, in the phrase "Perfectly Subjective", the word "Subjective" does not have the sense of "relating to the inward experience of an individual", but, rather, it has the sense of "Being Consciousness Itself, the True Subject of all apparent experience".

Pilgrimage and Retreat Sanctuaries   See **Sanctuaries**.

Pleasure Dome   Avatar Adi Da Samraj Speaks of the Way of Adidam as a "Pleasure Dome", recalling the poem "Kubla Khan", by Samuel Taylor Coleridge ("In Xanadu did Kubla Khan / A stately pleasure-dome decree . . ."). Adi Da Samraj points out that in many religious traditions it is presumed that one must embrace suffering in order to earn future happiness and pleasure. However, by Calling His devotees to live the Way of Adidam as a Pleasure Dome, Avatar Adi Da Samraj Communicates His Teaching that the Way of heart-Communion with Him is always about present-time Happiness, not about any kind of search to attain Happiness in the future. Thus, in the Way of Adidam, there is no idealization of suffering and pain as presumed means to attain future happiness—and, consequently, there is no denial of the appropriate enjoyment of even the ordinary pleasures of human life.

Avatar Adi Da also uses "Pleasure Dome" as a reference to the Ultimate and Divine Love-Bliss-Happiness That Is His own Self-Nature and His Gift to all who respond to Him.

"Practice"   As the quotation marks around the capitalized word "Practice" suggest, the psycho-physical expression of the process of Divine Enlightenment is a "Practice" only in the sense that it is simple action. It is not, in contrast to the stages of life previous to the seventh, a discipline intended to counter egoic tendencies that would otherwise dominate body and mind.

Avatar Adi Da uses quotation marks in a characteristic manner throughout His Written Word to Indicate that a particular word is a technical term, to be understood in the unique and precise language of the Way of Adidam, carrying the implication "as per definition". However, in other cases, His quotation marks carry the implication "so to speak", as in the case of the term "Practice" and are, therefore, not to be understood as precise technical terminology of the Way of Adidam.

prana/pranic   The Sanskrit word "prana" means "life-energy". It generally refers to the life-energy animating all beings and pervading everything in cosmic Nature. In the human body-mind, circulation of this universal life-energy is associated with the heartbeat and the cycles of the breath. In esoteric Yogic Teachings, prana is also a specific technical name for one of a number of forms of etheric energy that functionally sustain the bodily being.

Prana is not to be equated with the Divine Spirit-Current, or the Spiritual (and Always Blessing) Divine Presence of Avatar Adi Da Samraj. The finite pranic energies that sustain individual beings are only conditional, localized, and temporary phenomena of the realm of cosmic Nature. Even in the form of universal life-force, prana is but a conditional modification of the Divine Spirit-Current Revealed by Avatar Adi Da, Which Is the "Bright" (or Consciousness Itself), beyond all cosmic forms.

R

"radical"   The term "radical" derives from the Latin "radix", meaning "root", and, thus, it principally means "irreducible", "fundamental", or "relating to the origin". In *The Dawn Horse Testament Of The Ruchira Avatar*, Avatar Adi Da defines "Radical" as "Gone To The Root, Core, Source, or Origin". Because Adi Da Samraj uses "radical" in this literal sense, it appears in quotation marks in His Wisdom-Teaching, in order to distinguish His usage from the common reference to an extreme (often political) view.

Ramakrishna   See **Lineage, Avatar Adi Da's**.

Ramana Maharshi   A great sixth stage Indian Spiritual Master, Ramana Maharshi (1879-1950) became Self-Realized at a young age and gradually assumed a Teaching role as increasing numbers of people approached him for Spiritual guidance. Ramana Maharshi's Teaching focused on the process of introversion (through the question "Who am I?"), which culminates in conditional Self-Realization (or Jnana Samadhi), exclusive of phenomena. He established his Ashram at Tiruvannamalai in South India, which continues today.

Rang Avadhoot   Rang Avadhoot (1898-1968) was a Realizer in the tradition of Dattatreya. In *The Knee Of Listening*, Avatar Adi Da describes the brief but highly significant meeting that occurred between Himself and Rang Avadhoot in 1968.

Real God   Avatar Adi Da uses the term "Real God" to Indicate the True and Perfectly Subjective Source of all conditions, the True and Spiritual Divine Person (Which can be directly Realized), rather than any ego-made (and, thus, false, or limited) presumptions about God.

Re-cognition   "Re-cognition", which literally means "knowing again", is Avatar Adi Da's term for "the tacit transcending of the habit of 'Narcissus'". It is the mature form into which verbal self-Enquiry evolves in the Devotional Way of Insight. The individual simply notices and tacitly "knows again" (or directly understands) whatever is arising as yet another species of self-contraction, and he or she transcends (or feels beyond) it in Satsang with Avatar Adi Da.

renunciate orders   Avatar Adi Da has established two formal renunciate orders: The Ruchira Sannyasin Order of the Tantric Renunciates of Adidam (or, simply, the Ruchira Sannyasin Order), and the Lay Renunciate Order of Adidam (or, simply, the Lay Renunciate Order).

The senior practicing order in the Way

of Adidam is the Ruchira Sannyasin Order. This order is the senior cultural authority within the formal gathering of Avatar Adi Da's devotees. "Sannyasin" is an ancient Sanskrit term for one who has renounced all worldly bonds and who gives himself or herself completely to the Real-God-Realizing or Real-God-Realized life. Members of the Ruchira Sannyasin Order are uniquely exemplary practitioners of the Way of Adidam who are (generally) practicing in the context of the ultimate (sixth and seventh) stages of life. Members of this Order are legal renunciates and live a life of perpetual retreat. As a general rule, they are to reside at Adidam Samrajashram. The Ruchira Sannyasin Order comprises the first congregation of Avatar Adi Da's devotees.

The members of the Ruchira Sannyasin Order have a uniquely significant role among the practitioners of Adidam as Avatar Adi Da's human Instruments and (in the case of those members who are formally acknowledged as Avatar Adi Da's fully Awakened seventh stage devotees) as the body of practitioners from among whom each of Avatar Adi Da's successive "Living Murtis" (or Empowered human Agents) will be selected. Therefore, the Ruchira Sannyasin Order is essential to the perpetual continuation of authentic practice of the Way of Adidam.

The Founding Member of the Ruchira Sannyasin Order Avatar Adi Da Himself.

In "The Orders of My True and Free Renunciate Devotees" (in *The Lion Sutra*), Avatar Adi Da describes the Lay Renunciate Order as "a renunciate service order for all intensively serving (and, altogether, intensively practicing) lay practitioners of the total (or full and complete) practice of the Way of Adidam".

All present members, and all future members, of the Lay Renunciate Order must (necessarily) be formally acknowledged, formally practicing, significantly matured (tested and proven), and, altogether, especially exemplary practitioners of the total (or full and complete) practice of the Way of Adidam. They must perform significant cultural (and practical, and, as necessary, managerial) service within the gathering of all formally acknowledged practitioners of the four congregations of the Way of Adidam. Either they must live within a formally designated community of formally acknowledged practitioners of the Way of Adidam or, otherwise, they must be formally designated serving residents of one of the by Me formally Empowered Ruchira Sannyasin Hermitage-Retreat Sanctuaries or one of the by Me formally Empowered Pilgrimage and Retreat Sanctuaries for all formally acknowledged practitioners of the Way of Adidam. And they must formally accept (and rightly fulfill) all the obligations and disciplines associated with membership within the Lay Renunciate Order. ["The Orders of My True and Free Renunciate Devotees"]

right side of the heart See **heart, stations of the heart**.

Ruchira Avatar In Sanskrit, "Ruchira" means "bright, radiant, effulgent". Thus, the Reference "Ruchira Avatar" indicates that Avatar Adi Da Samraj is the "Bright" (or Radiant) Descent of the Divine Reality Itself into the conditionally manifested worlds, Appearing here in His bodily (human) Form.

Ruchira Avatara Bhakti Yoga Ruchira Avatara Bhakti Yoga is the principal Gift, Calling, and Discipline Offered by Adi Da Samraj to all who practice the Way of Adidam (in all four congregations).

The phrase "Ruchira Avatara Bhakti Yoga" is itself a summary of the Way of Adidam. "Bhakti", in Sanskrit, is love, adoration, or devotion, while "Yoga" is a Real-God-Realizing discipline (or practice). "Ruchira Avatara Bhakti Yoga" is, thus, "the Divinely Revealed practice of devotional love for (and devotional response to) the Ruchira Avatar, Adi Da Samraj".

The technical practice of Ruchira Avatara Bhakti Yoga is a four-part process of Invoking, feeling, breathing, and serving Avatar Adi Da in every moment.

For Avatar Adi Da's essential Instruction in Ruchira Avatara Bhakti Yoga, see the *Da Love-Ananda Gita (The Free Gift Of The Divine Love-Bliss)*, Part Five, verse 25, and Part Six; *Hridaya Rosary*

(Four Thorns Of Heart-Instruction), Parts Four and Five; and *What, Where, When, How, Why and <u>Who</u> To Remember To Be Happy*, Part Three, "Surrender the Faculties of the Body-Mind To Me" and "How to Practice Whole Bodily Devotion To Me".

Ruchira Avatara Satsang   The Hindi word "Satsang" literally means "true (or right) relationship", "the company of Truth". "Ruchira Avatara Satsang" is the eternal relationship of mutual sacred commitment between Avatar Adi Da Samraj and each true and formally acknowledged practitioner of the Way of Adidam. Once it is consciously assumed by any practitioner, Ruchira Avatara Satsang is an all-inclusive Condition, bringing Divine Grace and Blessings and sacred obligations, responsibilities, and tests into every dimension of the practitioner's life and consciousness.

The Ruchira Buddha   The Enlightened One Who Shines with the Divine "Brightness".

The Ruchira Buddha-Avatar   The "Bright" Enlightened One Who is the Incarnation of the Divine Person. (See also **Avatar**.)

Ruchira Buddhism   "Ruchira Buddhism" is the Way of devotion to the Ruchira Buddha—"the 'Bright' Buddha", Avatar Adi Da Samraj (or, more fully, "the Radiant, Shining, 'Bright' Illuminator and Enlightener Who Is Inherently, or Perfectly Subjectively, Self-Enlightened, and Eternally Awake").

Ruchira Samadhi   "Ruchira Samadhi" (Sanskrit for "the Samadhi of the 'Bright'") is one of the references that Avatar Adi Da Samraj uses for the Divinely Enlightened Condition Realized in the seventh stage of life, Which He characterizes as the Unconditional Realization of the Divine "Brightness".

Ruchira Sannyasin Order   See **renunciate orders**, and see also p. 326.

Rudi / Swami Rudrananda   See **Lineage, Avatar Adi Da's.**

S

"Sadhana Years"   In Sanskrit, "Sadhana" means "self-transcending religious or Spiritual practice". Avatar Adi Da's "Sadhana Years" refers to the time from which He began His quest to recover the Truth of Existence (at Columbia College) until His Divine Re-Awakening in 1970. Avatar Adi Da's full description of His "Sadhana Years" is Given in *The Knee Of Listening*.

Saguna   "Saguna" is Sanskrit for "containing (or accompanied by) qualities".

Sahaj   "Sahaj" is Hindi (from Sanskrit "sahaja") for "twin-born", "natural", or "innate". Avatar Adi Da uses the term to indicate the Coincidence (in the case of Divine Self-Realization) of the Inherently Spiritual and Transcendental Divine Reality with conditional reality. Sahaj, therefore, is the Inherent (or Native) and, thus, truly "Natural" State of Being. (See also **Samadhi**.)

Sahaj Samadhi   See **Samadhi**.

sahasrar   In the traditional system of seven chakras, the sahasrar is the highest chakra (or subtle energy center), associated with the crown of the head and beyond. It is described as a thousand-petaled lotus, the terminal of Light to which the Yogic process (of Spiritual ascent through the chakras) aspires.

During His "Sadhana Years", Avatar Adi Da spontaneously experienced what He calls the "severing of the sahasrar". The Spirit-Energy no longer ascended into the crown of the head (and beyond), but rather "fell" into the Heart, and rested as the Witness-Consciousness. It was this experience that directly revealed to Avatar Adi Da that, while the Yogic traditions regard the sahasrar as the seat of Enlightenment, the Heart is truly the Seat of Divine Consciousness.

Avatar Adi Da's account of the severing of the sahasrar in His own Case is Given in chapter eighteen of *The Knee Of Listening*.

Saiva Siddhanta "Saiva Siddhanta" is the name of an important school of Saivism which flourished in South India and survives into the present.

Samadhi The Sanskrit word "Samadhi" traditionally denotes various exalted states that appear in the context of esoteric meditation and Realization. Avatar Adi Da Teaches that, for His devotees, Samadhi is, even more simply and fundamentally, the Enjoyment of His Divine State, Which is experienced (even from the beginning of the practice of Adidam) through ego-transcending heart-Communion with Him. Therefore, "the cultivation of Samadhi" is another way to describe the fundamental basis of the Way of Adidam. Avatar Adi Da's devotee is in Samadhi in any moment of standing beyond the separate self in true devotional heart-Communion with Him. (See "The Cultivation of My Divine Samadhi", in *The Seven Stages Of Life*.)

The developmental process leading to Divine Enlightenment in the Way of Adidam may be marked by many signs, principal among which are the Samadhis of the advanced and the ultimate stages of life and practice. Although some of the traditionally known Samadhis of the fourth, the fifth, and the sixth stages of life may appear in the course of an individual's practice of the Way of Adidam, the appearance of all of them is by no means necessary, or even probable (as Avatar Adi Da Indicates in His Wisdom-Teaching). The essential Samadhis of the Way of Adidam are those that are uniquely Granted by Avatar Adi Da Samraj—the Samadhi of the "Thumbs" and seventh stage Sahaj Samadhi. All the possible forms of Samadhi in the Way of Adidam are described in full detail in *The Dawn Horse Testament Of The Ruchira Avatar*.

Samadhi of the "Thumbs" "The 'Thumbs'" is Avatar Adi Da's technical term for the invasion of the body-mind by a particular kind of forceful Descent of His Divine Spirit-Current. Avatar Adi Da describes His own experience of the "Thumbs" in *The Knee Of Listening*:

. . . I had an experience that appeared like a mass of gigantic thumbs coming down from above, pressing into my throat (causing something of a gagging, and somewhat suffocating, sensation), and then pressing further (and, it seemed, would have expanded without limitation or end), into some form of myself that was much larger than my physical body. . . .

The "Thumbs" were not visible in the ordinary sense. I did not see them then or even as a child. They were not visible to me with my eyes, nor did I hallucinate them pictorially. Yet, I very consciously experienced and felt them as having a peculiar form and mobility, as I likewise experienced my own otherwise invisible and greater form.

I did not at that time or at any time in my childhood fully allow this intervention of the "Thumbs" to take place. I held it off from its fullest descent, in fear of being overwhelmed, for I did not understand at all what was taking place. However, in later years this same experience occurred naturally during meditation. Because my meditation had been allowed to progress gradually, and the realizations at each level were thus perceived without shock, I was able at those times to allow the experience to take place. When I did, the "Thumbs" completely entered my living form. They appeared like tongues, or parts of a Force, coming from above. And when they had entered deep into my body, the magnetic or energic balances of my living being reversed. On several occasions I felt as if the body had risen above the ground somewhat, and this is perhaps the basis for certain evidence in mystical literature of the phenomenon of levitation, or bodily transport.

At any rate, during those stages in meditation the body ceased to be polarized toward the ground, or the gravitational direction of the earth's center. There was a strong reversal of polarity, communicated along a line of Force analogous to the spine. The physical body, as well as the Energy-form that could be interiorly felt as analogous to but detached from the physical body, was felt to turn in a curve along the spine and forward in the direction of the heart. When this reversal of Energy was allowed to take place completely, I resided in a totally different body, which also contained the physical body. It was spherical in shape. And the sensation of dwelling as that form was completely peaceful. The physical body was completely relaxed and polarized to the shape of this other spherical body. The mind became quieted, and then there was a movement in consciousness that would go even deeper, into a higher conscious State beyond physical and mental awareness. I was to learn that this spherical body was what Yogis and occultists call the "subtle" body (which includes the "pranic", or natural life-energy, dimension and the "astral", or the lower mental and the higher mental, dimensions of the living being).

In the fullest form of this experience, which Avatar Adi Da calls "the Samadhi of the 'Thumbs'", His Spirit-Invasion Descends all the way to the bottom of the frontal line of the body-mind (at the bodily base) and ascends through the spinal line, overwhelming the ordinary human sense of bodily existence, infusing the whole being with intense blissfulness, and releasing the ordinary, confined sense of body, mind, and separate self.

Both the experience of the "Thumbs" and the full Samadhi of the "Thumbs" are unique to the Way of Adidam, for they are specifically signs of the "Crashing Down" (or the Divine Descent) of Avatar Adi Da's Spirit-Baptism, into the body-minds of His devotees. The Samadhi of the "Thumbs" is a kind of "Nirvikalpa" (or formless) Samadhi—but in descent in the frontal line, rather than in ascent in the spinal line.

Avatar Adi Da's extended Instruction relative to the "Thumbs" is Given in "The 'Thumbs' Is The Fundamental Sign Of The Crashing Down Of My Person". This Essay appears in a number of Avatar Adi Da's "Source-Texts" (*Hridaya Rosary, The Only Complete Way To Realize The Unbroken Light Of Real God, Ruchira Avatara Hridaya-Siddha Yoga, The Seven Stages Of Life,* and *Santosha Adidam,* as well as chapter twenty-four of *The Dawn Horse Testament Of The Ruchira Avatar* and chapter thirty-one of *The Heart Of The*

Dawn Horse Testament Of The Ruchira Avatar).

Savikalpa Samadhi and "Cosmic Consciousness"   The Sanskrit term "Savikalpa Samadhi" literally means "meditative ecstasy with form", or "deep meditative concentration (or absorption) in which form (or defined experiential content) is still perceived". Avatar Adi Da indicates that there are two basic forms of Savikalpa Samadhi. The first is the various experiences produced by the Spiritual ascent of energy and attention (into mystical phenomena, visions, and other subtle sensory perceptions of subtle psychic forms) and the various states of Yogic Bliss (or Spirit-"Intoxication").

The second (and highest) form of Savikalpa Samadhi is called "Cosmic Consciousness", or the "'Vision' of Cosmic Unity". This is an isolated or periodic occurrence in which attention ascends, uncharacteristically and spontaneously, to a state of awareness wherein conditional existence is perceived as a Unity in Divine Awareness. This conditional form of "Cosmic Consciousness" is pursued in many mystical and Yogic paths. It depends upon manipulation of attention and the body-mind, and it is interpreted from the point of view of the separate, body-based or mind-based self—and, therefore, it is not equivalent to Divine Enlightenment.

Avatar Adi Da's discussion of Savikalpa Samadhi is found in "Vision, Audition, and Touch in The Process of Ascending Meditation in The Way Of Adidam", in Part Four of *Ruchira Avatara Hridaya-Siddha Yoga.*

Avatar Adi Da's description of the varieties of experiential form possible in Savikalpa Samadhi is found in "The Significant Experiential Signs That May Appear in the Course of The Way Of Adidam", in Part Three of *What, Where, When, How, Why, and Who To Remember To Be Happy.*

fifth stage Nirvikalpa Samadhi
The Sanskrit term "Nirvikalpa Samadhi" literally means "meditative ecstasy without form", or "deep meditative concentration (or absorption) in which there is no

perception of form (or defined experiential content)". Traditionally, this state is regarded to be the final goal of the many schools of Yogic ascent whose orientation to practice is that of the fifth stage of life. Like "Cosmic Consciousness", fifth stage conditional Nirvikalpa Samadhi is an isolated or periodic Realization. In it, attention ascends beyond all conditional manifestation into the formless Matrix of Divine Vibration and Divine Light Infinitely Above the world, the body, and the mind. And, like the various forms of Savikalpa Samadhi, fifth stage conditional Nirvikalpa Samadhi is a temporary state of attention (or, more precisely, of the suspension of attention). It is produced by manipulation of attention and of the body-mind, and is (therefore) incapable of being maintained when attention returns (as it inevitably does) to the states of the body-mind.

Avatar Adi Da's Instruction relative to fifth stage conditional Nirvikalpa Samadhi is Given in chapter forty-two of *The Dawn Horse Testament Of The Ruchira Avatar*.

Jnana Samadhi, or Jnana Nirvikalpa Samadhi "Jnana" means "knowledge". Jnana Nirvikalpa Samadhi (sixth stage Nirvakalpa Samadhi, or, simply, Jnana Samadhi) is the characteristic meditative experience in the sixth stage of life in the Way of Adidam. Produced by the intentional withdrawal of attention from the conditional body-mind-self and its relations, Jnana Samadhi is the conditional, temporary Realization of the Transcendental Self (or Consciousness Itself), exclusive of any perception (or cognition) of world, objects, relations, body, mind, or separate-self-sense—and, thereby, formless (or "nirvikalpa").

Avatar Adi Da's Instruction relative to Jnana Nirvikalpa Samadhi is Given in "The Sixth and The Seventh Stages of Life in The Way Of Adidam" in *The Lion Sutra*.

seventh stage Sahaj Samadhi, or seventh stage Sahaja Nirvikalpa Samadhi Avatar Adi Da's description of seventh stage Sahaj Samadhi is Given in Part Four of *The All-Completing and Final Divine Revelation To Mankind*.

Samraj "Samraj" (from the Sanskrit "Samraja") is a traditional Indian term used to refer to great kings, but also to refer to the Hindu gods. "Samraja" is defined as "universal or supreme ruler", "paramount Lord", or "paramount sovereign".

The Sanskrit word "raja" (the basic root of "Samraj") means "king". It comes from the verbal root "raj", meaning "to reign, to rule, to illuminate". The prefix "sam-" expresses "union" or "completeness". "Samraj" is thus literally the complete ruler, the ruler of everything altogether. "Samraj" was traditionally given as a title to a king who was regarded to be a "universal monarch".

Avatar Adi Da's Name "Adi Da Samraj" expresses that He is the Primordial (or Original) Giver, Who Blesses all as the Universal Lord of every thing, every where, for all time. The Sovereignty of His Kingdom has nothing to do with the world of human politics. Rather, it is entirely a matter of His Spiritual Dominion over all and All, His Kingship in the hearts of His devotees.

samsara / samsaric "Samsara" (or "samsaric") is a classical Buddhist and Hindu term for all conditional worlds and states, or the cyclical realm of birth and change and death. It connotes the suffering and limitations experienced in those limited worlds.

Sanctuaries Avatar Adi Da has Empowered two Hermitage-Retreat Sanctuaries and two Pilgrimage and Retreat Sanctuaries as Agents of His Divine Spiritual Transmission. The senior Hermitage-Retreat Sanctuary is Adidam Samrajashram, the Island of Naitauba in Fiji, where Avatar Adi Da usually Resides in Perpetual Retreat. It is the place where Avatar Adi Da Himself and the senior renunciate order of the Way of Adidam, the Ruchira Sannyasin Order of the Tantric Renunciates of Adidam, are established. It is the primary Seat of Avatar Adi Da's Divine Blessing Work with the entire Cosmic Mandala.

Avatar Adi Da has Spoken of the significance of this Hermitage Ashram:

*AVATAR ADI DA SAMRAJ: Adidam
Samrajashram was established so that I
might have a Place of Seclusion in which
to do My Spiritual Work. This is the Place
of My perpetual Samadhi, the Place of My
perpetual Self-Radiance. Therefore, this is
the Place where people come to participate
in My Samadhi and be further Awakened
by It. My devotees come to Adidam
Samrajashram to magnify their practice
of right, true, and full devotion to Me,
to practice the Way of Adidam as I Have
Revealed and Given It for the sake of most
perfectly ego-transcending Real-God-
Realization.*

Tat Sundaram is a small Hermitage-
Retreat Sanctuary that provides a private
circumstance for Avatar Adi Da and members of the Ruchira Sannyasin Order.

The two Pilgrimage and Retreat
Sanctuaries (The Mountain Of Attention,
in northern California, and Da Love-
Ananda Mahal, in Hawaii—formerly
known as "Tumomama Sanctuary") were
principal sites of Avatar Adi Da's Teaching
Demonstration during the years of His
Divine Teaching-Work. Through His years
of Blessing-Infusion of each of these
Hermitage-Retreat Sanctuaries and these
Pilgrimage and Retreat Sanctuaries, He has
fully Empowered them for His devotees
throughout all time.

Santosha   "Santosha" is Sanskrit for "sat-
isfaction" or "contentment"—qualities
associated with a sense of completion.
These qualities are characteristic of no-
seeking, the fundamental Principle of
Avatar Adi Da's Wisdom-Teaching and of
His entire Revelation of Truth. Because of
its uniquely appropriate meanings,
"Santosha" is one of Avatar Adi Da's
Names. As Santosha Adi Da, Avatar Adi
Da Samraj is the Divine Giver of Perfect
Divine Contentedness, or Perfect
Searchlessness.

Santosha Avatar   As the Santosha
Avatar, Avatar Adi Da is the Very
Incarnation of Perfect Divine
Contentedness, or Perfect Searchlessness.

Sat-Guru   "Sat" means "Truth", "Being",

"Existence". Thus, "Sat-Guru" literally
means "True Guru", or a Guru who can
lead living beings from darkness (or non-
Truth) into Light (or the Living Truth).

Satsang   The Hindi word "Satsang" (from
the Sanskrit "Satsanga") literally means
"true (or right) relationship", "the company of Truth". In the Way of Adidam,
Satsang is the eternal relationship of
mutual sacred commitment between
Avatar Adi Da Samraj and each formally
acknowledged practitioner of the Way of
Adidam.

Savikalpa Samadhi   See **Samadhi**.

scientific materialism   Scientific materialism is the predominant philosophy and
worldview of modern humanity, the basic
presumption of which is that the material
world is all that exists. In scientific materialism, the method of science, or the
observation of objective phenomena, is
made into philosophy and a way of life
that suppresses our native impulse to
Liberation.

seeing   See **listening, hearing, and
seeing**.

self-Enquiry   The practice of self-
Enquiry in the form "Avoiding relation-
ship?", unique to the Way of Adidam, was
spontaneously developed by Avatar Adi
Da in the course of His own Ordeal of
Divine Re-Awakening. Intense persistence
in the "radical" discipline of this unique
form of self-Enquiry led rapidly to Avatar
Adi Da's Divine Enlightenment (or Most
Perfect Divine Self-Realization) in 1970.

The practice of self-Enquiry in the
form "Avoiding relationship?" and the
practice of non-verbal Re-cognition are
the principal technical practices that serve
feeling-Contemplation of Avatar Adi Da in
the Devotional Way of Insight.

Self-Existing and Self-Radiant   Avatar
Adi Da uses "Self-Existing and Self-
Radiant" to indicate the two fundamental
aspects of the One Divine Person (or
Reality)—Existence (or Being, or
Consciousness) Itself, and Radiance (or
Energy, or Light) Itself.

seven stages of life See **stages of life**.

Shakti, Guru-Shakti "Shakti" is a
Sanskrit term for the Divinely Manifesting
Energy, Spiritual Power, or Spirit-Current
of the Divine Person. Guru-Shakti is the
Power of the Guru to Liberate his or her
devotees.

Shaktipat In Hindi, "shaktipat" is the
"descent of Spiritual Power". Yogic
Shaktipat, which manipulates natural, conditional energies or partial manifestations
of the Spirit-Current, is typically granted
through touch, word, glance, or regard
by Yogic Adepts in the fifth stage of life,
or fourth to fifth stages of life. Yogic
Shaktipat must be distinguished from
(and, otherwise, understood to be only
a secondary aspect of) the Blessing
Transmission of the Heart Itself (Hridaya-
Shaktipat), which is uniquely Given by
Avatar Adi Da Samraj.

Siddha, Siddha-Guru "Siddha" is
Sanskrit for "a completed, fulfilled, or perfected one", or "one of perfect accomplishment, or power". Avatar Adi Da uses
"Siddha", or "Siddha-Guru", to mean a
Transmission-Master who is a Realizer (to
any significant degree) of Real God, Truth,
or Reality.

Siddha Yoga "Siddha Yoga" is, literally,
"the Yoga of the Perfected One[s]".

Swami Muktananda used the term
"Siddha Yoga" to refer to the form of
Kundalini Yoga that he taught, which
involved initiation of the devotee by the
Guru's Transmission of Shakti (or Spiritual
Energy). Avatar Adi Da Samraj has indi-
cated that this was a fifth stage form of
Siddha Yoga.

In "I (Alone) Am The Adidam
Revelation", Avatar Adi Da Says:

*. . . I Teach Siddha Yoga in the Mode
and Manner of the seventh stage of life (as
Ruchira Avatara Hridaya-Siddha Yoga, or
Ruchira Avatara Maha-Jnana Hridaya-
Shaktipat Yoga)—and always toward (or
to the degree of) the Realization inherently
associated with (and, at last, Most
Perfectly Demonstrated and Proven by) the
only-by-Me Revealed and Given seventh*

*stage of life, and as a practice and a
Process that progressively includes (and,
coincidently, directly transcends) all six of
the phenomenal and developmental (and,
necessarily, yet ego-based) stages of life
that precede the seventh.*

Avatar Adi Da's description of the sim-
ilarities and differences between traditional Siddha Yoga and the Way of
Adidam is Given in "I (Alone) Am The
Adidam Revelation", which Essay appears
in many of Avatar Adi Da's twenty-three
"Source-Texts".

siddhi "Siddhi" is Sanskrit for "power",
or "accomplishment". When capitalized in
Avatar Adi Da's Wisdom-Teaching,
"Siddhi" is the Spiritual, Transcendental,
and Divine Awakening-Power That He
spontaneously and effortlessly Transmits
to all.

"Sila" "Sila" is a Pali Buddhist term
meaning "habit", "behavior", "conduct",
or "morality". It connotes the restraint of
outgoing energy and attention, the disposition of equanimity, or free energy and
attention for the Spiritual Process.

**"simpler" (or "simplest") form of the
Way of Adidam** See **forms of practice
in the Way of Adidam**.

sleeping See **waking, dreaming, and
sleeping**.

"Source-Texts" During the twenty-seven
years of His Teaching-Work and
Revelation-Work (from 1972 to 1999),
Avatar Adi Da elaborately described every
aspect of the practice of Adidam, from the
beginning of one's approach to Him to
the Most Ultimate Realization of the seventh stage of life.

Avatar Adi Da's Heart-Word is summa-
rized in His twenty-three "Source-Texts".
These Texts present, in complete and con-
clusive detail, His Divine Revelations,
Confessions, and Instructions, which are
the fruits of His years of Teaching and
Revelation Work. In addition to this
"Source-Literature", Avatar Adi Da's Heart-
Word also includes His "Supportive Texts"
(comprising His practical Instruction in all

the details of the practice of Adidam, including the fundamental disciplines of diet, health, exercise, sexuality, childrearing, and cooperative community), His "Early Literature" (Written during His Teaching Years), and collections of His Talks. (For a complete list of Avatar Adi Da's twenty-three "Source-Texts", see pp. 398-408.)

spinal line, spinal Yoga The spinal (or ascending) line of the body-mind conducts the Spirit-Current of Divine Life in an upward direction from the base of the body (or perineal area) to the crown of the head, and beyond.

In the Way of Adidam, the spinal Yoga is the process whereby knots and obstructions in the subtle, astral, or the more mentally and subtly oriented dimension of the body-mind are penetrated, opened, surrendered, and released through the devotee's reception and "conductivity" of Avatar Adi Da's Transmission into the spinal line of the body-mind. This ascending Yoga will be required for practitioners of Adidam only in relatively rare cases. The great majority of Avatar Adi Da's devotees will be sufficiently purified through their practice of the frontal Yoga to proceed directly to practice in the context of the sixth stage of life, bypassing practice in the context of the "advanced" fourth stage and the fifth stage of life.

Spirit-Baptism Avatar Adi Da often refers to His Transmission of Spiritual Blessing as His "Spirit-Baptism". It is often felt by His devotee as a Current descending in the frontal line and ascending in the spinal line. However, Avatar Adi Da's Spirit-Baptism is fundamentally and primarily His Moveless Transmission of the Divine Heart Itself. As a secondary effect, His Spirit-Baptism serves to purify, balance, and energize the entire body-mind of the devotee who is prepared to receive It.

Spiritual anatomy / esoteric anatomy Avatar Adi Da Samraj has Revealed that just as there is a physical anatomy, there is an actual Spiritual anatomy, or structure, that is present in every human being. As He Says in *The Basket Of Tolerance*, it is

because of this structure that the "experiential and developmental process of Growth and Realization demonstrates itself in accordance with what I have Revealed and Demonstrated to be the seven stages of life".

Avatar Adi Da's extended Instruction relative to the Spiritual anatomy of Man is Given in *The Seven Stages Of Life* and *Santosha Adidam*.

Spiritual, Transcendental, Divine Avatar Adi Da uses the words "Spiritual", "Transcendental", and "Divine" in reference to dimensions of Reality that are Realized progressively in the Way of Adidam. "Transcendental" and "Spiritual" indicate two fundamental aspects of the One Divine Reality and Person— Consciousness Itself (Which Is Transcendental, or Self-Existing) and Energy Itself (Which Is Spiritual, or Self-Radiant). Only That Which Is Divine is simultaneously Transcendental <u>and</u> Spiritual.

Sri "Sri" is a term of honor and veneration often applied to an Adept. The word literally means "flame" in Sanskrit, indicating that the one honored is radiant with Blessing Power.

stages of life Avatar Adi Da has Revealed the underlying structure of human growth in seven stages. The seventh stage of life is Divine Self-Realization, or Most Perfect Enlightenment.

The first three stages of life develop, respectively, the physical, emotional, and mental/volitional functions of the body-mind. The first stage begins at birth and continues for approximately five to seven years; the second stage follows, continuing until approximately the age of twelve to fourteen; and the third stage is optimally complete by the early twenties. In the case of virtually all individuals, however, failed adaptation in the earlier stages of life means that maturity in the third stage of life takes much longer to attain, and it is usually never fulfilled, with the result that the ensuing stages of Spiritual development do not even begin.

In the Way of Adidam, however, growth in the first three stages of life unfolds in the Spiritual Company of Avatar Adi Da and is based in the practice of feeling-Contemplation of His bodily (human) Form and in devotion, service, and self-discipline in relation to His bodily (human) Form. By the Grace of this relationship to Avatar Adi Da, the first three (or foundation) stages of life are lived and fulfilled in an ego-transcending devotional disposition, or (as He describes it) "in the 'original' (or beginner's) devotional context of the fourth stage of life".

The fourth stage of life is the transitional stage between the gross (bodily-based) point of view of the first three stages of life and the subtle (mind-based, or psyche-based) point of view of the fifth stage of life. The fourth stage of life is the stage of Spiritual devotion, or devotional surrender of separate self to the Divine, in which the gross functions of the being are aligned to the higher psychic (or subtle) functions of the being. In the fourth stage of life, the gross (or bodily-based) personality of the first three stages of life is purified through reception of the Spiritual Force ("Holy Spirit", or "Shakti") of the Divine Reality, which prepares the being to out-grow the bodily-based point of view.

In the Way of Adidam, as the orientation of the fourth stage of life matures, heart-felt surrender to the bodily (human) Form of Avatar Adi Da deepens by His Grace, Drawing His devotee into Love-Communion with His All-Pervading Spiritual Presence. Growth in the "basic" context of the fourth stage of life in the Way of Adidam is also characterized by reception of Avatar Adi Da's Baptizing Current of Divine Spirit-Energy, Which is initially felt to flow down the front of the body from Infinitely Above the head to the bodily base (or perineal area).

The Descent of Avatar Adi Da's Spirit-Baptism releases obstructions predominantly in what He calls the "frontal personality", or the personality typically animated in the waking state (as opposed to the dream state and the state of deep sleep). This Spirit-Baptism purifies His devotee and infuses the devotee with His Spirit-Power. Avatar Adi Da's devotee is, thus, awakened to profound love of (and

devotional intimacy with) Him.

Eventually, Avatar Adi Da's Divine Spirit-Current may be felt to turn about at the bodily base and ascend up the spine to the brain core. In this case, the fourth stage of life matures to its "advanced" context, which is focused in the Ascent of Avatar Adi Da's Spirit-Baptism and the consequent purification of the spinal line of the body-mind.

In the fifth stage of life, attention is concentrated in the subtle (or psychic) levels of awareness in ascent. Avatar Adi Da's Divine Spirit-Current is felt to penetrate the brain core and rise toward the Matrix of Light and Love-Bliss Infinitely Above the crown of the head, possibly culminating in the temporary experience of fifth stage conditional Nirvikalpa Samadhi, or "formless ecstasy". In the Way of Adidam, most practitioners will not need to practice either in the "advanced" context of the fourth stage of life or in the context of the fifth stage of life, but will (rather) be Awakened, by Avatar Adi Da's Grace, directly from maturity in the fourth stage of life to the Witness-Position of Consciousness (in the context of the sixth stage of life).

In the traditional development of the sixth stage of life, a strategic effort is made to Identify with Consciousness Itself by excluding the realm of conditional phenomena. Avatar Adi Da Teaches, however, that the deliberate intention to exclude the conditional world for the sake of Realizing Transcendental Consciousness is an egoic error that must be transcended by His devotees who are practicing in the context of the sixth stage of life.

In deepest meditation in the sixth stage of life in the Way of Adidam, the knot of attention (which is the root-action of egoity, felt as separation, self-contraction, or the feeling of relatedness) dissolves, and all sense of relatedness yields to the Blissful and undifferentiated Feeling of Being. The characteristic Samadhi of the sixth stage of life is Jnana Samadhi, the temporary Realization of the Transcendental Self (or Consciousness Itself)—which is temporary because it can occur only when awareness of the world is excluded in meditation.

The transition from the sixth stage of life to the seventh stage Realization of Absolute Non-Separateness is the unique Revelation of Avatar Adi Da. Various traditions and individuals previous to Adi Da's Revelation have had sixth stage intuitions (or premonitions) of the Most Perfect seventh stage Realization, but no one previous to Avatar Adi Da has Realized the seventh stage of life.

The seventh stage Realization is a Gift of Avatar Adi Da to His devotees who have (by His Divine Grace) completed their practice of the Way of Adidam in the context of the first six stages of life. The seventh stage of life begins when His devotee Gracefully Awakens from the exclusive Realization of Consciousness to Most Perfect and Permanent Identification with Consciousness Itself, Avatar Adi Da's Divine State. This is Divine Self-Realization, or Divine Enlightenment, the perpetual Samadhi of "Open Eyes" (seventh stage Sahaj Samadhi)—in which all "things" are Divinely Self-Recognized without "difference", as merely apparent modifications of the One Self-Existing and Self-Radiant Divine Consciousness.

In the course of the seventh stage of life, there may be spontaneous incidents in which psycho-physical states and phenomena do not appear to the notice, being Outshined by the "Bright" Radiance of Consciousness Itself. This Samadhi, Which is the Ultimate Realization of Divine Existence, culminates in Divine Translation, or the permanent Outshining of all apparent conditions in the Inherently Perfect Radiance and Love-Bliss of the Divine Self-Condition (which necessarily coincides with the physical death of the body-mind).

In the context of practice of the Way of Adidam, the seven stages of life as Revealed by Avatar Adi Da are not a version of the traditional "ladder" of Spiritual attainment. These stages and their characteristic signs arise naturally in the course of practice for a fully practicing devotee in the Way of Adidam, but the practice itself is oriented to the transcending of the first six stages of life, in the seventh stage Disposition of Inherently Liberated Happiness, Granted by Avatar Adi Da's Divine Grace in His Love-Blissful Spiritual Company.

Avatar Adi Da's extended Instruction relative to the seven stages of life is Given in *The Seven Stages Of Life*.

Star Form   Avatar Adi Da has Revealed that He is "Incarnated" in the Cosmic domain as a brilliant white five-pointed Star, the original (and primal) conditional visible Representation (or Sign) of the "Bright" (the Source-Energy, or Divine Light, of Which all conditional phenomena and the total cosmos are modifications).

The apparently objective Divine Star can potentially be experienced in any moment and location in cosmic Nature. However, the vision of the Divine Star is not a necessary experience for growth in the Spiritual Process or for Divine Self-Realization.

Avatar Adi Da's discussion of His Star Form is found in *He-and-She Is Me*.

student-novice / student-beginner
A student-novice is an individual who is formally approaching, and preparing to become a formal practitioner of, the total practice of the Way of Adidam (as a member of the second congregation). The student-novice makes a vow of eternal commitment to Avatar Adi Da as his or her Divine Guru, and to the practice He has Given, and is initiated into simple devotional and sacramental disciplines in formal relationship to Avatar Adi Da. During the student-novice stage, the individual engages in intensive study of Avatar Adi Da's Wisdom-Teaching and adapts to the functional, practical, relational, and cultural disciplines of the Way of Adidam.

A student-beginner is a practitioner in the initial developmental stage of the second congregation of Adidam. In the course of student-beginner practice, the devotee of Avatar Adi Da, on the basis of the eternal "Bond" of devotion to Him that he or she established as a student-novice, continues the process of listening and further adaptation to the disciplines that were begun in the student-novice stage of approach.

subtle   See **gross, subtle, causal**.

"Supportive Texts"   Among Avatar Adi Da's "Supportive Texts" are included such books as *Conscious Exercise and the Transcendental Sun*, *The Eating Gorilla Comes in Peace*, *Love of the Two-Armed Form*, and *Easy Death*.

Swami   The title "Swami" is traditionally given to an individual who has demonstrated significant self-mastery in the context of a lifetime dedicated to Spiritual renunciation.

Swami Muktananda   See **Lineage, Avatar Adi Da's**.

Swami Nityananda   See **Lineage, Avatar Adi Da's**.

Swami Rudrananda   See **Lineage, Avatar Adi Da's**.

T

Tail of the Horse   Adi Da Samraj has often referred to a passage from the ancient Indian text *Satapatha Brahmana*, which He has paraphrased as: "Man does not know. Only the Horse Knows. Therefore, hold to the tail of the Horse." Adi Da has Revealed that, in the most esoteric understanding of this saying, the "Horse" represents the Adept-Realizer, and "holding to the tail of the Horse" represents the devotee's complete dependence on the Adept-Realizer in order to Realize Real God (or Truth, or Reality).

"talking" school   "'Talking' school" is a phrase used by Avatar Adi Da to refer to those in any tradition of sacred life whose approach is characterized by talking, thinking, reading, and philosophical analysis and debate, or even meditative enquiry or reflection, without a concomitant and foundation discipline of body, emotion, mind, and breath. He contrasts the "talking" school with the "practicing" school approach—"practicing" schools involving those who are committed to the ordeal of real ego-transcending discipline, under the guidance of a true Guru.

Tat Sundaram   "Sundara" is the Sanskrit word for "beauty", and "Sundaram" means "something which is beautiful". "Tat" is the Sanskrit word for "it" or "that". Thus, "Tat Sundaram" means "That Which Is Beautiful" or, by extension, "All Of This Is Beautiful", and is a reference to the seventh stage Realization of the Perfect Non-Separateness and Love-Bliss-Nature of the entire world—conditional and Un-Conditional. Tat Sundaram is also the name of the Hermitage-Retreat Sanctuary reserved for Avatar Adi Da in northern California.

Teaching-Work   For a description of Avatar Adi Da's Divine Teaching-Work, see pp. 16-17.

technically "fully elaborated" practice   See **forms of practice in the Way of Adidam**.

technically "simpler" (and even "simplest") practice   See **forms of practice in the Way of Adidam**.

three stations of the heart   See **heart, stations of the heart**.

the "Thumbs"   See **Samadhi**.

Thunder   The Divine Sound of Thunder (which Avatar Adi Da also describes as the "Da" Sound, or "Da-Om" Sound, or "Om" Sound) is one of Avatar Adi Da's three Eternal Forms of Manifestation in the conditional worlds—together with His Divine Star of Light and His Divine Spiritual Body.

Avatar Adi Da's principal Revelation-Confession about these three forms of His Manifestation is Given in *He-and-She Is Me*.

> . . . *I Am conditionally Manifested (First) As The everywhere Apparently Audible (and Apparently Objective) Divine Sound-Vibration (or "Da" Sound, or "Da-Om" Sound, or "Om" Sound, The Objective Sign Of The He, Present As The Conscious Sound Of sounds, In The Center Of The Cosmic Mandala), and As The everywhere Apparently Visible (and Apparently Objective) Divine Star (The Objective Sign*

Of The She, Present As The Conscious Light Of lights, In The Center Of The Cosmic Mandala), and (From That He and She) As The everywhere Apparently Touchable (or Tangible), and Apparently Objective, Total Divine Spiritual Body (The Objective, and All-and-all-Surrounding, and All-and-all-Pervading Conscious and Me-Personal Body Of "Bright" Love-Bliss-Presence, Divinely Self-"Emerging", Now, and Forever Hereafter, From The Center Of The Cosmic Mandala Into The Depths Of Even every "where" In The Cosmic Domain) . . . .

total practice of the Way of Adidam
The total practice of the Way of Adidam is the full and complete practice of the Way that Avatar Adi Da Samraj has Given to His devotees who are formal members of the first or the second congregation of Adidam (see pp. 321-27). One who embraces the total practice of the Way of Adidam conforms every aspect of his or her life and being to Avatar Adi Da's Divine Word of Instruction. Therefore, it is only such devotees (in the first or the second congregation of Adidam) who have the potential of Realizing Divine Enlightenment.

"True Prayer" "True Prayer" is Avatar Adi Da's technical term for the various forms of the "conscious process" that are practiced by His Spiritually Awakened devotees who have chosen the Devotional Way of Faith.
　　Avatar Adi Da's full Instruction relative to "True Prayer" is Given in *The Dawn Horse Testament Of The Ruchira Avatar.*

Turaga "Turaga" (Too-RAHNG-ah) is Fijian for "Lord".

"turiya", "turiyatita" Terms used in the Hindu philosophical systems. Traditionally, "turiya" means "the fourth state" (beyond waking, dreaming, and sleeping), and "turiyatita" means "the state beyond the fourth", or beyond all states.
　　Avatar Adi Da, however, has given these terms different meanings in the context of the Way of Adidam. He uses the term "turiya" to indicate the Awakening to the Consciousness Itself (in the context of

the sixth stage of life), and "turiyatita" as the State of Most Perfect Divine Enlightenment, or the Realization of all arising as transparent and non-binding modifications of the One Divine Reality (in the context of the seventh stage of life).

U

ultimate See **the advanced and the ultimate stages of life**.

Ultimate Self-Domain "Ultimate Self-Domain" is a synonym for "Divine Self-Domain". (See **Divine Self-Domain**.)

Ultimate Source-Condition The Divine Reality prior to all conditional arising, which is, therefore, the "Source" of all conditional worlds, beings, and things.

V

Vira-Yogi Sanskrit for "Hero-Yogi". (See **"Heroic"**.)

Vow For a description of the Vow and responsibilities associated with the Way of Adidam, see pp. 321-32.

W, X, Y, Z

waking, dreaming, and sleeping
These three states of consciousness are associated with the dimensions of cosmic existence.
　　The waking state (and the physical body) is associated with the gross dimension.
　　The dreaming state (and visionary, mystical, and Yogic Spiritual processes) is associated with the subtle dimension. The subtle dimension, which is senior to the gross dimension, includes the etheric (or energic), lower mental (or verbal-intentional and lower psychic), and higher mental (or deeper psychic, mystical, and discriminative) functions.
　　The sleeping state is associated with the causal dimension, which is senior to both the gross and the subtle dimensions. It is the root of attention, prior to any particular experience. (See also **gross, subtle, causal**.)

washing the dog Avatar Adi Da uses the metaphor of the "dog" and "washing the dog" to Indicate the purification of the body-mind in the process of Adidam. He addresses the presumption (as in the Kundalini Yoga tradition) that the Spiritual process requires a spinal Yoga, or an effort of arousing Spiritual Energy literally at the "tail" end of the "dog" (the bodily base, or the muladhara chakra), and then drawing It up (or allowing It to ascend) through the spinal line to the head (and above). In contrast, Avatar Adi Da Samraj has Revealed (particularly in His *Hridaya Rosary*) that, in reality, the human being can be truly purified and Liberated (or the "dog" can be "washed") only by receiving His Divine Blessing-Power (or Hridaya-Shakti) and Spiritual Person downward from Infinitely Above the head to the bodily base. This Process of downward reception of Avatar Adi Da is what He calls the "frontal Yoga", because it occurs in the frontal line of the body (which is a natural pathway of descending energy, down the front of the body, from the crown of the head to the bodily base). This necessary descending Yoga of the frontal line, once completed, is sufficient to purify and Spiritually Infuse the body-mind, and, in most cases, it allows the practitioner of the Way of Adidam to bypass the ascending Yoga of the spinal line (which is the complementary natural pathway of ascending energy, up the back of the body, from the bodily base to the crown of the head). The frontal line and the spinal line are the two arcs of the continuous energy-circuit that Avatar Adi Da calls the "Circle" of the body-mind.

AVATAR ADI DA SAMRAJ: You wash a dog from the head to the tail. But somehow or other, egos looking to Realize think they can wash the "dog" from the "tail" toward the head by doing spinal Yoga. But, in Truth, and in Reality, only the frontal Yoga can accomplish most perfect Divine Self-Realization, because it begins from the superior position, from the "head" position, from My Crashing Down.

The heart-disposition is magnified by My Crashing Down in your devotional Communion with Me. And the vital,

grosser dimensions of the being are purified by this washing from the head toward the "tail". If the Process had to begin from the bodily base up, it would be very difficult, very traumatizing—and, ultimately, impossible. The "dog" is washed, simply and very directly, by your participation in My Divine Descent, by your participation in this frontal Yoga. I am Speaking now of the Spiritually Awakened stages, basically. But, even in the case of beginning practitioners in the Way of Adidam—not yet Spiritually Awakened, not yet responsible for the truly Spiritual dimension of their relationship to Me—this "wash" is, by Means of My Avataric Divine Grace, going on.

Therefore, Spiritual life need not be a traumatic course. The "dog" should enjoy being bathed. Nice gentle little guy, happy to be rubbed and touched. You talk to him, struggle a little bit, but you gentle him down. That is how it should work. And, at the end of it, the "dog" sort of "wags its tail", shakes the water off—nice and clean, happy, your best friend. That is how it should work.

If you wash the "dog" from the "tail" up, you smear the shit from his backside toward his head. Basically, that "washing from the tail toward the head" is a self-generated, self-"guruing" kind of effort. The Divine Process can only occur by Means of Divine Grace. Even the word "Shaktipat" means the "Descent (pat) of Divine Force (Shakti)". But Shaktipat as it appears in the traditions is basically associated with admonitions to practice a spinal Yoga, moving from the base up. In Truth, the Divine Yoga in My Company is a Descent—washing the "dog" from head to "tail" rather than giving the "dog" a "bone", letting it wash itself from the "tail" to the head.

DEVOTEE: It is only Your Hridaya-Shakti that does it.

AVATAR ADI DA SAMRAJ: This is why you must invest yourself in Me. And that is how the "dog" gets washed. [August 13, 1995]

Avatar Adi Da's extended Discourse relative to "washing the dog" is "Be Washed, From Head to Tail, By Heart-Devotion To Me", in *Hridaya Rosary*.

Way of "Radical" Understanding
Avatar Adi Da uses "understanding" to
mean "the process of transcending
egoity". Thus, to "understand" is to simultaneously observe the activity of the self-
contraction and to surrender that activity
via devotional resort to Avatar Adi Da
Samraj.

Avatar Adi Da has Revealed that,
despite their intention to Realize Reality
(or Truth, or Real God), all religious and
Spiritual traditions (other than the Way of
Adidam) are involved, in one manner or
another, with the search to satisfy the ego.
Only Avatar Adi Da has Revealed the Way
to "radically" understand the ego and (in
due course, through intensive formal practice of the Way of Adidam, as His formally
acknowledged devotee) to most perfectly
transcend the ego. Thus, the Way Avatar
Adi Da has Given is the "Way of 'Radical'
Understanding".

**Witness, Witness-Consciousness,
Witness-Position**   When Consciousness
is free of identification with the body-
mind, it takes up its natural "position" as
the Conscious Witness of all that arises to
and in and as the body-mind.

In the Way of Adidam, the stable
Realization of the Witness-Position is associated with, or demonstrated via, the
effortless surrender (or relaxation) of all
the forms of seeking and all the motives
of attention that characterize the first five
stages of life. However, identification with
the Witness-Position is not final (or Most
Perfect) Realization of the Divine Self.
Rather, it is the first of the three stages of
the "Perfect Practice" in the Way of
Adidam, which Practice, in due course,
Realizes, by Avatar Adi Da's Grace, complete and irreversible and utterly Love-
Blissful Identification with Consciousness
Itself.

Avatar Adi Da's extended Instruction
relative to the Witness is Given in *The
Lion Sutra*.

Yoga   "Yoga", in Sanskrit, is literally
"yoking", or "union", usually referring to
any discipline or process whereby an
aspirant attempts to unite with God.
Avatar Adi Da acknowledges this conventional and traditional use of the term, but
also, in reference to the Great Yoga of
Adidam, employs it in a "radical" sense,
free of the usual implication of egoic separation and seeking.

Yogananda, Paramahansa
Paramahansa Yogananda (Mukunda Lal
Ghosh, 1893-1952) was born in Bengal,
the child of devout Hindu parents. As a
young man, Yogananda found his Guru,
Swami Yukteswar Giri, who initiated him
into an order of formal renunciates. In
1920, Yogananda traveled to America to
attend an international conference of religions in Boston. Subsequently he settled
in the United States, attracting many
American devotees. He Taught "Kriya
Yoga", a system of practice that had been
passed down to him by his own Teacher
and that had originally been developed
from traditional techniques of Kundalini
Yoga. Yogananda became widely known
through the publication of his life-story,
Autobiography of a Yogi.

The Sacred Literature of
Avatar Adi Da Samraj

Read the astounding Story of Avatar Adi Da's Divine Life and Work in *The Promised God-Man Is Here*.

The Promised God-Man Is Here:
The Extraordinary Life-Story,
The "Radical" Teaching-Work, and
The Divinely "Emerging" World-Blessing
Work Of The Divine World-Teacher
Of The "Late-Time", Ruchira Avatar
Adi Da Samraj

The profound, heart-rending, humorous, miraculous, wild—and true—Story of the Divine Person Alive in human Form. Essential reading as background for the study of Avatar Adi Da's books.

Enjoy the beautiful summary of His Message that Avatar Adi Da has written especially "for children, and everyone else".

What, Where, When, How, Why, and <u>Who</u> To Remember To Be Happy

A Simple Explanation Of The Divine Way Of Adidam (For Children, and <u>Everyone</u> Else)

Fundamental Truth about life as a human being, told in very simple language. Accompanied by extraordinarily vivid and imaginative illustrations.

The Five Books Of
The Heart Of The Adidam Revelation

In these five books, Avatar Adi Da Samraj has distilled the very essence of His Eternal Message to every one, in all times and places.

BOOK ONE:

Aham Da Asmi
(Beloved, I Am Da)

The "Late-Time" Avataric Revelation Of The True and Spiritual Divine Person (The egoless Personal Presence Of Reality and Truth, Which Is The Only Real God)

The most extraordinary statement ever made in human history. Avatar Adi Da Samraj fully Reveals Himself as the Living Divine Person and Proclaims His Infinite and Undying Love for all and All.

BOOK TWO:

Ruchira Avatara Gita
(The Way Of The Divine Heart-Master)

The "Late-Time" Avataric Revelation Of The Great Secret Of The Divinely Self-Revealed Way That Most Perfectly Realizes The True and Spiritual Divine Person (The egoless Personal Presence Of Reality and Truth, Which Is The Only Real God)

Avatar Adi Da Offers to every one the ecstatic practice of devotional relationship to Him—explaining how devotion to a living human Adept-Realizer has always been the source of true religion, and distinguishing true Guru-devotion from religious cultism.

BOOK THREE:

Da Love-Ananda Gita
(The Free Gift Of The Divine Love-Bliss)

The "Late-Time" Avataric Revelation Of The Great Means To Worship and To Realize The True and Spiritual Divine Person (The egoless Personal Presence Of Reality and Truth, Which Is The Only Real God)

Avatar Adi Da Reveals the secret simplicity at the heart of Adidam—relinquishing your preoccupation with yourself (and all your problems and your suffering) and, instead, Contemplating the "Bright" Divine Person of Infinite Love-Bliss.

BOOK FOUR:

Hridaya Rosary
(Four Thorns Of Heart-Instruction)

The "Late-Time" Avataric Revelation Of The Universally Tangible Divine Spiritual Body, Which Is The Supreme Agent Of The Great Means To Worship and To Realize The True and Spiritual Divine Person (The egoless Personal Presence Of Reality and Truth, Which Is The Only Real God)

The ultimate Mysteries of Spiritual life, never before revealed. In breathtakingly beautiful poetry, Avatar Adi Da Samraj sings of the "melting" of the ego in His "Rose Garden of the Heart".

BOOK FIVE:

Eleutherios
(The Only Truth That Sets The Heart Free)

The "Late-Time" Avataric Revelation Of The "Perfect Practice" Of The Great Means To Worship and To Realize The True and Spiritual Divine Person (The egoless Personal Presence Of Reality and Truth, Which Is The Only Real God)

An address to the great human questions about God, Truth, Reality, Happiness, and Freedom. Avatar Adi Da Samraj Reveals how Absolute Divine Freedom is Realized, and makes an impassioned Call to everyone to create a world of true human freedom on Earth.

The Seventeen Companions
Of The True Dawn Horse

These seventeen books are "Companions" to *The Dawn Horse Testament*, Avatar Adi Da's great summary of the Way of Adidam (p. 406). Here you will find Avatar Adi Da's Wisdom-Instruction on particular aspects of the true Spiritual Way, and His two tellings of His own Life-Story, as autobiography (*The Knee Of Listening*) and as archetypal parable (*The Mummery*).

BOOK ONE:

Real God Is The Indivisible Oneness Of Unbroken Light

Reality, Truth, and The "Non-Creator" God In The True World-Religion Of Adidam

The Nature of Real God and the nature of the cosmos. Why ultimate questions cannot be answered either by conventional religion or by science.

BOOK TWO:

The Truly Human New World-Culture Of Unbroken Real-God-Man

The Eastern Versus The Western Traditional Cultures Of Mankind, and The Unique New Non-Dual Culture Of The True World-Religion Of Adidam

The Eastern and Western approaches to religion, and to life altogether—and how the Way of Adidam goes beyond this apparent dichotomy.

BOOK THREE:

The Only Complete Way To Realize The Unbroken Light Of Real God

An Introductory Overview Of The "Radical" Divine Way Of The True World-Religion Of Adidam

The entire course of the Way of Adidam—the unique principles underlying Adidam, and the unique culmination of Adidam in Divine Enlightenment.

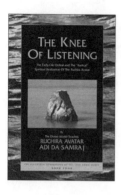

BOOK FOUR:

The Knee Of Listening

The Early-Life Ordeal and The "Radical"
Spiritual Realization Of The Ruchira Avatar

Avatar Adi Da's autobiographical account of the
years from His Birth to His Divine Re-Awakening
in 1970. Includes a new chapter, "My Realization
of the Great Onlyness of Me, and My Great
Regard for My Adept-Links to the Great Tradition
of Mankind".

BOOK FIVE:

The Divine Siddha-Method Of The Ruchira Avatar

The Divine Way Of Adidam Is An ego-Transcending
Relationship, Not An ego-Centric Technique

Avatar Adi Da's earliest Talks to His devotees, on
the fundamental principles of the devotional relationship to Him and "radical" understanding of the
ego. Accompanied by His summary statements on
His relationship to Swami Muktananda and on His
own unique Teaching-Work and Blessing-Work.

BOOK SIX:

The Mummery

A Parable Of The Divine True Love

A work of astonishing poetry and deeply evocative archetypal drama. This is the story of
Raymond Darling's birth, his growth to manhood,
his finding and losing of his beloved (Quandra),
and his ultimate resolution of the heart-breaking
"problem" of mortality. *The Mummery* is Avatar
Adi Da's telling of His own Life-Story in the language of parable, including His unflinching portrayal of how the
unconverted ego makes religion (and life altogether) into a meaningless mummery.

BOOK SEVEN:

He-and-She Is Me
The Indivisibility Of Consciousness and Light In The Divine Body Of The Ruchira Avatar

One of Avatar Adi Da's most esoteric Revelations—His Primary "Incarnation" in the Cosmic domain as the "He" of Primal Divine Sound-Vibration, the "She" of Primal Divine Light, and the "Son" of "He" and "She" in the "Me" of His Divine Spiritual Body.

BOOK EIGHT:

Ruchira Avatara Hridaya-Siddha Yoga
The Divine (and Not Merely Cosmic) Spiritual Baptism In The Divine Way Of Adidam

The Divine Heart-Power (Hridaya-Shakti) uniquely Transmitted by Avatar Adi Da Samraj, and how it differs from the various traditional forms of Spiritual Baptism, particularly Kundalini Yoga.

BOOK NINE:

Ruchira Avatara Hridaya-Tantra Yoga
The Physical-Spiritual (and Truly Religious) Method Of Mental, Emotional, Sexual, and Whole Bodily Health and Enlightenment In The Divine Way Of Adidam

The transformation of life in the realms of money, food, and sex. Includes: understanding "victim-consciousness"; the ego as addict; the secret of how to change; going beyond the "Oedipal" sufferings of childhood; the right orientation to money; right diet; life-positive and Spiritually auspicious sexual practice.

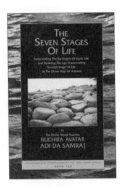

BOOK TEN:

The Seven Stages Of Life

Transcending The Six Stages Of egoic Life, and Realizing The ego-Transcending Seventh Stage Of Life, In The Divine Way Of Adidam

The stages of human development from birth to Divine Enlightenment. How the stages relate to physical and esoteric anatomy. The errors of each of the first six stages of life, and the unique ego-lessness of the seventh stage of life. Avatar Adi Da's Self-Confession as the first, last, and only seventh stage Adept-Realizer.

BOOK ELEVEN:

The All-Completing and Final Divine Revelation To Mankind

A Summary Description Of The Supreme Yoga Of The Seventh Stage Of Life In The Divine Way Of Adidam

The ultimate secrets of Divine Enlightenment—including the four-stage Process of Divine Enlightenment, culminating in Translation into the Infinitely Love-Blissful Divine Self-Domain.

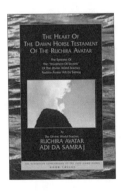

BOOK TWELVE:

The Heart Of The Dawn Horse Testament Of The Ruchira Avatar

The Epitome Of The "Testament Of Secrets" Of The Divine World-Teacher, Ruchira Avatar Adi Da Samraj

A shorter version of *The Dawn Horse Testament*—all of Avatar Adi Da's magnificent summary Instruction, without the details of the technical practices engaged by His devotees.

BOOK THIRTEEN:

What, Where, When, How, Why, and <u>Who</u> To Remember To Be Happy
A Simple Explanation Of The Divine Way Of Adidam (For Children, and <u>Everyone</u> Else)

A text written specifically for children but inspiring to all—with accompanying Essays and Talks on Divine Ignorance, religious practices for children and young people in the Way of Adidam, and the fundamental practice of whole bodily devotion to Avatar Adi Da Samraj. (The central text of this book is also available in a special illustrated children's edition—see p. 398.)

BOOK FOURTEEN:

Santosha Adidam
The Essential Summary Of The Divine Way Of Adidam

An extended overview of the entire course of the Way of Adidam, based on the esoteric anatomy of the human being and its correlation to the progressive stages of life.

BOOK FIFTEEN:

The Lion Sutra
The "Perfect Practice" Teachings In The Divine Way Of Adidam

Practice in the ultimate stages of the Way of Adidam. How the practitioner of Adidam approaches—and passes over—the "Threshold" of Divine Enlightenment.

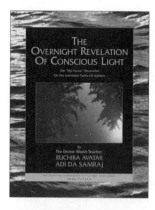

BOOK SIXTEEN:

The Overnight Revelation Of Conscious Light

The "My House" Discourses
On The Indivisible Tantra Of Adidam

A vast and profound "consideration" of the fundamental Tantric principles of true Spiritual life and the "Always Already" Nature of the Divine Reality. The day-by-day record of Avatar Adi Da's Discourses from a two-month period in early 1998.

BOOK SEVENTEEN:

The Basket Of Tolerance

The Perfect Guide To Perfectly <u>Unified</u>
Understanding Of The One and Great
Tradition Of Mankind, and Of The Divine
Way Of Adidam As The Perfect <u>Completing</u>
Of The One and Great Tradition Of Mankind

An all-encompassing "map" of mankind's entire history of religious seeking. A combination of a bibliography of over 5,000 items (organized to display Avatar Adi Da's grand Argument relative to the Great Tradition) with over 100 Essays by Avatar Adi Da, illuminating many specific aspects of the Great Tradition.

The Dawn Horse Testament Of The Ruchira Avatar

The "Testament Of Secrets"
Of The Divine World-Teacher,
Ruchira Avatar Adi Da Samraj

Avatar Adi Da's paramount "Source-Text", which summarizes the entire course of the Way of Adidam. Adi Da Samraj says: "In making this Testament I have been Meditating everyone, contacting everyone, dealing with psychic forces everywhere, in all time. This Testament is an always Living Conversation between Me and absolutely every one."

See My Brightness Face to Face

A Celebration of the Ruchira Avatar, Adi Da Samraj, and the First Twenty-Five Years of His Divine Revelation Work.

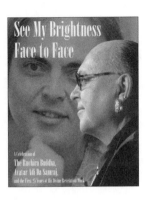

A magnificent year-by-year pictorial celebration of Ruchira Avatar Adi Da's Divine Work with His devotees, from 1972 to 1997. Includes a wealth of selections from His Talks and Writings, numerous Stories told by His devotees, and over 100 color photographs. **$19.95**, 8-1/2" x 11" paperback, 200 pages.

The "Truth For Real" series

Brief Essays and Talks by the Divine World-Teacher, Ruchira Avatar Adi Da Samraj

13 individual booklets on topics such as ecstasy, death, and the impulse to Happiness.
3-3/4" x 6", **$1.95** each

The Basket Of Tolerance Booklet series

6 individual essays on the religious traditions of humankind from *The Basket Of Tolerance.*
3-3/4" x 6", **$1.95** each

INDEX

RUCHIRA AVATARA HRIDAYA-SIDDHA YOGA

(Adi Da Samraj continued)
as Divine Person (principal Demonstration of), **54**, **64**, **66**, **75**, **92**, **172**
and Divine Self-"Emergence", 17, **92**, **189**, **278**, 368-69
and embrace and transcendence of both Emanationist and Transcendentalist schools, 99
feeling-Contemplation of, **307-309**, 364, 370
as first, last, and only Avataric Divine Adept-Realizer, Adept-Revealer, Adept-Revelation of the seventh stage of life, 91
as Grace of Love-Bliss, **177**
here to Intervene, **184**, **185**
His Touch, **193**
His Voice, **257**
is Standing Free, **179**
as Liberator in "late-time" or "dark epoch", **68**, **69**
not a "public" Teacher, **55**, **56**
and Ramana Maharshi as a connecting link to aspects of the Great Tradition, **142-43**
and refusal to be "man in the middle", **59-60**, **61**, **64**, **65**, **68**
and relationship to Kundalini Shakti during childhood and teenage years, **242-43**
and relationship to Swami Muktananda after Divine Re-Awakening
  and Adidam as form of Siddha Yoga, **149-51**, **152**
  assumption of His Divine Work institutionally independent of Swami Muktananda, **149**, **151-52**
  completion and fulfillment of Siddha-Yoga tradition, 95
  and continued sending of simple messages of love, **143-44**
  and discussions regarding Adi Da Samraj's seventh stage awakening, **115-20**, **140**, **141**, **142-43**, **144**, **145**, **146-47**, **149**
  and distinctions in point of view that were basis of His Divine Work independent of Swami Muktananda, **147-49**
  and ending of outer relationship immediately after September 1970, **100**
  unbroken Spiritual relationship to, **152**, **166**
and Rudi, continued relationship with, **107**
and "sadhana years" of Avataric Ordeal of Divine Re-Awakening of, **93**, **100**, 385
  Christian visions of and their interpretation, **131-34**
  completion of on September 10, 1970, 16, **115**, **139**, **166**, 368
  and demonstration of Yogi, Saint, and Sage characteristics, **106**
  and Divine "Cosmic Goddess" ("Ma"), **114**, **115**, **117**, **166**, 377, **377**
  entirely a demonstration for the sake of all others, **167**
  and experience of ego-death in spring of 1967, **166**
  and experiences of Savikalpa Samadhi or internal visions, **122-23**, **131-34**
  his personal experience of the "Thumbs", **271-73**
  and lineage of Gurus who passed Him on hierarchically one to the next, **165-67**, 376-77
  and passing beyond fifth stage "Witnessing" to Divine Self-Realization, **119**
  and practice and completion of ascending Yoga with Swami Muktananda, 1968-1970, **100**, **113**, **144-45**, 377
  and practice of descending or frontal Yoga with Rudi, 1964-1968, **100-101**, **165**, 376-77

and Rang Avadhoot, **100**, **109**, **113-14**, **165**
  sixth stage Transcendental Realization of always occurred spontaneously, **166**
  and sudden completely ascending Nirvikalpa Samadhi of 1968, **114**, **123**, **138**, **139**
  and Swami Nityananda, **100**, **113**, **165**, **166**, 377
  and the "Thumbs", **271-72**, 386-87
  and written acknowledgement of Siddha-Yoga authority by Swami Muktananda, **110-12**
and seventh stage Realization, **170**
  completes Spiritual Process of present and past lifetime lineages, **170**
  as first to realize and demonstrate what is a new way, **170-71**, **188**, **273**
  as only fulfillment of Gifts received from His Lineage Gurus and all received in past lifetimes, **170**
  as paradigm or patterning case of demonstration of, **92-93**
  unique Gift of, 350n14
  as Source, Inherently Perfect, **228**
Spiritual Bodies of, **246**, **259**
Teaching Work of, 12, 16-22, 27, 28-29, **55**, **292-93**
and visual perception of His Subtle bodily (human) Form, **250**, **254**
Admonition, Great, of Adi Da Samraj, **219**
adolescent patterns, 364
Advaita Vedanta, 360
  and admonition given to Adi Da Samraj by Swami Muktananda, "You are the One Who Is the Witness", **117-18**
  and historical encounter with Kashmir Saivism, 98
  and link to Emanationist tradition of Siddha Yoga, **143**
  as non-Emanationist or Transcendentalist tradition, **98**, **118**
  Swami Muktananda's philosophical opposition to, 95
Advaitayana Buddha, **172**, 360
advanced stages of life and practice, **196**, 360
  and in-Filling by Adi Da Samraj, **285-86**
Agents of Adi Da Samraj's Blessing Work, **227-28**, 361
Aham Da Asmi, 361
  in "First Word", **53**, **64**, **70**
  in "My Divine Disclosure", **75**
Ajna Door, **226**, 357n48
  and allowing of heart-feeling and attention to be carried towards and into in ascending Yoga, **259-60**
  and finger pressure in ascending Yoga, **255-56**
all and All/All and all, 361
always already, **52**, **78**, **79**, **91**, **115**
  Consciousness is, **303**, **304**
  God is, **184**, **185**
  and Happiness, 16, **78**, **297**
Amma (Pratibha Trivedi or Swami Prajnananda), **107-108**, **109**, **111**
  as example of fourth stage devotional bliss development of Siddha Yoga, **109**
  and involvement with Swami Muktananda's written teaching, **107**, **145**
  and name Love-Ananda, **151**
  relationship and service to Swami Nityananda and Swami Muktananda, **107**
  relationship to Adi Da Samraj, **107-8**
Amrita Nadi, 45, **203-4**, 361
  and discussion of with Swami Muktananda, **141**
  "Maha-Bindu" as upper terminal of, **136-37**, **141**
  "Regenerated" form of, **141**
anatomy, structural of human beings, 391

410

Index

Arrow, **260**, 357n47
 Hridaya-Shakti originates prior to, **207**
ascending meditation
 and vision, audition, and touch, **248-61**
 and vision of great Mandala of cosmic domain, **250**
 See also deep meditation
ascending Yoga, **125**, **226**, **230**, **249**
 Adi Da Samraj's own practice of, **100**
 and auditory phenomena, **256-58**
 and encounter with conceptual thoughts and gross
  bodily sensations, **249**
 may be unnecessary, **230**, **269**
 and non-concern for mapping or categorizing, **254**,
  258
 practiced in a unique manner in Adidam, **181**
 and practice in response to appearance of visual
  objects, **253-55**
 and rare sudden completely ascending Nirvikalpa
  Samadhi of Adi Da Samraj in 1968, **138**
 and touch, **258-59**
 traditional, as exclusive effort not necessary for
  Divine Enlightenment, **178**
 and visual perception of Adi Da Samraj's bodily
  (human) Form, **250**, **254**, **255**
 and visual perception of Cosmic Mandala, **251-52**,
  254, **255**
 and visual phenomena, **249-56**
asceticism and traditional approach to "money, food,
  and sex", 21
Ashtavakra Gita
 Amma pointing out to Adi Da Samraj, **108**
 as "premonitorily 'seventh stage'" text, **108**,
  350-51n14
Ati-Ruchira Yoga, **261**
"Atma-Murti", **297**, **308**, 361-62
attention, **154**, **298**, **392**
attractiveness of Adi Da Samraj's Form, Presence, and
  State, **212**
audition
 and ascending Yoga, **256-58**
 as primary sensation, **249**, **258**
 range of described in *The Dawn Horse Testament*,
  355-56n44
auditions. *See* Divine Sound; sound
Avadhoot, **101**, 362
Avatar, 14, 362
Avataric
 bodily (human) Divine Form, Spiritual Presence, and
  Perfectly Subjective State, **307-309**
 Divine Realizer, Revealer, and Self-Revelation, Adi Da
  Samraj as, **53**, **92**
 Incarnation, **53**, **70**, **75**, **83**, **85**
 and process of the "Bright" and the "Thumbs",
  277-78
 Self-Manifested Divine Self-Revelation of the seventh
  stage of life, **89**
 Self-Revealed Divine Person and Blessing-Work, **64**
 Self-Revelation beyond the cosmic play, **80**
avoidance of relationship, transcendence of, 362

B

Basket Of Tolerance, The, 350-51n14, 352-53n28
beginners and presumed involvement in phenomenon
  of advanced and ultimate stages of life, **280-81**,
  290
belief, 12
bewilderment, **57**
Bhagavad Gita, **74**, **126**, 352n25
Bhagavan, 362

Bhagavata Purana, **126**
bhakta, 362
"Big Bang", **136**, 353n29
bindu
 definition of, **103**, 362-63
 and Swami Muktananda, **103**, **137**
Blessing. *See* Spiritual Blessing
Blessing-Work of Adi Da Samraj, **56**, **206**, **246-47**, 363
"blue pearl" or "blue bindu", **137**
"blue person", **126**
body
 relationship to in Adidam, **286**
 roundness of and Witness as its shape, **274**
body-brain-mind-self
 abstract pattern of as universal, **135**
 bringing into condition of Energy, **220**
 first six stages developed on basis of structure of, **90**
 necessarily duplicates primary pattern of cosmic
  domain, **135-36**
 wild without devotion to a True Master, **165**
 and Yogic process of progressive experiencing of
  total pattern of structural forms of, **137-38**
"Bonding" to Adi Da Samraj, **228**, 363
brain core
 and ascending Yoga, **260**
 knot in, **230**
"Bright", the, 15, 363-64
 and the Cosmic Mandala and Amrita Nadi, **293-94**
 definition of, **139-40**, 363-64
 known as a child and Spiritual Signs of, **241-42**
 and Realization of Union of Self-Condition and Spirit-
  Energy, **203**
 Re-Awakening to, **139**, 353n32
 and Ruchira Avatara Hridaya-Shaktipat, **151**
 Spherical Space of seventh stage of life, **267**
 and "Thumbs" as Adi Da Samraj's unique Avataric
  Divine Characteristic, **167**, **271**, **277-78**, 363-64,
  386-87
"Bright"-Field photography, 39-41
"Brightness", Adi Da Samraj's Sphere of, **70**, **115**
Brihadaranyaka Upanishad, **187**
Buddha, Adi Da Samraj's Titles using term, **172**, 364
Buddhism
 and adoption of fourth and fifth stage doctrines and
  practices as a result of encounter with Kashmir
  Saivism, **98**
 Advaitayana, 360
 and Kashmir Saivism's use of language similar to, **96**,
  98
 Swami Muktananda philosophical opponent of, **95**

C

Camera Illuminata, 39-41
capitalization, and Adi Da Samraj's "Source-Texts",
  29-31
causal
 body or dimension, **127**, **128-29**, 372
 knot, **129**
 and root-self or ego, 155
celibacy, as expected sign of institutionalized Sacred
  Authority, **110**
center, **57-59**
cerebro-spinal fluid, **230**
changes, cycle of, **78-80**
Chidakasha Gita (Nityananda), **101-105**, 349n5
 acknowledgement of, **102**
 summary of teachings of, **103-105**
childish patterns, 364
Chinmayananda, Swami, **102**, 349n6

Index

and hearing and seeing allows reception of, **180**
and His Divine Spirit-Energy, 178-79
and in-Filling process, **285-86**, **287**
not a search, **189**
and pressure on the head and sense of Adi Da
    Samraj surrounding the body, **285**
and purification occurs by reception of, **181**
and Signs of psycho-physical openings, **288**
uniqueness of, **180**, **189**
descent
    by Adi Da Samraj to wander in Hell to account for
        much and many, **293**
    in frontal domain in fourth stage of life, **125**, 392
    and practice in frontal line, **226**
    "Thumbs" as sign of Avataric Crashing Down of Adi
        Da Samraj, **269**, **277-78**, 387
desire, **76**
"de-throning", **57-58**
devotees of Adi Da Samraj
    and Awakening within ordinary human life, **63**
    called to turn life-functions outward, **62**
    and making Satsang available, **55**
devotees of Real God, ask for nothing but God, **188**
devotional relationship to Adi Da Samraj, **60**, **62**, **77**,
    306-309, 316
    as "Atma-Murti", **297**, 361-62
    based not on illusions but recognition and right
        understanding of egoity, 317
    as foundation of Adidam, 10, 13, 16
    giving oneself over to, **220-21**
    magnification of as practice of beginners, **220**
    practiced from the beginning, **190**
Devotional Way of Faith/Insight, 367
devotion to a True Master, necessity of, **164**
Dharma, 367
"difference", **76**, **277**, **307**, 367
    and causal body, **129**
    and human suffering, **153**
    transcendence of concept of, **203**
disciplines. See life-conditions
discriminative self-understanding, **62**
Divine Being, 367-68
Divine Conscious Light, 39
Divine Enlightenment, 22, 317, 368
Divine Ignorance, 368
Divine Indifference, **261**, 371
Divine Light, **61**, **92**
Divine Person
    Adi Da Samraj as, **54**, **64**, **66**, **75**, **92**, **105**, **172**,
        228
    presumption of, **61**
Divine Self-Domain, **229**, **231**, **252**, 369, 371
Divine Self-"Emergence" of Adi Da Samraj, 17, **92**, **189**,
    278, 368-69
Divine Self-Realization, 22, 317
    only seventh stage Realization qualifies as, **93**
Divine Self-Recognition, **148**, **161**, 368
    of all conditions, **120**, **202**
    of self and world in seventh stage, **204-205**, **306**
    and seventh stage of life, **97**, **305**
Divine Sound, **191**, **195**, 394
    Divine Self-Recognition of, **203**
    mass of or "Om", "Da-Om", or "Da", **201**
    passage into and through, **248**
Divine Spiritual Baptism, 43-44
    See also Spirit-Baptism
Divine Spiritual Body, 394-95
    of Adi Da Samraj is Hridaya-Shakti, **246**
    and Adi Da Samraj's Touch, **192-93**

and "Bright" Spherical Space of the "Thumbs",
    267, **271**
definition of, **273**
direct experiencing of, **193-94**
Identification with, **273**
"Locating" of, 45
and Spirit-Current or Presence, **259**
Divine Star, **195**, **250**, 369, 393, 394-95
    as Adi Da Samraj's Attractive Force, **191**
    Divine Self-Recognition of, **203**, **252**
    and Divine Translation, **252-53**
    passage into and through, **248**
    and practice when it appears, **254**
    stands above the head, **202**
    visual perception of, **250**
    See also Star
Divine State of Adi Da Samraj, 24
    even from the beginning always Self-Revealed, **217**
    Spiritual Transmission of, **215-16**
Divine Thunder
    as Adi Da Samraj's Penetrating Force, **191**
    and Divine Sound, **195**, 394
Divine Transfiguration, **261**, 371
Divine Transformation, **261**, 371
Divine Translation, **201-202**, **261**, **278**, 371
    is accomplished by Love, **253**
    and Amrita Nadi, **204**
    and the Divine Star, **201**
    process of, **252-53**
    visions and auditions experienced on the way to, **201**
Divine Way of Adidam, **182**
Divine World-Teacher, **170**, **172**, 369
Divine Yoga of Spiritual reception of Adi Da Samraj, **186**
Divine Yogic Process, **287**, **292**
    necessarily life-long and beyond, **290**
dog, of self-contracted body-mind, **81-82**, **85**, 396
"dog, washing of", **283**
dreaming state, 395
duality
    illusion of, **90-91**
    and use of language, 30-31

E

Earth, and Moon as its coin, **275**
ecstasy, **220**, 369
ego
    group as, **57**
    social, **101**
ego, three forms of, **155-60**
    "brain-mind ego", **155**, **159**
        and fourth and fifth stages of life, **155**
        and Realization of Spiritual nature of cosmic
            existence, **159**
        and subtle or higher self, **155**
    "money, food, and sex", **101**, **155**, **157-58**
        and first three stages of life, **155**
        and gross or lower self, **155**
        and realization of inherent unity of gross
            conditional existence, **157-58**
    "root-ego", **156**, **159-60**
        and root-self or causal, **155**
        and sixth stage of life, **156**
    transcendence of, **156**, **185**
ego-"I", **52**, **69**, **81**, 369
    and Adi Da Samraj's use of language, 30
    is not what It Is That Is Happening, 26
    little heart of, **83**
    psycho-biography of, **93**, **180**
    and separation, **59**, **68**

413

love
for and by Adi Da Samraj, 16-17, **77**, **78**, **185**, 317
and Divine Translation, **253**
and Spirit-Current, **259**
Love-Ananda, 379
name given by Swami Muktananda, **151**
Love-Ananda Avatar, 379
Love-Ananda Avatara Hridaya-Shaktipat, **151**
Love-Ananda Avatara Hridaya-Shaktipat Yoga, **151**
Love-Ananda Avatara Hridaya-Siddha Yoga, **151**
Love-Bliss and Consciousness, **305**, **306**
love-surrender to a True Master, **163-64**

M

"Maha-Bindu", **136-37**
and Amrita Nadi, **136-37**, **141**
penetration of, **138**
Maha-Jnana, **109**
Mahamantra meditation, 357n51
Maharastra Spiritual tradition, **123**, **126**, **127**, **128**
Maharshi, Ramana, **142**, 353n33, 385
Adi Da Samraj and Swami Muktananda's
discussion of, **142-43**
as Nirguna Jnani, **105**
Swami Muktananda as opponent of, **118**, **142**
mandala, 379-80
See also Cosmic Mandala
"man in the middle", **57-58**
and Adi Da Samraj's existence beyond, **68**, **69**
Adi Da Samraj's refusal to be, **59-60**, **61**, **64**, **65**
as ego's scapegoat, **67**
tendency to make Adi Da Samraj into, **64**
Mary, Virgin, **134**
Masters, True, **163-65**
materialistic orientation, 389
matter and things and light, **275**
meditation, **287**, 321-22, 380
See also ascending meditation; deep meditation
"Method of the Siddhas", **152**, 353-54n35
"money, food, and sex"
ego, **101**
and ego-transcendence in midst of, 21-22
Moon, Consciousness is face of this side of, **275**
Mountain Of Attention (California), 333
Muktananda, Swami (Baba), **94**, **168**, 377
and abstract internal lights, **121**
and "blue bindu" or "blue pearl", **137**
and interpretations based on Hindu traditions and
his own mental and karmic predilections,
126, **130**, **131-32**
and interpretation via colors, dimensions, and
waking, dreaming, and sleeping states, **127**,
128, **130**, **137**
and acknowledgement letter of 1969 of Adi Da
Samraj as True Siddha-Guru and extending to
Him Siddha-Yoga Authority, **110-12**, 377
and Nirvikalpa Samadhi of 1968, **114**
non-necessity and limited basis of, **111-12**
as unique and unprecedented gesture, **112**
and adherence to philosophical tradition of Kashmir
Saivism, **95**
and Adi Da Samraj's "Sadhana Years" with and declaration in 1968 that Adi Da Samraj was a Divinely
Awakened Master and would be teaching in a
year, **111**
and indication that Adi Da Samraj's Work was
uniquely His Own and He should do it independently, **162**

instruction to Adi Da Samraj that "You are the One
Who Is the Witness", **117-18**
and Nirvikalpa Samadhi experience of 1968, **114**
and passing of Adi Da Samraj on to Swami
Nityananda, **165**
and Adi Da Samraj's unbroken relationship and
honoring of, **152**, **166**
and conflict between Hindu exotericism and esoter-
cism, **125-26**
and contemplation of emanations of "Cosmic Goddess",
120
"Description of the 'Bodies of the Soul'" (chart), **127**
and discussions with Adi Da Samraj relative to His
seventh stage Awakening, **115-20**, **140**, **149**
and distinctions requiring Adi Da Samraj's independent Work, **147-49**, **151**
and fifth stage requirements for Siddha Yoga, **145**, **146**
and fifth stage use of term "Witnessing" as observer,
118-20
and "Gift of blows" and sending out alone to do
His Work, **116**, **120**
and his lack of embrace of the Divine "Cosmic
Goddess", **117**
and inability to confess seventh stage Divine Self-
Realization, **100**, **117**, **120**, **140**, **146-47**
and inability to see limitations of phenomena of
absorptive mysticism, **116-17**, **141**, **144**, **146-47**
and presumption that Adi Da Samraj was departing
Siddha Yoga for Advaitism, **143**
and Ramana Maharshi, **118**, **142-43**
and "Regenerated" form of Amrita Nadi, **141**
and distinction and difference between Emanationist
and non-Emanationist traditions, **94**
as fifth stage Realizer of a high but not fully
ascended degree, **99**, **102**, **141**
fourth-to-fifth stage Emanationist point of view of, **100**
and internal vision, **103**
and Blue Person, **126**
of higher and lower worlds reported from a
personalized Hindu point of view as if categorically true and objectively existing, **122**, **126**
and interpretations of Yogic Spiritual experiences
in terms of Hindu cultural models, **126**
and Kundalini-Shaktipat tradition, **94**, **236**
as opponent of Transcendentalist philosophical traditions of Advaita Vedanta and Buddhism, **95**, **118**
and Rang Avadhoot, **114**, **165**
reported sexual activities of, **110**
as Saguna Siddha-Yogi, **99**, **102**, **122**
Siddha-Yoga teachings of attention-based and object-
oriented and ego-based with focus on Sahashrar
or brain, **140**
and Emanationist affirmation "I am Siva" or "I and
the world are Divine", **148**
as fifth stage internal sensory phenomena oriented
example of Siddha-Yoga process, **109**, **116**
as fourth-to-fifth stage Hindu religious practice, **125**
and Maharastra region of India, **123**, **126**, **127**, **128**
prejudiced and limited relative to anything beyond
fifth stage, **144**
and prejudice toward Savikalpa Samadhi and
against Nirvikalpa Samadhi, **121-22**, **123**
as product of his own point of view, **118**, **126**
view that Realization requires phenomenal experiences as a support, **140**
and Swami Prakashananda, **110**, 351n17
Mummery, The (Adi Da Samraj), 27
"Murti, Living", **283**, 379, 380
Murti-Form of Adi Da Samraj, **283**

Index

and fourth stage devotional bliss, **109**
and Kundalini-Shaktipat fourth-to-fifth stage development of, **94**
and no institution can claim ownership of, **149**
open form of taught by Swami Muktananda during Adi Da Samraj's "sadhana years" with him, **145**
and sudden complete rather than progressive ascent to Nirvikalpa Samadhi, **138**
and Swami Muktananda's fifth stage requirements for based on meetings with Adi Da Samraj in 1970 and 1973, **145**, **146**
and Swami Muktananda's fourth-to-fifth stage school of, **150**
as taught by Adi Da Samraj—Ruchira Avatara Hridaya-Siddha Yoga and completion of by extending into sixth and seventh stages, **95**, **145**, **146**
descriptive names and references of, **151**
and Hridaya-Shaktipat, **151**, 390
and potential development into sixth or Transcendentalist stage of life, **94**
and transcendence of attention and all of first sixth stages, **154-55**
and unique descriptive language of, **150**
and unique process of seventh stage of life, **151-52**
of un-"Veiling" of pattern of cosmic domain through progressive experiencing of pattern of all structural forms of body-mind-self, **137-38**
Siddhis, Divine, of Adi Da Samraj, 390
sinoatrial node, **137**, 373
sin of relating to the Adept-Realizer as an ordinary man, **66**
Siva, **126**
skin of "Thumbs" and Witness Consciousness, **274**, **275**, **276**
smell, secondary to seeing and hearing, **249**
social sphere and cult-making, 57
Society of Advocates of the Adidam Revelation, The Transnational, 330-31
"solid" type
and analytic mental non-surrender, **279-80**, **291**
presumption that Spiritual Yoga not necessary, **292**
and presumptuous identification with the sixth stage, **280**, **291**
sound
and ascending Yoga, **256-58**
and experiencing of Adi Da Samraj, **192-93**
as primary sensation, **249**
Source, Adi Da Samraj as Inherently Perfect, **228**
Source-Condition, **69**, **85**, **92**
"Source-Texts" of Adi Da Samraj, 17, 27-38, 51, 390-91
and capitalization, 29-31
and description of unique characteristics of His Avataric Divine Teachings, **106**
practice in Heart-Manner of, **253**
punctuation in, 31-32
titles and subtitles of the twenty-three, 34-38
vocabulary in, 29
sphere and the "Thumbs", **263-64**, **271**, **274**, **276**, **277**
spinal line, 391, 392, 396
Spirit-Baptism, **227-29**, 391, 392
Adi Da Samraj's Avataric Divine, **177**
and beginning of Spirit-"Conductivity" practice, **227**
"Cosmic" versus "Divine", 43-44
as distinguished from natural life-energies, 42
as Hridaya-Shakti-Kripa, **206-207**
and John the Baptist and Jesus of Nazareth, **132**
and necessary association with the "Thumbs", **263-64**, 387

and "shaking" of newly seeing devotee, **222**
two camps of "Cosmic" form of, 43
See also Crashing Down
Spirit-Blessing, beginners not able to stably receive, **220**
Spirit-"Conductivity", 46
in Adidam a searchless purification, **178**
and ascending Yoga, **259-60**
beginning of in Spirit-Baptism, **227**
Spirit-Current or Energy, **209**, **217**, 392
attention given to, **218-19**
is Divine Spiritual Presence, **259**
and touch as principal sensory means, **258-59**
Spirit-Power, as Divine matter, 42
Spiritual Blessing of Adi Da Samraj
and always standing as Divine State, **217**
appears or is revealed in progressive stages, 216-17
and His bodily (human) Divine Form, **216**
is direct and constant Spiritual Transmission, **215-16**
received according to present time stage of life of devotee, **216**
as Spirit-Current, **217**
Spiritual Conversion, **228**
Spiritual Presence of Adi Da Samraj, **196**, **275**, 316
and Blessing-Work, **206**
and capability to Identify moment to moment, **220**, **221**
comes from Adi Da Samraj and not ego, **289**
conducting and conserving of through the stages of life, **228-29**
"effects" of, **211-12**
forever transmitted by Adi Da Samraj via Instruments and Agents, **227-28**
and head-pressure, **279-93**
and infusion of faculties of the body-mind, **221**, **222**
and invasion of frontal line, **262-64**
is Divine Spirit-Current, **259**
and Realization of Oneness with Self-Condition in seventh stage, **203**
and Spirit-Baptism, **228-29**
and the "Thumbs", **273**
Spiritual sensitivity, **282-83**, **287**
Spiritual Transmission
of Divine Being, **215**
original, ultimate, and primary form is Divine State, **215-16**
Sri, 391
stages of life
summary of, 391-93
first stage, 391
second stage, 391
third stage, 391
first three stages, 391-92
and exoteric religious traditions which are also contextually associated with rudimentary aspects of the fourth stage, **124**
and "money, food, and sex" ego, **155**
fourth stage, 392
"basic" context, 392
"advanced" context of, 392
and descent of Spiritual Force in frontal domain, **125**
and direct transition into context of sixth stage, **268**, **274**
and exoteric and esoteric religion, **124-25**
and progressive development of the "Thumbs", **263**
fourth and fifth stages
and brain-mind ego, **155**
and Emanationist mode of Realization, **94**, **96**

421

Index

I do not simply recommend or turn men and women to Truth. I _Am_ Truth. I Draw men and women to Myself. I _Am_ the Present Real God, Desiring, Loving, and Drawing up My devotees. I have Come to Be Present with My devotees, to Reveal to them the True Nature of life in Real God, which is Love, and of mind in Real God, which is Faith. I Stand always Present in the Place and Form of Real God. I accept the qualities of all who turn to Me, dissolving those qualities in Real God, so that _Only_ God becomes the Condition, Destiny, Intelligence, and Work of My devotees. I look for My devotees to acknowledge Me and turn to Me in appropriate ways, surrendering to Me perfectly, depending on Me, full of Me always, with only a face of love.

I am waiting for you. I have been waiting for you eternally.

Where are you?

AVATAR ADI DA SAMRAJ

1971